David Lampe

ACIS
April '97

Patrick Kavanagh

Richard Fallis, Series Editor

PATRICK KAVANAGH

A Critical Study

Antoinette Quinn

SYRACUSE UNIVERSITY PRESS

Published in the United States of America by Syracuse University Press,
Syracuse, New York 13244–5160, by arrangement with Gill and Macmillan Ltd
Printed in Great Britain

Library of Congress Cataloging-in-Publication Data
Quinn, Antoinette.
    Patrick Kavanagh: a critical study / Antoinette Quinn.
    p.   cm. – (Irish studies)
    Includes bibliographical references (p.   ) and index.
    ISBN 0-8156-2549-9
    1. Kavanagh, Patrick, 1904–1967 – Criticism and interpretation.
2. Ireland in literature.   I. Title.   II. Series: Irish studies (Syracuse, N.Y.)
PR6021.A74Z88   1991
821'.912 – dc20   91–4284
                                                                                              CIP

*For my mother
and
in memory of my father*

Contents

Acknowledgments

I wish to thank the many people who contributed to the preparation of this book: my editor, Professor Terence Brown, without whose patient insistence it would probably still be a work in progress; my mother, Mrs M. Quinn, who lent me books and supplied information; Professor Brendan Kennelly, who also lent me books, and whose enthusiasm for Patrick Kavanagh was a perpetual stimulus; Dr Ruth Sherry, who shared her knowledge and ideas about Frank O'Connor and about *The Bell*; Geraldine Mangan, secretary of the Department of English, who offered much practical assistance, as well as that sympathetic support for which she is, by now, renowned; Laureen Coffey, the late Harriet Cooke, Bonnie Cotter, Lee Guckian, Tamsin Hargreaves, Edna Longley, the late Gerry Rafferty, Ian Ross, my colleagues in the Centre for Women's Studies, Trinity College, Dublin, all of whom helped in various ways, and Brian Crowley, who was 'always there'; the courteous librarians of Trinity College, Dublin, the National Library of Ireland, the Royal Irish Academy, the British Library at Collindale, the Macmillan Archive at Basingstoke, the Agricultural Library and the Kavanagh Archive at University College, Dublin. My very special thanks to Professor Nicholas Grene of the Department of English, Trinity College, Dublin, who read this book in its first and final drafts, and whose valuable advice and kind encouragement were so important to me.

I owe a scholarly debt to Patrick Kavanagh's bibliographers, biographers, critics and editors, whose work I consulted in the preparation of this book. Since it did not seem appropriate on this occasion to enter into a dialogue with the numerous scholars who have written essays about Kavanagh, I thank them collectively here. Those predecessors, who have written books on Kavanagh, are acknowledged in the

Bibliography. Special thanks are due to Kavanagh's bibliographers, Dr Peter Kavanagh and Professor John Nemo, whose work was of such assistance in the tracing of primary source materials. Like all Kavanagh's readers, I am particularly indebted to Dr Peter Kavanagh for publishing so much of his brother's work.

All quotations from Patrick Kavanagh's poetry and prose are by kind permission of the trustees of the estate of the late Katherine Kavanagh, c/o Peter Fallon, Literary Agent, Loughcrew, Oldcastle, County Meath, Ireland. The Patrick Kavanagh Award, administered by Trinity Trust, helped to defray the cost of quotation.

Some material in this book, particularly in chapter 6, 'Parochialism', previously appeared in 'Patrick Kavanagh's Parish Myth' in *Tradition and Influence in Anglo–Irish Poetry*, edited by Terence Brown and Nicholas Grene, Macmillan, London 1989. It is reproduced by kind permission of the editors.

Bibliographical Note

In the case of poems collected in *Ploughman and Other Poems* (1936), *A Soul for Sale* (1947) and *Come Dance with Kitty Stobling* (1960), all quotations from or allusions to Patrick Kavanagh's poetry are based on these volumes, with the exception of *The Great Hunger* (1942), where I have followed the unabridged Cuala Press edition.

In the case of poems published, but uncollected in these volumes, I have followed the first published version. For unpublished poems I have followed the MS. version.

Quotations from *The Green Fool* (1938) are from the edition published by Martin Brian and O'Keeffe Ltd, London 1971, except where otherwise stated.

Quotations from *Tarry Flynn* (1948) are from the edition published by Martin Brian and O'Keeffe Ltd, London 1972, except where otherwise stated.

Quotations from *Self-Portrait* (1964) are from the edition published by The Dolmen Press, 1975.

All other quotations from or allusions to Patrick Kavanagh's prose are based on the first published version, except where otherwise stated.

1
Homeward:
Songs by the Way

Introduction

'I SCARCELY believe in the theory of the mute, inglorious Milton', Patrick Kavanagh once declared, and his life-story seems designed to demonstrate that Gray was, indeed, wrong; that it is possible to plough 'the stubborn glebe', wake 'to ecstasy the living lyre', and finally make it back to the country churchyard when the curfew tolls. It was Kavanagh's opinion that 'If the potentialities are there it is almost certain that they will find a way out; they will burst a road.'[1] His own progress from mute ingloriousness to literary fame, although slow and tortuous, was a remarkable triumph over almost insuperable odds.

Patrick Kavanagh was born on 21 October 1904, to a poor family in the townland of Mucker in the parish of Inniskeen, Co. Monaghan. Mucker is about a mile from the small village of Inniskeen, which is situated approximately half-way between the market towns of Carrickmacross and Dundalk. Places and place-names from this region were to feature prominently in Kavanagh's writings. The future poet had 'no literary background' whatever.[2] His mother despised reading as a form of idleness and regarded her son's 'curse o' God books' as a threat to his worldly advancement; his father, who enjoyed a local reputation as a knowledgeable man, was a cobbler who stuck to his last and confined his reading to the newspapers. The couple had seven daughters and two sons, and their highest ambition for their elder son was that he should learn to ply his father's trade and supplement his income by subsistence farming. So Patrick Kavanagh's formal schooling at Kednaminsha primary school came to an end at the age of thirteen when he joined his father at the cobbler's bench and, as the able-bodied son of a sixty-one-year-old man, was set to work on the family smallholding. For then on he 'grabbed an education',[3] poring over whatever books and journals he could lay his hands on and memorising stanzas from the poems in schoolbooks.

Inniskeen, now relatively prosperous, was in Kavanagh's youth and early manhood a backward, impoverished parish. The poet has described his neighbours as '*scraidins* of farmers', struggling to rear large families on a few hilly or boggy acres. Their lives were 'barbaric', materially deprived and culturally unenlightened.[4] Such a hard-pressed and undereducated community set little store by scholarship other than as an exceptional means of escape from drudgery into a salaried profession like schoolteaching. It was a milieu hostile to non-utilitarian endeavour, unaccustomed to artistic cultivation, uncomprehending of literature or literary composition.

It seems scarcely credible that a poet should have discovered and nurtured his talent in so uncongenial an environment. Yet such is the imperative of genius that, despite inadequate schooling, in defiance of parental discouragement and local disincentive, and in the total absence of role models or fosterers, Patrick Kavanagh, at the age of twelve, 'took to the poeming'[5] and persevered until, with the publication of *Ploughman and Other Poems* by Macmillan in 1936, he had finally 'burst a road' from Inniskeen to London. Once his poetry had begun to appear in quality journals from 1930 onwards, his progress was rapid, eased by literary advice, gifts of books and the stimulus of friendship with other authors. In August 1939 he finally abandoned farming and cobbling and took up residence in Dublin as a full-time writer.

Patrick Kavanagh was not a poet who lisped in numbers but one who through sheer dedication and hard graft transformed himself from an uncouth rhymester into a competent versifier and gradually found his own individual voice.

Between 1 September 1928, when his poetry first appeared in print, and August 1939, when he finally became a full-time professional writer, Kavanagh composed over 120 poems that were either published or submitted for publication. At its most fluent much of this verse is derivatively smooth rather than innovative or adventurous. At its less accomplished its factitious subject matter and defective technique betray its writer's inexperience in both life and literature. Only occasionally did Kavanagh focus on issues that genuinely affected him. Rarely did he dare to defy literary orthodoxies, write out of his peculiar, individual situation, speak in a personal idiom and accent.

This chapter charts the first phase of his poetic development: his slow, arbitrary, and, for the most part, unhelpful process of self-education, the models he imitated in his dogged effort to master literary skills, the influences to which he consciously or unconsciously subjected himself, his progress from local balladry and poet's corner versifying to publication in serious Irish and English journals and his first collection, *Ploughman and Other Poems* (1936).

Dabbling in Poetry

Patrick Kavanagh was 'so deeply involved' with poetry for most of his life that he found it difficult to visualise his own poetic prepubescence, the 'virginal time before' he 'had ever thought of writing a verse'. There was 'nothing deliberate or conscious' about his poetic beginnings. According to his own account, 'It all happened like an accident.'[6] He dabbled in poetry, he says, not realising that it was to be his life. The inconsequential connotations of that verb 'dabble' are somewhat misleading. Kavanagh from an early age apprenticed himself to the trade of verse with far greater assiduity than to his ostensible trade of cobbling, educating himself and practising his craft late into the evening after a long day's work at the bench or on the farm. His tenacity is evident from the fact that he devoted twelve years to his chosen vocation before achieving even the minor gratification of being among the runners-up in a weekly newspaper competition for budding poets. It was only after a further eight years of persistent effort and a total aesthetic re-education that he was rewarded by seeing his first slim volume in print.

A manuscript selection of Kavanagh's 1929–1940 poems in the National Library of Ireland is prefaced by a note from the poet asking the reader to bear in mind 'the conditions under which these verses were written':

> They are my roots in Monaghan sitting at the end of the day upstairs in a cold corner by the light of a candle. A mother's voice calling every now and then: 'Come down and throw a lock of turnips to the unfortunate cows . . .'[7]

Kavanagh is probably craving the reader's indulgence towards his early verses here, but this prefatory note was also necessitated by the fact that there is almost nothing in the poetry of the first decade to acquaint us with his personal circumstances. Such a comic realistic sketch of his situation as a farmer-poet, with its dramatisation of the conflict between the practical mother and her scribbler son and its easy use of local dialect, would probably have seemed to the young poet a violation of literary decorum, if not a *trahison des clercs*.

Some might expect a poet who left school at the age of thirteen to be an untutored genius 'warbling his native wood notes wild'. However, in Kavanagh's case the end of his formal schooling appears to have coincided more or less with the beginning of his poetic education. 'Simplicity' was an imaginative condition only arrived at after a lengthy period of complexity and imitation and, moreover, a condition whose merit was at first not recognised and which was, therefore, not sustained. The image of the rustic poet as a simple singer piping down the valleys wild is, as Kavanagh pointed out, an absurd sentimentalisation, since poetic simplicity is 'the ultimate in sophistication'[8] and derivativeness is the common failing of self-taught poets:

> When a country body begins to progress into print he does not write out of his rural innocence—he writes out

of Palgrave's *Golden Treasury* . . . The first step out of total rurality is complexity—imitation.

The young County Meath poet, Francis Ledwidge, for instance, whose circumstances were quite similar to Kavanagh's, 'did not write out of his Meathness, he wrote out of John Clare'.[9]

His own poetic 'roots' were 'in the schoolbooks'. So excited was he by these school texts that in later years he could still recall the colours of their covers and sniff again their 'particular smell'. At primary school Kavanagh was taught that poems existed to be memorised and recited, and after leaving school he continued to learn passages of poetry 'by heart', expressing affection through assimilation. Because of this mnemonic approach he absorbed the language and rhythms of nineteenth-century verse: Thomas Hood's 'The Dream of Eugene Aram', Tennyson's 'Locksley Hall', Bret Harte's 'Dickens in Camp', Longfellow's 'My Lost Youth' and 'The Children's Hour'.[10] In the Sixth Book of a Royal Reader, found in a neighbour's smoky chimney nook, he first encountered 'A Song for St. Cecilia's Day', 'The Deserted Village', Gray's 'The Bard', the 'Ode to a Nightingale' and the opening passage of 'Endymion'.[11] His sister, Lucy, attended the convent secondary school in Carrickmacross and her Intermediate Certificate English Poetry and Prose text served as his first *ars poetica*.[12] This schoolbook was probably the source of his lifelong fascination with the sonnet.

The print-hungry youth devoured whatever books or journals he could come by: trashy popular reading matter like the *Messenger of the Sacred Heart* and *Old Moore's Almanac*, Carleton's *Traits and Stories of the Irish Peasantry*, which he reread again and again, volumes of the English classics, Milton, Pope, Burns, Shelley, Byron, which were occasionally to be found reposing among the parlour ornaments in neighbours' houses.[13] However, the collected editions of the poets were too valuable to their owners to be readily lent out, so it was the short lyrics or the excerpts from longer poems in school anthologies that provided the young Kavanagh's staple poetic diet.[14] Surprisingly, he displayed no enthusiasm for Shakespeare at this point.

Although, reminiscing about his youth, he associates the schoolbook poets with local places and place-names, Thomas Hood with summer time on a privet-hedged lane bordering a turnip field and Longfellow with an October evening in a field called Lurgankeel,[15] the effect of his total immersion in eighteenth- and nineteenth-century verse was, in fact, to blind and deafen Kavanagh to the literary potential of the life, landscape and language of his own neighbourhood. Poetry provided an alternative to his everyday concerns. Reading and writing were private pleasures snatched from the rough and tumble of family life and the numerous chores that fell to the lot of an elder son in a houseful of girls. Nothing in his primary school education or subsequent autodidacticism suggested that he should write out of his Monaghanness. Kavanagh is a blatant example of how the young Irish writer was, on Daniel Corkery's analysis, disadvantaged or disabled by a longstanding tradition of colonial education, bereft of realist Irish models, and, therefore, convinced that 'what happens in his own fields is not stuff for the Muses'.[16] There was no Irish precursor to whom the youthful Inniskeen poet could turn for inspiration or example. He himself had to make the pioneering discovery that what happens in an obscure country parish in Ireland is a valid poetic subject. Kavanagh was, in effect, as he claimed in 'Dictator's Genealogy', his 'own ancestors'.

When the young poet wrote about local places, people and happenings, he did so in verse intended as 'entertainment only', and his role model was the local balladist, John McEnaney (1872–1943), known as the Bard of Callanberg. The Bard was a 'rapscallion' and 'scandal-monger' who made ryhmes about his neighbours, such as his flyting of the Inniskeen grocer who refused him credit:

> The welkin was ringing
> And off I went singing

For in Inniskeen I'm well pleased for to be
But in less than an hour
Male, pollard and flour
Was whipped off me cart by consaitey Magee . . .[17]

From the age of twelve Kavanagh, too, made up ballads in his head and sang or recited them to the neighbours, 'useful ballads telling about football matches, dances etc.'[18] One which survived for at least thirty years was about a wedding dance which a number of men had tried to crash:

Farrelly fell over the barrow
At the gable-end of the house
And the singing and ructions were awful
Around the half-barrel of stout . . .[19]

The schoolbooks, on the contrary, spoke of subjects and emotions outside Kavanagh's own experience, quaint refinements remote from cobbling, subsistence farming, local football matches and 'hoolies'. The words and phrases they used, many of which belonged to poetic diction rather than to standard English in any case, were doubly strange to the Inniskeen youth, almost a foreign language compared to the local dialect he heard around him every day. The apprentice poet saw no connection between 'the world and the book'. By entering into an obsessive relationship with the eighteenth- and nineteenth-century muses he became something of a cultural Jekyll and Hyde, his literary personality totally at odds with his everyday bearing.

Kavanagh's first printed verses all too obviously expose their roots in the schoolbooks. This was a series of poems published in the *Irish Weekly Independent* between 1 September 1928 and 8 June 1929. The paper offered a weekly prize of half a guinea for the best contribution to its poetry column, 'A Selection of Irish Verse'. Patrick Kavanagh was fifteen times published as one of a number of runners-up but never succeeded in winning the half guinea. A few samples from these *Independent* poems will suffice to reveal the archaic imagery and outmoded poetic diction resulting from his imitation of nineteenth-century models:

> O break, cold heart!
> Thou'rt lost
> For want of wine.
> Why dost thou beat when I
> Have given the sign? . . .
>> ('The Pessimist', 22 September 1928)

> From Memories's garden I cull fair blooms
> To deck in splendour my heart's bare rooms.
>> ('In October', 10 November 1928)

> I knocked at your door and craved
> One grain of gold,
> It would not ope to my knocking,
> The night was cold.
> I lay where the vanquished lie,
> Now as of old.
>> ('To Fame', 2 March 1929)

As the mature poet humorously observed, 'The Assyrian has come down like a wolf' on such amateur versifying.[20] Another perceptible influence, especially on his love poetry, were the popular sentimental ballads and waltz tunes of the period:

> Away to dreamy places I
> Would steal at sundown's gleaming
> To smother a deep bosom sigh,
> And live my life a-dreaming . . .
>> ('Freedom', 1 September 1928)

Kavanagh's first published attempt at adapting schoolbook verse to Inniskeen conditions[21] was 'Address to an Old Wooden Gate', printed in his local newspaper, *The Dundalk Democrat*, on 2 February 1929:

Battered by time and weather, scarcely fit
For firewood; there's not a single bit
Of paint to hide those wrinkles and such scringes
Break hoarsely on the silence — rusty hinges.
A barbed wire clasp around one withered arm
Replaces the old latch with evil charm,
That poplar tree you hang upon is rotten
And all its early loveliness forgotten.
This gap ere long must find another sentry
If the cows are not to roam the open country . . .
Here have I kept fair tryst and kept it true
When we were lovers all and you were new.
And many a time I've seen the laughing eyed
Schoolchildren, on your trusty back astride.
But Time's long silver hand has touched our brows
And I'm the scorn of women, you of cows . . .

It was possibly the exigencies of rhyme that compelled the young poet to include the local dialect word 'scringes' among the poeticisms, 'ere long' and 'fair tryst', and to arrive at the unconventional pairing of 'sentry' with 'country'. The precursor poem here is 'The Deserted Village' and Kavanagh copies its heroic couplets and crudely catches its tonal blend of elegy and whimsy. It would appear that he was beginning to take literary notice of such familiar objects as 'rusty hinges', 'barbed wire', and 'cows' but he was still only semi-serious about his local poetry. It was appropriate for a Dundalk newspaper, not for the national weekly where he was publishing his 'serious' verses.

A new aesthetic influence, which had begun to supersede his schoolbook poetics, ensured that several more years would elapse before Kavanagh became imaginatively involved with the sights and sounds of his own neighbourhood. In August 1925 he was suddenly made aware of the existence of contemporary literature when he chanced upon *The Irish Statesman*, the weekly journal of arts and ideas edited by AE, in a Dundalk newsagents. The first issue he read introduced him to the names of James Joyce and Gertrude Stein.[22] Here also he encountered his first modern poem, AE's 'Cities'. From then until its demise in April 1930 *The Irish Statesman*, which he purchased every week, was the isolated Inniskeen poet's sole link with the world of contemporary letters.

Kavanagh now came under the aesthetic guidance of that kindly patron and fosterer of so many young Irish writers, AE, mystic and intellectual, the 'most famous Irishman living permanently in Ireland'. A founding father of the Literary Revival, AE, early in his poetic career, had decided that the twilight verse of the 1890s was his appropriate mode. He was a visionary, his 'heart drunk with a beauty' that his 'eyes could never see', and his poetry was preoccupied with the creation of a dream world. Its indistinct images, vague diction and other-worldly aspirations were the debased remnants of a Shelleyan poetics and its metrics owed much to Swinburne and Morris. 'Cities', which so excited the twenty-year-old Kavanagh, represents AE's Celtic twilit approach to an urban theme:

Faery shall dance in
The streets of the town
And from sky headlands
The Gods looking down.

The Waste Land might as well not have been written. A poem with the promising realist title, 'The Things Seen', is as Swinburnian in its pervasive immaterialism as in its rhythm:

The shadows drifted apart leaving the shadowless soul;
A high, winged, glittering airy creature of the sky.
What had we known of it but a fugitive flash of wing.
We had been drowned in our own shadows, you and I . . .
(*The Irish Statesman*, 7 September 1929)

The poems published in *The Irish Statesman* were usually idealistic, dreamy or incantatory lyrics and translations or adaptations of Gaelic verse. Short lyrics with rhymed, four-line stanzas predominated. It was a poetry at odds with the texture and idiom of contemporary life. Even the 'Nocturne' of a Modernist like Thomas McGreevy conformed to AE's predilection for cosmic vagueness:

> I labour in a barren place,
> Alone, self-conscious, frightened, blundering;
> Above me stars wheeling in space,
> About my feet, earth voices whispering.
> (*The Irish Statesman*, 18 September 1929)

The apprentice poet avidly seeking a literary education in the pages of *The Irish Statesman* from 1925 until 1930 was indoctrinated in the poetics of late Romanticism. His views on poetry were shaped by such authoritative aesthetic pronouncements as the following:

> ... it is out of the dream consciousness that poetry is born ... As your aspiration so is your inspiration.
> (*The Irish Statesman*, 29 August 1925)

> In what way did Shelley, Keats, Coleridge, or Wordsworth mirror the life of their time? When they dealt with it directly they were rarely practical. They were at their highest in creating romantic or ideal worlds, and it is possible that the greatest of American writers to come may turn from their swollen cities to nature, and seek refuge in spiritual depths from those riotous surfaces.
> (*The Irish Statesman*, 10 October 1925)

> Prose comes from the conscious mind, while verse comes from the subconscious or dream mind, whose creations seem timeless ...
> (*The Irish Statesman*, 17 October 1925)

He was taught that poetry deserving of praise is 'simple and fresh', 'touched with wonder', 'naively joyous or sad', 'ingenuously credulous of the incredible', and he must have been comforted to learn that 'the peasant, who has no subtle words to express what he sees, does yet see more often than the city dweller the Eternal Phantom in air, sea and earth . . .'[23]

After approximately four years of such indoctrination Kavanagh had learned how to write to the *Irish Statesman* formula and AE accepted three of his poems for publication, 'The Intangible', 'Ploughman' and 'Dreamer'. 'The Intangible', which appeared on 1 February 1930, was Kavanagh's first published poem proper and, despite its ineptitudes, it is not surprising that AE should have printed it, since it is so obviously a product of the *Irish Statesman* school:

> Rapt to starriness — not quite
> I go through fields and fens of night,
> The nameless, the void
> Where ghostly poplars whisper to
> A silent countryside.
> Not black or blue,
> Grey or red or tan
> The skies I travel under.
> A strange unquiet wonder.
> Indian
> Vision and thunder.
> Splendours of Greek,
> Egypt's cloud-woven glory
> Speak no more, speak
> Speak no more
> A thread-worn story.
> Two and two are not four
> On every shore.

The very title of this poem indicates its immaterialism and avoidance of the sensuous. Its locale is 'the nameless, the void': trees are spectral, the countryside, dark and silent, and colour is clumsily dismissed in the second stanza. Kavanagh wisely omitted the naively anti-rationalist concluding couplet from the 1936 version. It is all too easy to find fault with this early poem but it does show the unmistakable influence of AE's vague, mystical muse, not least in the young poet's erasure of Inniskeen and substitution of 'Indian/Vision and thunder'.

AE was a literary father figure to Kavanagh, the first editor of a quality journal to have encouraged and published him. After *The Irish Statesman* had folded Kavanagh went to Dublin to visit this 'great and holy man' in December 1931, seeking further advice and patronage. He walked the sixty-odd miles instead of travelling by train, exaggerating his role of 'country gobshite' in order to impress on the Literary Revival elder his peasant status.[24] AE regarded the Inniskeen poet proprietorially as his discovery, 'a new young genius . . . whose verses' had 'a wild and original fire in them', but recognised that he was uneducated and thought that 'it would be years before he' was 'able to make his wild intuitions into art'. He immediately began to supervise Kavanagh's education, unloading 'three dozen books on him', including such authors as Melville, Emerson, Whitman, Dostoyevsky, Victor Hugo and James Stephens.[25] Through AE, Kavanagh met other Irish writers, among them Frank O'Connor, who endorsed the sage's opinion of Kavanagh's talent and, after AE's departure from Dublin in 1933, took him under his wing. He also became friendly with Seán O'Faoláin, who was soon to play an influential role in Irish cultural life and in Kavanagh's literary career.[26] An introduction to the poet, Seumas O'Sullivan, editor of *The Dublin Magazine*, had the practical advantage of securing an Irish outlet for his poetry in the decade after the closure of *The Irish Statesman*. From now on the formerly isolated Inniskeen poet was in touch with the world of Irish letters. Between 1931 and 1939 he made frequent trips to Dublin to expand his literary acquaintance and receive artistic stimulation and guidance.

From 1930 new influences began to compete with, though not to oust, the aesthetic Kavanagh had learned from AE in the *Irish Statesman*. His horizons now broadened to include the English and American literary scene. In 1931 he published poems in two English journals, the *Spectator* and *John O'London's*.[27] He was reading Hopkins, Edward Thomas, Pound, Gertrude Stein, Archibald McLeish, and poring over back copies of *Poetry* (Chicago). He now began experimenting with a more sharply focused, hard-edged verse. 'Gold Watch' (1931) is an early instance of this newly acquired interest in rendering 'objective reality':[28]

> Engraved on the case
> House and mountain
> And a far mist
> Rising from faery fountain.
>
> On inner case
> No. 2244
> Elgin Nath . . .
> Sold by a guy in a New York store.
>
> Dates of repairs
> 1914 M. Y., 1918 H. J.,
> She has had her own cares . . .

'Gold Watch' fluctuates between Celtic mists and fairies and tough American realism. The most personalised of these 'eye on the object' poems is 'My Room' (1933):

> 10 by 12
> And a low roof
> if I stand by the side wall
> my head feels the reproof.
>
> Five holy pictures
> hang on the walls—
> The Virgin and Child
> St. Anthony of Padua
> St. Patrick our own
> Leo XIII
> and the Little Flower . . .

'Tinker's Wife' with its precise ugly images and its free rhyme is the most modern of Kavanagh's early thirties' pieces, one of a few poems in which he 'praises by showing' without any intrusive first-person commentary.[29]

> She searched on the dunghill debris,
> Tripping gingerly
> Over tin canisters
> And sharp-broken
> Dinner plates.

Some poems from the sequence, 'Seven Birds' (later 'Four Birds'), and 'To a Late Poplar' (1934) imitate the Imagist mode inaugurated by Pound in that they present a fusion of two disparate experiences in one objective image:

> Not yet half-drest
> O tardy bride!
> And the priest
> And the bridegroom and the guests
> Have been waiting a full hour.

> The meadow choir
> Is playing the wedding march
> Two fields away,
> And squirrels are already leaping in ecstasy
> Among leaf-full branches.

As in several of Pound's Imagist poems the title of this piece, 'To a Late Poplar', explains the latent subject, and the poem proper is entirely devoted to the presentation of the image. Yet because its language and poetic stance have not been sufficiently modernised, this poem teeters between fanciful rural metaphor and Imagism. The apostrophe, emphasised by the vocative 'O', one of Kavanagh's favourite techniques in the early 1930s, is a leftover from his nineteenth-century phase.

Long years in the wilderness had left Kavanagh hungry for recognition and he was touting a collection from as early as

1933. Eventually, in April 1936, Macmillan undertook to publish *Ploughman and Other Poems* in its Contemporary Poets Series. This was a paperback series selling at a shilling, primarily intended to introduce new poets to the public. Later, Macmillan's letter of acceptance promised, this small first collection might be augmented by a second group of poems and the combined collection sold in the usual cloth-bound volume at a higher price.[30] It was less distinction than Kavanagh had hoped for, but probably as much as his work at this stage merited, though the sonnet, 'Inniskeen Road: July Evening', first published in *Ploughman*, is the first poem in which he discovers a distinctive voice and remains one of his finest lyrics.

Ploughman and Other Poems, a collection of thirty-one poems, which appeared in summer 1936, might euphemistic-ally be described as eclectic. 'They're fake', AE is reputed to have said of the poems in the ur-collection, despite his great affection for Kavanagh.[31] He was presumably referring to the absence of any sense of a characteristic preoccupation, style, form, attitude or voice in these lyrics. Kavanagh's next collection, which was not published by Macmillan until 1947, did not include any of his *Ploughman* poems, probably because a decade later he already regarded these brief lyrics as juvenilia.

In the meantime he had submitted two collections of forty poems to John Gawsworth for publication in a series of booklets he was editing for the Richards Press: *The Seed and the Soil*, Second Poems (1937) and *To Anna Quinn*, Third Poems (1938). Gawsworth would have published a selection of these poems had the series not come to an untimely end.[32] No clear sense of direction is manifest in either Kavanagh's Second or Third Poems. He is still floundering between various models and the quality of the poetry is markedly uneven, as if he were more concerned to publish almost everything and bring the number of poems up to forty in each case than to prune and discard.

However, certain themes, stances and mannerisms do

recur in Kavanagh's thirties' verse, some of which would persist in a modified form throughout his mature poetry. There are also some really fine poems in which he stumbled into originality or, what he later called, 'the right simplicity', though at the time he was 'too thick to take the hint'.[33] Since no clear linear progress is discernible in Kavanagh's poetry from the early 1930s to 1939, there is no point in pursuing a chronological approach any further. A more enlightening view of his sporadic development will emerge from a study of some of his varied poetic preoccupations and strategies as he tacked and veered on his uncertain course throughout the decade.

I divide Kavanagh's thirties' poems into three groups, though the distinction between them is sometimes blurred and there are some instances of overlapping. The first is a group of reflexive poems culminating in 'Inniskeen Road: July Evening'. The second and third are both groups of 'ploughman' poems, lyrics written in the persona of farmer-poet; the second is a study of the Georgian and religious strains in this rural verse and includes 'Poplar Memory' and 'Threshing Morning'; the third considers Kavanagh's 'peasant' poetry in an Irish post-Revival context and focuses on his own best-loved thirties' poem, 'Shancoduff'. Kavanagh's development throughout the 1930s was spasmodic because he was usually frightened of venturing outside the norms of the poetically respectable. It is remarkable that the only poems in which he risks offending against contemporary taste are all set in Inniskeen. The imaginative excitement of moving in his familiar local world energised him into kicking the traces of poetic politeness, freeing himself from inhibiting orthodoxies of phrase and image.

Tradition and the Individual Talent

(i)

Almost every poem in Kavanagh's first decade is a lyric, presented from a first-person, present-tense perspective.

Almost none achieves individuality. This is because they are for the most part safe formula-poems, written in conformity with existing models of the poetic, with modes of perception that prevent the poet from expressing something new. Poetry, as William Carlos Williams remarked, 'needs some tincture of disestablishment', is 'subversive of life as it was before'. The new hasn't time to be correct and Kavanagh was still seeking literary orthodoxy. The principal obstacle to individuality for the young Kavanagh was his perception that his personal situation and idiom were unsuited to poetry. He purposely copied stances and styles that seemed legitimately literary, he cultivated derivativeness. Rather than admit any hint of his actual circumstances into his first-person verse, he preferred to don ready-made masks, play expected roles, adopt conventional attitudes, disguise his speaking voice, hide behind clichéd metaphors.

His poetry was so dependent on literary models for its validity that he sometimes did not bother to conceal its bookish associations. An old white goat strays into his verse, not as a familiar local beast, but because he reminds the poet of a goat encountered 'seven years ago' in a James Stephens lyric. Even love pangs require explicit literary legitimisation:

> Her name was poet's grief before
> Mary, the saddest name
> In all the litanies of love
> And all the books of fame.
>
> I think of poor John Clare's beloved
> And know the blessed pain . . .
>
> ('Mary')

In 'To M' the unrequited lover consoles himself with the recollection that there is an honourable literary tradition of sublimated passion:

> Keats to his Fanny Brawne of dream mated
> And Dante a nobler Beatrice won
> And Mangan calling to his Nameless One

> And the pensive poets of the Gael
> Embracing the stars of True Beauty . . .

In his thirties' verse Kavanagh favoured the equation of poet and pre-Freudian, Romantic dreamer because it denied poetry any realist dimension. He reverted to the Romantic symbolist identification of lyricism and birdsong, saluting the blackbird as a fellow poet and depicting the kestrel as a 'true artist'. AE's transcendentalism was attractive because it allowed him to transport his verse from his everyday surroundings to some vague never never land. Georgianism and Imagism offered a contrary inducement, enabling him to single out some appropriate scene or object and focus on it in isolation from its context; Imagism, of course, had the apparent advantage of eliminating subjectivity. However, despite occasional experiments with 'eye on the object' verse, he was less a descriptive nature poet than a neo-Romantic, less concerned with 'objective reality' than with subjective reaction.

Kavanagh was inhibited from a direct presentation of his unique personal situation in the 1930s by the absence of appropriate poetic precedents, by a Victorian sense of poetic decorum and by a desire to protect his own privacy. The last is offered as an explanation of his obliquity in 'Snail', where the speaker's 'Self' remains exultantly inaccessible, enclosed in his 'twisted habitation',[34] allowing the public to view only his misleading printed trail:

> I know the shadow-ways
> Of Self
> I know the last sharp bend
> And the volleyed light.
>
> You are lost
> You can merely chase the silver I have let
> Fall from my purse,
> You follow silver
> And not follow me.

Yet Kavanagh's thirties' verse, however non-autobiographical, is obsessively self-referential and reflexive. Its first-person speaker is a poet and frequently named as such. Its subject is usually the poet's lonely pursuit of his vocation. Its stance is self-justifying, self-consoling, self-pitying. Throughout his life Kavanagh was to subscribe to the high Romantic creed that the poet is set apart from ordinary mortals, privileged or cursed by his gift. This sense of his poetic specialness helped to sustain him in his chosen career during those difficult neophyte years in the unsympathetic and uncongenial environment of Inniskeen. He portrays himself as a loner, kindred to the blackbird, not to 'Earth's sad children', a 'pagan poet' in a Catholic parish; he aspires to be 'Brother to no man'. What his thirties' poetry conveys either explicitly or implicitly is his self-imposed aesthetic isolation from the life of his neighbourhood, his suppression of his own sensuousness in the cause of art, his occasionally regretful but unwavering commitment to the role of poet.

An insistence on divorcing art from life impelled the young poet to distance his literary personae, situations and language from his normal personality, everyday milieu and ordinary speech cadences. The 'I' figure in his thirties' poems passes most of his brief lyric life in pursuit or avoidance of capitalised abstractions and personifications, posturing in improbable metaphorical conditions, speaking in hortatory tones, solemnly addressing the reader, admonishing himself, or apostrophising. One of Kavanagh's poetic models was the Shelleyan quest for the ideal. The speaker in his short thirties' lyrics is often a 'scorner of the ground', a diminished Alastor, dissatisfied with the actual and striving after an undefined and unattainable goal. Images of yearning and unfulfilment proliferate. The lyricist hungers for 'the wisdom that grows/ In the other lands'; the 'potion of charm' is always 'out of reach'. A recurring image of remote, desirable beauty is the star, also a favourite with AE. Star-gazing, a strategy for directing poetic attention away from the earthly, usually results in a poetry that is vague and unrealised:

Beauty was that
Far vanished flame,
Call it a star
Wanting better name.

And gaze and gaze
Vaguely . . .

('A Star')

Following the Shelleyan model the quest for the unattainable
is depicted in imagery of unsuccessful pursuit:

I follow the blind dog
Crying to my star; O star
Of a passionate pagan's desire
Lead me to the truths that are.

('Blind Dog')

or

I followed Wisdom
A night and a night
And a day and a day
Clay-knowing to spite . . .

Yet never I
Caught up with slow-footed
Wisdom who took
The lanes deepest rutted . . .

('The Chase')

Such straining after absolutist abstractions like beauty, wisdom and truth only covertly suggests aesthetic ambitions and
insecurities, the aching longing for adequacy. Personal and
literary anxieties are accommodated in generalised terms to
ensure privacy as well as poetic propriety. Kavanagh was
slow to relinquish this attitude of yearning. As late as 1938 he
was still writing about the 'Pursuit of an Ideal'.

The obverse of Shelleyan aspiration in these thirties' lyrics
is deprivation. Poverty is presented defensively as a voluntary or desirable condition for the dedicated poet:

That in the end
I may find
Something not sold for a penny
In the slums of Mind.

That I may break
With these hands
The bread of wisdom that grows
In the other lands.

For this, for this
Do I wear
The rags of hunger and climb
The unending stair.

('Ascetic')

'Soft Ease', originally entitled 'Beggar's Ease', makes comfort inimical to poetic endeavour, not an opinion that the older Kavanagh would readily have endorsed.

Wisdom, an undefined condition signifying knowledge, rationality, poetic adequacy or even adulthood, is sometimes sought after in these poems, sometimes spurned. It is customarily represented negatively when contrasted with folly or innocence. One of the poet's favourite thirties' roles is that of fool, the title role adopted in his 1938 autobiography, *The Green Fool*. In his poetry the figure of the fool is invoked not, as one might expect, to suggest low self-esteem but, rather, inverted superiority. The exaltation of the fool is closely connected with Kavanagh's cult of anti-intellectualism and irrationality in poems where the speaker is a 'high dunce', intent on avoiding 'the drouth of desert knowledge', anxious not to awaken 'the academic scholars' and not to purchase what is on offer in 'the slums of Mind'. From one lyric, at least, it is evident that anti-intellectualism compensates for a sense of educational deficiency:

Once the Golden Book was open to me
And I read

The Answer to the Riddle
And I, an unschooled rustic
Was wise
As fool's laughter in an academy . . .

('Poet')

In 'Street Corner Christ', the most self-congratulatory of the 'fool' poems, Christ is depicted as an unkempt beggarly poet and the fool triumphs by being the only one to penetrate his disguise. The role of fool, beggar, pariah or naif generally serves as a self-inflationary pose in Kavanagh's thirties' verses, a mask concealing genuine merit from the unappreciative gaze of the vulgar or a lowly condition voluntarily endured for the sake of higher spiritual gains. By 1938 he represents himself clinging to the role of fool, fearful that 'dignified ways' will prove disastrous.[35] This particular self-image, in fact, was about to disappear from his verse. In *The Great Hunger* (1942), the contrast between wisdom and folly is playfully dismissed in a throw-away couplet:

Two cyclists pass
Talking loudly of Kitty and Molly—
Horses or women? wisdom or folly?

The cult of the irrational, however, remained a feature of Kavanagh's poetry to the end.

In his thirties' verse, wisdom was also presented negatively when coupled with innocence. Innocence, for Kavanagh, connotes regression into childhood as a refuge from sexuality and self-knowledge:

Child do not go
Into the dark places of soul,
For there the grey wolves whine,
The lean grey wolves . . .

('To a Child')

It was Pound who later taught him that poetry is not an affair of prolonged adolescence, that the full range of adult

experience is available to the poet.[36] The speaker in Kavanagh's primitivist thirties' verse recoils from both the adult and
the urban: childhood and unsophisticated 'meadow ways',
sexual depravity and city life, are sometimes found in
conjunction:

> God keep you child
> When you go down
> The faithless streets
> Of Pleasure's town . . .

('Orthodox')

Dublin is destructive of laughter and innocence ('To a Child')
while New York and Paris are sexually corrupt, red light
districts where

> The no-good dames
> Tattoo my flesh with the indelible
> Ink of lust.

('At Noon')

Kavanagh's primitivist verse is righteously puritanical.
Like the sexually inhibited Patrick Maguire of *The Great
Hunger* the young poet

> saw Sin
> Written in letters larger than John Bunyan dreamt
>   of . . .

This anti-sensuous bias in his thirties' poetry is related, in
some measure, to its abstraction and immaterialism. Sexuality is perceived as a threat to poetic incorporeality, so
woman is depicted as a 'Siren' who tempts the poet into
descending from his 'spiritual heights' only to destroy him:

> And I came down and my house came down
> Stone and slate and rafter
> And unhoused I wandered in Woman's town
> Beggared by Woman's laughter.

Here there is an oblique recognition of the connection
between poetry and sexual sublimation. As the 1930s progressed, Kavanagh occasionally betrayed a momentary impatience with the narcissism of his verse:

Everything I look upon
I make
A mirror of
Wherein to see myself in all its seasons.

('Mirrors')

He became more sympathetic to the idea of a 'clay-sensuous' art, to the image of the artist as 'Pygmalion' or as lover. The 1938 sonnet, 'Pursuit of an Ideal', is complemented by another sonnet, 'In the Same Mood', which concludes:

I want by Man, not God, to be inspired.
This year O maiden of the dream-vague face
You'll come to me, a thing of Time and Space.

Failure in poetry and in love are conjoined in the most epigrammatically succinct of the thirties' poems, 'Sanctity':

To be a poet and not know the trade,
To be a lover and repel all women;
Twin ironies by which great saints are made,
The agonising pincer-jaws of Heaven.

This terse quatrain sentence lays out its dual inadequacies in two paratactic parallel clauses; in the remaining two lines these are joined to fashion an excruciating instrument of torture in which both converge to pincer the martyr. Whatever about his success as a lover the masterly use of compression here shows remarkable proficiency in the trade of poetry.

The cult of asceticism in Kavanagh's thirties' verse derives in part from a genuine conflict between sensuous enjoyment and artistic discipline. As an after-hours apprentice poet he had to forego many of the pleasures of young manhood to find the leisure to read and write, and one of the themes of his reflexive lyrics is the human cost of being a poet. In 'Poet' the speaker is a reluctant 'monk' and poetry, a cloistered, celibate art:

Winter encloses me
I am fenced

> The light the laugh the dance
> Against.

Such sacrifice of manhood to poethood is more circumstantially and more complexly treated in 'April Dusk':

> It is tragic to be a poet now
> And not a lover
> Paradised under the mutest bough.

Shades of Milton's Adam and Eve or Keats's 'Bold lover' may hover here, but Kavanagh's poem focuses on a personal frustration, the plight of the 'silenced poet' who, like a silenced priest, is still vowed to celibacy though unable to perform his ministry:

> An unmusical ploughboy whistles down the lane
> Not worried at all about the fate of Europe
> While I sit here feeling the subtle pain
> That every silenced poet has endured.

The interplay of sound and silence increases this poem's resonance. Tunefulness or discord matters little to the carefree 'ploughboy' the poet might have been. The poet, on the contrary, appraises his world in terms of sound and silence, displacing the 'subtle pain' of his own inarticulateness on to the 'mutest bough' which dumbly witnesses the lover's pleasure yet does not participate in it. It would be a further twelve years before Kavanagh 'worried' about the relationship between his poetry and the 'Phoney War'.

Resentment at his self-imposed seclusion from 'The light, the laugh, the dance' provoked one of Kavanagh's finest thirties' lyrics, 'Inniskeen Road: July Evening', a sonnet in which he dares to write out of his peculiar personal circumstances, as a young Inniskeen man whose poetic gift excludes him from the normal pleasures enjoyed by his neighbours:

> The bicycles go by in twos and threes—
> There's a dance in Billy Brennan's barn to-night,

And there's the half-talk code of mysteries
And the wink-and-elbow language of delight.
Half-past eight and there is not a spot
Upon a mile of road, no shadow thrown
That might turn out a man or woman, not
A footfall tapping secrecies of stone.

I have what every poet hates in spite
Of all the solemn talk of contemplation.
Oh, Alexander Selkirk knew the plight
Of being king and government and nation.
A road, a mile of kingdom, I am king
Of banks and stones and every blooming thing.

For the first time Kavanagh has the confidence to give his poetry a local habitation and local names, to situate the 'I' in the parish of Inniskeen, reacting to everyday happenings, gestures, talk. As he sets his poem in a familiar scene it takes on a new specificity. Even in the title he is conscious of time and place and the passage of the half-hour as opposed to the passing of 'Time' is a feature of the poem's movement. The particularity here is of a different order than in Kavanagh's other realist/imagist experiments. There the objects presented were detached from their context; here 'a world comes to life'. This is a peopled poem where neighbours chat and flirt as they cycle past and a sense of localisation is casually achieved by the mention of 'Billy Brennan's barn'. The speaker is simultaneously an insider and an outsider, fully conversant with the drama of local life yet denied any share in it. This alienated poet is himself a dramatic character rather than a rhetorical figure, refreshingly honest and humorously rueful about the anomaly of being a poet in Inniskeen.

The move to local realism is accompanied as in other 'eye on the object' experiments by a relaxation from the artificialities of poetic diction into a spoken idiom, especially in the opening lines. In his description of this ordinary scene the speaker uses 'and' twice to slacken the conjunction and repeats the limp introductory phrase, 'There's', but the language also shows a new linguistic ease and vitality in the coinage of colloquial turns of speech out of monosyllables and commonplace words in 'half-talk code' and 'wink-and-elbow language'. From line 5 the speech rhythm becomes more rhetorical, swelling and diminishing, falling and rising, controlled by checks and pauses that enhance its emotive effects. This change to a rhetorical mode coincides with the disappearance of everyday life and speech, the shift from neighbourhood to landscape.

That Kavanagh's first public act of poetic self-disclosure should have been expressed through the medium of a sonnet may appear remarkably proleptic to those familiar with his later poetry. Most of his thirties' verse was rhymed and formally regular, usually consisting of three, four or five short-lined stanzas. The form he found most challenging was the sonnet, and he returned to it repeatedly throughout the decade in, for instance, 'After May', 'Morning', 'Pygmalion', 'Primrose', 'Pursuit of an Ideal' and 'In the Same Mood'. ('Worship' is a sestet.) He was to retain a lifelong fascination with the sonnet, not merely because it is 'the most popular vehicle for the expression of love' but because 'it forces the mind to moral activity but is not itself forced'.[37] Purists might object that in 'Inniskeen Road' he combines a Shakespearian rhyme scheme with a Petrarchan dual structure, but this mixed form is perfectly adapted to the thematic movement of his poem. Setting the scene on a mile of road enables him to populate it in the first quatrain of the octet, depopulate it in the second and focus on the singular 'poet' in the sestet, and the present tense lends immediacy to this unfolding action. The customary disjunction between the octet and sestet of the Petrarchan sonnet is exploited to direct attention away from the villagers and towards the 'poet', marking the change from external presentation to internal reaction, from description to reflection. So the spatial separation of the two parts of the sonnet on the printed page reinforces the theme of the 'poet's' apartness from his fellow villagers.

In the first quatrain Kavanagh focuses on the shared

delights from which the 'poet' is excluded and the emphasis is on community and communication. The villagers cycle in 'twos and threes' on their way to a communal revel, the barn dance. Theirs is a conspiratorial vernacular, incomprehensible to outsiders, composed of hints and gestures, part metaphysical, part body language. By coining new phrases to convey this language, Kavanagh is bending standard English to accommodate local speech.

The second quatrain is transitional, emphasising the sense of emptiness and quiet that follows on the revellers' exit, straining after human images and messages. Here negatives build towards a conclusive silence; all movement and music are concentrated in the far-off dance; the sonnet slows down to a standstill, petrifies. The octet concludes with a peculiarly haunting line, 'not/A footfall tapping secrecies of stone', where the code of line 3 is given added meaning and a more profound resonance.

After a blank wordless interval the sonnet resumes with a new surge of energy. The withdrawn observer now takes the centre stage, soliloquising on his isolation. In this highly sound-conscious and language-conscious poem the speaker is separated from his fellow villagers both by a silent space in the text and by a language barrier of his own devising. What the soliloquist foregrounds is the unwelcome divergence between poetic discourse and Inniskeen speech, the contrast between the 'solemn' and solitary 'talk of contemplation' and the semi-articulate 'half-talk' that is the condition of companionable local conversation. He dramatises himself into a marooned Alexander Selkirk, a voluntary castaway for poetry's sake, magnifying his deserted village into a desert island. The sestet subverts the already subversive opening stanza of Cowper's 'Verses Supposed to be written by Alexander Selkirk', adapting it half seriously, half tongue-in-cheek, to the 'poet's' unsociable life in Inniskeen:

> I am monarch of all I survey
> My right there is none to dispute

> From the centre all round to the sea,
> I am lord of the fowl and the brute.
> O solitude! where are the charms
> That sages have seen in thy face?
> Better dwell in the midst of alarms,
> Than reign in this horrible place.

Cowper's balancing of spurious regal dignity and painful social ostracism provides a perfect analogue for the Inniskeen 'poet's' blend of Romantic superiority and human loneliness, yet the element of parody gives an air of playfulness to his inflationary self-dramatisation. The poet/speaker crowns himself insistently and repetitively in the closing lines of the sonnet but its concluding line and rhyme mock his autocratic pretensions. Whereas Cowper's Selkirk opposed an Augustan concern with social relations to a philosophical tradition that privileged private contemplation, Kavanagh's Selkirk is an anti-Romantic, debunking the Wordsworthian aesthetic that ennobled the poet's solitary communion with nature. Though the 'solemn talk of contemplation' promoted by poets is now devalued by comparison with 'the half-talk code' enjoyed by ordinary folk, the Inniskeen 'poet's' access to both literary and colloquial language makes possible the final pun on 'blooming', in which pretty poeticism is played off against slangy disparagement.

Kavanagh's thirties' verse is self-centred, while lacking any sense of identity, and self-irony is rare. The poet of 'Inniskeen Road' is the first incarnation of the character who gives his best poetry its distinctive personality; wry, self-mocking, cocking a snook at various orthodoxies, amusedly conscious of his nonconformist relationship with literary tradition, delighting in deflationary effects that only partially destabilise the grandiosities they pretend to undermine. The Kavanagh persona talks rather than sings, plays with various language registers to convey the impression of a quirky individuality, humorous yet offhandedly serious, claiming while apparently disclaiming.

There would appear to be as little territorial possessiveness in 'Inniskeen Road' as in Cowper's ode which values society far above landscape. The Inniskeen 'poet' has *faute de mieux* discovered his 'mile of kingdom' but dismisses it as a comic domain, an unwanted property. Or does he? Even as the poem concludes on a disengaged downbeat the disowned landscape is unobstrusively becoming the focus of attention, taking on plurality and organic life, displacing the convivial human community of the octet. The rhythm of the rhetoric is exultant though its language *seems* scornful. Seems, because the pun on blooming pinpoints the 'poet's' final ambivalence. Cowper's Alexander Selkirk was straightforwardly self-pitying, whereas the quizzical Kavanagh persona prefers to leave the reader guessing. The schoolbook verse that had once dominated the apprentice poet's consciousness is now subverted.

Kavanagh's appropriation of the sonnet is a further act of poetic maturity. Thematically versatile as the sonnet was by 1936 it, nevertheless, would have come as something of a shock to contemporary readers to find this venerable form located in Inniskeen and to have bicycles and Billy Brennan's barn wheeled into view in the opening lines. Kavanagh commandeers the sonnet, not with any parodic intent, but to conscript its services for his mile of kingdom. Whereas he once was governed by the classics of English verse he is now a 'king' who legislates for his own poetry.

(ii)

'Inniskeen Road: July Evening' is an exceptional poem in Kavanagh's first collection, *Ploughman and Other Poems*. While the title of the collection stressed the rurality of his poetry and he was generally publicised as a peasant poet in the 1930s, the poems of this decade are considerably less concerned with country matters than either his life or his public image would lead one to expect. *Ploughman and Other Poems* could have been entitled, with more justification, *The Intangible and Other Poems*. One of the most remarkable features of this poetry is the complete separation between the man who worked and the mind which created. Even the poems on rural subjects, on the whole, are totally lacking in agricultural realism and could have been written by an armchair pastoralist. Seán O'Faoláin has recorded that when Kavanagh visited Dublin in the 1930s he looked like a farmer who had come to town to buy seeds or implements, not like a poet. Reading his thirties' poetry, on the contrary, one almost forgets that he was a farmer-cum-cobbler and that ploughing and sowing were more than symbolic activities in his life. O'Faoláin quotes 'The Sower' to illustrate that it is always his own world of the fields that he [Kavanagh] transmutes into magic:

> I have scattered the grain over the brown clay
> Visioning hunger triumphant in darkling day
> Of a city builded in fields of terrible pain
> Crying out want and sorrow and crying in vain.
>
> I am the Giver's servant. Want and Sorrow
> Lie with their long teeth shattered by my harrow.
> Who sits at my table now and shares my crust
> Shall rise amongst starry fields on winged dust.[38]

If anything is clear from this terrible poem, however, it is that Kavanagh is interested only in the symbolic aspect of sowing and harrowing. Years of work in the fields have contributed nothing to this or to other poems where farm imagery is used figuratively, such as 'I May Reap' or 'Twisted Furrows'.

One of the major factors contributing to the absence of agricultural realism in so much of Kavanagh's thirties' poetry was his custom of drawing on rural images as religious

metaphors. While several of his Realist or Imagist experiments were competent within their limits their secular self-
containment was alien to his genius. His Irish Catholic
upbringing prevented his becoming a disciple of T. E.
Hulme's, contenting himself with a 'dry, hard' verse that
rejected mystery, infinity and transcendence.[39] Whatever his
occasional minor irritations with Catholicism and his posing
as a pagan poet in 'To a Blackbird' and 'Blind Dog', he was a
Catholic Romantic. The doctrines and liturgy of Catholicism
had from childhood inculcated in him a metaphoric attitude
to material reality, a tendency to read the world symbolically.
AE's mystical poetics reinforced this predisposition towards
the transcendental.

In Kavanagh's early poetry AE's Oriental and Romantic
immaterialism is christened:

> And in the green meadows
> The maiden of Spring is with child
> By the Holy Ghost.
>
> ('April')

or

> The trees were in suspense,
> Listening with an intense
> Anxiety for the Word . . .
>
> ('March')

The Romantic concept of the poet as priest is represented in
Eucharistic clichés:

> That I may break
> With these hands
> The bread of wisdom . . .
>
> ('Ascetic')

> O cut for me life's bread, for me pour wine!
> ('Worship')

> I too have eaten of the holy bread . . .
> ('Pioneers')

Literary positives and negatives are defined in Christian terminology: 'Seraphim', 'Heaven', the Garden of Eden versus 'the devil's contrition', and 'A hell-fantasy/From meadows damned/To eternal April'. To mention the pervasiveness of conventional Catholic imagery and vocabulary in Kavanagh's thirties' poems is merely to state the obvious. His reading of Hopkins, which had the deleterious effect of lumbering his verses with neologisms and awkward hyphenated coinages,[40] probably imbued him with confidence in the acceptability of Catholicism as a literary creed. Recent Irish poetry, with the exception of Joseph Campbell's, had tended to ignore the Catholic dimension of Irish country life. Despite one flash of scepticism about transcendental experience in the 1930s —

> A light that might be mystic or a fraud
> Played on far hills beyond all common sight . . .
>> ('After May')

— the mystical transfiguration of the actual was to be a recurring theme in Kavanagh's poetry to the end of his career.

Throughout the 1930s his Catholic transcendentalism usually reinforced his tendency towards vagueness in theme and image, encouraging his liking for inflationary abstract language and for apostrophe. Even in 'Ploughman', where he represents himself in the present tense as a working ploughman, he pays little attention to the job in hand and is more anxious to appear an aesthete and mystic than a farmer:

> I turn the lea-green down
> Gaily now,
> And paint the meadow brown
> With my plough.
>
> I dream with silvery gull
> And brazen crow.
> A thing that is beautiful
> I may know.

Tranquillity walks with me
And no care.
O, the quiet ecstasy
Like a prayer.

I find a star-lovely art
In a dark sod.
Joy that is timeless! O heart
That knows God!

Ploughing is presented as an aesthetic activity: 'I . . . paint the meadow brown/With my plough', 'I find a star-lovely art/ In a dark sod.' Twelve years later Kavanagh will re-create the kinetic exhilaration of ploughing: 'The pull is on the traces . . .'.Here he bypasses physical sensation to engage in transcendental posturings: 'Tranquillity walks with me', 'O, the quiet ecstasy/Like a prayer', 'O heart/That knows God'. Agricultural realities do not impinge on his imaginings. The gulls and crows who follow the ploughman are transformed into aesthetes and artifacts, fellow dreamers and static sculptures. 'Brazen' probably means 'impudent', but in conjunction with 'silvery' it too has a metallic clang, and the singular nouns enhance the effect of stylisation. The older poet would view crows and gulls in the ploughing field with a more observant and more disenchanted eye:

Here crows gabble over worms and frogs
And the gulls like old newspapers are blown clear of
the hedges, luckily.

In 'Ploughman', on the contrary, his aim is to transfigure the drab actualities of the small-farmer's life into a 'star-lovely art', to substitute the 'timeless' for the temporal. His anecdote about the origins of this poem in *The Green Fool* seems expressly designed to illustrate the discrepancy between the actual circumstances of his life and the ingredients of his art at this period:

Holding the handles of a rusty old plough that was drawn by a kicking mare I made a poem . . . I could not help smiling when I thought of the origin of my ploughman ecstasy. A kicking mare in a rusty old plough tilling a rood of land for turnips.

'To the Man after the Harrow' is a reflexive, hortatory poem about the necessity of erasing agricultural realities and focusing on their religious symbolism. Consequently, though is begins with two of his most farmer-like lines:

> Now leave the check-reins slack,
> The seed is flying far to-day . . .

it immediately moves into figurative and abstract language and finally concludes in a religious haze:

> For you are driving your horses through
> The mist where Genesis begins.

Kavanagh's criticism of Philip Francis Little's work is applicable to much of his own poetry at this period:

He is all tension, all anxiety to read eternal messages in the earthly symbol. He desired mystical experience but did not realize that the madness, which too intense desire of any kind is, needs to have in it a great deal of carnal method . . .[41]

It is not surprising that as a rural poet with religious proclivities Kavanagh should have found a congenial model in Georgian pastoral. Despite the Modernist eruption into the tranquil English poetic scene there was still a considerable vogue for this less flamboyantly intellectual and more technically conservative verse. Georgian poetry was meditative, smooth, low-keyed, a rural poetry that ignored messy particularities and focused on genteel images, generic symbols and spiritually elevating reactions. Kavanagh's attraction to this poetic model would have been strengthened by his friendship with John Gawsworth from the mid-1930s, for Gawsworth was 'Co-ordinator of the neo-Georgian lyric poetry movement' during that period.[42] The attraction was mutual since the Georgians were very sympathetic to Kavanagh's religio-rural effusions. To the anthologist, Thomas Moult, 'Ploughman' was among the best poems published in British, Irish and American periodicals between July 1929 and June 1930 and he included it in *The Best Poems of 1930*.[43] The less naif and more technically polished 'Plough Horses' was anthologised in John Gawsworth's *Fifty Years of Modern Verse*:[44]

> Their glossy flanks and manes outshone
> The flying splinters of the sun.
>
> The tranquil rhythm of that team
> Was as slow flowing meadow stream.
>
> And I saw Phidias's chisel there—
> An ocean stallion, mountain mare—
>
> Seeing with eyes the Spirit unsealed
> Plough-horses in a quiet field.

Kavanagh normally tried to market his Georgian pastoral poetry in England in the 1930s and restricted his Irish or localised rural poetry to Irish journals. *The Spectator*, for instance, published 'The Ploughman' where the ploughman speaker's sole function is to transpose a simplified physical landscape to a simplistic metaphysical schema:[45]

> And when a man's a ploughman
> As I am now
> An age is a furrow
> And Time a plough,
>
> And Infinity a field . . .

As the older poet observed,

> What proof have we that a man's poetical vision is genuine when we know that to the immediate scene he is totally blind?[46]

It is only when Georgian manner is allied to particularised personal and local circumstance as in 'Poplar Memory', an elegy for the poet's father, that elevation from a physical to a metaphysical dimension becomes more than a polite exercise:

> I walked under the autumned poplars that my father
>   planted
> On a day in April when I was a child
> Running beside the heap of suckers
> From which he picked the straightest, most
>   promising.
>
> My father dreamt forests, he is dead —
> And there are poplar forests in the waste-places
> And on the banks of drains.
>
> When I look up
> I see my father
> Peering through the branched sky.[47]

As usual with Kavanagh's home-based poetry the rhythm is conversational and he also uses the unpoetic 'heap' and substitutes the local word, 'drains', for streams. Unusually, the role of the 'I' is subordinated and the poem is emotionally reticent, its grief mediated through imagery. The traditional literary associations of the human and natural cycles are renewed by the autobiographical immediacy of this imagery, and the poem develops organically through its skilful grafting of the father's belatedly realised dreams on to the central image of the poplars.

Despite its Wordsworthian ancestry, Georgian poetry was more hospitable to expressions of 'spiritual sweetness' than to visionary illumination. It would seem that it was from Wordsworth himself, a poet whose exemplary influence he never acknowledged, that Kavanagh learned how to combine 'carnal method' with transcendental vision. Too many intimations from the Immortality Ode are detectible in the sonnet 'Primrose', with its meanest flower, celestial light, 'child

made seer', 'wonders in the grass' and lament for the passing
of childhood's mystical vision. 'Primrose' flowers in the mind
and its principal gesture towards the sensuous and immediate is the opening phrase, 'Upon a bank I sat'.

* However, the Wordsworthian model of particularised ped-
estrian progress towards epiphany is so well adapted to the
immediate scene in 'Threshing Morning' that the influence is
no longer obtrusive. This is a lyrical ballad in which Kavanagh evokes his life as a young farmer in Inniskeen with that
air of good-humoured casualness which was to be his declared poetic aim in his last years:

> On an apple-ripe September morning
> Through the mist-chill fields I went
> With a pitch-fork on my shoulder
> Less for use than for devilment.
>
> The threshing mill was set-up, I knew,
> In Cassidy's haggard last night,
> And we owed them a day at the threshing
> Since last year. O it was delight
>
> To be paying bills of laughter
> And chaffy gossip in kind
> With work thrown in to ballast
> The fantasy-soaring mind . . .

The movement and rhythm of the 'As I roved out' ballad
contribute to the carefree swing of this sensuous country
song. As with 'Inniskeen Road' its success is chiefly due to
the creation of a persona, here an irresponsible, yet respons-
ive young man, devil may care, relaxed, savouring his life as
a farmer. The poem quickly modulates from its lyrically
succinct autumnal opening to colloquial language, local
names, workaday metaphors and realist details, without any
loss of exhilaration. A Wordsworthian technique of combining walk and commentary helps to sustain an illusion of
improvisation and allows for that blend of specific recognition, remembrance and anticipation which authenticates this
presentation of a small farmer's consciousness:

> And I thought of the wasps' nest in the bank
> And how I got chased one day
> Leaving the drag and the scraw-knife behind,
> How I covered my face with hay.

Mood is all important in this poem, transforming ordinary farming chores into treasured occasions. 'Threshing Morning' culminates in a mystical transfiguration of happy autumn fields, yet even this visionary awareness is relayed with an offhand conviction, since the speaker takes the unexpected epiphany in his stride and does not pause to meditate on its significance:

> And then I came to the haggard gate,
> And I knew as I entered that I had come
> Through fields that were part of no earthly estate.

That final backward glance as the farmer-poet opens the gate and closes the poem illuminates all that has gone before. Ordinary, feckless living is retrospectively blessed. Such a delay in the visionary interpretation of events allows sensuous experience to be savoured for its own sake first and not immediately displaced by mystical insight as in 'Primrose'.

Although he included this poem in a manuscript collection of his 1929–1940 poems Kavanagh did not publish any stanzas from it until 1943.[48] Was he, perhaps, still uneasy in the 1930s about the validity of a poem that included such indecorous local facts as 'Cassidy's haggard', a 'wasps' nest' and a 'scraw-knife'? The farmer-poet of 'Threshing Morning' eventually evolved into the eponymous hero of the novel, *Tarry Flynn* (1948). Belatedly, Kavanagh discovered that in 'Threshing Morning' he had fashioned a poetry consonant with his own life as a farmer-poet, a poetry that combined the earthy, the numinous and the insouciant. Such was his high regard for this poem by the late 1940s that he took the unusual step of concluding his novel with it, presenting it as a summation and distillation of his fictional autobiography.

(iii)

From the mid-1930s, when Kavanagh came into increasing contact with other Irish writers,[49] Literary Revival ideology began to compete with Georgian neo-Romanticism as an influence on his country verses. He was reading Padraic Colum, F. R. Higgins, Frank O'Connor, James Stephens and Seumas O'Sullivan among others. Irish rural poetry in the wake of the Literary Revival was inhospitable to Roman Catholic transcendentalism and, especially, to agricultural realism. Though the merit of Joseph Campbell's folksy Catholic verses was recognised, the touchstone modern Irish rural poem was Padraic Colum's 'The Plougher', in which a farm worker observed from a reverential distance is portrayed as a noble savage, a primitive pagan, his thoughts 'of Pan, or of Wotan, or Dana'. So influential was this poem in providing a literary stereotype of the Irish countryman that even such an intelligent commentator on national affairs as Seán O'Faoláin depicted Kavanagh the man in Colum's terms.[50] By opening *Ploughman and Other Poems* with a poem about a ploughman Kavanagh emulated Colum's *Wild Earth* (1907), a ploy which provoked invidious comparisons between his poetry and Colum's.[51]

Despite the cult of folklore and peasant subjects in the Literary Revival there were no realist Irish models to nerve Kavanagh into drawing on the actualities of farm life for either his poetic themes or images. The peasant who featured in Literary Revival verse was too fully employed in a primitivist challenge to modern industrial values to have any time for spraying the potatoes or carting dung. He was a personified idea rather than a realist character. For most of the 1930s, Kavanagh, too, sidestepped 'the barrel of blue potato spray' and the 'cartloads of dung' to engage with more elevating ideas and images. So the title poem of his second collection, *The Seed and the Soil*, a title which once again misleadingly promises a strongly rural collection, is scarcely more concerned with agricultural realism than 'Ploughman':

> Somebody is moving across the headlands
> Talking to himself
> A grey thinker.

> The clay is whitening in the windy light
> Where the sparrows are bathing.
> Tomorrow surely
> The seed will go under the harrow
> Nothing must hinder
> The wooing of grain and clay.

The scene is more closely observed than in 'Ploughman' but nothing indecorously rural is allowed to disturb this tranquil pastoral.

Kavanagh may have been exaggerating somewhat when he wrote about the literary importance of peasantry in the Dublin of the 1930s:

> In those days in Dublin the big thing besides being Irish was peasant quality. They were all trying to be peasants. They had been at it for years but I hadn't heard. And I was installed as the authentic peasant . . .[52]

Nevertheless, the criterion of 'peasant quality' was such a literary commonplace in the aftermath of the Revival that in Abbey Theatre circles it was abbreviated to 'pq'. One effect of the Revival was to teach Kavanagh new strategies for avoiding agricultural realism. Sometimes he cultivates the 'backward look' favoured by Revivalists, a tendency to ignore contemporary actualities and focus on a vanished or vanishing cultural heritage. A furrow presented from a Revivalist metaphorical perspective is:

> A word in the black Book of Durrow
> Or anything of April-Gaelic story . . .
>
> ('Furrow')

Several thirties' poems praise the 'Old Men of Ireland' or eulogise the poetic forefathers of the hamlet:

> My fathers were a temple in the deep
> Hill-secrecies where I today roll blindly

The masonry of my generation
Has taken not kindly
To air and sick of time
I roll upon the ridge of tribulations
And the bulls paw the wind
Where once was rhyme and chime.

('Field Stone')

a poem which bears out the speaker's sense of his own
impotence only too well! In 'Hope' he depicts himself as the
heir to a declining folk culture, desperately attempting to
salvage something of his heritage:

Remembering, striving to hold against the dark-to-come
Some of the ballad-liveliness
When minds were supple
And there were poems hidden under the black-oak
couple . . .

Elsewhere Kavanagh breaks with Revival convention to
reveal an anguished awareness of his own lonely uniqueness,
the absence of any enabling rural literary tradition, however
primitive:

I am the hoarse cry of creatures who
Have never scratched in any kind of hand
On any wall the signs by which they knew
The endurable stone in the phantasmic land . . .

('Peasant')

That sense of poetic inadequacy, so often voiced in his
thirties' poems, now takes on a tribal dimension:

I have not the fine audacity of men
Who have mastered the pen
Or the purse.
The complexes of many slaves are in my verse.
When I straighten my shoulders to look at the world boldly
I see talent coldly

Damning me to stooped attrition.
Mine was a beggar's mission
To dreams of beauty I should have been born
   blind . . .

('The Irony of It')

In poems like these Kavanagh is at last cutting through the
Revivalist myth of a poetic Irish peasantry to reveal the
discouraging sense of cultural inferiority experienced by the
undereducated, underfunded countryman in his struggle
from illiteracy to literature. He would return to this theme in
one of his last poems, a still undernourished poet, biting the
hand that had beckoned the Irish peasant into English poetry:

Yes Yeats it was damn easy for you protected
By the middle classes and the Big Houses
To talk about the sixty-year old public protected
Man sheltered by the dim Victorian Muses.

('Yeats')[53]

Nevertheless, it was the Irish literary self-confidence nurtured by the Revival and, in particular, its promotion of Irish
peasant subject matter, that encouraged Kavanagh to continue writing verse with a peculiarly local flavour at a time
when London was his literary Mecca, most of his exemplars
were English or American, and he was consciously or unconsciously tempted to suppress his Irishness and Monaghan-
ness.

From the mid-1930s there is a thin trickle of poems with
local settings and a very few which, like 'Inniskeen Road: July
Evening' or 'Threshing Morning', are so specifically localised
as to mention place-names or personal names. Kavanagh's
emergent sense of the importance of locality in poetry is
evident in the reflexive 'Monaghan Hills', where his native
place is said to have determined the nature of his imagination. This is a jocularly defensive piece which claims that the
product of drumlin country needs must lower his sights and
settle for small scale achievements:

Monaghan hills
You have made me the sort of man I am
A fellow who can never care a damn
For Everistic thrills.

The country of my mind
Has a hundred little heads
On none of which foot-room for genius . . .

The carefree, happy-go-lucky persona encountered here is similar to the speaker in 'Threshing Morning', and, as is normally the case in Kavanagh's homegrown verse, the idiom is colloquially relaxed for some of the time at least. Even the retention of the archaic apostrophe seems playful. Unfortunately, he rarely made Monaghan's hills his imaginative terrain in the 1930s, though the best poems of the period clearly indicate that he was at his most original and most subtle when the subject was his ambivalent relationship to the ordinary familiar life of Inniskeen.

Kavanagh's favourite among his thirties' lyrics was 'Shancoduff', a farmer-poet's love poem to his own fields, but a complex love poem that questions the holiness of the heart's affections and allows worldly doubt to trouble poetic faith:

My black hills have never seen the sun rising,
Eternally they look north towards Armagh.
Lot's wife would not be salt if she had been
Incurious as my black hills that are happy
When dawn whitens Glassdrummond chapel.

My hills hoard the bright shillings of March
While the sun searches in every pocket.
They are my Alps and I have climbed the Matterhorn
With a sheaf of hay for three perishing calves
In the field under the Big Forth of Rocksavage.

The sleety winds fondle the rushy beards of Shancoduff
While the cattle-drovers sheltering in the Featherna Bush
Look up and say: 'Who owns them hungry hills
That the water-hen and snipe must have forsaken?

A poet? Then by heavens he must be poor'
I hear and is my heart not badly shaken?

'Shancoduff', as the Gaelicised spelling of the original title,
'Shanco Dubh', and the incorporation into the poem of the
translation 'black' would indicate, was influenced by the
Revivalist fascination with Irish country place-names and the
translation of Irish folklore. Orthodoxy stops short at the title,
however. Kavanagh is here expressing a love that previously
had not dared to speak its name in his published poetry, a
farmer-poet's attachment to his own land. No concession is
made to the cult of the picturesque in this new Monaghan
version of pastoral. Shancoduff is a north facing hill-farm
depicted at its wintry worst, frostbound, starved of grass,
swept by sleety winds. Yet the farmer-poet does succeed in
communicating his affection for these bleak, impoverished
acres. The fond possessive 'my' that prefixes every mention
of the hills, embraces their unrelenting grimness, the den-
igratoriness implicit in their very name; and their personification as 'incurious', 'happy' or cunning sustains the sense of
indulgent relationship. Even the sleety winds are shown
caressing them. This is no sultry southern passion but a
tender tribute to cussed individuality, a cherishing of a harsh
integrity that refuses to charm or seduce. Kavanagh's distrust
of the explicitly sensuous is here imaginatively related to his
dour local landscape. Lot's wife belongs with the yearning
personae of so many of his thirties' poems. The incuriously
self-sufficient Shancoduff personifies a new contentment
with his native air and his own ground. Ugly, sunless,
niggardly, begrudging, Shancoduff may be a poor thing but it
is his own. Actual place-names and the casual reference to
landmarks like Glassdrummond chapel, the Rocksavage fort
and the Featherna Bush, give this poem a peculiarly local
feel. The exotic and difficult of attainment are introduced
only to magnify the importance of the local and the ordinary:

They are my Alps and I have climbed the Matterhorn
With a sheaf of hay for three perishing calves
In the field under the big fort of Rocksavage . . .

However, these lines also mark the poem's turning point. Their climactic declaration of a faith that moves mountains strains beyond belief towards bathos and the farmer-poet is left perched on the slippery slopes between rhetorical inflation and deflation.

Downhill, in the final stanza, the cattle drovers from their less exposed position give uncompromisingly blunt expression to negatives latent in the farmer's endeared images and metaphors. Mercenary minded and rootless men, who only buy and sell the calves the farmer nurtures, they know nothing of the transfiguring power of proprietorial affection and evaluate worth solely in commercial terms. The drovers substitute the ungrammatical third-person demonstrative adjective 'them' for the caressingly repeated 'my', and, bereft of the bonds of relationship, the hills appear merely 'hungry' and their owner 'poor'.

'Shancoduff' originally included another stanza before this last stanza:

> My hills have never seen the sun rising,
> With the faith of an illiterate peasant they await
> The Final Resurrection when all hills
> Will face the East.

The first line here repeats the poem's original first line, introducing an element of artifice which interferes with the sense of spontaneous development, while the symbolic invocation of peasant piety is gratingly strident, upsetting the poem's semi-playful figurativeness.

From the mid-1930s Kavanagh was self-consciously modernising his poetic voice, aware that he had never fully sloughed off the artificial diction, inert rhythms and inhibiting postures of schoolbook verse:

> The weary horse on which I ride
> Is language vitiate
> That cannot take in its stride
> Bank, stream and gate.

> Its eyes have the blank look
> Of a memoried fool
> Or a Victorian book
> In a modern school.

What is being identified specifically here is an antagonism between his nineteenth-century poetics and his incipient interest in rural realism. It was usually the pressure of realism that compelled Kavanagh to use speech rhythms in verse. When he adopted the persona of Inniskeen poet or farmer, in particular, he shed anonymity and Victorian notions of decorum and felt free to move from textbook standard English nearer to his own more relaxed vernacular. The closer to home he brought his poetry the less its images and language could be made to conform to established usage. He was not only colonising a new region for English verse; he was connecting the illiterate and literary parts of himself.

'Shancoduff' is a dramatic poem in which Kavanagh speaks in two voices, the one colloquio-poetic, the purified language of the tribe, adapting the idiom and rhythm of ordinary speech and capable of accommodating figurative language without strain; the other colloquio-realist, mimicking Monaghan turns of phrase. His farmer-poet speaks as an idiosyncratic individual, and not as a representative peasant or *vox populi*. Kavanagh recognises the limitations of the clichés of everyday speech which can manage the common expletive, 'by heavens', but not the metaphoric inversion, 'Eternally they look north'. Like the poet of 'Inniskeen Road' his local poet maintains an eavesdropper's distance from local speech. In 'Shancoduff' the virtual dialogue between two kinds of language signifies a confrontation between two different mentalities, the one metaphoric and celebratory, the other demotic and derogatory.

As the poem concludes, does the imaginative landowner quail before the dismissive judgment of shrewd spectators, decline from confidence to diffidence, lapse from assertive affection to self-questioning doubt? Or is he merely entertaining, not committing himself to, the kind of response that Monaghan common sense would demand? Once again, as in 'Inniskeen Road', the quizzical Kavanagh persona leaves the reader guessing. Originally, the concluding line was more qualified, exclamatory rather than interrogatory, and referred to the speaker's 'faith', not his 'heart':

I hear, and is my faith not somewhat shaken!

In the revised version what is called in question is not the poet-farmer's convictions but his affections, his primal bonding with his own place.

'Shancoduff' is a reflexive poem in which Kavanagh dramatises his ambivalence towards localising his verse or exposing what is near and dear to the detached appraisal of outsiders. Sexuality is displaced into territorial bonding; aspiration has yielded to the troubled delight of homecoming. He has hacked his way clear of his roots in the schoolbooks but anticipates criticism of his innovative attitudes and material. The conflict between the very different values of indigenous poet and foreign audience, between imagination's imperative and the claims of orthodoxy, is the subtext of a poem set among the rushy hills of Inniskeen. While the farmer-poet apparently loses confidence in the validity of his enterprise and exits from the poem 'badly shaken', the rhetorical odds are so overwhelmingly in his favour that the reader wishes him to take heart and continue.

In Kavanagh's country verse, familiarity breeds affection and in 'Shancoduff', where he achieves a perfect marriage between the roles of farmer and poet, his insider's knowledge of small-farm life gives substance and specificity to his customary reflexiveness. Not a single abstraction intrudes into the poem. Yet his apprehension that critical reaction to his local poetry would be unfriendly proved correct. 'Inniskeen Road: July Evening' was ignored by most contemporary critics and Donagh MacDonagh noticed it only to lament its unfortunate conclusion.[54] John Gawsworth and Maurice Wollman both passed up the opportunity to anthologise

'Shancoduff'. Published in the *Dublin Magazine* in 1937, it was not collected until 1960.[55]

'Shancoduff' is radically innovative not only in its blend of agricultural realism and an unobtrusively Catholic ethos (Armagh, Glassdrummond chapel), but, more fundamentally, in its fashioning of a distinctively new poetic personality, affectionate, playful, vulnerable. This is not descriptive or symbolic verse; it is entirely self-creating, using others to distinguish the self. The rebarbativeness of the hill-farm, its commercial worthlessness, serve only to enhance its lover's eccentric individuality. What matters in this poem is not the object of affection, not literal place or literary materials; what matters is the poet persona's relationship with place or materials. It was presumably his later recognition of the poem's real purport that led Kavanagh to substitute 'heart' for 'faith' in the last line. The drama of 'Shancoduff' is the enactment of Kavanagh's hesitant realisation of the holiness of the poet's affections. It hovers diffidently on the brink of an aesthetic belief that the older poet would confidently and triumphally assert: 'Gods make their own importance'.[56] Creative artists require no external endorsement, either from an established value system or from the golden opinions of contemporaries; their role is to confer value and it is in the act of bestowing significance that they themselves become significant. Kavanagh's poetics not only asserts the importance of the author-God, it enshrines love as the cardinal creative principle; it affirms that the incarnation of individual feeling in poetry is primary and that reifying devices, words as signs, function as necessary signs of affection:

Naming a thing is the love act and its pledge.[57]

The poet may transform Inniskeen Road into 'a mile of kingdom', or Inniskeen land into 'fields that' are 'part of no earthly estate', but he must name specific places and objects, Billy Brennan's barn, Cassidy's haggard, Glassdrummond chapel, to give 'a substance and a life' to what he feels.

In an age when impersonality was avant-garde, when even

old-fashioned, ostensibly subjective, verse was only reticently and conventionally personalised, Kavanagh restored the communication of personal feeling to poetic centrality. As a lyricist who makes poetry an affair of attachments, the poet he most resembles is not the mandarin W. B. Yeats but the homely Thomas Hardy, though their very different personal situations, temperaments and philosophies obscure this *rapprochement*.

As early as 1937 Kavanagh was groping towards a formulation of the central tenet of his mature aesthetic. No wonder, then, that 'Shancoduff' became his favourite early poem. He had memorised, imitated and adapted Victorian and modern lyrics; had shed one influence in order to succumb to another; had slaved for twenty years to suppress his own identity and circumstances and invent a literary world more in conformity with pre-existing perceptions of what constituted the poetic; and, finally and somewhat tentatively, he had arrived at the moment of supreme daring when he was courageous enough to name the love of which he had been ashamed and to make his love and his shame the subject of his published verse. 'Shancoduff' was an accidental, isolated, aesthetic epiphany, however, and he might have remained 'too thick to take' its 'hint'[58] were it not for the confirmation and confidence accruing from a contemporary autobiographical venture, the writing of *The Green Fool*.

2
Paddy-Go-Easy:
The Green Fool as
Autobiography

Introduction

JUST as he had followed up his initial success in publishing his poetry in the *Irish Statesman* by visiting Dublin and making the acquaintance of AE and other Dublin writers, similarly after the publication of *Ploughman and Other Poems* Kavanagh journeyed to London in May 1937 to seek out literary contacts and employment. He called upon Thomas Moult and met up with John Gawsworth, both of whom had included his poetry in one of their anthologies. He also visited the writer and scholar, Helen Waddell, a friend of AE, who had read a selection of his poetry with a view to its publication in 1934. Moult proved completely unwelcoming. Gawsworth, with whom he lodged for a time, was keen to include some of Kavanagh's unpublished poetry in his Richards Booklets but the series ended suddenly and so the project came to nothing.[1] Helen Waddell suggested that he write a book about his life in Inniskeen for Constable, for whom she acted as reader. This book appeared in spring 1938 under the title, *The Green Fool*.

Since she herself had successfully managed the transition from poetry to discursive prose and fiction, Helen Waddell saw no reason to type-cast Kavanagh as a poet. An Ulster-woman with an abiding love for the northern countryside, she probably viewed her fellow countryman as an ideal native informant. He was an articulate peasant who had passed the thirty odd years of his life in a remote Ulster village and could furnish a colourful first-hand account of old-fashioned farming methods and quaint local characters and customs. The English translation of the Irish peasant

autobiography, *Twenty Years A-Growing*, Maurice O'Sullivan's account of life on the Blasket Islands, had proved
immediately successful when it appeared in 1933 and another
Blasket autobiography, Tomás O'Criomhtháin's *The Island-
man*, translated by Robin Flower, was published simultaneously in Dublin and London the following year. Moreover,
Kavanagh was also something of an Irish Robbie Burns and
the story of his progress from undereducated ploughman to
London-published poet promised a primitive Romantic tale
with a happy ending. So the commissioning of *The Green Fool*
was, for Constable, a sound commercial proposition. For the
comparatively young and inexperienced poet it was to prove
a crucial literary opportunity.

The Green Fool's categorisation as an autobiography has had
the unfortunate effect of focusing attention on its historicity,
almost to the exclusion of its artistry. It is more often consulted and quoted from as a memoir than assessed as an
aesthetic artifact. In devoting a chapter to *The Green Fool*, my
purpose is to reinstate this book as an integral and significant
part of Kavanagh's *oeuvre* and to bestow on it the kind of
critical attention normally reserved for his poetry. I read *The
Green Fool* as an autobiography but, since I believe that autobiography in general, and a writer's autobiography in particular, is closer to the art of fiction than to historiography, I am
less concerned by its accuracy than by its artifice.

In confronting the generic issues arising from Kavanagh's
choice of the autobiographical mode, this chapter places less
emphasis on the factuality of his record, than on his selection
and arrangement of material, on the question of the book's
'allobiographical' or autobiographical status,[2] and, in particular, on an aspect highlighted by the author himself, the
conventions of representation he chose to deploy. In *Self-
Portrait* (1964), Kavanagh denounced *The Green Fool* as a
'dreadful stage-Irish, so-called autobiography' written 'under
the evil aegis of the so-called Irish literary movement', a 'stage-
Irish lie' which gullible readers 'gobbled up' as if it were
the truth. The autobiographical implications of Kavanagh's

recourse to two such competing conventions as Literary Revival reverence and stage-Irish comedy will be explored in this chapter.

Much of the poetry collected in the unpublished *The Seed and the Soil* and *To Anna Quinn* was contemporaneous with *The Green Fool*. Though there was a time-lag between Kavanagh's extended prose description of life in Inniskeen and his poetic evocation of his own parish, it is significant that 'Shancoduff', in which he assumes the persona of farmer-poet, was quoted from in the book and published later in the same year. In the conclusion of this chapter I consider how the composition of *The Green Fool* contributed to Kavanagh's literary evolution.

Life and Literature

Prior to the writing of *The Green Fool* Kavanagh customarily turned to literature, not to life, for his inspiration; his goal was imitation rather than mimesis. 'Inniskeen Road: July Evening' apart, he was oblivious of local context in his published poetry. He was turning out short, smooth, shapely lyrics with a reflexive or transcendental bias and might well have remained imaginatively arrested in that solemn, rarefied phase so dismissively recalled in 'Leaves of Grass':

> When I was growing up and for many years after
> I was led to believe that poems were thin
> Dreary, irrelevant, well out of the draught of
>   laughter
> With headquarters the size of the head of a pin.
> I do not wonder now that my mother moaned
> To see her beloved son an idiot boy;
> He could not see what was before his eyes, the
>   ground
> Tumultuous with living, infinite as Cleopatra's
>   variety . . .

The Green Fool changed all that. This excursion into an untried prose medium proved an exhilarating and liberating experience for the young writer, enabling him to shed inhibiting notions of poetic decorum and to discover a more inclusive, realist mode. The very expansiveness of the project ensured his emancipation from the verbal and syntactical constrictions of the short lyric. Above all, the subject matter of *The Green Fool*, his thirty-three years a-growing in Inniskeen, compelled Kavanagh to reflect on and attempt to make sense of his own actual life and circumstances instead of hiding behind a vague persona. As the hero of a *Bildungsroman* he could not pass his entire time in the Selkirk-like solitude so wryly deprecated in 'Inniskeen Road'; his milieu was to be part of his message. An environment, which he had previously taken for granted, had now to be consciously registered and documented. Fields, lanes and ditches, seasonal crops and wild flowers, daily farming chores and pastimes, local rituals and superstitions, all these had to be introduced to an English public. He was also faced with the novel challenge of peopling his book, re-creating his domestic context and his neighbourhood. Lyrical and narrative modes would no longer suffice; he must experiment with the construction of dramatic scenes.

The precise, documentary particularity, which characterises *The Green Fool* from its first paragraph, is altogether new in Kavanagh's work. Though the opening chapter on his childhood is euphorically entitled 'Angelhood', the child-poet is prosaically encountered lying in a converted onion-box cradle, observing the 'sticky black-oak couples of thatched roof'. Throughout *The Green Fool* the claims of 'honest reality' frequently triumph over the desire to prettify or mythologise. This newly acquired capacity for an exact documentation that does not blink at ugly or sordid detail is noticeable in the depiction of local scenes:

> It was a dark lane that for a long time had not known the sharp discipline of a briar-hook. Trellised with wild-woodbine and roofed on places with wild roses, through which the songs and light of a high summer morning were strained. Baked and half-baked cakes of cow-dung

lay at my feet. In this cool place the cattle found shelter during the day from the gadflies and all the tormentors that come with beauty and love. Even now one old cow was coming up the lane. Far away on the New Line Road I could hear the wild cry of home-sick cattle.

At the end of the road Pat the Hack's fields began. Three poplar poles lay across the gap, but the upper two poles were broken down by the fly-goaded beasts . . .

The scene is filtered through the sensibility of a country dweller, not rendered with the merely pictorial accuracy of a camera-happy visitor. Such elaborate description is rare in *The Green Fool* where landscape is usually an unobtrusive presence, a backdrop to action, or an unsentimentally realised work-place.

The Green Fool combines a portrait of the artist with a portrait of his society; it is both an 'autobiography' and a work of popular anthropology. Kavanagh's newly acquired realism is displayed to best advantage in his evocation of his milieu. We see a local community at work, at play and at prayer. He presents an informed insider's report on the practicalities of farming: ploughing, sowing and threshing corn, thinning turnips, churning, turf cutting, driving cattle, slaughtering pigs. The commercial side of farming is also described: cattle fairs, a pork market, the purchase of a horse and cart at auction, the leasing of land on the con-acre system and a hiring fair at which there is a brisk trade in human labour. Marriage in the Irish countryside is shown as a business deal with small farmers almost beggaring themselves to provide dowries for marriageable daughters. There are lively accounts of wedding festivities, the rituals surrounding death, the annual pilgrimage to a holy well, gambling at the cross-roads, gaffing salmon, blackberrying, Christmas mumming. Several chapters are devoted to chronicling local superstitions about cures, ghosts and fairies.

The Green Fool includes not only some lengthy set pieces on farm life, such as the pig-slaughtering episode in chapter 23;

it also abounds in short passages full of authentic detail about ordinary rural chores, as in chapter 12 where a paragraph on churning is immediately followed by one on thinning turnips. Here Kavanagh enlivens exposition through dramatisation, lacing his narrative with colloquial dialogue:

> The dash churn stood near the door because the weather was hot. Michael's wife poured three pan-crocks full of cream into it. She tightened down the lid with a crack of her fist's heel.
>
> 'Now in the name of God,' she said.
>
> 'I'll take the first brash,' Michael said.
>
> Churning with a dash-churn is heavy work. I was tired when we had finished. Michael's wife took the lid off and looked into the churn. 'God bless it, but it's lovely,' she said.
>
> She scooped up a plateful with her hand and mixed some salt through it. Twice or three times she put her buttery finger in her mouth to test the butter's saltiness.
>
> 'It's a little pale,' the old woman said.
>
> 'More like goat's butter,' Michael remarked.

Representative episodes are thus briefly recounted as theatrical anecdotes or presented as virtual playlets, not ponderously weighted with information.

While the mandate to describe a way of life he knew so intimately gave Kavanagh access to a wealth of new material, the autobiographical mode simultaneously placed severe constraints on its use. His was the usual problem of the comparatively young autobiographer; his cast of characters was still alive, jealous of its reputation and liable to turn litigious. Inniskeen, in particular, was, as he later phrased it, a 'lawbred country',[3] where neighbours were in the habit of taking each other to court to settle their differences. More immediate and almost as frightening as the prospect of libel suits was the threat of severing friendly relations with family and neighbours. An entry in a notebook in which he made preparatory jottings for *The Green Fool* shows that Kavanagh was aware from the outset of the risks involved in auto-biography:

> A man who writes a book libelling his own people is burning his bed. The fragments cannot be put together again.[4]

No sooner had he conceived of Inniskeen as a literary source than he was obliged to reinvent it fictionally.

The Green Fool is necessarily unreliable as a biographical record. In the interests of preserving good relations with his family and community Kavanagh had to censor his reportage carefully, to suppress a good deal of relevant information, to distort or falsify some of his material out of all recognition and generally to engage in an imaginative rearrangement of the facts. His portrayal of his family in *The Green Fool* is markedly discreet, evasive rather than inventive. There must have been a tacit or explicit agreement that he would not exploit them for copy. The tale of his family's origins, written down by his father, has been conveniently lost, and the father's illegitimacy is thereby concealed.[5] Kavanagh was always coy about his age so his refusal to divulge his date of birth is not surprising, nor the minor misinformation that at the time of his father's death he was twenty-two, when he was actually nearer to twenty-five. More remarkable is his reticence about his siblings; none of his seven sisters is named or described and his relationship with them is scarcely touched upon. His brother, Peter, is given only a minor role. We learn very little about the day-to-day private life of the Kavanagh household. Their kitchen doubles as a cobbler's workshop and the writer focuses on its social instead of its domestic aspect. It is a communal meeting place where customers come and go and neighbours gather. Discretion about family matters may have been a factor in determining that the narrator, on one pretext or another, spends most of his time out of doors or away from home. While he pays tribute to his mother's thrifty ways she is seldom portrayed in a maternal role and usually appears as one of the chorus of rustics in the cobbler's workshop. Though the mother figure dominates in Kavanagh's later writings, in *The Green Fool* his father plays a more prominent part in the action, possibly because he was safely dead. His son writes of him affectionately and respectfully, delighting in his sceptical intelligence, knowledgeability, keen sense of humour and shrewd business acumen. Indeed the book is something of a hagiographical memorial tribute.[6]

As regards his re-creation of his neighbourhood, Kavanagh could probably have prefaced his book with the usual novelistic disclaimer that his characters bear no resemblance to any living person. Incidents in which specific local individuals could be readily identified were avoided. As a further precaution against identification some names were changed between draft and final version. Substitutes were found for such common local surnames as Agnew, Doran, Meegan and Tuite in certain instances; Kelly's public house became King's; key characters were called by the locally inauthentic Christian names, George and Michael, instead of the original Barney and John T.; and 'my neighbour Terry' was changed to 'my neighbour Owen' in chapters 12 and 23 because one of the Kavanaghs' neighbours was named Terry Lennon.[7]

Ironically, Kavanagh succeeded in avoiding local litigation only to have a libel action brought against him from an unexpected quarter. Oliver St John Gogarty took exception to the poet's remark that on his first visit to Dublin he 'mistook Gogarty's white-robed maid for his wife — or his mistress' expecting 'every poet to have a spare wife'. This observation is more revealing of its author's *naïveté* than of Gogarty's connubial mores and it may well be that what actually offended Gogarty was a slighting comment a few lines earlier. When he inquired in the National Library for the address of any Dublin poet and was offered Gogarty's, Kavanagh tells us that his reaction was 'Is that the best you can do?' Surprisingly, a London court found in Gogarty's favour on 21 March 1939 and the book was withdrawn from circulation.[8] When *The Green Fool* was serialised in *The Irish Weekly*, from 3 December 1938 to 13 May 1939, Kavanagh's, or possibly the editor's, nervous caution was such that, in addition to the deletion of the entire Gogarty passage, the names of Helen Waddell and John Gawsworth and some of the comments on Seán O'Faoláin were also omitted; Oul' Quinn was changed to Oul' Casey; the Inniskeen public house, MacNello's, was renamed Daly's; and a local estate, Rocksavage, was referred to as Rocklawn. On negative evidence the fact that no libel suits were pressed by Kavanagh's neighbours probably testifies to the fictionality of *The Green Fool*.[9]

The omissions and fabrications necessitated by social tact and legal nicety only partially account for *The Green Fool*'s untrustworthiness as a book of evidence. It is primarily a literary work, not a literal record. Verisimilitude, not veracity, was Kavanagh's aim. While his late rejection of the book as a 'stage-Irish lie' is widely known, his earlier claim that it is 'one of the truest books ever written' has been forgotten:

> A thing is not true in literature merely because it happened. A thing is true in literature when it could happen—to anybody. That is the basis of the trueness of *The Green Fool*.[10]

Here Kavanagh is distinguishing between historical and artistic truth, classifying *The Green Fool* as a work of fiction rather than an accurate source of biographical information.

In *The Green Fool* a world is turned into words; thirty-three years of living are distilled into 350 pages of text. Facts had to be omitted, rearranged, improved upon in the interests of representative significance and formal coherence. Because of the seasonal and cyclical nature of small-farm life, for instance, annual occurrences had to be telescoped to avoid monotonous repetition. As a consequence narrative organisation tends to oscillate between chronological progression and documentary stasis and many chapters pay scant attention to the hero's development and focus on aspects of country living. His autobiographical role on such occasions is subordinate to his role as narrator. His ubiquitous presence serves as a linking device in a work that is highly episodic and diverse. In many episodes the first-person narrator is deployed to invest reportage with immediacy and authenticity. Consequently, accounts of common rural activities are sometimes prefaced by a perfunctory introductory dialogue validating his presence in the ensuing action:

> 'Were you ever at holy well?'
> 'I never was', I answered, 'and I'd like to go'.
> Well, you can come with us', Corbett said . . .

or

> He was looking for me to come and wheel turf.
> 'To-morrow mornin', if all goes well, we'll be startin', he said.
> 'To be sure. I'll come', I said . . .

or

> The previous evening Pat the Hack had come to our house and asked my parents if they would let me go with him to the fair.
> 'He'll go and welcome, Pat', they said.

Such incidents are sometimes based on cumulative experience, presented as singular episodes to avoid cluttersome repetition. Sometimes they are entirely fictional as in the case of the Lady Well pilgrimage.[11]

Narrative organisation imposed certain restraints on *The Green Fool*'s fidelity to fact and formal considerations occasionally took precedence over autobiographical truth. Objective documentation was further distorted, as Kavanagh recognised in *Self-Portrait*, by the conventions of representation he consciously or unconsciously applied. In 1937 he was strongly influenced by the still prevalent Literary Revival ethos. On the very first page of *The Green Fool* he displays a self-consciousness about folk tradition which clearly derives from a Literary Revival model: 'The house where I was born was a traditional wedge-shaped cabin.' The significance of the first adjective only becomes apparent when the second chapter describing the building of the Kavanaghs' new house is entitled 'Break with Tradition' and we are told that this was 'a modern dwelling cut off from the Gaelic tradition' and 'had no secret nooks where one might find an old prophecy or a forgotten ballad'. According to Peter Kavanagh's account the Kavanaghs did not knock down their cabin but simply added another storey to the existing structure, so that the lamented 'Break with Tradition' is a fictional invention.[12] Placed prominently towards the beginning of the book, the house-moving episode both salutes Literary Revival values and covertly signals Kavanagh's awareness that he does not conform to its cultural expectations; he is 'cut off from the Gaelic tradition'.

Kavanagh was particularly susceptible to Revivalist indoctrination on the literary importance of the Irish peasantry, for him a self-affirming and self-inflationary ideology. The available Literary Revival models for representing Irish country folk have been deftly summarised by John Wilson Foster:

> Pearse's peasantry is innocent, childlike, submissive, Catholic; Synge's romantic, primitive, artistic; Yeats's and Lady Gregory's mystical, otherworldly, traditionalist; Colum's and Stephens' bright, adaptive, quick-witted . . .[13]

And Kavanagh's peasantry? Throughout *The Green Fool* there is an unresolved conflict between a Revivalist romanticisation of country people and a comic realist representation. Kavanagh has recourse to double-speak when he writes about country people, referring to them as 'farmers' or 'peasants' according to whether the situation is realist/comic or Revivalist. Although the word 'peasant' is not an exclusively Revivalist term it belongs to literature rather than to life in Ireland, since Irish landowners who possess even a few acres are always referred to as farmers. Kavanagh employs the normal local word 'farmer' when he is reporting the speech of the people or writing about their day-to-day activities. So when his neighbours talk about the 1914–18 war they say, 'It's a great war for the farmer' and, when his cobbler father buys a nine-acre field, Kavanagh is told by way of congratulation, 'Yer a farmer's son now.' Elsewhere, commenting acerbically on social stratification in rural Ireland, he remarks, 'The blood of cobblers is inferior to the fluid in the veins of a five-acre farmer.' When he views his neighbours through Literary Revival lenses, however, regarding them as purveyors of Irish folk culture, he refers to them as 'peasants':

> The peasant folk knew the lore and strange knowledge of God and Greece that they didn't know they knew . . .

> . . . the secret archives of peasant minds of which no official document has ever been made . . .

> They (Connemara people) spoke Gaelic yet I felt that the English-speaking peasants of my own country were nearer to the old tradition . . .

Kavanagh is intermittently conscious of the disparity between his shrewd, tough, commonsensical neighbours, small farmers scraping a living from a few scrawny acres, and the various versions of literary peasantry available for his imitation. He is caught between local piety, a desire to present the Inniskeen small farmer as the equal of his colourful, lyrical, Revivalist counterpart and a rueful recognition that literary orthodoxy bears little relation to Mucker fact, that Inniskeen is not Innisfree.

The success of Synge's dramatic experiments with Hiberno–English dialect had established the linguistic orthodoxy that Irish country speech was as 'fully-flavoured as a nut or an nut or an apple'. Kavanagh later complained that such emphasis on tangy rural speech retarded his appreciation of the actual flavour of ordinary country talk. This may indeed be the case, but it is equally probable that it was the Revival's obsession with rural language which stimulated his initial interest in Inniskeen speech. The inclusion of local dialect in *The Green Fool* was not simply a natural consequence of writing about Inniskeen; it was a conscious decision. Possibly in imitation of his Revivalist antecedents Kavanagh, the 'peasant', actually collected Inniskeen phrases in a notebook.[14] Occasionally his dialogue betrays its notebook origins. It is obvious that he is merely stringing well-worn phrases together to add linguistic colour to his narrative in this compilation of neighbourly verdicts on a newly purchased horse and cart:

> Out of the gabble a few illuminating phrases emerged.
> 'Her teeth's a foot long, she'll grind no oats with them spikes.'
> 'She has a spavin.'
> 'Looka the two pockets over her eyes, ye could put a pint of water in each of them. The rale sign of oul' age.'
> 'There's a damn good straddle.'
> 'It is that. Pity to have it on such a scram.'
> 'The cart-wheels are a bit dished. I wouldn't like to chance them over a bad pass.'
> 'That's a bleddy good axle' . . .

However, one of the strengths of *The Green Fool* is the local dialect that animates almost every episode and brings a refreshing authenticity to conventional situations. It is through his language that Kavanagh best achieves a sense of 'Monaghan-ness' in the book, catching every turn and nuance of local speech and even attempting to mimic the Inniskeen accent in his spelling. *The Green Fool* is as densely populated as a Breughel canvas and all its characters are talkers, always ready with an opinion, a proverb, a local cliché or commonplace. Narrative as well as dialogue is so larded with local saws and sayings that the genuine 'voice of the people' insists on making itself heard and Inniskeen *parole* usually manages to overwhelm Revivalist *langue*.

Dialogue in *The Green Fool* is sometimes deliberately introduced to communicate a local mentality. Inniskeen people's habitual secrecy about illness in man or beast and the malicious curiosity this provokes is illustrated by the following exchange between two women on the death of a cow:

> 'Did yez sell yon bracket cow, Judy?'
> 'Oh, we did to be sure,' Judy Brown answers. 'The jobbers came round and when the price was good we thought we'd be as well lit her go.'
> 'Well, in troth, I heard she died on yez.'
> 'Deed aye! The bad story is the quickest goes round. How is Peter's chist?'
> 'Peter, thank God, is grand, not the laste catch on him now.'
> 'Isn't that the blessin'!'

Kavanagh is now sensitive to speech tones, to that loaded significance invested in a word or phrase in the act of utterance which cannot be reproduced on the page without annotation. Here he is recording the reactions of two 'oldish girls' to the news of another girl's forthcoming wedding:

> 'Well she's not much and the fella that's marryin' her must be a fool.'
> 'Sure, some girls would take anyone.'
> 'I wonder is she gettin' married decent.'
>
> 'Just.'

This word 'just' was much more eloquent than it appears on paper. It was steeped in the venom of a thousand repressed desires.

Whereas Aran cabin dwellers and Wicklow servant girls were prepared to indulge Synge's eavesdropping ways,

Inniskeen dialect speakers, apparently, proved less co-operative:

> Old men and women colloguing in groups along the poplar-lined laneway would suspend their conversation as I passed. Across the conversational breach they would hang a suspension bridge formed by the word 'and'. 'Aaa . . . nnn . . . ddd.' Through the wide eyes of this bridge they would survey me with puzzled looks.
> 'And . . . as I was sayin', she came up to me . . . Is that Paddy Kavanagh? Would he be gettin' a bit odd of himself?'

Sophisticated linguistic comedy is created out of the neighbours' insulting manipulation of dialogue and the narrator's manipulation of metaphor.

Although, on the whole, he is appreciative of the terse reductiveness of local dialect in *The Green Fool*, Kavanagh also, on occasion, displays a neo-Revivalist attraction to colourful language, a self-consciousness about the poetic qualities of rural speech. 'Simple old women' are credited with 'phrases of whimsical prophecy and exciting twists of language'; Biddy Murphy's 'language had spiritual riches deep in its gutteral folds' and ass dealers at Carrickmacross fair speak 'an ancient language'. Significantly, no examples of such picturesque language are cited. It was almost impossible for Kavanagh to represent his hard-pressed, down-to-earth neighbours as a 'poetry loving people' and he sometimes admits that by Revivalist standards Inniskeen's Hiberno–English is an impoverished language:

> The talk among us was poor. The folk who knew how to make conversation were dead.

One reason advanced for this cultural decline anticipates his far from idyllic depiction of rural life in 'The Great Hunger':

> There was no love for beauty. We were barbarians just escaped from Penal days. The hunger had killed our poetry.

Kavanagh's romanticisation of itinerants in *The Green Fool* probably derives from the Revivalist cult of the nomadic for, as he states in *Self-Portrait*, his 'poverty-stricken upbringing' had actually inculcated a 'belief in respectability—a steady job, decency'. In *The Green Fool*, however, journeymen cobblers are revered as 'the wandering poets of cobblerland' and beggars, too, are idealised as 'richly coloured', 'fantastic' and 'quaint' creatures, 'real romantic people of the roads', 'the living records of a poetry-loving people'. In order to dissociate himself from the prosaic life of cobbling and farming Kavanagh claims a nomadic lineage: 'the blood of tramps was in my veins; my father's father had come from the west'. The mythological lore popularised by the Revival adds a touch of epic glamour to his grandfather's journey north:

> He had taken the road Queen Maeve took when that cattle-fancier was on the chase of the Brown Bull of Cooley.

A practical farmer, for all his literary inclinations, Kavanagh timed his own western odyssey to coincide with 'the slack period of six weeks between the spring wheat sowing and the summer sowing of turnips'. His journey to Connemara in chapter 30 is in the nature of a literary pilgrimage since Connacht was the imaginative locus of the Literary Renaissance, 'near to the gate of heaven' for good Revivalists like Patrick Pearse. Kavanagh's own claim to Connacht ancestry mitigates the literary solecism of having been born in Ulster. His professed disillusionment with Connemara in *The Green Fool* marks a growing point in his literary evolution. That he was not impressed by its Gaelic-speaking inhabitants anticipates his later heterodox attitude to the Revival, although, as yet, the rivalry between Monaghan and Connemara is stated in Literary Revival terminology, the issue being which is 'nearer the old tradition'. He concludes that there is 'no culture in Connemara, nothing like County Monaghan where the spirit of the old poets haunted the poplars'. Local affection impels Kavanagh to take an independent stand on certain articles of the Revival creed though he adheres to its general ideology.

Among the few surviving links with a Gaelic past in English-speaking County Monaghan were its place-names. Naming was to play an important part in the evocation of locality in Kavanagh's poetry, but in *The Green Fool* he is more concerned with the Gaelic origins of names than with their evocative properties. He takes the Revivalist attitude that place-names 'told of the days when poetry was in the land' and displays his Gaelic scholarship by translating local place-names into English. 'Mucker', the name of his birthplace, is 'a corrupted Gaelic word signifying a place where pigs were bred in abundance', Bohar Bhee means 'the yellow road', Eden Bawn is translated as 'the bright face', Barragroom as 'the lonely road' and 'Shancoduff', black Shanco, is so called because its fields face north.

Douglas Hyde, Lady Gregory and W. B. Yeats had tended to regard peasants less as individuals than as living folklore archives, repositories of 'ballad and story, rann and song'. Kavanagh confesses the hideous truth that his parish was 'most unmusical' and that of the fifty members of the Inniskeen Sinn Féin Pipers Band he was the only one with an ear for music. Undeterred by this cacophonous state of affairs he makes a valiant effort to perpetuate the myth of a tuneful and poetry-loving peasantry and declares that 'The rattle of a cart over rutted roads, or any roads, is the proper accompaniment for a ballad-singer.' Among the snatches of ballad quoted in the book are two of the best-known local verses:

> It wasn't the men from Shercock
> Or the men from Ballybay,
> But the dalin' men from Crossmaglen
> Put whiskey in me tay.

and

> The Castleblaney besoms, the best that ever grew
> Were sold for two a penny on the Hill of Mullacrew.

The turf-cutting episode is probably located in Ardee to establish a connection with the popular song, 'The Turfman from Ardee'. Most of the songs quoted from or referred to in *The Green Fool* are not indigenous and even the beggar-woman, Biddy Dundee, more attuned to her Scottish name than to her role as 'one of the living records of a poetry-loving people', sings 'Loch Lomond'.

In the matter of folklore Kavanagh's reading of what Yeats termed 'the book of the people' differs from that of the Revivalists. George, the only adult in the book to believe in fairies, is a comic character whose stories of the 'Wee Fellas' are dismissed as 'rubbish' by his daughter. Kavanagh's own father lacks faith in local cures and some of his neighbours are ready to offer rational explanations of ghostly apparitions. Revivalist obsession with recording folklore is neatly turned on its head when a local farmer tells the poet stories of old Ireland quoted verbatim from Father Burke's *Lectures and Sermons*. 'Romantic Ireland's dead and gone' but no new rural model has yet emerged, so the invented peasantry of the Revival still provides the ideal against which to measure small-farm life in Inniskeen.

The writer of *The Green Fool* is conspicuously bookish, obsessed by others' imaginings. While he consciously resists James Stephens's 'beautiful rhythms', Kavanagh succumbs to the literary influence of F. R. Higgins and Padraic Colum. So the ass dealers at Carrickmacross fair are referred to as a 'dark breed', a phrase deriving from the title of one of Higgins's collections of poems; Biddy Dundee is compared to Colum's 'old woman of the roads'; and he himself twice identifies with Colum's 'Drover'. Yet his growing scepticism about the Revival's rural model is also clearly manifest. It provides a literary orthodoxy with which the facts of small-farm life seldom square. That rough beast, Patrick Maguire, slouches about the text, waiting to be born.

However, *The Green Fool* never crosses the shadow-line into the dark, tragic region of *The Great Hunger*; its prevailing tone is comic. Kavanagh's choice of a comic framework might seem at odds with his espousal of Literary Revival orthodoxy, yet his authorial perspective is sufficiently uncontrolled to allow such contradictory conventions to flourish in close proximity and, of course, the humour of the book derives, in part, from Inniskeen's failure to measure up to Literary Revival norms. That *The Green Fool* should have been written from a comic perspective is an unexpected volte-face on the part of the hitherto solemn lyric poet. Only in 'Inniskeen Road' had he previously revealed his sense of humour. The liberating effect of the transition from brief lyric to extended prose narrative may have been partly responsible for the change of mood. He could sustain a serious pose over a few stanzas, but over 350 pages his natural 'humorosity' could not be restrained.[15] In 1937 Kavanagh was a successful young writer with one London-published book to his credit and another under way. The years of struggle and obscurity were over; he was confident, exuberant, brimful of irrepressible good spirits. All was right with his world; how should he not feel celebratory? Much of the book was drafted in London and temporary exile may have made the drumlins of home seem greener and his attitude to his absent neighbours fonder. Even enemies and detractors now had the status of potential literary characters. He could appease a sometimes painful past by converting it into a comic text. The comic mode registers his social reconciliation. It would seem, then, that the genial tone and comic perspective that characterise *The Green Fool* express an inner autobiographical truth about its author's disposition at the time of writing.[16]

Kavanagh, on the contrary, has disparaged the book's humour as 'stage-Irish', dictated less by an inner psychological imperative than by external pressure, the need to manufacture an exportable literary commodity tailored to the requirements of the English market:

> The English literary critics refused until recently in a few cases to have anything to do with the authentic Irish

article. If you didn't come as an 'Irishman' you didn't come at all . . .[17]

An 'Irishman' was, of course, a stage-Irishman, an entertaining buffoon with the gift of the gab, and even Shaw 'had to do a bit of clowning'.[18] So the young Kavanagh felt obliged to distort his material to pander to the comic expectations of his English readers. He does, indeed, aim at keeping the reader almost continually amused and the text bears several tell-tale signs that it was written with an English public in mind since it comments on national customs and explains common Irishisms.

The choice of the comic mode in *The Green Fool* may also have been strongly influenced by the example of William Carleton's *Traits and Stories of the Irish Peasantry* and, to a lesser extent, his *Autobiography*. Carleton, who hailed from the neighbouring county of Tyrone, remained one of Kavanagh's favourite authors to the end of his life. Indeed, one of his final literary tasks was to write the preface for an edition of Carleton's *Autobiography*. When Kavanagh 'was growing up', he tells us, 'Carleton was popular among the people, for a good many had not been corrupted, and so were happy to look in the mirror that their poet had presented'.[19] So Carleton provided an appropriate model for the rendering of small-farm life in Ulster. The impact of the *Autobiography* and the *Traits and Stories* on *The Green Fool* may not be immediately obvious because the narrator of the *Autobiography* is a hedge scholar, obsessed with classical erudition, while the *Traits and Stories* take the form of a series of short fictions set in pre-famine Ireland. Kavanagh, who admired the *Traits and Stories* for their 'vivid pictures' of 'landscape and character' and their 'racy' and 'authentic' dialogue,[20] probably learned from Carleton how to populate his narrative with a multitude of characters and make them live through dialogue rather than through action. Above all, Carleton taught him how to keep the reader entertained and amused. It is the continual movement of characters on and off stage and in and out of earshot that makes *The Green Fool* such a lively book. No subject is dwelt on at length and the thematic variety, the to-ing and fro-ing of so many characters, the frequent inter-ruptions of commentary by conversation, ensure that there is hardly a dull moment. The picaresque form of much of Carleton's *Autobiography* would have directly inspired the chapter on 'Tramping' and, in the case of Kavanagh's walk to Dublin, life was copying literature. *The Green Fool's* emphasis on incident, adventure and anecdote imitates the episodic nature of Carleton's narrative. Kavanagh personally identi-fied with Carleton, the poor man from a backward Ulster village who, though despaired of as a lazy ne'er do well, wrote his way to fame, if not to fortune. The happy-go-lucky narrative persona he adopts in *The Green Fool* and the book's friendly relaxed narrative tone both derive from the *Auto-biography* and the *Traits*. He overlooked William Carleton's polemical broadsides as unfortunate lapses and instead mod-elled himself as narrator on the feckless, sunny-tempered, good-natured Billy Carleton. Scarcely a hint of his future bitterness is detectible in *The Green Fool*. All is for the best and Inniskeen the best of all possible worlds. He is 'Paddy-Go-Easy', a cheerful, genial, native informant, affectionately amused at the vagaries and rascalities of his characters and at his own shortcomings, utterly content with the course his life has taken.

Whatever the mix of motives governing Kavanagh's choice of the comic mode the generic traditions of comedy enforced certain procedures and strategies in his approach to his subject. In common with Literary Revival conventions, the conventions of comedy were not amenable to authenticity of portrayal. Neither allowed for psychological complexity in characterisation; each demanded that rustics perform, enter-tain. Accordingly, *The Green Fool's* supporting cast consists of a gallimaufry of grotesques, caricatures and country hu-mours. These include the 'trickster', Michael, who cheats the corn factor with a false sample of his wares, George, the credulous five-acre farmer, hen pecked by his daughter over his superstitious beliefs, the village schoolmistress with her notorious black cloak and the tin whistler whose 'job when he wasn't playing the tin whistle was to prove beyond doubt or cavil his wife's fantastic tales'. Although Kavanagh avoids poking fun at his immediate family he does include a comic sketch of his grandfather, an octogenarian given to proclaiming that 'only wastrels die and people who couldn't eat fat bacon'. The only prominent child character, apart from the narrator, is that fit inhabitant of a rogues' gallery, John Gorman, who among other feats boils a pigeon's eggs and returns them to the nest. Colourful characters are even introduced in the concluding chapter, which is set in London. The 'kicking mare', a fully animated cartoon character, introduces an element of horse-play. Comic caricature is at odds with the illusion of naturalism and the demands of social realism. The narrator excuses this comic limitation on the verisimilitude of his text by declaring that he remembers only 'the quaint and the bizarre'. It would seem that he is catering for a literary tourist trade, readers who seek 'quick returns of the picturesque and the obvious'.[21]

In his later *Self-Portrait* Kavanagh scorns any temptation to show that his background and his childhood were 'out of the common'. There he informs us that his 'childhood experience was the usual barbaric life of the Irish poor'. The colourful, talkative folk who crowd the pages of *The Green Fool* are portrayed in *Self-Portrait* as a poor, anxious and unenlightened breed, 'scraidins of farmers' trying to eke out a livelihood from 'their watery little hills'. In *The Green Fool* the horror, the grinding poverty, the frustration, the claustrophobia and intrusiveness of village life are screened out. 'Scraping poverty' and 'vicious neighbourly hatreds' rate only a fleeting mention. 'Real elementalism' was 'more tawdry', 'resentful, mean and ungenerous'[22] than comedy would countenance:

> The keynote of simple folk is bad manners, familiarity. They intrude on one's private soul. The only tolerable

simple people are those we have manufactured in our evocative memories . . .[23]

Even in 1937 Kavanagh must have been aware of the possibility of a less benign alternative text, but comedy prompted him to look the other way. Laughter was a defence against unpalatable truth. In any case non-idyllic recollections were disallowed by his English publishers. Reminiscences about cruelty to insects and peeing into cans of blackberries were suppressed. A pathetic tale of a fifty-year-old bachelor's punishment for threatening the stability of the family home by falling in love was also censored.[24] Realism was permissible only within the clearly defined limits that it did not make for tedious, shocking or disturbing reading, and was not libellous. So *The Green Fool* is set in the greenwood where 'life is most jolly'.

Comedy insists that we relax our concern about characters' lives, refuses to allow us to take them seriously. The comic, as opposed to the satiric pact, is such that the reader exculpates moral failings and delinquencies. Kavanagh's characters may cheat, poach, steal and rob with impunity. *The Green Fool* tends to diminish the way of life it celebrates. Controversial topics, such as religion or politics, are treated lightheartedly. Although the poet passed his teens in a Border village during the armed struggle that preceded and succeeded Partition, he is almost indifferent to the nightmare of history and the fierce passions and enmities of those years are hardly adverted to or are trivialised into amusing adventures and youthful larks. Three men are shot off stage but on stage the action is usually mock-heroic; guerrilla attacks turn into escapades and danger is reduced to embarrassment or loss of face. The breakdown of law and order is represented as a period of comic misrule. As *The Green Fool* had been commissioned by an English publisher some degree of tact in the approach to Irish politics was *de rigueur*. Yet Kavanagh already manifests something of his later cynical attitude towards patriotism; a political demonstration turns into a party fight, an election is blatantly rigged, and raids and hold-ups are staged by local lads on the make, not by committed idealists funding their cause.

For most of *The Green Fool* 'Motley's the only wear'. One of the narrator's principal roles is that of comic hero and he consciously exploits his name and place of origin to align himself with the caricature stage-Irishman. He is Paddy from the piggery, a buffoon, indolent and feckless, ready for any adventure or prank, prone to cutting a ridiculous figure and to failing in most of his undertakings, utterly insouciant about his manifest deficiencies. His parents' shrewdness, responsibility and respected status in the local community allow their son to perpetuate his adolescence, and maturity is not noticeably thrust upon him by his father's death. So he is an irresponsible comic raconteur, perpetually in holiday mood, oblivious of the grimmer, darker realities of country life. In short, he is given a fool's licence to entertain and amuse.

The epithet, 'green', in the book's title, which reinforces the term, 'fool',[25] points to the hero's narrative function as the naif who is initiated into various aspects of country life and lore, as well as indicating his virginity, and, above all, his rusticity and his Irishness. In London he is the innocent abroad, the Romantic Irish primitive who is alienated by urban materialism, godlessness and carnality. The Ireland to which he returns is created in his own likeness—'green and chaste and foolish'.

Kavanagh drew upon several of the historical and literary conventions surrounding the 'fool' in *The Green Fool*,[26] deploying this figure to connect the role of comic hero with that of poet or literary hero. The various connotations he attaches to the term, 'fool', are rehearsed in the opening chapter:

> The people didn't want a poet, but a fool, yes they could be doing with one of these. And as I grew up not exactly 'like another' I was installed the fool.

I was the butt of many an assembly. I hadn't then read the wisdom of King Cormac Mac Art. 'Never be the butt of an assembly'. At wake, fair, or dance for many years I was the fellow whom the jokers took a hand at when conversational funds fell low. I very nearly began to think myself an authentic fool. I often occupied a position like that of 'The Idiot' in Dostoevsky's novel. I do not blame the people who made me their fool; they wanted a fool and in any case they lost their stakes.

Being made a fool of is good for the soul. It produces a sensitivity of one kind or other; it makes a man into something unusual, a saint or a poet or an imbecile.

As 'fool', Kavanagh is singled out, however derogatorily, from the other villagers who sense that he does not share their model of reality; is less pragmatic, less worldy, more individualistic and imaginative. Kavanagh's antic disposition is, in some measure, a rhetorical ploy to endear him to his audience, to offset the egotism of his autobiographical project. Yet he cannot resist anticipating the conclusion of his narrative, the final comic reversal when, against all the odds, the underdog triumphs and the comic hero is transformed into a successful author. There is also a considerable element of self-preening in parading himself as Dostoevsky's 'Idiot'.

The role of fool was one Kavanagh several times assumed in his early poems, usually humbling himself in order to exalt himself. Two journal entries from a notebook of miscellaneous jottings reveal a private obsession with the subject of foolishness and a connection between folly and introspection dating at least as far back as 1927. The first, undated, passage is entitled 'Wisdom from weakness':

When we are most foolish then is the time to study our real selves. That is the time to peer in the recesses of our minds and ask the question 'where is my worth'. I write thus because I have played the seer and been made a fool of by those whom I considered fools. When

people 'buttonhole' you think calmly, when people tell a
fishy story think awhile and use the proverbial 'grain of
salt'.

The second entry is dated 11 June 1927:

> On this day I was fooled twice the cattle tricksters, and
> then the gay boys whose names I shall not forget FLTL.
> Beware of thy wisdom for it is dangerous, subtle, puffing
> us up with wind, leading us away from all that makes for
> real strength and worth . . .[27]

On both occasions being made a fool of prompts Kavanagh to
engage in self-analysis and self-admonition, though here the
image of the fool touches an exposed nerve as it is not
permitted to do in his published writings. In *The Green Fool* he
is conscious of the Pauline paradox that folly is superior to
wisdom and is particularly alert to the fool's theopneustic
potentialities. He refers, for instance, to 'the essential fool on
which all poets are built'.

The figure of the fool is as close as Kavanagh comes to self-
definition in *The Green Fool*. He is not much given to introspection and does not probe the inner reaches of the self.
The book does not succeed as autobiography because it is not
primarily focused on its author's personality and identity; the
drama of self-discovery or self-expression is not its overriding
plot. It lacks the 'self-regarding, self-interpretative element
that lies at the heart of the [autobiographical] genre whenever
it is exploited to its fullest'.[28]

This is due in part to the choice of the comic mode. One of
the principal roles assigned to the autobiographical 'I' is that
of comic hero, buffoon, prankster, loser, clown. The emphasis on incident, adventure and anecdote arising from this
comic role results in a good deal of concentration on external
caricature and a dearth of inwardness and reflectiveness. The
book's numerous comic character sketches do not contribute
to the central self-portrait. Comedy's function in *The Green*

Fool is to entertain the reader, not to serve as a vehicle of self-revelation.

The narrator of *The Green Fool* is also the social hero of a comic fiction, incorporated into his community, a mediator between his society and the reader. As the original publisher's blurb claimed

> The life of the community is made as vivid as the life of the person through whose eyes it is presented.

Such bifocalism is responsible for much of the book's inadequacy as an autobiography. It fails to achieve the necessary autobiographical balance and tension between outer and inner, objective and subjective. Its narrator is both native informant and self-analyst and the representation of the external world is too often given precedence over self-interpretation. Though the autobiographical subject cannot exist in a vacuum and some evocation of his milieu is necessary, Inniskeen in *The Green Fool* is portrayed as significant in its own right and is not usually appropriated as the context of the narrator's self-construction. It is a foreground rather than a background. Because Kavanagh assumes that his milieu is at least as important to the reader as his self-portrayal he frequently casts himself in a self-effacing, passive, reportorial role. The realisation of his neighbourhood contributes only in a general way to our sense of his growth and development and many episodes were selected more for reasons of anthropological inclusiveness than because they are integral to the *Bildungsroman*. Occasionally, Kavanagh is willing to sacrifice biographical truth to sociological documentation as in the episode of the hiring fair in chapter 15.[29] Often the autobiographical 'I' is a merely technical hero, a pervasive or ubiquitous presence investing a disjointed, episodic narrative with a semblance of coherence.

Some subordination of self to social milieu may have been dictated by the commissioning publisher, since Kavanagh, however successful in his own eyes, was a virtually unknown thirty-three year old whose only claim to fame was that his first slim volume of poems had been included in a Macmillan 'young hopefuls' series. An autobiography in such a case in normal circumstances would have seemed somewhat premature; it was the primitiveness of the poet's background and upbringing that justified the enterprise. The book was marketed as 'an entirely fascinating picture of the adolescence of a young man in a patriarchal society in Ireland, capturing the very essence of Irish rural life'.

Whatever *The Green Fool*'s qualified success in focusing on a specific society it is notably discreet on the subject of adolescence. Remarkably little extra-literary private experience is included;[30] the emphasis on jocularity precludes any serious self-scrutiny or airing of *angst*. The episode of the narrator's illness and hospitalisation, for instance, rapidly tumbles into farce with the rebellious hero and an obstreperous deaf mute challenging hospital discipline.[31] Such youthful fantasies of heroic achievement as found their way into the draft version were factitious and implausibly narrated and were rightly suppressed. The original concluding chapter, entitled 'Love', was condensed into a page.[32] In fact, Michael Joseph, to whom Constable passed on the manuscript when they decided against publishing it themselves, agreed to bring out the book only on condition that this concluding chapter was withdrawn and replaced.[33] The poet was probably too close to the experience to achieve authorial objectivity in discussing his failure in love and the narrative at this point was maundering and uncontrolled. Kavanagh was possibly too young and too immature at the time of writing *The Green Fool* to have assimilated his own past or possibly he was shy of autobiographical self-exposure. In any case he displays very little self-knowledge or self-awareness. His sense of individuation is expressed, for the most part, in terms of his difference from the local community, being not 'like another'. His identity is closely bound up with his literariness.

In so far as *The Green Fool* has a coherent autobiographical plot it is a portrait of the artist as a young man. This

Kuntslerroman theme is conducted as a separate plot and only occasionally relates to the narrative's anthropological or comic concerns. The poet's intellectual and imaginative life is carried on almost independently of and in isolation from his milieu. He is both a social hero and a solitary, and the narrative is fractured to accommodate this double life.

As a portrait of the artist, *The Green Fool* is largely an autodidact's tale, a story of bookish influences and poetic experiments, its climactic epiphany being his first encounter with contemporary literature in the *Irish Statesman*. As a schoolboy he is, predictably, attracted by emphatically rhythmic lyrics and narrative poems: 'Let Erin Remember', 'L'Allegro', 'The Lady of the Lake'. Later, he is dependent for reading matter on the books he occasionally comes upon on a country parlour table and resorts to his sister's Intermediate Certificate English textbook as a writer's manual. Small wonder that his chance encounter with the *Irish Statesman*, a weekly source of contemporary literature and literary criticism, is greeted so rapturously and accorded the status of a Romantic revelation:

> . . . it had a meaning and a message that had come from hills of the imagination far beyond the flat fields of common sense.

Though he is under no external pressure to invent or fictionalise in those parts of *The Green Fool* which portray his own imaginative development, Kavanagh tampers with chronology in order to create the impression that the verses he contributed to the *Irish Weekly Independent*'s poetry competition pre-dated his acquaintance with *The Irish Statesman*. In fact, his Poet's Corner verse began to appear three years after he had first started reading *The Irish Statesman* and continued on for a further year. It only stopped when AE's first rejection slip accompanied by an encouraging request for further poems signalled that better times were round the corner. The book, therefore, presents a false paradigm of Kavanagh's literary evolution, an account of how it should have been, not how it was.

On the other hand, *The Green Fool* is fascinating in its unselfconscious revelation of how Kavanagh's gradual emergence from illiteracy into literariness disqualified and devalued his own personal and local experience and drew him into compensatory, fictional worlds. He turns an upstairs bedroom into the poor man's approximation of an ivory tower and constructs a hedge school in the fields, stocking the bushes with journals and cuttings of poems. Far from being troubled by the anxiety of influence, he anxiously seeks out models, 'as if his whole vocation were endless imitation'. He tries out literary roles: the child visionary from the 'Immortality Ode', Dostoevsky's 'Idiot', the peripatetic hero of *Gil Blas* or Carleton's *Autobiography*, Padraic Colum's 'Drover'. He falls willing victim to intertextuality, thinking in others' ready-made phrases: 'footprints on the sands of my memory', 'thoughts that lie too deep for tears', 'my candle of vision'. His haphazard, arbitrary education leads him to substitute one set of influences for another: nineteenth-century English and American are succeeded by Literary Revivalist Irish models and in the concluding pages he is excited by the American modernists, Ezra Pound, H.D. and, especially, Gertrude Stein. His progress is uneven, to-ing and fro-ing between the popular culture in which his upbringing has saturated him and the literary culture in which he is consciously immersing himself. An earlier draft of *The Green Fool* was, apparently, entitled *The Grey Dawn was Breaking*,[34] a phrase based on a popular sentimental ballad, 'Kathleen Mavourneen, the grey dawn is breaking'. The phrase, which partially survives as a chapter title, is deployed without any trace of irony to indicate Kavanagh's breakthrough into contemporary literature and from apprentice-poet to poet proper. The book originally concluded with the sentence:

The grey dawn has broken and it will soon be noon.[35]

Kavanagh's intoxication with Modernism was merely a stimulus to experimentation with new techniques; his aesthetic, probably reinforced by that of his mentor, AE, remained deeply imbued with nineteenth-century Romanticism. The literary self-images he projects in *The Green Fool* are those of visionary, mystic, dreamer; he extols the imagination as the poetic faculty, par excellence; he sees 'a strange beautiful light on the hills' and observes 'beauty' where his unenlightened fellows see only an ordinary scene. He backdates this propensity towards the visionary to his schooldays when his most memorable poetic experience was overhearing a recitation of Mangan's 'A Vision of Connaught in the Thirteenth Century'. The songs and hymns that haunt him usually refer to starlight.

One of the dilemmas that Kavanagh fails to resolve, or even to address, in *The Green Fool* is that his poetics lags behind his literary practice. Despite the fact that he is constructing a comic realist narrative he still defines literature as a discourse remote from everyday life: 'a world where only spectres flit', 'a cold ghost-wind blowing through Death's dark chapel'. Poetry is separated from literature but it, too, is detached from mundane experience and associated with dream, mysticism, vision, 'beauty too rare for carnal words'. Dream is used in vague, neo-Romantic fashion to divorce literary inspiration from everyday living, or as a sign of inwardness and reflectiveness. His etherealising poetics blinds Kavanagh to the concept of a referential literature, to the aesthetic issue of reification or representation. Consequently, *The Green Fool* is curiously unreflexive. He has not assimilated his parish imaginatively and it has little literary relevance for him. Even as he writes he is still in the process of discovering Inniskeen as a fictional resource. It is only towards the end of the book that he becomes reflexively aware of his neighbours' potential as dramatic characters and alert to the possibilities for 'kitchen comedy' in everyday scenes and dialogue:

Such a scene and such talk was common in the country, yet I had not observed its humour before. Now I was the half of one remove from the people and developing a sense of perspective.

The conclusion of an autobiography always presents a problem since the writer has to create an illusion of conclusiveness out of his life's continuum, and in the case of a youthful autobiographer the problem is exacerbated. Kavanagh originally arrived at a double conclusion: the end of a love affair and the launch of his literary career:

> And curved in mid-air, having leaped for love, I end my tale. The grey dawn has broken and it will soon be noon.[36]

The final two chapters, portraying the poet's conflict between his attachment to home and locality and his ambition to detach himself from his roots and become a professional writer, apparently arose from the necessity of concocting a new ending to satisfy his new publisher. Kavanagh thus arrived at the first expression of one of his most obsessive personal myths, his departure from Inniskeen, a theme replayed in various registers to the last years of his life. Where later works focus on the drama of leavetaking, *The Green Fool* ends happily with the return of the native:

> And when I wandered over my own hills and talked again to my own people I looked into the heart of this life and I saw that it was good.

Already Kavanagh is assuming an attitude of proprietorial affection towards his parish. His pose of happily returned exile may be something of a popular Irish cliché and he is certainly not fully aware of the relationship between his art and his locality but, somewhere in the margins of the closing chapters, a grey dawn is breaking.

The Green Fool is, to some extent, an updated version of *Traits and Stories of the Irish Peasantry*. In inviting an inexperienced countryman to re-create the life of a remote Ulster farming community, Helen Waddell performed a similar role for Kavanagh as Caesar Otway had for William Carleton. Perhaps the literary example of such friends as Frank O'Connor and Seán O'Faoláin might eventually have counteracted AE's etherealising influence, yet up to the publication of *Ploughman and Other Poems* both had been content to endorse Kavanagh's poetic stance, O'Connor attempting to interest various publishers in a collection of his verse[37] and O'Faoláin quoting that etiolated, metaphorical lyric, 'The Sower', as an example of poetry drawn from the poet's 'own world of the fields'.[38] O'Connor and O'Faoláin, who demanded realism in fiction, appear to have judged poetry by different criteria in the 1930s and to have been uncritical of the vague, derivative symbolism of much of Kavanagh's early verse.

The writing of *The Green Fool* was a consciousness-raising exercise in which Kavanagh established a working literary relationship with himself and his environment. While he still retained his image of the poet as a dreamer and solitary visionary, the exigencies of theme and audience compelled him to suspend his transcendental attitude towards the countryside and to realise something of its earthy reality. The champion of the local and the ordinary as the most appropriate subjects for literature underwent his gestation in the pages of *The Green Fool*. Though he had not yet found a suitable convention to represent the actualities of local life, and was further impeded by the libellous potential of the autobiographical mode, Kavanagh's parochial vision may not have been as restricted as his text suggests. The composition of *The Green Fool* may, indeed, have alerted him to the existence of an alternative text, the drab, tragic contrary of his resolutely cheerful rural comedy.

As a psychodrama *The Green Fool* is, undoubtedly, short on self-analysis and self-knowledge. A multiplicity of thematic and fictionalising pressures distract Kavanagh from self-contemplation. He is too busy playing various narrative roles to engage in confessionalism and shows very little self-awareness. Nevertheless, his early experimentation with *Bildungsroman* probably exercised a considerable formal influence on his work. Many of the poems contemporaneous with or written soon after *The Green Fool* are retrospective lyrics. More fundamentally, this introduction to the autobiographical mode launched Kavanagh on a life-long preoccupation with himself as 'hero' and taught him to project himself as the central character in a drama of his own devising.

Writing *The Green Fool* introduced the decorous, limited, inhibited lyricist to the more expansive world of prose fiction, to characterisation, dialogue, drama, documentation, comic techniques, to the structural problems of organising a lengthy narrative. The onus of entertaining and amusing readers also released his repressed sense of fun and compelled him to attempt to strike a balance between his lyrical and his comic gifts. Although he published only one novel, *Tarry Flynn* (1948), he tried his hand at several, the first of which, *Stony Grey Soil*, was drafted by summer 1941. Soon after *The Green Fool* he also began to experiment with combining his lyrical and fictional skills, embarking on the long, documentary and dramatic narrative poems, 'Why Sorrow?', *The Great Hunger*, *Lough Derg*.

Whether Kavanagh would ever have realised his imaginative potential without undergoing his literary apprenticeship as 'green fool' may be debatable. In addition to its considerable interest as an antecedent narrative, generative of later, more accomplished fictions, *The Green Fool* is not without merit in its own right and cannot simply be dismissed as a 'stage-Irish lie' or a Literary Revival romance. It may exclude, distort, diminish or embellish its material but, so precise is the description of local mores, so particularised the naming of places and objects, so persistent the presence of local dialect, that something authentically Inniskeen-like survives the superimposition of comic and Revivalist conventions.

The Green Fool's contemporary reception was overwhelmingly congratulatory. It was in circulation for almost a year before Gogarty won his libel action and even this setback would hardly have blighted Kavanagh's burgeoning self-confidence. Whatever the commercial effects, it would have earned him a good deal of notoriety and sympathy in literary circles. The book was enthusiastically reviewed in England, Ireland and the United States.[39] Such international acclaim must have been very heartening and gratifying for the author and the success of *The Green Fool* probably influenced his decision to abandon all pretence of farming and cobbling and establish himself as a full-time professional writer.

3

Return in Departure:
Towards *The Great Hunger*

'O blessing
For the return in Departure'
('Auditors In')

Introduction

*T*HE *Green Fool* concluded with the return of the native, a
closure that asserted the superiority of rural simplicity
over metropolitan meretriciousness and served as a final
fictional enactment of the writer's faith in his local subject
matter. Kavanagh's real-life situation was less idyllic. His
homecoming had been dictated by financial exigency rather
than primitivist preference; he could not afford to continue
living in London while he was completing *The Green Fool*. He
was restive and unsettled, even less well adapted than before
to the socially claustrophobic and culturally stunted life of
Inniskeen where, as writer-in-residence, he was a marked
man, a dishonoured prophet, 'the butt of many an assembly'.
Whenever possible he absented himself and visited Dublin or
London. In 1939 he made a last attempt to support himself as
a free-lance writer in London, hoping that he could capitalise
on the success of *The Green Fool*. He even accepted the rather
improbable patronage of two lady café owners in Gerrards
Cross. When this parody of life at Coole Park came to an
abrupt, angry conclusion in August 1939 he decided to try his
literary fortunes in Dublin, availing himself of the hospitality
of his schoolteacher brother, Peter. Thus, almost eight years
after his neophyte literary pilgrimage to the Irish capital,
Kavanagh made a definitive break with Inniskeen and settled
in Dublin as a professional writer.

Whether or not the threat of European war precipitated his departure from London, Kavanagh's arrival in Dublin almost coincided with the onset of hostilities, a coincidence exploited in one of his early forties' poems, 'Peace', in which life in Inniskeen is rendered in tranquil, peacetime images, while his subsequent struggle to establish himself in Dublin is presented in the contrasting metaphor of warfare:

> Out of that childhood country what fools climb
> To fight with tyrants Love and Life and Time.

The move to Dublin is characterised as ambitious folly in this sonnet and the city is imaginatively effaced, substituted for by capitalised abstractions, while Inniskeen, though idealised as 'childhood country', is sharply visualised:

> Upon a headland by a whinny hedge
> A hare sits looking down a leaf-lapped furrow
> There's an old plough upside-down on a weedy ridge
> And someone is shouldering home a saddle-harrow . . .

Such precise agricultural imagery and such erasure of the urban are typical of the poems of Kavanagh's early years in Dublin, though nostalgia for his rural past is by no means their only emotional register.

Later, he would grumble less lyrically about the mistiming of his departure from Inniskeen, describing it as 'the worst mistake' of his life, a 'waste of four glorious years' which he could have spent more profitably working his border farm and carrying on a little smuggling on the side.[1] If Kavanagh did lose financially by his move to Dublin then such loss was not without abundant recompense, for once he was at a physical remove from his home place he experienced a Romantic 'return in Departure' and 1939 to 1942 were four glorious years for his poetry. Now that he had abandoned his few paternal acres he was at last content to breathe his native air and to farm the land imaginatively in poem after poem. Once again he sprayed the potatoes on a warm June day or picked them in October, teasing out the tangled skeins of stalk with 'mud-gloved fingers'; he shivered in a 'cold, old black wind . . . blowing from Dundalk' as he ploughed in March or was warmed in November by the steam from a cart-load of dung; his verse danced to 'the music of milking'. This was country poetry, not nature poetry; it teemed with specific images drawn from an insider's knowledge of living in a country parish and working as a tillage farmer.

Nevertheless, the subject of Kavanagh's early forties' poetry is less rural realism than the portrayal of an emotional relationship with home, parish and land. Inniskeen is not so much a geographic terrain as a heartland. The exiled poet is torn between homesickness and relief at having escaped, between mourning and spurning his past. His native village is Eden, the land of lost content, his childhood home the 'garden of the golden apples'; alternatively, Inniskeen is a 'stony grey soil' where the best the field labourer may expect is hell on earth, 'to be damned and yet to live'. A persistent tension in Kavanagh's personality between love and condemnation, celebration and satire, latent in his previous writings, though surfacing in 'Shancoduff' and *The Green Fool*, now began to find expression in the contraries of his early forties' verse.

A significant shift in this verse, closely associated with his antithetical literary moods, is a transition from personal lyricism to sociological narrative. AE's dreamy, asocial acolyte, the carefree prose purveyor of stage-Irish humours, was converted into an angry, socio-literary radical. Kavanagh's reorientation from nostalgic evocation to *saeva indignatio* is in keeping with a general reaction in Irish letters against Literary Revival Romanticism and against the obscurantism and self-congratulatory smugness of the Irish Free State. The outsider status he had always implicitly cherished, even while he explicitly affected to deplore it, predisposed Kavanagh to become a social rebel; his dissociation from a village ethos was easily inflated into outspoken opposition against the Irish literary, cultural and political establishment. The coincidence of his friendship with Seán O'Faoláin, Frank

O'Connor and Peadar O'Donnell, all relentless critics of the cultural status quo, and his move to Dublin at the height of the government's promotion of Ireland as a primitivist paradise, were the catalysts that transformed the hitherto transcendental or comic writer into the author of Ireland's major twentieth-century poetic dystopia, *The Great Hunger* (1942).

Yet Kavanagh was never totally or permanently to shed either the influence of AE's idealism or of Carleton's comic self-portrayal and dramatisation of rural manners. The three roles of socio-literary critic, visionary and comic realist, were each temperamentally congenial and, throughout his career, each was to be vehemently justified or just as vehemently jettisoned as an aesthetic credo. That

> Fair and foul are near of kin
> And fair needs foul . . .

was not a belief to which Kavanagh readily subscribed. He usually preferred outrageous indulgence and righteous repentance to fruitful tension, and whether his subject is a heavenly mansion or a foul sty depends on the literary perspective of the moment. His is a career punctuated with enthusiams embraced and discarded, professions of faith and denials, conversions and recantations. At one time comedy is in the ascendant, at another, tragedy; pastoral has its day and so also has satire; irony is overtaken by empathy, self-irony by self-pity. Yet the shifting emotional and literary registers that his varied allegiances commanded do occasionally meet and intersect, introducing a subtly angled obliquity, an antinomy of attitude, that is characteristic of his finest work.

Literary mood swings are a marked feature of Kavanagh's writing from the late 1930s. His presentation of Inniskeen and of the Irish Catholic way of life is unstable, prone to reversals from fair to foul and foul to fair. These instabilities, the product of a new emotional and descriptive honesty, would be even more obvious had he not suppressed, for one reason or another, the larger portion of the prose and poetry he wrote at the time. Literary works published between September 1939 and the end of 1942 consist of a handful of short lyrics and the long poem, *The Great Hunger*. Unpublished works include a novel, *Stony Grey Soil*, and two long poems, 'Why Sorrow?' and *Lough Derg*. Chapters 3 and 4 focus on the poetry Kavanagh published between 1939 and 1942; the remaining poetry and fiction emanating from this period and either revised for subsequent publication or published posthumously will be discussed in chapters 5 and 6.

This chapter explores the imaginative genesis of Kavanagh's rural masterpiece, *The Great Hunger*. The first part is devoted to a study of the brief, benign lyrics published between 1939 and 1942, some of them among his best poems, in which 'remembered country' first becomes Kavanagh's definitive subject. The second part reveals the presence of a contrary, condemnatory perspective on Inniskeen in his short lyrics prior to the poetically powerful indictment of small-farm Ireland in *The Great Hunger*. It also examines the broader Irish literary context out of which Kavanagh's long poem emerged, the crucial constituency of dissent which writers such as Seán O'Faoláin, Frank O'Connor and Peadar O'Donnell represented in Ireland during the insular, introverted years of the Second World War.

Foul is Fair: Lyrics 1939–1942

Inniskeen is a mere sixty miles or so from Dublin; for the twenty-seven-year-old poet it was even within walking distance. However, the literary importance of Kavanagh's exile, the imaginative mileage he got out of it, is utterly disproportionate to the facts of geographical distance. His migration from Inniskeen was pivotal in his writings for almost a decade, approached from different angles in different poems and, in addition, providing the fictional climax of his novel, *Tarry Flynn*. When the older poet looked back over his literary career in his last great creative phase he summarised it as a circuitous progress from Monaghan to Dublin's Grand

Canal, and in his *Self-Portrait*, published three years before his death, he was still pondering the repercussions of deracination. Metaphorical projection of his life as a journey, pilgrimage, exodus or hegira, was the most enduring of Kavanagh's personal myths. The 'pain of roots dragging up' proved the most traumatic emotional experience of his life for the farmer-poet whose love affair with places was as intense as other men's sexual passions. Where Tennyson was imaginatively energised by the death of Arthur Hallam and Hardy by the death of his wife, Emma, the severing of a thirty-five year attachment to home was the painful pressure that finally released the poet in Kavanagh. For all three it was better to have loved and lost than not to have lost at all.

Kavanagh actually compared himself in his early years away from Inniskeen to one who had suffered a bereavement, wanting to banish grief-provoking memories at first, but soon consoling himself by constructing mental 'pictures of the past'.[2] Exile and elegy are associated, in fact, in one of his late 1939 poems, 'Memory of My Father'.[3] The poet's father had died ten years previously but the sundering of his primal bond with home probably reactivated the trauma of being orphaned. Whereas in 'Poplar Memory' the father was situated in familiar surroundings, a fertile patriarch, in 'Memory of My Father' he is translated from harvest fields to city streets and appears an elderly, enfeebled figure, incapable of offering paternal protection or support:

> Every old man I see
> Reminds me of my father
> When he had fallen in love with death
> One time when sheaves were gathered.
>
> That man I saw in Gardner Street
> Stumble on the kerb was one,
> He stared at me half-eyed,
> I might have been his son.

And I remember the musician
Faltering over his fiddle
In Bayswater, London,
He too set me the riddle.

Every old man I see
In October-coloured weather
Seems to say to me:
'I was once your father.'

The poet's father haunts the poem through rhyme and assonance, as well as through image. Even its Dublin and London place-names were probably selected for their asson-antal associations, and the last line of the first stanza was revised from 'Ten years ago in Monaghan' for the sake of the rhyme, as much as for the poignant harvest image. Kavan-agh's father had died in August yet his presence is recalled in 'October-coloured weather', an impressionistic phrase that exploits the traditional mournful connotations of autumn and also resonates with 'old'. Not only is imagery of home trans-ferred to city pavements in this poem, but the displaced psyche senses a kinship with ailing and vulnerable male figures. Whether the 'half-eyed' stare of the Inniskeen spectre is kindly or reproachful is not recounted. When he finally speaks it is to affirm his parental role, yet simultaneously to relegate it to the past. Nevertheless, this poem performs no rite of exorcism; it raises ghosts rather than lays them. It is both a valediction to a disavowed heritage and a testimony to its continually reasserted presence.

Exile stimulated that poetic definition of his relationship to Inniskeen in which Kavanagh had already sporadically en-gaged in 'Inniskeen Road' and 'Shancoduff'. When he first arrived in Dublin he had 'no system, no plan'. His subject discovered him, obsessed him, overwhelmed him. Inniskeen images came teeming and tumbling in, crowding out the present scene, compelling him to expand beyond rhymed quatrains into the more generous latitudes of long narrative poems and novels. Some he could not immediately accommodate and they sprawled beyond the story line of 'Why Sorrow?'

In *The Green Fool* Kavanagh had frequently belied his own ground; falsifying his perceptions so that they would conform with accepted views of Irish rusticity, selecting and presenting images and scenes in accordance with established aesthetic criteria. Paradoxically, it may have been his very success in adhering to prescribed formulae in *The Green Fool* that allowed him to break with literary precedent. On all sides his peasant proprietorship was now acknowledged: in Ireland there was no one to challenge his patrimony; in England his status as a latterday Robbie Burns was assured. Relieved of the need to establish his credentials he no longer felt obliged to conform to existing models of peasant literature; he had earned the right to stand his own ground and dictate his own terms. In *The Green Fool* he was still an apprentice writer fulfilling his first commission; now he could rework the same terrain as a free-lance artist. A recognised authority on peasant Ireland, he was at liberty to discard others' versions of pastoral. Though he quickly developed into an iconoclast, it was as an image-maker that Kavanagh set out.

Personal deracination from his 'dear, perpetual place' served to root his imagination all the more firmly there; for the first time his poetry was continuously localised. This 'return in Departure' went beyond the merely scenic or descriptive. What Kavanagh was attempting to write was a love-poetry about a place and its way of life. Later, he would observe that 'roots in the soil' did not mean knowledge of 'people living close to nature, struggling for survival on the small farm':

> Real roots lie in our capacity for love and its abandon. The material itself has no special value; it is what our imagination and our love does to it . . .[4]

Though he was too immersed in his new subject to arrive at

such a formulation in the early 1940s, it defines what he was attempting to achieve in these years, a local poetry indelibly marked by the passionate commitment that had led to its conception. He was seeking out forms and rhythms which would not only make a previously disregarded locality visible and audible, but would also communicate a sense of it as a place intimately known and intimately loved or loathed.

He resorted to a combination of personification and apostrophe to pay court to and to part company with his native place in the paired poems, 'Kednaminsha' and 'Stony Grey Soil'.[5] Such rhetoric was calculated to convey a personal relationship with place; unfortunately, it was not conducive to descriptive particularity. The sonnet, 'Kednaminsha', begins flirtatiously yet no clear picture of this artfully dressed place emerges:

> You wore a heather jumper then,
> A hat of cloud and on your feet
> Shoes made by craft-gods out of peat . . .

The retrospective Romantic mode, which allowed for a partnership between realist evocation and subjective 'emotion recollected', was the mode Kavanagh most often turned to in his short early forties' lyrics, most of which include an explicit reference to their own retrospectiveness:

> Like this my memory saw . . .
> Yet I recall . . .
> In the glass of memory plain can see . . .
> I recover now the time . . .
> Remembering the lime and copper smell . . .
>   Now and then
> I can remember something . . .

Place is here inseparable from autobiographical association; unavoidably personalised rather than personified. Such poetry relies for its innovativeness on the realisation of local particularity and/or on the characterisation of the first-person

narrator. What Kavanagh tends to emphasise are local individuality and the transformative powers of the endeared
imagination. Nomenclature plays a significant part in this
poetry: personal names, place-names, names of familiar objects. Naming serves an introductory function, acquainting
the reader with a neighbourhood and its way of life. More
importantly, however, for Kavanagh, naming is also a poetic
rite of intimate intercourse.

His first-person narrator is distinguished by his attraction
to ugly or ordinary aspects of country living, to what literary
convention had dismissed as poetically unworthy. The disfig-
ured bones of his subjects usually gape through the figurative
clothing that adorns them; homely metonyms are revealed
both naked and metaphorised. Readers are made aware, as in
'Shancoduff', that intrinsically unpoetic material is being
glamourised; that what matters is less the material than what
imagination and love do to it.

This defiant, unconventional love affair with the objects of
others' scorn draws attention to its own novelty and unorthodoxy, to the individuality of its narrator's perceptions. It is
both sophisticatedly knowing, and innocent. Kavanagh combines plain honesty with gorgeous or elevating fancy; the
realist and figurative dimensions of his narratives remain in
tension. This is a poetry that succeeds in annexing a new
terrain for Irish verse by adapting the Romantic mode at a
time when English poetry was, itself, espousing impersonality and turning for new subject matter to the urban, the
industrial and the political. Kavanagh's country poetry consciously addresses neglected and deprived areas of Irish
experience. When not subversive of Romantic ruralism it is a
deliberately interlinear poetry, positioning itself in textual
spaces left vacant by English Romanticism or by the Irish
Literary Revival's cult of the peasant. Its 'common people'
inhabit:

The unwritten spaces between the lines . . .[6]

'Christmas   Eve   Remembered',   Kavanagh's   earliest

re-creation of his own parish, published the Christmas after
his arrival in Dublin in 1939,[7] is not altogether successful:

> I see them going to the chapel
> To confess their sins; Christmas Eve
> In a parish in Monaghan.
> Poor parish! and yet memory does weave
> For me about those folk
> A romantic cloak.
>
> No snow, but in their minds
> The fields and roads are white;
> They may be talking of the turkey markets
> Or foreign politics, but to-night
> Their plain hard country words
> Are Christ's singing birds.
>
> Bicycles scoot by; old women
> Cling to the grass margin:
> Their feet are heavy but their minds fly
> In dreams of the Mother Virgin
> For One in Bethlehem
> Has kept their dreams safe for them.
>
> 'Did you hear from Tom this Christmas?'
> 'These are the dark days'.
> 'Maguire's shop did a great trade,
> Turnover double—so Maguire says.'
> 'I can't delay now, Jem
> Lest I be late in Bethlehem' . . .

The impulse to present both an impoverished, realist picture
of Inniskeen and an imaginative transformation of the same
unpromising subject matter is evident here. While the realist
dimension is well represented through visualisation and
dialogue, the transformational dimension is defensive, sentimentalised and extrinsic, 'a romantic cloak'. One reason for
this imaginative failure is the choice of a detached narrator, a
commentator and interpreter, who maintains a distance from

his material, condescends to it, confers a somewhat egotistical significance on it:

> Like this my memory saw,
> Like this my childhood heard . . .

In his next Christmas poem, 'A Christmas Childhood', Kavanagh solved the problem of combining contrary perspectives by presenting country life from a child's viewpoint. Instead of serving as a generalised symbol of prelapsarian rural innocence, childhood is now invoked to provide a dual perspective on the limited world of home and townland, a foreshortened and uncontaminated awareness, accompanied by a transfiguring vision achieved through simple Christian faith. However, the introductory section of 'A Christmas Childhood', first published as an independent piece, is not an entirely happy addition to the poem.[8] It includes some remarkable instances of Kavanagh's use of childhood perception to transform the mundane into the marvellous:

> Again
>
> The tracks of cattle to a drinking-place,
> A green stone lying sideways in a ditch
> Or any common sight the transfigured face
> Of a beauty that the world did not touch.

Yet, despite such 'wonderful' and 'magical' rural images, an adult narrator bewailing the loss of his childhood Eden is an obtrusive presence, unnecessarily justifying these glimpses

> of the gay
> Garden that was childhood's . . .

Like 'Christmas Eve Remembered', the second part of 'A Christmas Childhood' compares an Irish parish with Bethlehem, but here the religious metaphor is incarnated in the poem's realist texture. Originally, this second part was a separate poem, showing 'the wonder of a Christmas townland' through the eyes and ears of a six-year-old child:

My father played the melodeon
Outside at our gate;
There were stars in the morning east
And they danced to his music.

Across the wild bogs his melodeon called
To Lennons and Callans.
As I pulled on my trousers in a hurry
I knew some strange thing had happened.

Outside in the cow-house my mother
Made the music of milking;
The light of her stable-lamp was a star
And the frost of Bethlehem made it twinkle . . .

An atmosphere of childhood excitement pervades this Christmas poem. Despite the past tense it retains an air of unmediated *naïveté* and reads like the unaided effort of 'my child poet'. Detail is picked out with a crisp, frosty clarity; yet the apparent arbitrariness of its ordering, the limpid simplicity of the spoken language, the brief quatrains with their unobtrusive assonantal rhymes, sustain the illusion of childhood experience. The poem radiates outwards from a domestic interior to gate, cowshed, road, bogland, neighbourhood, townland; a world awakening to music. Its child poet, inscribing on frost-silvered stone or making his mark on the doorpost, will inherit the rural rhythms of his parents. This child's perspective is that of the insider, completely at home, familiar with the people and places of his small world. Since a townland is the boundary of the known universe to him he accommodates the exotic to the local, associates the name and position of a distant star with a neighbour's surname and farm:

Cassiopeia was over
Cassidy's hanging hill . . .

(The two near homonyms are also confused through the linear division of 'overhanging').

This poem's transfiguration of an ordinary townland into Bethlehem is not laboured, and the conflation of stable, star and wise kings with the homely and local images of cow house, stable lamp and whin bushes is credible as the fantasy of an Irish Catholic child reared on the Christmas story. The numinous is here offset by comedy: a humorously affectionate glimpse of the six year old dressed in his Sunday best, skulking shyly in the doorway, proud of his adult penknife with its blade for cutting tobacco. 'A Christmas Childhood' ends with a harmonious family triptych:

> My father played the melodeon,
> My mother milked the cows,
> And I had a prayer like a white rose pinned
> On the Virgin Mary's blouse.

The only full rhyme occurs in this last stanza, linking the mother figure with the Virgin Mary, ordinary farmyard chores with religion, a commonplace happening with an image of emotional fulfilment. Music modulates into prayer. Yet the unexpected flowering at the close of this poem is a sudden incarnational miracle that brings heaven down to earth, transforms the Virgin into a village sweetheart, and with a chastely sexual flourish, half out of fairy-tale, half out of country courtship, turns a delicately poised lyric into a simple and beautiful Christmas gift.

'The Long Garden' (December 1941)[9] draws on the inventive make-believe element in childhood play to metamorphose the ordinary and the ugly into the rich and strange. A long garden, bounded by thistly hedges, shared with farm animals and full of household rubbish, is transformed by childhood imagination into the Hesperides, thereby suggesting a connection between childish fantasy and adult myth-making:

> It was the garden of the golden apples,
> A long garden between a railway and a road,

In the sow's rooting where the hen scratches
We dipped our fingers in the pockets of God.

In the thistly hedge old boots were flying sandals
By which we travelled through the childhood skies,
Old buckets rusty-holed with half-hung handles
Were drums to play when old men married wives.

Adult wish-fulfilment obtrudes awkwardly, however, in the lines

The racing cyclists' gasp-gapped reports
Hinted of pubs where life can drink his fill . . .

Although childhood country in this poem is the poet's own, identifiable through a series of local references, details are accumulated less for evocative than for doctrinaire purposes. This is a schematic poem where Kavanagh is intent on underlining the disparity between the real and the imagined to show what can be made of the most unpretentious subject matter. Substitution of plural for singular, first-person narration increases the effect of generalisation. While it offers some vividly realised images of a materially impoverished and fantastically rich rural childhood, 'The Long Garden', which was extracted from the unfinished sprawl of 'Why Sorrow?',[10] is spoiled by its formulaic and rhythmic predictability.

From the beginning Kavanagh's autobiographical rural verse tended towards reflexiveness. In 'Spraying the Potatoes' and 'Art McCooey' it is even programmatically local.[11] What happens in Inniskeen fields is now 'stuff for the Muses'. 'Spraying the Potatoes' is based on the recollection of a specific farming occasion, and the urban present, adverted to only briefly and negatively in the last stanza, is immediately overwhelmed by the magic of the past.

The barrels of blue potato-spray
Stood on a headland of July

Beside an orchard wall where roses
Were young girls hanging from the sky.

The flocks of green potato-stalks
Were blossom spread for sudden flight,
The Kerr's Pinks in a frivelled blue,
The Arran Banners wearing white.

And over that potato-field
A lazy veil of woven sun.
Dandelions growing on headlands, showing
Their unloved hearts to everyone.

And I was there with the knapsack sprayer
On the barrel's edge poised. A wasp was floating
Dead on a sunken briar leaf
Over a copper-poisoned ocean . . .

The poem opens flatly and prosaically. An ordinary farming chore, which might seem peculiarly resistant to lyricisa-
tion, is being appropriated for poetry. 'Spraying the Potatoes' soon blossoms into a colourful, sensuous, almost erotic,
evocation of a warm July day on the farm, a lyric which
anticipates a poetics formalised in the mid-1950s:

. . . nothing whatever is by love debarred
The common and banal her heat can know . . .[12]

The farmer-poet's lost potato fields are provocatively titivated
and memory beckons with a come-hither look. His attitude is
amorous; the poem is 'in heat'. This sexual undertow,
charging recollection with excitement, is mediated through
weather images, metaphor and narrative transference: noon-
time warmth, a tropical becalmment; roses personified as
dallying girls peeping over a wall; potato stalks decorated
with feminine fripperies; dandelions in the pathetically expect-
ant role of wallflowers; reminiscence about cornfield courtship displaced on to an old man. That transitional metaphor

The axle-roll of a rut-locked cart
Broke the burnt stick of noon in two . . .

so descriptively evocative, slow paced, hot, and slyly sexual, is a paradigmatic turning point. Afterwards tension winds down, the experience gradually slips out of focus and dialogue disappears into vaguely celebratory phrases, 'a theme of kings,/A theme for strings'.

The concluding stanza combines the programmatic with the sensuous:

> And poet lost to potato-fields,
> Remembering the lime and copper smell
> Of the spraying barrels he is not lost
> Or till blossomed stalks cannot weave a spell.

Here the word 'lost' is pivotal, advanced in the first line, withdrawn in the third. An elegiac mood is summoned only to be dismissed as Kavanagh confidently proclaims that personal loss has paradoxically resulted in imaginative gain, that he has now found his bearings as an autobiographical poet.

'Art McCooey' confirms this finding. It is a manifesto poem which, under the guise of rural reminiscence, explains the literary importance of Kavanagh's Inniskeen period. Here he has chosen as his ostensible subject a farming chore even less prepossessing than spraying potatoes, carting dung:

> I recover now the time I drove
> Cart-loads of dung to an outlying farm—
> My foreign possessions in Shancoduff—
> With the enthusiasm of a man who sees life simply.
>
> The steam rising from the load is still
> Warm enough to thaw my frosty fingers.
> In Donnybrook in Dublin ten years later
> I see that empire now and the empire builder . . .

'Art McCooey' begins urbanely: an older poet's benign amusement at his younger self, rendered in comically inflated images; simplicity mediated through experienced narration.

Affectionate humour also plays over the poem's subsequent recollections, misleading the reader into underestimating its ultimate seriousness. This is the work of a poet who has come to terms with his local subject matter and is completely at his ease. The younger self portrayed here is a small farmer, whose horizons, like those of 'my child poet' in 'A Christmas Childhood', are bounded by his parish. His talk is of local scandals; he can name the owner of every house and field; he is interested in the trivia of neighbours' lives, can identify a man's shout, tell the time by the distant laughter of children just released from school; his speech is flavoured with localisms like 'Brave and cool' or 'wangel'; he looks ahead only as far as teatime or the chat after second mass on Sunday; his day ends with the sordid business of cleaning out the dung cart. The embryonic poet is presented as an ordinary country lad, registering his local milieu unawares, not realising that here is life and food for future years. He is still in the preconscious, pre-natal phase of his poetic formation:

> Wash out the cart with a bucket of water and a wangel
> Of wheaten straw. Jupiter looks down.
> Unlearnedly and unreasonably poetry is shaped
> Awkwardly but alive in the unmeasured womb.

This concluding stanza exploits the shock-value of having the president of the Immortals oversee the sordid business of cleaning out a dung cart. The dialect word, 'wangel', is deliberately juxtaposed with Jupiter, a meeting of the local and the universal, the 'thick-tongued' and the classical. Two years after his arrival in Dublin, Kavanagh, in 'Art McCooey', is distancing himself by a decade from his rural past and fashioning a Romantic myth about his own poetic formation which emphasises the ordinary, the ugly and the comic aspects of his early experience. What the myth stresses is the unlikelihood of his translation from farmer into poet. A slow and painful process of autodidacticism is erased at a stroke in the phrase, 'unlearnedly and unreasonably'; whom the gods

love cart dung. In later life Kavanagh claimed that he had
been born as a poet on the banks of the Grand Canal in 1955,
but the poetry testifies to an earlier Dublin birth in 1940.
Implicit in 'Art McCooey's' concluding metaphor of gestation
is the recognition that the farmer-poet is now delivering the
verse conceived and nurtured in his foolish Inniskeen years.

'Art McCooey' offers a myth of cultural as well as personal
poetic origins. On Kavanagh's ancestral stair we encounter
not 'Goldsmith and the Dean, Berkeley and Burke', but an
eighteenth-century Irish Catholic poet of small-farming stock.
Art McCooey, 'Art of the Songs', who hailed from the parish
of Creggan, a few miles from Inniskeen, was, like William
Carleton, a local literary hero. In writing a poem about his
memories of carting dung Kavanagh is clearly identifying
with this Irish-speaking poet who occasionally worked as a
farm labourer. One of the best-known folk traditions about
Art McCooey is that once, when employed by a farmer to cart
dung, he became so absorbed in composing a poem that he
drove the same cartful four or five times between the manure
heap and the place where he was supposed to deposit his
load, until he was eventually caught in the act by his enraged
employer and brought back to earth with a few rough words.
'Owney Martin's splitting yell', sharp enough to 'knife the
dreamer that the land begets', doubtless recalls McCooey's
irate master. Kavanagh, whose knowledge of the Irish language was rudimentary, nevertheless, felt a warm regard for
the Gaelic poets of his native region because as Catholic,
small-farm poets they were his 'rude forefathers', anticipating to some extent his aesthetic programme of localisation:

> ... though they were not great poets, they absorbed the
> little fields and lanes and became authentic through
> them.[13]

'Úir Chill an Chreagáin', the lyric for which Art McCooey is
best remembered is an *aisling*, an Irish poetic mode in which
the poet, almost oblivious of his surroundings, describes a
visionary encounter with a female personification of Ireland.

Kavanagh, despite his tribute to local poetic tradition in 'Art McCooey', is writing a primarily autobiographical poem full of evocative realistic detail and his literary ancestor is not any local or even Irish poet but the William Wordsworth of the *Prelude*, chronicler of the apparently ordinary trivia that contribute to poetic formation. Wordsworth's was an influence which Kavanagh had ingested during his reading of nineteenth-century schoolbook poetry and of which he appears to have been unconscious.

What is distinctive about Kavanagh's early forties' Romanticism is its discovery of a new, unworked ground, its consistent localisation and imaginative insistence on the importance of the poet's intimate relationship with his own home and parish, its 'awkwardly but alive' quality which refuses smooth English pentameter speech rhythms, and its occasional creation of a self-ironic yet serious persona with a sharp eye for country humours and a keen ear for Inniskeen dialect.

Almost as soon as he had realised that a whole rural hinterland lay waiting to be imaginatively reclaimed, Kavanagh abandoned the poetics of happy retrospection. One would have expected his series of rustic idylls to continue for years. Instead, by 1941 he was already turning from his brief lyrics with their naif personae and correspondingly simple quatrains to explore, through the medium of more expansive structures, that ambivalence in his own response to the countryside which had made departure from Inniskeen both difficult and desirable. The ugly actualities, metonymically present, though metaphorically flattered, in his celebratory country lyrics are now usually denuded of 'celestial light' or fanciful apparel, and adult desires and frustrations, hitherto repressed, disturb and complicate the emotional register of his fictions.

(ii) Fair is Foul: Towards *The Great Hunger*

In November 1941, the same year in which he published 'The Long Garden' and 'Art McCooey', Patrick Kavanagh submitted his long poem, *The Great Hunger* (then named 'The Old Peasant'), for part publication in *Horizon*'s January 1942 number on Ireland. The nostalgic exile, who had evoked Inniskeen as a lost Eden or a significant poetic source, had been transformed into an embittered, impassioned critic of rural Ireland. It would appear that suddenly and simultaneously the hitherto self-absorbed poet had acquired a social conscience, abandoned affectionate pastoralism for harsh naturalism and shifted from a lyrical to a fictional narrative mode. He had also vastly expanded his poetic range and repertoire. Where previously his favourite forms had been the lyric in rhymed quatrains or the sonnet, and none of his poems had run to more than fifty-four lines, *The Great Hunger*, a poem divided into fourteen irregular parts, was 758 lines long,[14] and was composed of a collage of poetic styles and forms. Yet *The Great Hunger* does not represent an unforeseeable volte-face, either in its author's own *oeuvre* or in early forties' Irish literature. It is a poem thematically and formally anticipated in Kavanagh's writings, though several of the links in its evolutionary chain were not visible at the time. It is, also, as Geoffrey Taylor immediately recognised, the poem Ireland had been waiting for,[15] the progeny of a post-Yeatsian school of socio-literary criticism. It is bred of a new iconoclastic movement in Irish letters, a realist revolution against anachronistic and destructive national fantasies.

The *saeva indignatio* that powers *The Great Hunger* was first unleashed in Kavanagh's savage onslaught on his rural past in 'Stony Grey Soil' (October 1940). This, and its companion poem, 'Kednaminsha', both of which apostrophise his native place and personify it as female, seem designed to convey two conflicting relationships with Inniskeen. Of the two, 'Kednaminsha', a flattering and nostalgic sonnet, is by far the weaker, a negligible poem which Kavanagh did not bother to collect or republish. 'Stony Grey Soil', on the contrary, is charged with poetic conviction, rhythmically confident, packing imagistic punch after punch, impelled forward with a righteous and relentless emotional momentum, a raw energy that eventually dissipates itself in self-pity and a sad sense of irretrievable loss. Whereas in 'Spraying the Potatoes' and 'Art McCooey' Inniskeen is portrayed as a fertile poetic terrain and the years devoted to cultivating it, guarding it against blight or manuring it, are regarded as time well spent, in 'Stony Grey Soil' Inniskeen appears a psycho-sexual and poetic wasteland, a graveyard of aborted desires, and the years passed there misspent, a squandering of precious youth:

> O stony grey soil of Monaghan
> The laugh from my love you thieved;
> You took the gay child of my passion
> And gave me your clod-conceived.
>
> You clogged the feet of my boyhood
> And I believed that my stumble
> Had the poise and stride of Apollo
> And his voice my thick-tongued mumble.
>
> You told me the plough was immortal!
> O green-life-conquering plough!
> Your mandril strained, your coulter blunted
> In the smooth lea-field of my brow.
>
> You sang on steaming dunghills
> A song of cowards' brood,
> You perfumed my clothes with weasel itch,
> You fed me on swinish food.
>
> You flung a ditch on my vision
> Of beauty, love and truth.
> O stony grey soil of Monaghan
> You burgled my bank of youth . . .

'Stony Grey Soil' anticipates *The Great Hunger* in its bitter exposure of the falsity of the pastoral myth. Its infertile, dreary, yet compelling 'soil' will become the dispirited 'clay' that dominates all rural life in *The Great Hunger*. Throughout the poem 'grey' is contrasted with 'gay'. Though 'Stony Grey

Soil' is a lyric in which the land's victim is the farmer-poet, while *The Great Hunger* is a fictional narrative in which the hungry fiend's prey is the ordinary Irish farmer, represented by the dramatic character, Patrick Maguire, the two poems occupy the same psycho-sexual terrain. Like *The Great Hunger*, 'Stony Grey Soil' portrays the bond between the farmer and his land as wronghearted, a displaced sexual relationship, and the poet whose place-attachment delayed his removal from Inniskeen is, like Patrick Maguire, a man who made 'a field his bride'. Here the land is personified as a scheming, ingratiating, possessive woman who has used her female wiles to hold on to her man and trick him out of self-fulfilment. She also takes on the role assigned to Mrs Maguire in *The Great Hunger*, that of 'wife and mother in one'. Homeland in 'Stony Grey Soil' is maternal as well as seductive, supposedly mature, wise, reassuring, trustworthy. The farmer-poet is simultaneously a prodigal son fed on swinish husks and a beguiled traveller bewitched into brutish stagnation by the charms of a dunghill Circe. This doubly treacherous female relationship suggests deep duplicity, and the farmer-poet is fiercely angry at his own capacity for being deceived. Sexual imagery suggests a perverted ('strained') eroticism; the earth that had its way with the complainant for so long was intrinsically unattractive. Like Patrick Maguire, this farmer-poet is characterised as a passive, involuntary victim. In 'Stony Grey Soil' all past action and initiative are attributed to the female land who deprived, deceived, seduced, impeded, thieved. Youth's 'hours of pleasure' are passively 'lost', not actively neglected.

Though 'Stony Grey Soil' and *The Great Hunger* both centre on the metaphor of sexual frustration and both associate it with farming and misplaced trust in a female power, the earlier lyric is altogether more evasive than the later fiction, despite the apparent directness of its accusatory tirade. Where attachment to the land and psycho-sexual unfulfilment in *The Great Hunger* are presented objectively and dramatically, 'Stony Grey Soil' resorts to the more old-fashioned

verbal masks adopted in Kavanagh's thirties' poetry: personifications, abstractions, metaphorical generalisations. The
metonymic dimension which was becoming a feature of his
contemporary verse is abandoned and the poem proceeds by
a series of metaphoric correlatives whose subjective referents
are sometimes difficult to determine. The fact that the undeceived hero of 'Stony Grey Soil' is both man and poet
complicates his grievance. Its metaphoric strategy renders
'Stony Grey Soil' fundamentally elusive on the connection
between poetic and sexual frustration; it shifts about between
decrying sexual sublimation through poetry and through
place-attachment, and between bewailing poetic limitation,
lost laughter and lost lovers, as if all these were almost
interchangeable disabilities. The 'gay child of my passion'
modulates into the 'first gay flight of my lyric'; the 'clod-
conceived' changeling is assonantally connected with the
'clogged' poetic feet of the apprentice rhymester. Is the
'immortal' plough a reflexive allusion to 'Ploughman': the
plough, once perceived as an aesthetic instrument, painting
the meadow, now a murderous weapon, fatal to young life?
The most puzzling of the poem's metaphors is the abrupt
introduction of a male monster into an otherwise female
terrain in the sixth stanza and the near-oxymoronic reference
to him as a monster who should, preferably, be caressed:[16]

> Lost the long hours of pleasure
> All the women that love young men
> O can I still stroke the monster's back
> Or write with unpoisoned pen

> His name in these lonely verses
> Or mention the dark fields where
> The first gay flight of my lyric
> Got caught in a peasant's prayer.

The monster remains a private, inaccessible metaphor, an
extreme instance of this poem's psycho-analytic covertness.

In the poem's favour it must be said that its metaphorical
strategy enables it to zone in quickly on psychic territory, to

communicate swiftly and surely through freshly minted images, ('You flung a ditch on my vision . . . You burgled my bank of youth') and to suggest the interrelatedness of creative and psycho-sexual repression. Incompatibility between imaginative transcendence ('vision', 'gay flight') and the constraints imposed by country living ('clogged', 'ditch', 'caught') foreshadows a similar tension in *The Great Hunger*, as does the thwarting of aspiration by peasant piety. While the precise identity of child and changeling may not be explicit in the opening stanza, the exchange of a gay love child for a 'clod conceived' also gestures towards the stifling materialism/ maternalism of *The Great Hunger*.

Although it is a relatively young man's poem, 'Stony Grey Soil' shares something of *The Great Hunger*'s sense of belatedness. Unlike Maguire, the disillusioned farmer-poet has only temporarily made 'a field his bride' and his poem ostensibly focuses on the termination of the relationship, not on its prolongation past the point of no return, yet its form, tone and structure subtly suggest that he has not quite made his escape. 'Stony Grey Soil' is a saying of the unforgivable, an ugly, unseemly row, that seems intended to prevent any future reconciliation. However, the farmer-poet is still locked in dialogue with the matrix/mistress he is leaving, still absorbed in his past life when the poem ends. The hold this heartland has over him may be deduced from his persistent emotional engagement, the angry vehemence of the first part of the monologue and the deepening feeling of bereavement in the three concluding stanzas. The ambivalent nature of this valedictory quarrel is very evident in the closing lines:

> Mullahinsha, Drummeril, Black Shanco—
> Wherever I turn I see
> In the stony grey soil of Monaghan
> Dead loves that were born for me.

Naming introduces a tone of amorous intimacy. On the point of departure, the farmer-poet is drawn back into the thrall of his old passion. Monaghan earth may be transformed into a cemetery like the potato field of *The Great Hunger*, but it is fertile as well as funereal. The land is finally, if obliquely, acknowledged as a source, as well as a fatal stranglehold.

'Stony Grey Soil' is a love poem disguised as a hate poem (a poet killing the thing he loves), or a hate poem that discovers what it loves in the act of destroying it. Either way it is not as straightforward as it may at first appear. A seemingly spontaneous overflow, its spate is powerfully checked by formal restraints. Emotionally, it is as controlled and balanced as a Petrarchan sonnet, five angry, accusatory stanzas, then a *volta*, signalled by inversion, followed by a change of tonal register from aggression to lament. However, its metaphors mingle across stanzaic boundaries, setting up internal tensions and correspondences, and the paradoxical concluding line fails to bury the past, indeed, affirms the local, rooted nature of the farmer-poet's 'loves'. Interestingly, this poem's title is the same as that of Kavanagh's near-contemporary, unpublished novel about a young farmer's failure in love, suggesting further interrelatedness between place-attachment and heterosexual relationship in his early forties' writings.

In *The Great Hunger* the personal anger and anguish of 'Stony Grey Soil', its private rhetoric of invective, denunciation and lament, are redirected into a public, socio-literary indictment of small-farm Ireland. A complex emotional response to Inniskeen is transposed into a powerful, despairing vision of lost human potentialities. The first-person narrator champions the cause of his inarticulate, suffering fellow countrymen and countrywomen, the Maguires of Ireland, trapped in a lonely, loveless, laborious existence, dumbly acquiescing in their slow extinction.

In 'Peasant' (1936), Kavanagh had already envisaged himself as 'the representative of those/Clay-faced sucklers of spade-handles'. In 'The Hired Boy' (1936), he had exposed the constricted, brutalised life of the country labourer with embittered realism:

He knew what he wanted to know —
How the best potatoes are grown
And how to put flesh on a York pig's back
And clay on a hilly bone.
And how to be satisfied with the little
The destiny masters give
To the beasts of the tillage country —
To be damned and yet to live.

(Proleptically, the hired boy works for one John Maguire of Donaghmoyne.) In 'My People' (1937), in which a country poet dialogues with an urban stranger, metropolitan myths about peasant Ireland are harshly dismissed. The stranger conceives of country people romantically as elemental heroes:

Great in despair,
Simple in prayer,
And their hard hands tear
The soil on the rock
Where the plough cannot go

The poet, in his role of native informant, is quick to disillusion him:

They till their fields and scrape among the stones
Because they cannot be schoolmasters —
They work because judge Want condemns the drones.
Dear stranger, duty is a joke
Among my peasant folk.

The poet's role and stance here anticipate those of the *Great Hunger*'s narrator, while the misguided urban stranger will be that poem's implicit audience. Whereas *The Green Fool* was still heavily influenced by stage-Irish or Revivalist conventions, poems like 'The Hired Boy' and 'My People' are the first signs of the Inniskeen poet's involvement in an Irish literary counter-Renaissance, a cultural revolution against the oppressions of primitivist and heroic misrepresentation, which was rapidly gaining momentum throughout the 1930s, spearheaded by Seán O'Faoláin and Frank O'Connor.

The second stanza of 'To a Child' (1935) originally read:

> Child remember this high dunce
> Had laughter in his heart and eyes
> A million echoes distant thence
> Ere Corkmen taught him to be wise.[17]

The 'Corkmen', later erased from the poem, were O'Faoláin and O'Connor, Kavanagh's friends, mentors and promoters during the 1930s and early 1940s, and the wisdom they imparted was that the business of literature is social criticism. O'Faoláin and O'Connor, both of whom were disillusioned veterans of the War of Independence and ex-disciples of the extreme cultural nationalist, Daniel Corkery, had emerged in the 1930s as the spokesmen of a new post-Independence and post-Revival generation of Irish writers. Both conceived of literature as a socially engaged, realist art, holding the mirror up to the unglamorous actualities of contemporary Ireland. Their aesthetic programme was subversive of the prevailing xenophobic, puritanically Catholic and primitivist pietas fostered by the alliance of church and state in the 1930s and 1940s, and deliberately discontinuous with what they perceived as the romantic, heroic myths of the Literary Revival.

For several decades after Independence, Ireland remained self-consciously chauvinistic, obsessed with fashioning or consolidating a separatist ethnic identity. De Valera, whose Fianna Fáil government came to power in 1932, was anxious to establish the twenty-six counties as an economically self-sufficient, politically and culturally independent state, totally liberated from its English colonial past; 'not merely free but Gaelic as well'. His ideal Irish Ireland was a nation largely rural and agricultural rather than urban and industrialised, piously Catholic rather than materialist, Gaelic-speaking or, at least, bilingual, and fostering a distinctively ethnic culture. The Irish were to be a poor but proud people, heartened by a long history of heroic resistance to colonial domination; a nation of small farmers, diligent, sober, God fearing, content with simple pleasures. De Valera's was a national dream which the Catholic hierarchy, who had, not so long before, excommunicated his party, was happy to endorse.[18] By 1940 'de Valera's government had complete control inside the country' and was insulated against outside liberal criticism of its social or cultural programme by the Second World War.[19] Ireland's neutrality in this war fulfilled de Valera's isolationist ambitions only too well. Withdrawal from Europe reinforced Irish post-Independence tendencies towards morally censorious Catholicism, obscurantism and cultural xenophobia.

The most powerful and most relentless critic of the prevailing nationalist Catholic ethos in the 1930s and 1940s was Seán O'Faoláin, who had returned to Dublin from Harvard in 1929, fired with zeal to stir 'this sleeping country, those sleeping fields, those sleeping villages'.[20] He immediately set about dispelling consolatory Romantic fantasies about the glories of Irish nationhood, using short stories, novels, biographies and essays as vehicles for historical and social analysis. In his short story, 'A Broken World', O'Faoláin created a prototype of Patrick Maguire, an indifferent, somnolent, scarcely conscious farmer, who appears to find his way by 'animal magnetism'. His biography of Daniel O'Connell, *King of the Beggars* (1938), masterfully disposed of Ireland's proudest and most politically and culturally synthesising myth: that modern Ireland was the continuator of Gaelic Ireland. According to O'Faoláin's persuasive thesis, modern Ireland was the nineteenth-century invention of the pragmatic, anti-Gaelic leader, Daniel O'Connell, who had disciplined a horde of socially and culturally disadvantaged beggars into a potential citizenry.[21] In *An Irish Journey* (1941), O'Faoláin toured the country, acquainting his readers with the often unattractive face of contemporary Ireland. His response to neutral Ireland's introverted isolation in the Second World War was to launch *The Bell* in October 1940: a monthly journal aimed at conducting a documentary and literary exploration of various facets of Irish life and opening 'Irish windows to the world beyond its shores'. *The Bell*'s vision of Ireland was pluralist, embracing all creeds and classes as manifestations of Irish reality and according no ethnic monopoly to Catholics, neo-Gaels or small farmers. In O'Faoláin's view, Ireland's absorption with its own past was pernicious, an ostrich-like escape from the urgent needs of the present. The structures of Irish society were disintegrating in the wake of Independence and no vital initiatives or institutions might be expected from a ruling class which was content to 'wail for the past like John Ball'.[22] He deplored the Irish inclination to take cultural refuge in the artistic grandeurs of a bygone era and consigned the Literary Revival to the imaginary museum. Essays such as 'Yeats and the Younger Generation' (1942) emphasised the generation gap between contemporary Irish writers and the Revivalists. The 'younger generation'

> were faced with problems far more insistent: social, political and even religious problems. They had grown up in a period of revolution, were knitted with common life, and could not evade its appeal . . .[23]

'Curiously, O'Faoláin's influence is most strongly marked not on any novelist', Frank O'Connor notes, 'but on the poetry of Patrick Kavanagh'.[24] Kavanagh was invited to contribute to the first number of *The Bell*, which carried that love-hate pair of poems about his native place, 'Kednaminsha' and 'Stony Grey Soil', the latter dedicated to O'Faoláin. Subsequent issues during O'Faoláin's editorship included the lyrics, 'A Christmas Childhood', 'Art McCooey', 'Bluebells for Love', and three excerpts from a draft version of *Tarry Flynn* under the appropriate *Bell* title, 'Three Glimpses of Irish Life'. O'Faoláin praised the precise rural imagery of 'Spraying the Potatoes',[25] which was published in the *Irish Times*, as was 'Memory of Brother Michael',[26] a poem undoubtedly influenced by O'Faoláin's views on the deleterious effects of Irish historiography.

More substantial evidence of a developing community of interest between O'Faoláin and Kavanagh may be deduced from the fact that the latter's first novel, *Stony Grey Soil*, was based on the 'Inniskeen dance-hall case' which O'Faoláin considered 'so typically illuminating' of contemporary Irish country life as to merit narrating in *An Irish Journey*:

> Some local boys got the idea of erecting a dance-hall. So, unfortunately, did the Parish Priest. The two halls were started. Just then the P.P. had to leave his parish on a spiritual retreat. While he was away the local boys built as no man ever built before, so that when the P.P. returned he found the rival building almost completed. The next Sunday there was a sermon fit to scald the hair off a cannon-ball. The local boys' dance-hall became known thereafter as the Anti-Christ Hall. Undaunted, the local boys went ahead and finished their hall.
>
> Then came the fateful question, 'Which would get a licence?' The local boys applied to the courts for their licence and were, of course, opposed by the P.P. The Justice supported the P.P. and refused a licence. In due course the P.P. finished his hall and applied for a licence. It is not too much to say that he got it *con brio, fortissimo,* and *suaviter in modo*. Now the local boys may survey their hall and wonder what they are going to do with it, and how they can ever hope to pay for it, while the strains of revelry by night come to their ears from the triumphant jazz-palace beside the church.

For O'Faoláin this story illustrated 'better than a Blue Book the power of the Church in Ireland'.[27]

It is hardly pure coincidence that it was in a novel based on this case that Kavanagh first revealed a sociological interest in his native parish. His initial reaction had been to appreciate the humour of the situation. 'Great fun over Halls surely', he wrote in a letter of 1 August 1939 to his brother,[28] but, most probably under O'Faoláin's guidance, he came to regard it as an affair of sufficient import to serve as the basis of his first novel about life in rural Ireland. Several drafts survive of this novel, which was finally completely rewritten and published as *Tarry Flynn* in 1948.[29] None of the extant drafts appears either as coherent or as devoid of comedy as the version Frank O'Connor had read by 1941, so it may well be that his reading was affected more by the latent or potentially serious message of the novel than by any actual sustained tone of despair. On the other hand, Kavanagh did claim that this novel was anti-clerical: 'The novel belonged to my anti-clerical period. Anti-clericalism was part of the jag.' So the version Frank O'Connor saw may well have been different from the extant drafts.

O'Connor read Kavanagh's novel as a story of young people 'in conflict with the furious piety and Puritanism of Catholic Ireland' and summarised its plot as follows:

> In it he describes the life of a country boy in a north of Ireland village which is dominated by an ignorant, good-natured old parish priest. The story begins with an attempt by a group of boys and girls to establish a village hall in which they can meet and exchange ideas. The hall is a symbol of the life they would really like to lead, but which they never can lead because the old village tyrant opposes the licensing of the 'Anti-Christ Hall' as he calls it, and there is no one strong enough to defeat him. And so we see the principal character, in love with a decent girl whom he can never meet under decent conditions, masturbating his soul away until the girl he loves is seduced by the local Don Juan (though, except for this once his Don Juanism has never been anything but a mental exercise), while the hero settles down in comfort with a cow of a girl who has a little fortune, and the Anti-Christ Hall becomes a cattle-shed.[30]

It is doubtful whether the thesis of Kavanagh's first novel was as consistent or as sociologically symbolic as O'Connor suggests. The poet was still his own hero (albeit fictional-ised), and the novel's anti-clericalism was intertwined with a new version of that failed romance which Michael Joseph had caused to be excised from *The Green Fool*. Extant drafts are rambling and confused and their tone is comic. What O'Connor's interpretation, like O'Faoláin's documentation of the dance-hall case, illustrates, is the sociologically biased reading of rural life customary in Kavanagh's Dublin milieu. O'Connor ranked Kavanagh's unpublished novel with O' Faoláin's *Bird Alone* (1936), his own *The Saint and Mary Kate* (1932), Gerald O'Donovan's *Father Ralph* (1913) and Joyce's *Portrait of the Artist as a Young Man* (1916), all disenchanted realist fictions in an anti-Revivalist mode. A concern with the 'facts' of Irish life was, for O'Connor, an interrupted tradition in Irish literature, inaugurated with George Moore's *The Untilled Field* (1903), continued by Joyce, and resumed in the 1930s and early 1940s by O'Faoláin, Kavanagh and himself. The three latter were 'merely the strayed revellers of the Irish Literary Revival, and by the early 1940s this was all over and done with'.[31]

An important figure is absent from this thirties' and early forties' triumvirate. O'Faoláin's and O'Connor's influence on Kavanagh at this time was augmented by that of Peadar O'Donnell, managing editor of *The Bell* from 1940 until 1946, when he succeeded O'Faoláin as editor. O'Donnell, who was a friend of Kavanagh's during the lifetime of *The Bell*, came from a very similar background; he was reared on a small farm near Dungloe, Co. Donegal. Like O'Faoláin and O'Connor he had been involved in the War of Independence, had been an activist on the Republican side in the Civil War, and had turned into a fierce opponent of de Valera. O'Donnell was a socialist who had hoped that the Republican side would bring about a workers' and small farmers' Republic. In 1935 he ended his involvement with IRA politics, but he remained a dedicated socialist to the end. The principal socio-economic issue that concerned him, both inside and outside the pages of *The Bell*, was the poverty of the small farmers in the west of Ireland.[32] O'Donnell had described the life of poor country people in his novel, *Islanders* (1927), and his literary and ideological commitment to the poor and underprivileged must have contributed in no small measure to the awakening of Kavanagh's social conscience. O'Donnell's humane zeal helped to inspire Kavanagh's poetic compassion for the plight of the small-farming class in *The Great Hunger*, as well as fuelling his detestation of the prosperous middle classes and his sympathy for the urban unemployed in *Lough Derg*.

O'Connor has elected 1940, the year after Kavanagh's move to Dublin, as 'the crucial year for any study of modern Irish literature'. By this time 'the intellectual darkness of the country was almost palpable'.[33] Yeats was dead and so, too, was Romantic Ireland. The 'emptiness and horror of Irish life' had begun to dawn on any Irish writer who was not 'a rogue or an imbecile'. Irish literature had 'reached the end of a period', he advised at the beginning of 1942, and Irish writers 'must be prepared to come into the open . . . have done with romanticism . . . and let satire have its way'.[34]

However dubious the documentary credentials of Kavanagh's maundering first novel, in the distilled fictionality of *The Great Hunger*, which probably followed on it, he suddenly arrived at a searingly authoritative exposure of life in rural Ireland. It is a masterpiece, apparently written at white heat,[35] powered by a fierce, sustained rage at the primitivist fantasies so pervasive in Dublin's political and literary circles. In it Kavanagh is subverting de Valera's small-farm pieties as much as the perpetuation of Revivalist myths. It is significant that the poem should have appeared in 1941 during Fianna Fáil's wartime campaign to promote tillage farming and potato growing. It is also significant that it should have been first entitled, 'The Old Peasant', an ironic usage, since 'peasant' was, as Kavanagh had implicitly noted in *The Green Fool*, a purely literary term in Ireland, where the normal real-life word was 'farmer'. Seán O'Faoláin had already observed of de Valera's primitivist ideology that he and his party could not be forgiven 'for leaving out of their philosophy everything in life that is magnificent and irrelevant and proud and luxurious and lovely'.[36] Kavanagh once remarked that he had never met anyone so out of touch with the realities of Irish life as de Valera, and his poem is an impassioned denunciation of this politician's rural Eden, a vision of a small-farm Ireland, stripped of all love, beauty, dignity and aspiration. Patrick Maguire, *The Great Hunger*'s anti-hero, a timid elderly bachelor, tied to his fields and to his mother's apron strings, sexually frustrated and imaginatively stunted, also represents a drab realist alternative to the more colourful folksy heroes favoured by Revivalists and neo-Revivalists, Synge's 'Danny', Yeats's Red Hanrahan and 'wild, old wicked man', Colum's 'Drover' and 'Plougher', Campbell's 'Horse-Breaker' and 'Fighting-Man' and F. R. Higgins's 'Dark Breed' and 'Gallivanter'. In addition, something of the anti-clericalism that Frank O'Connor detected in *Stony Grey Soil* appears to have seeped into *The Great Hunger*, a poem that illustrates the Church's oppressive power over the minds and hearts of the 'too-faithful'.

'Disillusion is also a form of revelation', wrote Seán O'Faoláin, 'but to see clearly is not to write passionately . . . It is not enough for an artist to be clinically interested in life: he must take fire from it.'[37] In *The Great Hunger* Kavanagh achieved a new kind of poetry, bred of the disenchanted realism advocated by O'Faoláin and O'Connor and charged with the polemical zeal of the recently converted, yet altogether different from and independent of the fictions of his mentors, a visionary as well as a documentary poem. Frank O'Connor immediately recognised that *The Great Hunger* was a poetic masterpiece in the anti-Romantic mode and he set about actively promoting it. It was he who suggested to Cyril Connolly that part of the poem should be included in the Irish number of *Horizon* in January 1942,[38] and as a member of the editorial board he was largely responsible for the Cuala Press's publication of the entire poem in April of the same year.[39] However, *The Great Hunger* is not merely a social and literary critique, a realist satire of chauvinist fantasies. It offers what the age demanded of its writers but considered impossible of achievement: 'a portrait, a judgment, and an ideal'.[40] Moreover, its ideal, its vision of possibilities, far transcends its cultural occasion and its 'breathtaking honesty'[41] and adventurous technique mark a watershed in Irish poetry. *The Great Hunger* is one of the finest long poems of the twentieth century.

4
Voice of the People:
The Great Hunger

IN *The Great Hunger* Kavanagh returns to a terrain he had already lightheartedly traversed in *The Green Fool*. Once again his narrator is a native informant taking the reader on a conducted tour of his own neighbourhood. On this occasion his parish is named Donaghmoyne rather than Inniskeen but, since these two parishes were once, in fact, united, both autobiography and poem present the same people and the same land. Only four years separate the two works. Yet all has changed utterly; a terrible hideousness, inconceivable to the genial narrator of *The Green Fool*, has been born, a terrifying vision of a way of life that had once seemed full of blessings. *The Great Hunger* subverts the benign narrative of *The Green Fool*. To turn from its concluding pages to the opening lines of *The Great Hunger* is not simply to enounter an alternative version of the same text; it is to change imaginative worlds. It is to move from this:

> As we picked up the tubers the smells rising from the dry brown clay were a tonic to revive the weariest body, the loneliest spirit. Turning over the soil, our fingers were turning the pages in the Book of Life . . .

to this:

> Clay is the word and clay is the flesh
> Where the potato-gatherers like mechanised
>   scarecrows move
> Along the side-fall of the hill—Maguire and his men.
> If we watch them an hour is there anything we can
>   prove

Of life as it is broken-backed over the Book
Of Death?

The rhetoric here is biblical, the voice that of the angry prophet, crying out in an Irish wilderness, railing against the desecration of sacred human life. His opening words shock the complacent Irish reader out of his *laissez-faire* lethargy with their powerful perversion of a fundamental tenet of Christian faith:

And the Word was made flesh . . .

Twice daily the Angelus bell reminded country Catholics of the reality of Christ's incarnation, yet the ethos of the small farm daily denied the evangelical truth in which all professed to believe. What they worshipped was a false God made of clay, sacrificing body and soul in his service. The land of Ireland is deconsecrated in this deeply religious poem, where clay connotes the negation of body and soul and of all human and divine intercourse, the victory of death over life; and the Irish farmer is reduced to a corpse ('a bag of wet clay'), his fields to a cemetery.

The Great Hunger may seem to be a reading from the Book of Death, yet its prophetic condemnation of rural Ireland as a wasteland is inspired by an intensely Christian interpretation of the holiness of human life. Christ's incarnation is here envisioned not as some far off divine event but as a present metaphysicality, a quickening spirit that sanctifies the flesh. The poem's vision is Johannine in its identification of God as light and life and *Logos*. Its God is, above all, a creative God, rejoicing in human sensuality, sexuality, fertility; not a repressively puritanical deity, approving the closed lips, closed legs and closed minds of the Irish poor. In a parish where 'five hundred hearts' are 'hungry for life' and women proffer unwanted wombs, the tabernacle is 'pregnant', for 'God's truth is life'. The cautious, thrifty, prudish gospel emanating from a rural 'Respectability that knows the price of all things' (and, presumably, the value of nothing) and 'marks God's truth in pounds and pence and farthings' is apocryphal. According to Kavanagh's evangel what God abhors is sexual inhibition, not sexual licence:

> For the strangled impulse there is no redemption.

Kavanagh's God is not some remote, unattainable, abstract absolute; he is immanent in life's ordinary quotidian round, in 'the bits and pieces of Everyday'. The farm folk, 'hurrying' to Sunday mass, ignore the sacramentality of their weekday lives. They dissociate the eucharist from their daily bread, failing to recognise that

> In a crumb of bread the whole mystery is.

Their God has been distorted into the custodian of a post-Famine peasant ethos, wanting his people to endure rather than enjoy, rewarding the respectable with a church collecting-box, or lighting the farmer's way to the grave with a blessed candle when he finally reaches the end of his long day's dying. A peasant priesthood colludes with this peasant version of Catholicism in which economic prudence and material self-interest masquerade as morality. The country chapel has been converted into a coffin, grimly clamping down on human desires, 'pressing its low ceiling over them'. The fierce anger that empowers *The Great Hunger* is the wrath of the biblical seer, lifting 'a moment to Prophecy/Out of the clayey hours'. He concludes with oracular authority, warning of the terrible 'apocalypse' in store for a land that has blasphemed against the incarnate Christ by raising up a false clay god in his stead.

The Great Hunger is as visionary in its critique of a historical epoch as Blake's 'America: A Prophecy', though it substitutes figurative fiction for mythic abstraction. The living death of small-farm Ireland is represented through the biography of the elderly bachelor farmer, Patrick Maguire. His name, ironically combining that of the national apostle and the parish priest of Inniskeen,[1] marks him out as a typical Irish country Catholic. Patrick Maguire is an overworked slave, brutalised, vegetised even, by a life of unremitting drudgery, culturally deprived, compelled to be chaste, and forbidden to marry until impotent from age. He is the victim of a religiously enforced rural economy which values property and propriety at the expense of love and self-fulfilment. Maguire's human energies are gradually absorbed by devotion to his fields, while his psycho-sexual yearnings are simultaneously suppressed to the point of extinction. Human fertility is sacrificed to agricultural productivity:

> He lives that his little fields may stay fertile when his
> own body
> Is spread in the bottom of a ditch under two coulters
> crossed in Christ's Name.

As a tale of wasted human potential *The Great Hunger* centres on Maguire's celibacy, focusing with grim relentlessness on a lifetime of sexual evasions pathetically interwoven with aspirations towards marriage (or, in his later years, even some groping of unsuspecting schoolgirls), and eventually culminating in a lonely, hopeless, sterile old age. His failure to achieve the normal expression of his manhood is attributed to the reinforcement of sexual timidity and inexperience by economic and ecclesiastical precept:

> Religion, the fields and the fear of the Lord
> And Ignorance giving him the coward's blow . . .

Maguire's predicament is exacerbated by a combination of filial obligation and maternal manipulation. He is trapped in a pernicious Irish rural system of belated male marriage which he himself, if he were not doomed to perish childless, would be condemned to perpetuate. His widowed mother is only twenty six years his senior; the farmhouse is her home. It is in her interest to blackmail her son into celibacy, exploiting the dictates of economic expediency and Catholic morality to maintain her dominant position as head of the household, fearful that if her son's sexual curiosity is encouraged she will be unable to deter him from marriage. Mrs Maguire trusts that 'the push of nature' will thwart her efforts in the long term but, instead, her son is slowly emasculated by matriarchy. He procrastinates, masturbates, sublimates. Patrick Maguire has fallen victim to the stereotypical Irish mother/ son relationship that precludes all other relationships, a grotesque Oedipal parody in which she is 'wife and mother in one' and he upholds their marriage contract. By the verbal sleight of substituting 'to' for 'until' Kavanagh makes such fidelity tantamount to being 'faithful to death'. When Mrs Maguire dies, aged ninety-one, 'the knuckle-bones' are 'cutting the skin of her son's backside' and he is sixty-five. The Maguires' case is extreme, but not untypical. Such a sustained, sterile, mutual dependency violates the natural order all around them:

> The cows and horses breed,
> And the potato-seed
> Gives a bud and a root and rots
> In the good mother's way with her sons;
> The fledged bird is thrown
> From the nest—on its own.
> But the peasant in his little acres is tied
> To a mother's womb by the wind-toughened
>   navel-cord . . .

Patrick Maguire's biography is presented, for the most part, in an extended flashback. He is already an old mechanised scarecrow when first encountered in his potato field and because his role is that of representative subsistence farmer, his childhood and adolescence are disregarded. What the poem sets out to evoke is the texture of his adult life, not only his doings and sayings but his most private fantasies, fears and frustrations. Kavanagh could get under the skin of the tillage farmer because, to some extent, it was his own skin too, yet Maguire is an autonomous dramatic creation and not a disguised self-portrait. Poet and character differ not only in the matter of age in that Maguire's biography begins at approximately the age where Kavanagh's rural autobiography left off. They differ fundamentally in that Maguire is emphatically neither a poet nor an intellectual, merely an 'illiterate, unknown and unknowing'. Though 'not born blind' and 'not always blind' ('sometimes ... these men know God the Father in a tree'), the peasant, with very rare exceptions, is deprived of that visionary imagination which transfigured the Inniskeen landscape for Kavanagh and enabled him to transcend the horror and the boredom of country life. Peasantry in *The Great Hunger* is defined, as the poet would much later define it in *Self-Portrait*, less as a station in life than as a state of semi-consciousness, remote from imaginative awareness. The peasant is a 'half-vegetable', little better than the potatoes he picks,

> Who can react to sun and rain and sometimes even
> Regret that the Maker of Light had not touched him
>   more intensely.
> Brought him up from the sub-soil to an existence
> Of conscious joy ...

Nevertheless, a shared Christian name indicates Kavanagh's recognition that poet and character have something in common. The aged, resigned slave who will never escape from the tyranny of his little tillage fields embodies a fate which, but for the grace of imagination, might have been the poet's own. Possibly the dire alternative over which, as elder son and mainstay of a female household, he brooded as he struggled to free himself from the bonds of home. Certainly, the narrator of *The Great Hunger* renders the deprivations and limited consolations of Maguire's life from young manhood to old age with the familiarity of one who has foreknown and foresuffered all.

Whereas the narrator of *The Green Fool* was also the book's hero, in *The Great Hunger* Kavanagh takes advantage of his own recent professional distance from subsistence farming to sever the relationship between poet and farmer. The poet figure now serves as an interpreter of country life, mediating between an uninitiated urban or non-Irish readership and an illiterate peasantry. Maguire's biography is filtered through a controlling narrative consciousness; it is a realist but also an exemplary fiction. Maguire is an Irish rural Everyman and the omniscient narrator's prophetic role is to witness to his story's representativeness and to warn of its consequence. He is both angry on his character's behalf and ironic at his expense.

Though Maguire is a pathetic or derisory spectacle displayed for the reader's empathy or enlightenment, the structural metaphor of tragic theatre, invoked in the poem's opening lines to separate commentator and character, is misleading. It does signal an important change of literary direction from the lyrical and comic genres Kavanagh had formerly deployed. To invest small-farm misery with the dignity and gravity of tragedy was a way of elevating a humble situation by assigning it to an aggrandising literary category, just as, ten years later, he would defiantly entitle a sonnet about a 'local row', 'Epic'. Here he draws attention to his own subversiveness by declaring that Maguire's case history demands a redefinition or a revision of the tragic category. What *The Great Hunger* presents is a realist or 'true tragedy', neither heroic nor spectacular. It is a drama of non-event, telling a 'weak' and 'washy' tale; its hero is an anti-hero, lacking in vision, energy, courage or resolve. It treats of an obscure life passed in an ugly world, brutal, lonely, wretched, downcast; a life that is really a protracted death; not 'mad hooves galloping in the sky', but 'A sick horse nosing around the meadow for a clean place to die'. The heavens do not blaze forth the death of Irish farmers.

While *The Great Hunger* sometimes calls for an empathetic response to Maguire's plight, it does not do so with any consistency. 'Let us salute him without irony', the narrator demands in part XIII, before he reintroduces his tragic metaphor. A change of tone is called for because here, as throughout much of the poem, sympathy is blocked by narrative irony. At thirty-five Maguire 'could take the sparrow's bow'; at sixty-five his whistling saddens his terrier dog; and the applause that greets the conclusion of his biography is less cathartic than ironic, more a boo than a boo hoo, a zany whoop of relief that 'The story is done'. If the poem must be assigned a genre, then it comes closer to tragicomedy than to tragedy and, probably, closer to black comedy than to either.

Kavanagh refers to his narrative enterprise in theatrical metaphors, yet fictional technique in *The Great Hunger* is really cinematic,[2] rather than dramatic, short on dialogue, highly visual and scenically mobile. The narrator substitutes for both camera and sound recording and also serves as a voice-over. Its cinematic technique prevents this poem from settling into either tragedy or comedy, for gravity is often displaced by irony, a pathetic image spliced with a comic. It is a destabilising technique, even threatening the prophetic voice-over through undignified realist juxtaposition. The poem, organised as a montage, is extraordinarily flexible, continually altering angle and direction, zooming from a long shot of farm workers on the side-fall of a hill to a close up of a dog lying on a torn jacket under a heeled-up cart, cutting from breakfast time in the Maguire kitchen to a headland at dawn, from Maguire at mass to his occasion of sin in the Yellow Meadow, from a night's card-playing in a firelit kitchen to a frosty February morning in bleached white fields. Maguire's life is framed with rapid changes of focus and from a deliberately diverting play of angles. The camera tracks him as he ducks and weaves, his 'dream' fluctuating 'like the cloud-swung wind'.

It is to a large extent its innovatory technique that liberates the poem from the conventions of Abbey 'peasant quality' (the notorious 'pq'), enabling Kavanagh to achieve a more documentary presentation of small-farm life. Moving out from the confines of the proscenium arch he covers new ground. He shoots a good deal of outdoor footage, accompanying the farmer into the fields as he collects 'the scattered harness and baskets' after a day's potato picking, gathers 'the loose stones off the ridge', walks 'among his cattle' or loads 'the day-scoured implements on the cart/As the shadows of evening poplars crookened the furrows'. His presentation is selective, avoiding the tedium of a full scale presentation, panning from the hills, where neighbours watch 'with all the sharpened interest of rivalry' as Maguire ploughs in a black March wind, to a close up of the headland:

> Primroses and the unearthly start of ferns
> Among the blackthorn shadows in the ditch,
> A dead sparrow and an old waistcoat . . .

The camera eye does not distinguish between pretty and ugly images and here neither is edited out. *The Great Hunger* abounds in authentic shots of country life: savants swapping knowledge in the pub; heavy-headed ruminants nodding at the crossroads; Maguire on the railway slope watching children picking flowers; girls 'sitting on the grass banks of lanes/ Stretch-legged and lingering staring'; a dying mother reaching 'five bony crooks under the tick' to find five pounds for masses; Agnes picking her steps through wet grass, holding her skirts 'sensationally up' for Maguire's benefit. Selectivity is exercised with such unobtrusiveness that there is no sense of an imposed order or a measured comprehensiveness. The delightful redundance of Kavanagh's approach is evident, for instance, in the February morning sequence in part XII, which pans from the frozen white hills to a candid camera shot of Maguire clapping his arms, prancing on crisp roots, shouting to warm himself, buckleaping about the potato pit. Such quirkiness takes the didacticism out of documentary.

By clever cutting, occasional brief flashbacks, and dispensing with linking narrative, Kavanagh solved the problem of organisation he had already confronted in *The Green Fool*, the difficulty of combining the linearity of biography with the repetitiveness of agricultural cycles and rural routines. Whereas in *The Green Fool* he felt compelled to treat of a farming chore in some detail in one chapter and never revert to it, his new technique permitted him to return to the same locations, chapel, tillage field or potato pit, and the same actions, ploughing or potato harvesting, varying the camera angle and distance or the length, pace and detail of a sequence. Again and again Maguire is filmed with his dog and there are brief late allusions to such earlier sequences as the card playing or his masturbation over the kitchen hearth. So *The Green Fool*'s artificial division of labour is avoided, a better sense of the repetitive texture of the farmer's life is conveyed, recurrence is exploited to indicate monotony or the repeated evasion of opportunity, and the turning of the rural calendar marks 'the slow and speedier' passage of time. *The Great Hunger*, despite its deliberate discontinuities, is a unified coherent whole, in which each sequence is inspired by the same religious vision, designed to show an aspect of the same rural catastrophe.

The skilfully edited chapel episode in part IV reveals Kavanagh's narrative technique at work. A self-contained sequence it, nevertheless, refers backwards and forwards into the poem and contributes both playfully and seriously to its central theme of the meaning and misunderstanding of Christ's incarnation:

> Maguire knelt beside a pillar where he could spit
> Without being seen. He turned an old prayer round:
> 'Jesus, Mary and Joseph pray for us
> Now and at the Hour.' Heaven dazzled death.
> 'Wonder should I cross-plough that turnip-ground.'
> The tension broke. The congregation lifted its head
> As one man and coughed in unison.
> Five hundred hearts were hungry for life—
> Who lives in Christ shall never die the death.
> And the candle-lit Altar and the flowers
> And the pregnant Tabernacle lifted a moment to
>   Prophecy
> Out of the clayey hours.

Maguire sprinkled his face with holy water
As the congregation stood up for the Last Gospel.
He rubbed the dust off his knees with his palm, and
    then
Coughed the prayer phlegm up from his throat and
    sighed: Amen.

The sequence opens with a comic, realist close-up of
Maguire at mass, obliquely noting his omission of the allusion to death in his routine prayer and taking amused
cognisance of the fact that the colourful religious spectacle
may distract him from the fear of death, but not from his
agricultural preoccupations. The subject of death, a central
symbolic obsession in this poem, is introduced by the narrator but evaded by the character's ellipsis. He overlooks death
and concentrates on a heavenly afterlife, or displaces the
grave with his 'turnip-ground'. Yet his prayer is one that
ironically conjoins the immediate present and the hour of
death.

The narrative then cuts to the moment after the Elevation
and the camera is turned on the rest of the congregation,
comically clearing their throats after the obligatory ritual
silence. What is emphasised about this humorous rustic
chorus is its 'unison'. Maguire is here both 'one man' and
everyman. The narrator now shifts into his vatic mode to
provide a visionary interpretation of the eucharist, seeing the
consecrated bread and wine as the divine satisfaction of the
parishioners' appetite, presenting transubstantiation as an
image of divine incarnation. The title metaphor is defined as a
people's hunger for life and love. Life in Christ is opposed to
death but the Christian triumph of life is acknowledged to be
as momentary as the elevation itself for this rural congregation. Christ has not impregnated their world; before and after
the elevation stretches a horizontal plane of 'clayey hours'.
Significantly, the chapel sequence is preceded by the fields'
message that 'only Time can bless' and succeeded by
Maguire's failure to avail of the sexual blessing he is offered

in the Yellow Meadow which he, puritanically, mistranslates as sexual temptation. The spirit quickens but the letter kills and sexual sin is writ large in Maguire's Catholic consciousness. As the narrator interprets the prophetic meaning of the divine incarnation the camera focuses on the aesthetically beautiful altar, candle lit and flower adorned.

Abruptly the screenplay cuts to the Last Gospel and to the chapel porch where Maguire, as was customary among less devout males, is making an early escape. He is caught in slow motion, gesturing towards blessing himself, cleaning the dust off his good Sunday trousers (he has probably been kneeling on the floor at the back of the chapel so that he can slip out easily) and indulging the smoker's cough he was restraining during mass. His actions are both comic, realist and, also, ironic because he is shaking off and expectorating whatever religious experience he has just undergone. 'Amen', the last word in the passage, is an apt word to fade out on. It signals the conclusion of Maguire's devotions, the separation of mass from the world outside the chapel, and his passive, fatalistic, 'So be it' attitude to life. The sequence reveals the narrator's religious vision and his character's blindness to it. Maguire emerges completely unaffected from a potentially transcendental occasion. This passage illustrates Kavanagh's mastery of a narrative technique that combines comic realism with a visionary critique that embraces humour, irony, compassion and prophetic faith. His narrator mediates between the *Logos* and the clay words of everyday. By virtue of its cinematic art *The Great Hunger* presents an almost unbearably bleak biography in an entertainingly varied manner, with subtle modulations or outrageous transitions between shots and numerous changes of pace and mood.

To praise *The Great Hunger* for its 'breathtaking honesty' has become something of a critical commonplace, but its documentary authenticity never stops short at realism. Kavanagh's is a visionary and fiercely moral imagination, obsessed with meaning, finding God or the 'hungry fiend' 'in the bits and pieces of Everyday'. His God is not 'all/In one place, complete and labelled like a case in a railway store',[3] a piece of baggage to be deposited in the 'Left Luggage' office, when inconvenient. He is not pre-packaged for Sunday consumption. From the outset *The Great Hunger* is concerned not just with daily 'life as it is' realistically, but with what scene and action signify religiously. 'Is there anything we can prove . . .?' is the poem's first question. The potato gatherers of the opening lines move between metaphors. Cinematic technique enabled Kavanagh to apply what he called a 'carnal method' to his visionary critique of Irish rural society.[4] Where previously he, like Maguire, often 'read the symbol too sharply', so that objects tended to fade and disappear in the light of his religious or aesthetic vision, the camera which converts everything into image, gives a metonymic dimension to his metaphoric readings.

There is often so little disjunction between realist detail and figurative interpretation in *The Great Hunger* that metaphor is unobtrusive and even contributes to the documentary process: the farmer's spirit is 'a wet sack flapping about the knees of time' or 'the mark of a hoof in a guttery gap'; a deep-drilled potato field or two coulters lying crossed in a ditch suggest a grave and headstone; morality is like 'a bush' in a gap 'weighted with boulders'; 'the green of after-grass' symbolises life's aftermath; the bachelor is an unbroken colt trembling his head and running free of the halter. Maguire sighs 'like the brown breeze in the thistles' and the mumble of rural speech is compared to 'the rumination of cows after milking' or to the rumbling of 'laden carts'. Metonymy often contributes an ironic edge to the poem's symbolism as when a biblical 'strait way' is achieved for the peasant's passage to the afterlife 'by the angles/Where the plough missed or a spade stands, straitening the way'. The reader is frequently 'diverted' by such angles. Its splicing of metonymy and metaphor creates a continuity and coherence between *The Great Hunger*'s documentary and visionary dimensions. Only when the voice-over is too predominant, the freeze-frame too prolonged, does the poem's palpable design become too obtrusive.

The primary contraries in *The Great Hunger* are life and death; its symbolic drama is the defeat of spirituality and sexuality by inertia, cowardice, enslavement to matter and a perverted morality. In Kavanagh's christened world psycho-sexual energies are sacred; sexual intercourse is as sacramental as matrimony; to refuse the claims of the flesh is sacrilegious. It is a Blakean universe where 'everything that lives is holy/Life delights in life'. Before this late arousal of his sexual imagination Kavanagh's poetry had inhabited a land where 'flesh was a thought more spiritual than music'. He had side-stepped the sexual by adopting a childhood perspective or projecting himself as poet rather than man. Although girl-ish presences hover in 'Spraying the Potatoes' and 'Art McCooey', they are never brought to 'lust nearness'. The poet is merely playing with 'the frilly edges of reality'; he is 'lost in the mists where "genesis" begins'. *The Great Hunger*, however, is explicitly and insistently sexual in thought, word, deed and omission. Now ordinary farm images are invested with phallic significance:

> A dog lying on a torn jacket under a heeled-up cart,
> A horse nosing along the posied headland, trailing
> A rusty plough. Three heads hanging between
>   wide-apart
> Legs. October playing a symphony on a slack wire
>   paling . . .

Or less droopily, Maguire raping the earth that an earlier Kavanagh ploughman had painted brown:

> The twisting sod rolls over on her back—
> The virgin screams before the irresistible sock . . .

Planting seed takes on connotations of 'sensuous groping'; picking potatoes becomes an occasion for sexual innuendo:

> What is he looking for there?

> He thinks it is a potato, but we know better
> Than his mud-gloved fingers probe in this
>   insensitive hair . . .

Harrowing is a phallic activity; a horse eating clover lips 'late passion'; cows and foal mare are surrogate wives; Maguire's devotion to his farm is uxorious, making 'a field his bride'. The repressed Irish country Catholic displaces his sexual energies on to his crops and his stock. He ekes out his sterile days in a fecund, burgeoning, teeming world where cows and horses breed, grass and corn flourish, potatoes and weeds proliferate.

To refuse the 'fruited Tree of life' in *The Great Hunger* is to indulge a perverse appetite for death. Necrophilia and a prostrate worship of a life-denying scripture are fused in the image of the potato gatherers bent 'broken-backed over the Book of Death'. Kavanagh exploits the metonymic connections of clay with agriculture, inhumation and the decomposed corpse to establish a metaphoric association between farming and the funereal, devotion to the land and death wish. His peasant is ground down and buried alive: the 'mud-walled space' allocated to him in part XI is a coffin; the potato pit he pats smooth in part XIV is 'a new-piled grave'. The poem's black comedy is at its most macabre in its ironic fantasia on Maguire's 'afterlife': his comfortable familiarity with a subterranean existence or his compensatory posthumous paradise, full of exhilarating alternatives to his present deprivations. The story concludes with the grim acknowledgment that there may be no 'unearthly law'; that Maguire has not sufficient spirit to be either damned or glorified; that he is not alive enough to warrant reincarnation. So the poem circles back to the image with which it had begun, that of the potato field as a graveyard, the bitter truth being that in the Irish farmer's case there is little to choose between being over it or under it.

There is now no 'ditch' on Kavanagh's 'vision'. No scene or event is too mean or trivial or ugly to be included in his verse.

Nothing human is foreign to him, no place or action so unsanctified as to be off-limits. Maguire spits, grunts, coughs, cleans his arse, masturbates. In 1941 such realism in Irish poetry was revolutionary. Kavanagh's flouting of literary decorum was too extreme even for Macmillan who had already published Yeats's late, physically explicit verse. Unaccountably, they permitted the masturbation sequences but drew the line at allowing Maguire to clean his arse with grass, and all but the first eight lines of part II were bowdlerised when the poem was collected in *A Soul for Sale* (1947). In Ireland, surprisingly, *The Great Hunger* escaped the censor, probably because it was originally published in a limited edition of 250 copies, or because Mrs O'Grundy rarely read poetry.[5]

The passage of time is frequently marked throughout *The Great Hunger*: the time of day, the month or season, the flight of years, hallooed away like greedy crows. April and October are key months in Maguire's calendar. April, the time for sowing seed, is a cruel month, reminding him and the reader that, through an obsession with ensuring the fertility of his fields, he himself is failing to propagate. He has sacrificed parenthood to protect 'the seed of an acre'. October is the symbolic month in which *The Great Hunger* begins and ends. Not only does it herald the approach of winter, even more significantly, it is a time when potatoes are picked and, therefore, a crucial month in Irish folk mythology. Through title, timing, location and the use of the potato as a recurrent motif Kavanagh establishes a consistent analogy between the psychic and sexual deprivation that is depopulating and destroying rural Ireland in the twentieth century and the Famine that ravaged the country in the mid-nineteenth century. *The Great Hunger* is almost a Famine centenary poem.

Famine is a potent, anti-heroic national myth, stirring atavistic fears, rousing racial memories of extreme indignity and humiliation as well as of impoverishment, suffering and death. The victims of the Famine, were, as in *The Great Hunger*, the ordinary Irish poor, people who lived in degradation and died ignominiously. Like T. S. Eliot's *Waste Land* myths this Irish historical disaster myth embraces both place and people, the physical and the psychic, connecting natural and human disease and decay; but Kavanagh's method, unlike Eliot's, is not allusive. The title of *The Great Hunger* provides the only direct clue to the poem's central historical symbol and contemporary parallels are subtly suggested, not explicitly adverted to, throughout the text. Knowledge of the poem's prior myth is taken for granted and readers are invited to discover implicit historical comparisons and ironies. The supreme historical irony, which Kavanagh appears to have intuited and which social historians have since largely substantiated, is that the infrequency or belatedness of marriages in twentieth-century rural Ireland was a consequence of the Famine.[6] Previously, so the historical argument runs, an agreeable carelessness had prevailed in matters of land and marriage; afterwards, the economics of survival took precedence over all other considerations, and agricultural prosperity was achieved at the cost of self-expression and self-fulfilment. That cult and culture of the potato so savagely mocked in *The Great Hunger* had set in. The potato crop flourished but human lives were blighted.

In *The Great Hunger* a civilisation and its discontents are revealed rhetorically, fictionally and symbolically. Kavanagh had read Joyce for the first time in 1937, and *The Great Hunger* may be read as a rural sequel to *Dubliners*, a poetic version of the *Provincials* that Joyce probably recognised he lacked the necessary experience to write. Joyce, whom O'Faoláin and O'Connor opposed to Yeats as the contemporary Irish writer's exemplary author, would have disapproved of Kavanagh's narrative technique with its all too visible narrator. Nevertheless, Maguire is the Dubliner's country cousin, psychologically paralysed, immobilised by an inertia endemic in his rural acculturation.

His entrapment is enacted in the poem's structure and reiterated through image and metaphor. The technique of extended flashback predestines him to a lifetime of sexual failure. His ambitions and aspirations to escape misery through marriage are foredoomed. The reader watches him writhe on a death-baited hook, with that almost unbearably unrelieved pessimism which only dramatic irony can induce. He is caught in the noose of the poem's circular narrative and also circumscribed by the narrator's insistence on applying circular metaphors to his routine existence. He is compared to an athlete running round and round a grass track where there is no finishing line, a goat mooching about the tree stump to which it is tethered, a sick horse nosing around a meadow looking for a clean place to die. So accustomed is he to a treadmill existence that he hopes for nothing better in the future than a different circle, one 'curved to his own will'. Maguire's immobility is further emphasised through such narrative metaphors as being gripped, 'tied', 'tethered', 'stuck in the slot'. The narrator is cruelly ironic about his failure to recognise that he is a farmer under field-arrest and a prisoner of conscience to boot when he is prevented from acting out his sexual fantasies by a fear of jail, scathingly rendered as a reluctance to 'serve . . . time'. Even the ordinary farmyard chore of locking and unlocking the henhouse acquires disturbing metaphoric overtones when Maguire finally reaches the claustrophobic awareness that he himself is both brutalised and incarcerated:

> Oh Christ! I am locked in a stable with pigs
>   and cows forever.

The desperate narrative question, 'Is there no escape?' elicits the doubly emphatic negative response, 'No escape. No escape.'

Monotony is suggested through the metaphor of unvarying melody. 'A new rhythm is a new life' and Maguire cannot change his tune. Seasonal recurrence is exploited to symbolise repetitiveness, not renewal, with the adjective 'another' ironically connoting sameness as well as transience:

> A year passed and another hurried after it . . .

and

> Another field whitened in the April air . . .

Time cannot bless. It is experienced as a continuum because there is nothing to look forward to:

> There is no tomorrow
> No future but only time stretched for the mowing of
> the hay
> Or putting an axle in a turf-barrow . . .

For all its morbid inevitability, its structural trajectory from cemetery to cemetery, *The Great Hunger* is not an unmitigatedly grave poem. Though it writes the obituary of a man and a culture, its tone is not elegiac. Its narrative modes are too versatile, its moods too changeable, its cinematic technique too flexible, to induce a continuously mournful response. In fact, there is a good deal of comedy interspersed throughout the *saeva indignatio* of this poem. Maguire's mother may be the wicked witch of the north, an ugly domineering harpy, but, pictured in the kitchen and even in her last illness, she is a comic grotesque. The deathbed scene is blackly humorous. No keening voices exhort the 'men from the fields' to 'tread softly, softly'. Kavanagh later complained that Colum's rendering of peasant death was charming but superficial, based on 'cliché-phrase and -emotion'.[7] Here he disperses 'old sentimentality' by the realist detail of sending Mary Anne 'to boil the calves their gruel', and by his reductive, un-Lycidas-like play with water imagery:

> The holy water was sprinkled on the bed-clothes
> And her children stood around the bed and cried
> because it was too late for crying.

A mother dead! The tired sentiment:
'Mother mother' was a shallow pool
Where sorrow hardly could wash its feet . . .

Crowd scenes in the pub, at the crossroads and the card playing, the rival farmers perched on neighbouring hills as Maguire ploughs, may reveal the intellectual limitations, boredom and intrusiveness of village life, but they are also very funny. The poem includes several such amusing sequences: rosary time in Barney Meegan's; Maguire's promotion to the position of church collector; the whist playing in Duffy's and the elderly bachelor's autobiographical reflection, 'I should have led that ace of hearts.'

Structurally, *The Great Hunger* is divided into fourteen parts, perhaps to suggest the epic dimensions of the subject, though as befits a poem, whose theme is the death wish of a culture, it begins well past the *in medias res* phase of its antihero's life. The first and last parts, both of which have an outdoor October setting, provide a structural frame, establishing the narrator in his role of commentator, inappropriately applying the metaphor of theatre to the intervening action, introducing Maguire at the beginning, and at the end projecting his posthumous fate and proclaiming the doom of the rural culture he represents. Formally, *The Great Hunger* is even more versatile and varied than its fourteen-part structure might suggest, most parts consisting of a montage of different sequences, with successive sequences separated by paragraphing as well as by variations in line length, rhyming and rhythmic patterns.

Kavanagh also exploits the abrupt transitions of montage to effect unexpected juxtapositions and disconcerting connections between the poem's successive parts. So the mercenary religious arithmetic with which part III concludes:

                         O to be wise
      As Respectability that knows the price of all things
      And marks God's truth in pounds and pence and
          farthings.

is reversed at the beginning of part IV:

> April, and no one able to calculate
> How far is it to harvest . . .

Maguire's lewd nocturnal indoor dreams at the end of part V are immediately contrasted with his more conventional and, even religious, outdoor, daytime dreams in part VI. Here his three wishes also echo the half religious/half fairytale aspirations of Barney Meegan's daughter in part V, an echo which serves to show that, though Maguire is no bisexual Tiresias figure, his fantasies and frustrations are shared by country parishioners of both sexes. The narrator's prophetic observation, 'In a crumb of bread the whole mystery is', almost chokes on its irreverent recollection of the chunk of loaf Maguire consumed with his cocoa before masturbating. A striking image of sexual and creative frustration at the end of part VI, the 'speechless muse', is instantly displaced by the scheming, manipulative accents of Mrs Maguire, conning her son into sexual abstinence at the beginning of part VII. The 'intellectual life' of the pub in part X reflects sardonically on the transmission of oral culture at the conclusion of part IX. Such structural interplay, which is a feature of Kavanagh's narrative throughout *The Great Hunger*, introduces a subtle quirkiness into his formal presentation. Despite his retention of a central protagonist and a controlling narrator, his technique is modernist, discontinuous and multifaceted.

Rhyme, almost always unobtrusively present, is only occasionally foregrounded, usually for comic or satiric effect, as in those lines which Macmillan expurgated from part II:

> O he loved his mother
> Above all others.
> O he loved his ploughs
> And he loved his cows
> And his happiest dream
> Was to clean his arse
> With perennial grass
> On the bank of some summer stream;

> To smoke his pipe
> In a sheltered gripe
> In the middle of July—
> His face in a mist
> And two stones in his fist
> And an impotent worm on his thigh.

The rhythmic beat is mockingly accentuated here and in part VIII where the use of an improvisational jazz technique points up Maguire's psychological paralysis:

> Sitting on a wooden gate,
> Sitting on a wooden gate,
> Sitting on a wooden gate
> He didn't care a damn.
> Said whatever came into his head,
> Said whatever came into his head,
> Said whatever came into his head
> And inconsequently sang.
> Inconsequently sang
> While his world withered away . . .

Here the repetitive monotony of Maguire's life is playfully transposed into a series of lilting refrains, yet the narrator is also ironic about his character's insouciant mood. The frivolity of popular song, with its privileging of rhythm over meaning, captures the sense of frittered time and opportunity as Maguire masturbates in a land where love is freely available and 'young women' run 'wild' and dream 'of a child'. Maguire here uses religion to rationalise his inhibitions, so his effort to secure his sexual position on the gate is highly ironic:

> He locked his body with his knees . . .

Kavanagh deploys a technique of free indirect narration interspersed with direct narrative commentary to catch his character's mood and to condemn it, yet since both are played to the same tune, not only are the transitions less obvious but the effect is more chilling. One of the unfortunate Maguire's few interludes of well-being is uncomfortably counterpointed. The sequence concludes by replaying its introductory refrain, this time accompanying it with a still musical, yet sardonic, sexual thrust:

> But while he caught high ecstasies
> Life slipped between the bars.

The Great Hunger's ludic 'wooden gate' melody is a far cry from 'Address to an Old Wooden Gate', twelve years previously. Eliot's 'Shakes-pe-her-ian rag' may echo behind Kavanagh's satiric refrains but, if so, the influence has been so well absorbed as to be inaudible. The modernisation of Kavanagh's muse seems to have been hastened by his admiration for the 'fresh young attitude and vocabulary' of Stephen Spender, Dylan Thomas and W. H. Auden, whose poetry was transfused with 'the blood of life-as-it-is-lived'.[8] Kavanagh learned from Auden how to zoom in on the precise images that evoke a way of life and to reproduce the speech rhythms that catch the texture of a particular culture. He knew how to adapt from the English middle-class ambience and tone of well-bred disdain in

> Pardon the studied taste that could refuse
> The golf-house quick one and the rector's tea[9]

to register with comic neutrality the shriller refusals and niggardly kindliness of Irish Catholic farmers. In an understatedly ironic sequence Maguire and his sister, childless, unmarried, sexually frustrated by their prudent Catholicism, confront the children whom the church sends fund raising to their door:

> His sister Mary Anne spat poison at the children
> Who sometimes came to the door selling raffle
>   tickets
> For holy funds.
> 'Get out you little tramps!' she would scream

As she shook to the hens an apronful of crumbs,[10]
But Patrick often put his hand deep down
In his trouser-pocket and fingered out a penny
Or maybe a tobacco-stained caramel.
'You're soft' said the sister 'with other people's
     money
It's not a bit funny' . . .

While the brief lyric, 'War and Peace', is embarrassingly derivative of Auden's 'O What is that Sound?', in *The Great Hunger* this new literary influence is unrecognisable.[11]

What is remarkable about the changing rhythms of this long poem is their adaptability to a wide diversity of narrative situations, moods and voices. Most impressive of all, perhaps, is Kavanagh's ability to create a conversational rhythm that not only mimics the Monaghan accent but is attuned to his characters' unvoiced moods. In the crossroads sequence in part V, for instance, the narrative captures the men's vacuous apathy through simile and documentary realism, the slight stir of uneventful events; and through a sluggish pacing that imitates the almost stationary inertia it evokes:

Evening at the cross-roads —
Heavy heads nodding out words as wise
As the rumination of cows after milking.
From the ragged road surface a boy picks up
A piece of gravel and stares at it — and then
He flings it across the elm tree on to the railway.
It means nothing,
Not a damn thing.
Somebody is coming over the metal railway bridge
And his hob-nailed boots on the arches sound like a
     gong
Calling men awake. But the bridge is too narrow —
The men lift their heads a moment. That was only
     John,
So they dream on.

A double interruption of drowsiness by insignificant action, accompanied by a double interruption of long lines by lines of four syllables, four monosyllables on two occasions, mimes the occasional jerking into wakefulness of these somnolent revellers. The boy's sense of futility is particularly well enacted through falling rhythms and a minimally negative colloquial speech. Such subtle adaptation of narrative commentary to country speech patterns and moods shows that in addition to a sharp eye for the authentic images that summon up a country scene and an ear alert to the nuances of local speech, Kavanagh was also sensitive to the inner psychic rhythms of the country farmer. Without any intrusive narrative moralising he succeeds in conjuring up a drab and dreary ambience, evoking the disspiritedness that is his central theme. Meaninglessness and damnation are unobtrusively allied in the boy's action, which repeats one of the elderly Maguire's futile actions in part I. Dream in *The Great Hunger* has not the Romantic connotations it had in Kavanagh's early lyrics; it now refers to fantasy, particularly sexual fantasy, or, more often, to 'things half-born to mind', the submerged, subconscious psycho-sexual longings of an oppressed people:

And sensual sleep dreams subtly underground . . .

By replacing the stage Irishman with a cinematic Irishman, Kavanagh not merely freed himself from comic convention, static, indoor presentation, and theatrical propriety; more importantly, for his purposes, he shifted the emphasis from dramatic dialogue to dumb show, found a way of portraying muteness and repression. Unlike the stage-Irishman, the cinematic Irishman does not have to talk entertainingly to earn his literary keep. He need hardly speak aloud at all. Exhausted and oppressed by fourteen-hour days of drudgery, he need only mutter a few clichés from the betting shop, pub or card game, by way of social intercourse:

'A treble, full multiple odds . . . That's flat porter . . .

or

'Cut for trump'.

Maguire is silent throughout most of *The Great Hunger*. The only subject on which he waxes even a little eloquent, is work. On this topic he sometimes manages two or three consecutive lines and once even rises to eleven:

> 'Move forward the basket and balance it steady
> In this hollow. Pull down the shafts of that cart, Joe,
> And straddle the horse' Maguire calls.
> 'The wind's over Brannagan's, now that means rain.
> Graip up some withered stalks and see that no
>   potato falls
> Over the tail-board going down the ruckety pass—
> And *that's* a job we'll have to do in December,
> Gravel it and build a kerb on the bog-side. Is that
>   Cassidy's ass
> Out in my clover? Curse o' God—
> Where is that dog?
> Never where he's wanted' . . .

After this Maguire 'grunts and spits' and lapses into his customary incommunicativeness. This is the realist speech of rural Ireland as Kavanagh heard it, neither imaginatively lyrical nor rumbustiously wordy, the terse practical language of a culture obsessed by a work ethic and by economy, control and constraint. Maguire's is the voice of a man 'bounded by the hedges of [his] little farm', the peasant proprietor, preoccupied by the job in hand or the job to follow, vigilant about his crops, angered by wastefulness or neighbourly exploitation, moved to utterance by the necessity to issue orders and protect what he owns.

Speech is never, where Maguire is concerned, a vehicle for communicating private hopes, disappointments, fears and anxieties. These remain repressed, unvoiced. It is the narrator who makes us privy to the frustrations and fantasies that trouble his consciousness. In public Maguire conceals his worries and his lusts, masks the desires he cannot master, learns to adopt a guise of 'respectability and righteousness'. With supreme narrative irony he is portrayed in 'an old judge's pose' immediately after he has decided to substitute masturbation for the groping of schoolgirls, a secret 'crime'

The law's long arm could not serve with 'time'.

The Great Hunger's rural community is scarce with words because what matters most cannot be spoken. Taciturnity is inseparable from repression. To venture beyond the limits of local cliché, of communal passwords, would be an act of self-identification or self-discovery, and self-denial is their established code: 'No' is 'in every sentence of their story'. For all its devotion to 'pq' the Abbey could not enact what Kavanagh envisaged as the tragedy of rural Ireland, because dialogue was essentially false to the close-mouthed, suppressed suffering he wished to see articulated. Silence was for him the Irish countryman's most personal speech.

Ireland's language crisis was not, for Kavanagh, as for so many of his contemporaries, the seemingly inexorable disappearance of Gaelic; it was the absence of any real verbal communication. So great was the divergence between the official, imprimatured version of Irish conduct and the impermissible, instinctual impulse towards extra-marital sexuality or maternity in a land of late marriages that a whole countryside was quietly dying. Rural Ireland had become a place of full bellies and empty wombs. In *The Great Hunger* even the female body-language of loosed buttons and 'skirts lifted sensationally up' is a one-sided dialogue that elicits no answering male sign. The capitalised, religiously inhibiting word, 'Sin', intervenes between sexual invitation and response. Kavanagh's Ireland is silent as a graveyard; its people are censored into vegetal muteness; their deepest instincts lie buried:

The tongue in [their] mouth is the root of a yew.

His potato-picking epic sets out to unearth a different hidden Ireland than nationalist cultural historians like Daniel Corkery wished to reveal. The hugely disproportionate ratio of commentary to speech in *The Great Hunger* may sometimes make the narrative appear over-determined, yet it is also its most powerful medium of condemnation. These people require a narrator; they are incapable of even beginning to tell their own story. They need an interpreter who understands the sign-language of the deaf and dumb.

The narrator of *The Great Hunger* is acutely aware of the undone vast, all the unscripted lives whose misery will never be chronicled. The life-in-death of Patrick Maguire to which he witnesses is only one among the numerous unwritten biographies of countrymen and women; his uneventful drama is representative of a tragedy being mutely re-enacted in 'every corner of this land'. Not even the full story of Maguire's silent suffering can be told; there is much that is irretrievable, illegible:

> Nobody will ever know how much tortured poetry
>   the pulled weeds on the ridge wrote
> Before they withered in the July sun,
> Nobody will ever read the wild, sprawling,
>   scrawling mad woman's signature,
> The hysteria and the boredom of the enclosed nun
>   of his thought.
> Like the afterbirth of a cow stretched on a branch
>   in the wind
> Life dried in the veins of these women and
>   men . . .

Here 'the pulled weeds on the ridge' suggest marginalisation, unwanted fertility, the destruction of what is alive but unloved. Self-identification and loss of sexual control both signify lunacy. The mad-woman-in-the-attic image modulates into the religious image of the enclosed nun, with its connotations of a secret life hidden behind defensive walls, vowed to silence and to celibacy, frustrated yet self-prevented from participation in human intercourse, an entombment exalted by country Catholicism:

> Religion's walls expand to the push of nature.
>   Morality yields
> To sense—but not in little tillage fields . . .

Repressed within the subconsciousness of the Irish rural male is the image of his female counterpart (mad woman, nun) whose human fulfilment he denies, a secret knowledge of the torments he is inflicting on her in the process of torturing himself. *The Great Hunger* is populated with neglected, uncourted women: Eileen Farrelly, the girl in the Yellow Meadow, Agnes, Kitty and Molly, Barney Meegan's daughter, Kate, who minds the kitchen fire while the men play cards; girls laughing like 'fillies in season', sitting 'stretch-legged and lingering staring', praying for 'health and wealth and love', or running 'wild' dreaming 'of a child'. Their fate is embodied in Maguire's own sister, Mary Anne, who endures the 'purgatory of middle-aged virginity', turns into an embittered spinster, spitting 'poison at . . . children' and ends her days, tight-legged, tight-lipped and frizzled up 'like the wick of an oil-less lamp', an unwise biblical virgin relocated in Donaghmoyne. Behind these women stands the Catholic icon of the Blessed Virgin, 'Queen of Heaven, the ocean's star', symbolising the Church's ideal of chastity, an ideal that has contributed to Maguire's sexual inhibition:

> Which of these men
> Loved the light and the queen
> Too long virgin?

The cult of the virgin queen may well be indistinguishable from worship of the 'hungry fiend'. Today, the Irish Constitution champions the rights of the unborn. In Kavanagh's terrible prophetic vision the born in rural Ireland are reduced from persons to animal 'afterbirths', their lives stretched out in the fields, disregarded, until they dry up and wither silently away.

'A man is what is written on the label', but what if he cannot communicate, or what if the 'passing world' refuses to 'look closer' and decipher his illiterate scrawl? In *The Great Hunger* Kavanagh takes on the literary responsibility he had envisaged in 'Peasant', to articulate the 'hoarse cry' of his people, to represent those who

> Have never scratched in any kind of hand
> On any wall . . .

In this poem we hear the muffled language of a submerged, suppressed race:

> Their voices through the darkness sound like voices
>   from a cave,
> A dull thudding far away, futile, feeble, far away . . .

We read the 'left-handed' message they wish to write on the page, a more sinister text than the received version of pastoral.

The Great Hunger exposes a nationwide conspiracy of lies, secrecy and silence: a false paradisal perception of Irish country life sponsored by post-colonial chauvinism and national economic expediency, and enforced by a combination of religious precept and a cautious, thrifty, small-farm ethos. What this angry poem demonstrates is that the cover-up connived at by state, church, literary convention and peasant morality is tantamount, not just to the burial of a problem, but to the burial of a race. The solution to Maguire's puzzlement over his distorted, misshapen, paralysed existence:

> Who bent the coin of my destiny
> That it stuck in the slot?

is written into the title and central symbolism of the poem. Kavanagh's rural Ireland is caught in a time-warp, still traumatised by the economic shock of the Famine. As he wrote, neutral Ireland was isolated from world history, psychologically stagnant, frozen 'for want of Europe', undergoing a self-inflicted genocide. Kavanagh had a lifelong dislike of journalistic notions of the important, so it is not surprising that he bypassed the 'headlines of war' to focus on life in a backward Irish village. He could not have known about the concentration camps yet if he had, on the evidence of his later 'Epic', he would still have written as he did, recognising that a people can be suffocated to death in other ways than in the gas chamber.

The Great Hunger bypasses official Irish national history, even more blatantly than European war, which at least gets a mention in the pub sequence. The rise and fall of Parnell, the 1916 Rising, the Treaty, the Civil War, all would have occurred in the lifetime of a character who was sixty-five some time before 1941. However, Maguire's life goes onward the same though dynasties pass. Ageing is presented as a prolongation of personal misery, a repetition of personal despair, not as a device for chronicling nationally important events. In the Ireland of 1941 social history still tended to be marginalised by political history and heroic biography. What Kavanagh is inventing is an Irish social history in the guise of a social critique, recording the way common country people lived in the 'unwritten spaces between the lines' of orthodox history books, bringing to his documentation the persuasiveness of the prophetic historian.

At the conclusion of *The Great Hunger* the camera pans from the lone figure of the aged Maguire to the horizons of Ireland:

> He stands in the doorway of his house
> A ragged sculpture of the wind
> October creaks the rotted mattress
> The bedposts fall. No hope. No. No lust.
> The hungry fiend
> Screams the apocalypse of clay
> In every corner of this land.

Here Maguire stands freeze-framed, more image than man, a silent icon shaped by adverse weather. His raggedness recalls his scarecrow attitude at the beginning of the poem, though this soul will not clap its hands and louder sing for every tatter in its mortal dress. Instead part VIII's inconsequential song has ceased; part I's October symphony plays a different, though equally ironic, sexual tune. Lust's disappearance is equated, through apposition, with hopelessness. The hunger of the title is now personified as an anti-Christ; the farmer's field has been metamorphosed into a fiend. A poem that began with a perverse parody of divine revelation concludes with the annunciation of an anti-Logos. Word disintegrates into a wordless scream. This final scream echoes the scream of Maguire's unborn children and of the excited girls 'in season' in part I, the 'hysteria' of the unmated woman of Maguire's fantasy in part IX, but it is also the cry of the victims of Ireland's twentieth-century famine. It is the voice of the oppressed and repressed from every country parish, clamouring to be heard and heeded, and resonating beyond the poem into *après-texte* Ireland: the terrible primal protest of a whole people being buried alive, before the clay finally smothers them.

In *The Great Hunger* the people's need has created a voice. Its narrative gives utterance to inarticulate peasant Ireland, as if the very stones were crying out, speaking the unspoken and unspeakable, defying the taboo that keeps desperation quiet, unsaying the pastoral platitudes, gainsaying the literary myths of the noble savage and the prelapsarian peasant. The 'speechless muse' has found a language.

If *The Great Hunger* aimed at changing the fanciful establishment view of rural Ireland as a primitivist Eden, it was not immediately successful. Almost a year after its publication de Valera made his notorious St Patrick's Day broadcast to the Irish people in which he communicated his political fantasy of small-farm Ireland:

That Ireland which we dreamed of would be the home of a people who valued material wealth only as a basis of right living, of a people who were satisfied with frugal comfort and devoted their leisure to the things of the spirit; a land whose countryside would be bright with cosy homesteads, whose fields and villages would be joyous with sounds of industry, the romping of sturdy children, the contests of athletic youths, the laughter of comely maidens; whose firesides would be the forums of the wisdom of serene old age.[11]

De Valera's vision of small-farm Ireland is indeed such stuff as politicians' and poets' dreams were made on before the advent of *The Great Hunger*. How anachronistically hollow his oratory sounds by contrast with the bleak honesty of Kavanagh's poem. One of *The Great Hunger*'s claims to the status of major poem, as the cultural historian, Terence Brown, has pointed out, is its antenna-like sensitivity to 'the shifts of consciousness that determine a people's future'.[12]

Had Kavanagh intended to broadcast to the nation would he have been content to publish his poem in a semi-private edition and not reprint it until 1947? However, it was its social concern that led him to repudiate *The Great Hunger* in his last years. He condemned it for its preoccupation with 'the woes of the poor' which prevented it from achieving 'the nobility and repose of poetry'. It was, he declared, a 'tragedy' and 'Tragedy is underdeveloped Comedy, not fully born.' Such a definition of the tragic aesthetic is undoubtedly debatable. What is certain is that his dismissal of *The Great Hunger* as tragedy has some validity within the context of his own poetics where comedy represents a detached, disengaged art, and tragedy, as its aesthetic contrary, represents an engaged, committed art. That *The Great Hunger* was 'visible to policemen', the older poet considered, betrayed its 'kinetic vulgarity'. It had the obviousness of a poem addressed to a mass audience; whereas 'a true poet', as opposed to a rhetorician, 'is selfish and implacable', content to state 'the position' and 'not care whether his words change anything or not'.[13]

This is not merely a sensational recantation of an early masterpiece; it is a criticism that focuses unerringly on the poem's central weakness, its over-determined narrative. It is, indeed, the case that *The Great Hunger* is at its least persuasive when it is at its most audience-conscious, when its designs on the reader are too palpable; specifically, when the role of the narrator upstages that of the chief protagonist. A conflict between rhetoric and drama is, however, inherent in the nature of the poem.

The Great Hunger is formally problematic when the control exercised by its ubiquitous and dictatorial narrator is too obtrusive. Sometimes this failure is one of tone as in the overly pedagogic approach in the first paragraph, 'is there anything we can prove' or the patronising, 'He thinks ... but we know better', later in part I. Sometimes the narrator is unduly reflexive as when, conscious that he is taking poetry into a new terrain, he invites Imagination to accompany him in the opening and closing parts of the poem. Sometimes he abandons exemplary fiction for a more direct rhetorical engagement with his reader as in his appeal for empathy in part XI or his ironic attack on primitivism in part XIII. His hortatory stance in part XI:

> Let us kneel where he kneels
> And feel what he feels ...

might be attributed to a lack of confidence in his own fictional powers of evocation, a failure to see that the pity is in the poetry already. One might argue that *The Great Hunger* is weakened by Kavanagh's failure to contain his new anti-Romantic and anti-Revivalist polemic within the confines of his fiction. When Maguire 'grunts and spits/Through a clay-wattled moustache' the reader detects a mischievous gibe at idyllic life on Innisfree. However, the satiric representation of primitivism in such lines as

> *There* is the source from which all cultures rise,

And all religions,
There is the pool in which the poet dips
And the musician.
Without the peasant base civilisation must die,
Unless the clay is in the mouth the singer's singing is
    useless.
The travellers touch the roots of the grass and feel
    renewed
When they grasp the steering wheels again . . .

does not stop short at sneering at tourists and trippers and debunking a Revivalist ideology, triumphally proclaimed by Yeats:

John Synge, I and Augusta Gregory, thought
All that we did, all that we said or sang
Must come from contact with the soil, from that
Contact everything Antaeus-like grew strong . . .

More fundamentally, it disposes of a literary myth of the importance of peasantry which had flourished in English poetry since Wordsworth published the preface to the *Lyrical Ballads*. Nevertheless, such a frontal rhetorical assault was unnecessary because Kavanagh had by then almost completed the alternative fiction that demythologises peasantry, had demonstrated that having 'roots in the soil' is uncomfortably close to vegetable status.

Unfortunately, the rhetorical defects of *The Great Hunger* are almost inseparable from its virtues. It is primarily a dogmatic poem; its fiction is not autotelic and is only a means to its didactic end. By dehyphenating his customary role of poet-farmer and distributing it between two characters Kavanagh created a non-autobiographical poet figure, a lay narrator with no function other than that of commentator. The authoritativeness of this narrative voice is due, in large measure, to the fact that it is disembodied, rhetorical rather than dramatic. It does not provide a partial or limited view such as that of the cattle drovers in 'Shancoduff'; it presents a reliable, responsible overview. One of the principal functions assigned to the narrator is to compensate for the myopia or partial sightedness of the poem's fictional characters by the clarity and comprehensiveness of his own religious vision. He supplies a dimension absent from, or usually concealed from view, in the poem's fictional world, a visionary criterion by which this world can be judged and found wanting. Maguire is perturbed by his inability to arrive at a mathematical religious certitude, a 'certain standard, measured and known'. The narrator enjoys just such certitude since he is a religious prophet, representing God's viewpoint: registering divine anger and amusement, pronouncing divine judgment, promising divine retribution. The poet who had loitered palely around the altar in his early verse has become a theologian and mounted the pulpit. To take away the 'messianic compulsion'[14] that Kavanagh later complained of is to diminish the poem. Message and medium, vision and rhetoric, are inseparable in *The Great Hunger*.

The emotional instability of the narrator's response, which varies between anger, irony, amusement and compassion, may be identified with the complexity of Kavanagh's own emotional attitude to life in Inniskeen, or, to give him greater credit, with his dramatisation of such an attitude. It is an attitude aphoristically summed up in a phrase he quotes from Chesterton, to 'love the city enough to set fire to it'.[15]

Kavanagh did love the country enough to burn it. A love almost indistinguishable from hatred and a destructiveness bred of love: this is the complex of passions to which Maguire's drama is essential, yet subsidiary. Donaghmoyne is but a combustible to Kavanagh's fiery prophetic vision. *The Great Hunger* is a marriage of heaven and hell.

5

Writing Catholic Ireland: Pilgrimage

Introduction

CATHOLICISM is integral to the small-farm world that Patrick Kavanagh celebrated in his early forties' lyrics and condemned in *The Great Hunger*. When first encountered in these verses the poet's neighbours are 'going to the chapel/ To confess their sins' on Christmas Eve. On Christmas morning their mass-going feet are heard crunching the wafer-ice on a pot-holed country road. In both 'Christmas Eve Remembered' and 'A Christmas Childhood' Inniskeen is so saturated with Catholicism that it is transfigured into Bethlehem. Even in 'Art McCooey', which might appear a secular poem presided over by a pagan deity, Catholicism is unobtrusively present as part of the social fabric of country living. Young farmers stopping for a chat on the roadside know that they'll meet up again at the chapel on Sunday:

> 'I'll see you after Second Mass on Sunday.'
> 'Right-o, right-o' . . .

This casual exchange of farewells affords a quick glimpse of a mentality in which Catholicism is taken for granted as part of the normal weekly round.

These first representations of rural Irish Catholicism appear instinctive rather than programmatic. Kavanagh writes not as a social realist but as an autobiographer whose Catholic community is part of his background and upbringing. Home and parish are evoked as a personal context. His subject is really himself; his Catholic neighbours are an extension of his family romance.

No sooner did Kavanagh arrive at the point where his lyricism was grounded in a communal Catholic substratum, transfusing the collective into the individual, than social concerns began to weigh heavily on his poetry. Under the tutelage of O'Connor and O'Faoláin he learned that 'in dreams begin responsibilities'. So in *The Great Hunger* Inniskeen is fictionalised as Donaghmoyne to divest it of personal relevance and the Catholic parish, instead of providing an autobiographical context, serves in a representative capacity as a microcosmic expression of national deprivation. With the publication of *The Great Hunger* Kavanagh emerged as a conscious interpreter and critic of Irish rural Catholicism. He had embarked on a socio-literary programme of writing Catholic Ireland.

From being the peasant-subject of Irish literature, Kavanagh had been transformed into its author. Unlike earlier Irish Catholic poets, such as Padraic Colum, who had made a similar transition, he assumed the authority that authorship conferred. Colum had adhered servilely to Revivalist conventions in his representations of Irish countrymen. In his most celebrated peasant poem, 'The Plougher', he maintained a patronising, interpretative distance from his subject; his ennobling of the farmer as a figure of primitive iconography denied him realism. Colum refused imaginative empathy with his ploughman, suppressing his Catholic consciousness, dismissing his speech, compelling him to conform to the poet's ritualised script:

> Surely your thoughts are of Pan, or of Wotan,
>   or Dana? . . .

> What matter your foolish reply! O man standing
>   lone and bowed earthward,
> Your task is a day near its close Give thanks to the
>   nightgiving god . . .

Colum's 'plougher' makes a glorious exit but he is elevated to an alien, archaic, pagan splendour, remote from the 'living pieties' of Irish small-farm life. In Colum's case, the native

Irish Catholic turned author reinforced existing literary stereotypes about his fellow countrymen.

In *The Great Hunger*, Kavanagh, on the contrary, was a
revisionist Irish writer, re-seeing the peasant-subject of so
much Romantic and Revival literature, knowingly taking
'Imagination' into new cultural and psychological ground.
This communication of a communal Catholic consciousness
involved an excommunication of the admiring observer, the
reverential iconographer. Kavanagh knew that in acting as
tribal spokesman, in taking advantage of his status as an
insider in the Catholic community, he was altering the pact
between people and poet in Ireland. He had invented a new
narrative, whose focus was the Irish Catholic consciousness.
From the beginning an anti-Romantic, anti-Revivalist, aesthetic polemic was inseparable from Kavanagh's realist
representation.

The cultural imperative to imagine rural Catholic Ireland
and the concomitant marginalisation of Revivalist and neo-
Revivalist reportage were already present in Daniel Corkery's
Synge and Anglo–Irish Literature (1931). Corkery had established a dichotomy between 'the literature of the Ascendancy
writer' and that of 'the writer of the Irish people'. Ascendancy writers were many and often world famous, yet they did
not share in the Irish national consciousness, 'in the people's
emotional background', and were incapable of expressing
Ireland to itself. The native Catholic writers were a submerged few, usually unknown except to the Irish, artistically
flawed, yet theirs was the only literature 'in which undereducated Ireland discovers its own image'. To Corkery Revival poetry was exotic, not indigenous; it was impertinent as
a representation of rural reality, bypassing Ireland's 'living
pieties' — 'the white-walled houses, the farming life, the hill-
top chapel, the memorial cross above some peasant's grave'.
What had shaped 'the Irish national being' and, therefore,
what distinguished the Irish mentality, for Corkery, were
three great forces: '(1) The Religious Consciousness of the
People; (2) Irish Nationalism; (3) The Land.' The Irish

Catholic consciousness which, he claimed, had never been adequately articulated in Anglo–Irish fiction was 'so vast, so deep, so dramatic, even so terrible a thing' that he wondered if it were possible for 'a writer to deal with any phase whatever of Irish life without trenching upon it'. The 'conventions of Anglo–Irish literature' had 'cut out the heart of the mystery' by omitting Catholicism or by substituting for it 'the wraith-like wisps of vanished beliefs'. 'We may perhaps know', concluded Corkery,

> that genuine Anglo–Irish literature has come into being when at every hand's turn that religious consciousness breaks in upon it, no matter what the subject . . .[1]

Acknowledging the inadequacy of Anglo–Irish representations of the Irish psyche, James Joyce had already set about forging 'the uncreated conscience' of his race. His enterprise was unacceptable to Corkery who was too exclusively concerned with realist, rural and residential writers. Joyce's was an intellectual, urban Catholic sensibility which in the persona of Stephen Dedalus pronounced itself sophisticatedly repelled and atavistically unnerved by the Gaelic-speaking western peasant, Mulrennan. However, Patrick Kavanagh, who in 1931 was still an apprentice poet, only too eager to be accounted true brother of the Revivalists, by the 1940s seemed to be evolving into an incarnation of Corkery's literary ideal. An indigenous Catholic writer who had emerged from the under-educated underworld of rural Ireland, he had begun to defy neo-Romantic, Revivalist versions of pastoral and to evoke the Irish country parish realistically as he himself had experienced it. Kavanagh was not exercised by the doctrinal aspects of religion or by abstruse theological debate. What interested him was the imaginative representation of the popular piety in which he had been reared. Catholicism was intrinsic to his aesthetic programme of social realism and inseparable from his literary radicalism.

That Kavanagh should have corresponded so closely to Corkery's ideal is ironic, since he shared O'Connor's and

O'Faoláin's aversion for the older writer's extreme cultural nationalism. By contrast with Corkery's, Kavanagh's literary model was ahistorical and monoglot, unconcerned with Ireland's artistic, legendary or mythic past, with the adaptation of Gaelic literary techniques or the preservation of Gaelic literary discourse.[2] Even on the issue of the literary representation of Catholicism he differed from Corkery in that for him the religious consciousness of his people was neither 'dramatic' nor 'terrible'; rather it was as pervasive and unremarkable as air and as natural and normal as breathing. Kavanagh's harsh denunciation of the absence of a liberating Christian vision in rural Ireland in *The Great Hunger* is exceptional. His customary attitude is to appreciate the divine comedy of country Catholicism, its insistence on bringing heaven down to earth, involving God, the Virgin Mary and the saints in all the preoccupations of small-farm life, from the fattening of sows to the marriage of daughters. Conversely, Catholicism is such a real presence in the Irish country psyche that its transubstantiating power divinises the most earthy talk and thoughts:

> They may be talking of the turkey markets
> Or foreign politics, but to-night
> Their plain hard country words
> Are Christ's singing birds
>
> Bicycles scoot by; old women
> Cling to the grass-margin:
> Their feet are heavy but their minds fly
> In dreams of the Mother Virgin . . .
> ('Christmas Eve Remembered')

When the poet's mother talks to her son about farming chores in 'In Memory of My Mother' a transcendental presence hovers about her 'earthiest words':

> Going to second Mass on a summer Sunday—
> You meet me and you say:

'Don't forget to see about the cattle—'
Among your earthiest words the angels stray.

In *The Great Hunger* Maguire's intermingling of farming and prayer in the chapel sequence was presented as immediately comic and ultimately tragic, since it signified 'the grip of irregular fields' on his psyche. In 'In Memory of My Mother' that a woman should be preoccupied about cattle on the way to mass reveals that easy relationship between faith and farming which characterises daily life in small-farm Ireland. Both 'Christmas Eve Remembered' and 'In Memory of My Mother' are soft focus portraits of country Catholics. In his novel, *Tarry Flynn*, while still adhering to the comic mode, Kavanagh would depict the Catholic community in a harsher, more naturalistic light.

Of Corkery's submerged tradition of native Irish writers the only one who, it seemed to Kavanagh, had captured the comedy of country Catholicism was the renegade, William Carleton. Carleton's literary lapses from the faith of his fathers were condoned because he was 'incapable of being anything but a Catholic'. In *Traits and Stories of the Irish Peasantry* Carleton had recognised the inextricability of the sacred and the secular in small-farm life. His 'best work' was

> true to that medieval texture of Irish Catholic life in which the same breath that utters a Hail Mary suffices to shoo the chickens off the floor or the cat from the jug of cream.[3]

Yet Carleton's conversion to Protestant propagandist was a salutary warning to Kavanagh. Though separated by almost a century from this literary precursor and a migrant to a Dublin where Catholicism was the prevailing religion he, too, shared something of Carleton's artistic dilemma, torn between an instinctive affection and homesickness for his country parish and an intellectual disaffection and scepticism fostered by his Dublin literary milieu. To espouse the official Irish religion was, for Kavanagh, to ally himself with the censoriousness, obscurantism and moral hypocrisy of de Valera's theocracy.

In the unpublished narrative poem, 'Why Sorrow?', written during his first years in Dublin, the central character is a priest who is racked with religious *angst*, torn between the prior aesthetic claims of pagan love of nature and a dutiful Catholic pastoralism, between sympathy with the simple beliefs of country people and alienation from their limited creed and passive faith. 'Why Sorrow?', which revealed an antagonism between poetry and Catholicism on the one hand and between poetry and social responsibility on the other, was suppressed and, indeed, never completed. In concealing 'Why Sorrow?' from public notice Kavanagh hid his own religio-aesthetic doubts, his sense of divided artistic allegiance. The only section of the poem published in the early 1940s, 'The Long Garden', displayed nothing of its religious plot.[4] However, the fact that Kavanagh was unable to, or chose not to, finish 'Why Sorrow?' probably indicates that the subject ceased to engage him imaginatively. His most scathing condemnation of country Catholicism in *The Great Hunger* was conducted from a Catholic perspective, a Christian critique of a supposedly Christian land.

Unlike Carleton, who began his career as a free lance journalist by writing for the Evangelical periodical, *The Christian Examiner*, Kavanagh soon gravitated towards the staunchly Catholic daily newspaper, *The Irish Press*, to which he contributed a twice-weekly column, 'City Commentary', from September 1942 to February 1944. From February 1943 he overtly proclaimed his allegiance to Catholic journalism when he began contributing a regular feature, 'The Literary Scene', to the Catholic Sunday newspaper, *The Standard*. Although this feature was discontinued from June 1943, he retained an association with *The Standard* for which he acted as Editorial and Feature writer for three years from July 1945 and as film critic from February 1946 to July 1949. Granted that Kavanagh's motives in accepting such employment were financial rather than ideological and that he would have preferred to work as a columnist for the more prestigiously intellectual and literary *Irish Times*, despite its Protestant coloration, his acceptability to *The Irish Press* and, especially, to *The Standard* shows that he was regarded as a sound Catholic writer. His second volume of poems, *A Soul for Sale* (1947), was dedicated to the editor of *The Standard*, Peter Curry.[5]

Significantly, it was from the safe Catholic stronghold of *The Standard* that Kavanagh launched his first direct offensive on the unrepresentative, because ascendancy-inspired and non-Catholic, nature of Revival literature:

> The Anglo–Irish were, and are, the lookers-on. They are not part of the national conscience, but in an objective position outside it . . . The nearer they got to the essential truth of Ireland the less they wrote about it. None of them got very near, simply because, as Lady Gregory recognised, the only short cut to the soul of Ireland was via Rome. The Anglo–Irish are not English, much as a few of them might wish it, and there being no country called Anglo–Ireland it follows that they are without a fatherland.
>
> From Swift to Yeats the mouthpieces of this limbo-stranded class have had to search diligently wherever they might for the spiritual food of their creative need. Yeats was the fruit of many generations resident in Ireland, yet he was forced to adopt Ireland as his country. A people raises up a poet out of its silent necessity just as it raises a leader. Yeats was not pushed up by the under-drive of a nation; he saw the force and he allowed it to drive *him*. It was the same with Synge. Imagine the unnaturalness of Synge searching all round the world for something to write about and then finding the Aran Islands.[6]

Kavanagh's argument here is very similar to Corkery's, with its premise that art should articulate a national consciousness and its association of Irish nationality with Catholicism. His nativist aesthetic is obvious in his reference to the unnaturalness of non-national subject matter in the case of Synge. The Revivalists are turned into a composite father figure in order that Kavanagh may assert the end of their patriarchal claim to guide or instruct Irish writers, to teach Irish poets their trade. Like Corkery he is attempting to alter the reading of Revival texts by insisting on their minority cultural basis. He is deliberately decentralising the Revival to make room for another literary reality, a Catholic narrative more equivalent to the experience of the majority of Irish people. In challenging Yeats's credentials as Ireland's national poet, the writer of *The Great Hunger* is implicitly asserting his own claim to that office. He is the poet raised up by his countrymen's 'silent necessity', 'pushed up by the under-drive of a nation' to articulate the experience and aspirations of its people. He is the voice of oppressed Catholic Ireland.

In the early 1940s Kavanagh's aesthetic was ethnic, sectarian and class conscious. He regarded himself as the spokesman of the poor, obscure, downtrodden classes. Reviewing Seán O'Faoláin's *The Great O'Neill* in 1943 he disclaimed any interest in the book's ostensible subject and read this historical biography for what it might reveal of 'the secret history of the poor and humble and virtuous', the suppressed dimension of Ireland's national identity. He lamented the fact that the Irish had 'no historian of the poor like the author of *The Vision of Piers Plowman*, that Ireland's 'only social historian was Carleton' who 'submitted to a convention that barred some salutary truths'.[7] Since this review is contemporaneous with Kavanagh's 'City Commentary' column for *The Irish Press*, a social significance attaches to his adoption of the pen-name 'Piers Plowman' for this column. He was projecting himself as a combination of Catholic visionary poet and recorder of the unnewsworthy lives of ordinary people. On occasion his class bias even triumphed over his sectarian prejudice as when Sean O'Casey's realistic portrayal of the urban poor compensated for his Protestantism, enabling him to qualify as an Irish writer on Kavanagh's terms:

> And how Irish he is. Why shouldn't he be Irish? You might ask. There is a catch in it: O'Casey was born and

brought up a Protestant, and Irish Protestants—even the most liberal of them—have always been at one remove from the inner spirit of the ordinary people of Ireland. But there is one element which can break down all theological barriers and make the most spiritually opposed neighbours one—and it is common poverty. O'Casey was one of the people.[8]

Writing for the Catholic *Standard*, encouraged Kavanagh to indulge his religio-literary bigotry. For the remainder of his career he was to challenge the hegemony of the Literary Revival on sectarian grounds. He insisted on reading Irish literature from a Catholic standpoint, taking truth to the culture being represented as his artistic criterion, treating Irishness and Catholicism as interchangeable terms. In a series of hit and run journalistic assaults, the Protestant Revivalists were singly and collectively attacked, Yeats and Synge being the principal targets. Yeats was a 'doubtful Irishman' because

the one thing that vitally impregnates the whole of life in Ireland is Catholicism. How can a man be what is called Irish and be totally outside the mainstream of the people's consciousness?[9]

Synge suffered 'from a certain coarseness born of his Protestantism, the loutish superiority of a mediocre ruling class'.[10] He was an 'outsider' whose 'coarse mind never reached the heart of a people's repose'. Kavanagh pictured him 'sitting in the Aran cabin taking his superficial notes while the people were out at Mass on a Sunday'.[11] Synge's status as an Anglo–Irish dramatist he attributed to his having 'provided Irish Protestants who are worried about being "Irish" with an artificial country'.[12] In a notorious essay on F. R. Higgins, Kavanagh accused him of concealing his Protestantism and, worse still, of alluding to Catholic rituals in his work, in order to pose as an Irish writer:

If he were a really true poet . . . he would have written

about a Protestant church and a Protestant service and while it might not be as droll, it would have the merit of being sincere.

You get the same thing among Irish Protestant writers in general. It is not without point that the fathers of 'Irish wit and humour' (more inverted commas) have nearly all been Protestants. They were trying to by-pass Rome on their way to the heart of Ireland.

Their Protestantism has been a great tribulation to Irish writers of that persuasion.[13]

By basing literary authenticity on personal experience and refusing to allow Irish Protestant authors either to treat of or to ignore the majority faith Kavanagh introduced a sectarian split in Irish letters and attempted to marginalise the contribution of the mainly Protestant Revivalists.

It might appear that Kavanagh was suffering from an acute case of the anxiety of influence, as diagnosed by Harold Bloom, that finding 'all space filled with his precursors' visions' he was resorting 'to the language of taboo, so as to clear a mental space for himself'. He did acknowledge that his sweeping, destructive criticism was the negative aspect of his creative programme; according to his own agricultural metaphor he was clearing the field of weeds 'against the crop' he wanted 'to sow'.[14] Yet his boorish bigotry, his insistence on creed and class as a sign of literary difference, belong to a recognisable moment in Irish post-colonial history. The synthesis arising from national cultural resistance against an alien, occupying imperium had been disintegrating since 1922. This resistance had been spearheaded by a Protestant ascendancy who were originally part of the colonial system they helped to oust. Kavanagh's sectarian and class-conscious aesthetic was designed to distinguish the Anglo–Irish neo-colonists from the native Irish. His enterprise was to recover the land of Ireland from his colonial predecessors, imaginatively reclaiming it for the purposes of a new literary agendum. He wished to express the separatist identity of his own people, to elevate a Catholic subculture to artistic eminence. There was a fierce anti-colonial bias in Kavanagh's hostility to Irish literary Protestantism. Douglas Hyde, for instance, who as founder of the Gaelic League and collector and translator of the *Love Songs of Connacht*, might be considered to have earned the accolade of Irishness, he disparaged as a 'Cromwellian', probably the most abusive of Irish anti-colonial sobriquets.[15] The return of the repressed is inevitably angry and aggressive. Kavanagh's polemic against the Revival was an act of dispossession which was the literary equivalent of the burning of the Big House. 'An age is the reversal of an age', Yeats had written, and the older poet would have recognised in the younger a necessary antithesis, his anti-self, the 'gangling stock' grown great, the rough beast subverting custom and ceremony and pitching assiduously accumulated ancestral pearls in the sty.

Throughout the 1940s Kavanagh was preoccupied with finding literary modes for exploring and expressing the Irish Catholic consciousness. Though he was to define the poet as a theologian, one versed in the nature and attributes of God and in his relations with man and universe, what most concerned him in the 1940s was the portrayal of Catholicism as a communal faith and an integral part of the texture of Irish life. In the beginning he still deployed a nationalist rhetoric, subscribing to 'the myth of Ireland as a spiritual entity' that he was later to repudiate and attribute to the baneful influence of Yeats.[16] Kavanagh's long, socio-realist poem, *Lough Derg* (1942), which is the principal subject of this chapter, belongs to this ethnic phase. Through the documentation of a national pilgrimage he hoped to construct a profile of Irish Catholicism; but he was so dissatisfied with the poem that he never published it. The peripatetic and collective dimensions of national pilgrimage were totally at odds with the rooted, local aesthetic he was to espouse in his novel, *Tarry Flynn* (1948), and his most successful experiments with forging the uncreated Irish Catholic conscience were in what he christened the 'parochial' mode rather than in the peregrinatory mode of *Lough Derg*. Kavanagh's 'parish myth', which he opposed to 'the myth of Ireland as a spiritual entity', will be discussed in chapter 6.[17]

Pilgrim Poet: *Lough Derg*

The theme of pilgrimage had attracted Patrick Kavanagh from *The Green Fool* onwards but, apart from his account of a pilgrimage to Lady Well near Dundalk in the sixth chapter of this book, he never succeeded in publishing anything other than short newspaper articles on the subject. A projected book on Irish pilgrimages, which he persuaded Hollis and Carter to commission, was never written, indeed, was scarcely begun.[18] This project may have been a cynical fundraising exercise, to some extent, yet it did appear a feasible undertaking in view of his previous interest in pilgrimage and his literary commitment to Catholicism.

From the outset of his career as a free-lance journalist Kavanagh had from time to time cast himself in the role of religious affairs correspondent, reporting on pilgrimages for the Catholic national daily, *The Irish Independent*, and for the Catholic Sunday newspaper, *The Standard*. Summer was the open season for pilgrimages and he probably enjoyed the opportunity for a day's outing in fine weather, but his peregrinations were not merely frivolous. Observing his coreligionists was an essential part of that literary programme of coming to terms with the realities of Irish life on which, under the aegis of Seán O'Faoláin and Frank O'Connor, he had embarked since 1940.

In *The Green Fool*, the unofficial Lady Well pilgrimage, frowned on by the Catholic Church as a pagan observance, was depicted as a disorderly and unruly affair. The site was 'like a rowdy bazaar-ground'; comic songs replaced hymns; beggars proliferated; couples courted; men argued politics or bargained; kneeling pilgrims were pelted with clods. The scramble to fill bottles with newly risen well water was a superstitious scrimmage. Yet even here, Kavanagh, though sceptical about the miraculous origins of the holy water, took a lenient approach to the rumbustious antics of his fellow pilgrims. His Catholicism was comprehensive enough to embrace all forms of human behaviour and to welcome all comers:

> Our Lady was a real lady and human, she was not displeased, I knew, because some who pilgrimed in Her name were doubters and some cynics and a lot vulgar sightseers. She is kind and no doubt she enjoyed the comic twists in the pageant round Lady Well.

Kavanagh later denied that he had ever been to Lady Well.[19] Whether or not he was depending on hearsay evidence or exaggerating riotous unorthodoxy for comic effect, the non-puritanical stance he adopted here anticipated his later commendation of the mixed nature of the Catholic pilgrimage as part devotion, part entertainment.

The aspect of Irish pilgrimages that Kavanagh most frequently commented on in his realist reportage from 1940 was their intermingling of the sacred and the secular, piety and gaiety, prayer and pragmatism. This easy commerce between spiritual and worldly impulses he sometimes characterised, as in *The Green Fool*, by the adjective, 'medieval'. It was an epithet that enhanced and justified modern Irish Catholic practice by placing it in the context of pre-Reformation European mores. So, he compared the town of Westport in summer 1940 on the eve of the strenuous climb up Croagh Patrick to a scene from the middle ages:

> Croagh Patrick is flamboyant and colourful as some warm-faithed corner of medieval christendom. Westport tonight is like something one might read about but never experience: Christmas Day in a poet's childhood or a page of the Canterbury Tales.[20]

A pilgrimage to Knock in 1942, although less festive, demonstrated that 'the laughter and the ordinary business of life . . . is woven with religion in the texture of country life'.

On this occasion Kavanagh cited a typical example of unself-conscious transition from prayer to farm-speak:

> Star of the Sea, pray for us. Queen of peace, pray for us . . . That's a great craft, that bit of oats of Micky's down there . . . [21]

On pilgrimage to Our Lady's Island in south Wexford in 1945 the poet was moved to find himself praying in the open air with 'ordinary little tillage fields', 'whinny fences' and 'weed fringes' that reminded him of home all around.[22] Again faith and farm life were associated. Describing a return visit to Croagh Patrick in July 1952, when he was still forcibly struck by the blend of piety and gaiety on the eve of the pilgrimage, he claimed that he had come to regard the documentation of pilgrimages as an intrusive, insensitive type of reportage. At the beginning of the Croagh Patrick climb he felt himself to be 'at the source of material for literature as well as of grace'; by the end he was abashed at the crassness of capitalising on the religious fervour of his fellow pilgrims for literary copy. Ironically, his purpose in climbing the holy mountain at this juncture was to include an account of the pilgrimage in his projected book for Hollis and Carter. The death-knell of this particular publishing venture is sounded at the conclusion of his report:

> You are at the raw sensitive heart of the active Faith; too raw and sensitive perhaps for poetic exploitation . . .[23]

The pilgrimage that Kavanagh found most imaginatively intractable, despite its clearly attested existence in medieval times, was that most penitential and most protracted of all Irish pilgrimages, the painful ordeal of 'doing Lough Derg'. St Patrick's Purgatory, commonly known as Lough Derg, is an 'island-acre of greenstone'[24] in the middle of Lough Derg in County Donegal. Kavanagh's local hero, William Carleton, had inaugurated his literary career with the story, 'A Lough Derg Pilgrim'; his own attempts to derive copy from Lough Derg were conspicuously less successful. His first report on the pilgrimage for the *Irish Independent* in June 1940 was unpublishable. 'The moment you think of Lough Derg, your mind goes blank, your mind atrophies',[25] he wrote. It was probably this pilgrimage that prompted him to include a section on Lough Derg in his long, Catholic, crisis poem, 'Why Sorrow?'. With the inclusion of the Lough Derg material the poem foundered and was left unfinished. Though two excerpts from this poem were published, these did not include the Lough Derg sequence. Kavanagh returned to the island determined to write a poem about the pilgrimage in June 1942. The poem was concluded but neither published nor revised, completely abandoned, never quarried from. All that he salvaged from two pilgrimages to Lough Derg and five attempts to write about the subject was one newspaper report in the *Standard* (12 June 1942).

Kavanagh appears to have concluded that the subject of Lough Derg, though potentially interesting, was somehow imaginatively recalcitrant. Expressing his disappointment with Denis Devlin's 'Lough Derg' in 1946, he commented:

> It is a remarkable fact that Lough Derg does not lend itself to the literary spirit. There has yet to be written a great poem or book on this pilgrimage.

While he did not declare his interest, he was puzzling over his own failure as much as Devlin's, for he, too, had tried to extract 'from the stony austerity of Lough Derg the warm blood of abundant poetic life'.[26]

What partially vitiated Kavanagh's efforts to come to literary terms with Lough Derg was a humiliating incident connected with his first visit that jaundiced his outlook on the pilgrimage at the time and still rankled when he came to write his poem. Before leaving the mainland he had aroused 'peasant fear of the unconventional' by striking a poetic pose and gazing meditatively at the island. This 'bogus trance' was rudely interrupted by two suspicious ferrymen. It was the kind of embarrassing episode that could have been turned to comic use but the young poet was too insecure to dwell on its funny side. Instead he retaliated by abusing his fellow pilgrims in his subsequent unpublished report:

> The crowds which gather in such a place as Lough Derg act like one enormous creature, almost; and it is doubtful if one can develop a defence against it. The heart of this creature is one boiling mass of suspicious insult-ability . . .
> Lough Derg is typical of what may be called the Irish mind. No contemplation, no adventure, the narrow prim-itive piety of the small huxter with a large family.[27]

Clearly he himself shared that peasant 'insultability' he affected to despise. Alone among his own people, without a literary support group, he was at his most vulnerable. He was even incapable of summoning up sufficient professional detachment to write a few publishable column inches of devotional prose on Lough Derg for the *Independent*. Neverthe-less, it was probably because he considered Lough Derg so 'typical of the Irish mind' in 1940 that Kavanagh revisited it in June 1942 to continue the enterprise of creating the con-science of his race which he had initiated in *The Great Hunger*, published just two months previously. He was deliberately embarking on an imaginative excursion beyond 'the white-thorn hedges of the little farm'.

Lough Derg is Kavanagh's most sociologically and religiously ambitious poem, a serious attempt at an anatomy of Irish Catholicism. *The Great Hunger* had focused solely on rural Ireland but the life of the subsistence farmer was very different from that of the urban poor and unemployed or the upwardly mobile middle classes who, since he had turned city-dweller, had begun to impinge on his awareness. Kavan-agh probably chose Lough Derg as the locus of a poem on Irish Catholicism because he knew that on this field of folk he would encounter a representative cross-section of the Irish faithful, men and women from town and country, from all

parts of Ireland and from all walks of life, assembled together. The austerity of Lough Derg's penitential programme
is such that pilgrims are placed under severe physical and
psychological strain and this communal penance, which,
according to the poet, 'almost reaches the limits of human
endurance',[28] has the effect of rendering them vulnerable and
confessional and so breaking down social barriers. On Lough
Derg Kavanagh would have expected to achieve an insight
into the Irish racial psyche, the anxieties and aspirations,
loves and longings, pomps and privations, of his people.
Whereas other Irish national pilgrimages lasted only a few
hours and were relatively unstructured, the three-day
duration of the Lough Derg pilgrimage and its repetitive
routine of prescribed exercises would give the pilgrim-poet
time to familiarise himself with his subject. Being an island,
Lough Derg had the additional advantage of presenting that
subject to him in self-contained isolation, a vision of Ireland
at its most exclusively and intensely Catholic.

In order to arrive at a comprehensive summation of Irish
Catholicism in *Lough Derg* Kavanagh inverted the parochial
and temporal strategies of *The Great Hunger*. Now all Ireland,
north and south, is reduced to parish size and its emotional
and spiritual gamut charted over a three-day period. Men
and women from town and country and from twelve of the
thirty-two counties are represented: priests and laity, the
professional classes, civil servants, shopkeepers, farmers, the
urban and rural poor. A catalogue, listing pilgrims by profession and place of origin, is one economical method of
extending the poem's regional and social range of reference:

> A baker from Rathfriarland
> A solicitor from Derry
> A parish priest from Wicklow
> A civil servant from Kerry . . .

Lough Derg's linear narrative follows the time-scheme of the
pilgrimage and the frequent references to the time of day or
night at which the action takes place is both a documentary

and a mimetic device, chronicling the slow passage of the penitential ordeal. As in *The Great Hunger* Kavanagh's narrative mode is cinematic. Numerous shots of pilgrims at different named locations and in a variety of pious or relaxed poses, accompanied by snatches of prayer, hymns and dialogue, convey a realistic picture of life on the island. They are portrayed flocking into the chapel for Benediction on their first evening; queuing with outstretched arms to renounce the world, the flesh and the devil; tripping each other around the penitential gravel rings, almost mindless with hunger, fatigue and pain; pulling bare feet close to their bellies during the cold all-night vigil; stumbling bleary eyed from the hostel after their first night's sleep; waving and singing 'O fare thee well, Lough Derg' as they return to the mainland by boat, their purgatorial stint completed. The sociable side of Lough Derg is not neglected: homely chat, the exchange of confidences, even flirtation. Kavanagh was anxious to achieve more than mere cinematic reportage in his poem; he wanted to penetrate the minds and hearts of his pilgrims, to understand their motivations, their aspirations, their conception of the divine. Again as in *The Great Hunger* he assumes the role of privileged commentator, here penetrating the secret recesses of the pilgrims' consciousness, in particular, using prayer as an expository technique.[29] Although it is not divided into numbered sections *Lough Derg* otherwise imitates the irregular structure of *The Great Hunger*, being written in paragraphs or rhymed sequences of different lengths, with rhythm and rhyme sometimes obtrusive, sometimes almost disappearing under colloquial or rhetorical pressure from the commentator's voice.

Yet *Lough Derg* remains an interesting experiment, an ambitious failure rather than a masterpiece. It may seem unduly censorious to criticise a work which Kavanagh himself decided not to publish and appears not to have revised. However, its dual publication in 1978 has brought it from the oblivion to which its author consigned it into the public domain.[30]

As with *The Great Hunger* the principal problem in *Lough Derg* is its poet-narrator but, on this occasion, the difficulty is not one of over-persuasiveness, rather one of pervasive narrative uncertainty. Kavanagh is here confronting what attracted and repelled him in contemporary Catholic Ireland. The subject was probably too intimate or written up too soon after the event to allow sufficient artistic detachment. He approaches it with mixed feelings, as sceptic and believer, outsider and insider. The narrator's status in the text wavers between that of observer and pilgrim-poet; emotionally, he veers between alienation and empathy. Where *The Great Hunger* is sometimes flawed by a too strident polemicism, *Lough Derg*, ironically, fails because its prejudices do not amount to a sustained *parti pris*. Although the narrator is only occasionally an actor in his poem he is its most important character. His moody, mercurial presence dominates throughout. While not ostensibly a journey into his personal and poetic psyche, like Seamus Heaney's 'Station Island', *Lough Derg* is, nevertheless, either covertly or overtly confessional. Unlike Heaney, Kavanagh is not artistically in control of his introspective processes; he appears to be struggling with his own partialities and preconceptions in order to achieve some semblance of objectivity. *Lough Derg* is really an extended lyric in the guise of a cultural commentary. Its increasingly positive attitude toward pilgrimage and Catholicism is due to a more buoyant and charitable personal mood, a willing suspension of superiority. What it records is its narrator's disaffection from and return to religious communion.

Even Kavanagh's contemporary newspaper report of the pilgrimage, written for the *Standard*, betrays the uncertainty of response which incapacitates his poem. There he declared that his 'first and strongest impression' of Lough Derg was of the 'freshness and recency of Christianity', 'the excitement of this new truth ... stirring the imaginations of men and women', but he then proceeded in a contradictory vein by deploring the 'Victorian smugness' of the pilgrims, their impenetrable 'coat of heavy, protective piety', 'the absence of obvious mental or spiritual conflict' among them. The newspaper article is, of course, much briefer and more superficial than the poem and where both comment on the same phenomena the journalistic account is, predictably, more flattering. So the island basilica which has the prose virtues of 'usefulness and simplicity' is presented poetically as 'conventional' and even comical, with its concrete stilts 'spread like a bullfrog's hind paws'. Praise of the 'deep seriousness of every official' in the *Standard* is more tongue-in-cheek in the poem where the sexton, 'a man who knows the ins and outs of religion', adopts a 'heaven-sure stance' and the 'booted Prior', 'ignoring all the crowd', behaves 'suavily, goodily'.

Whether Kavanagh went to Lough Derg to scoff and remained to pray, his poem begins contemptuously and concludes compassionately, and the conflict between satiric superiority and pastoral charity ultimately destabilises the work. *Lough Derg* begins badly, its sneering authoritativeness undermined by inadmissible bias:

> From Cavan and from Leitrim and from Mayo,
> From all the thin-faced parishes where hills
> Are perished noses running peaty water,
> They come to Lough Derg to fast and pray and beg
> With all the bitterness of nonentities, and the envy
> Of the inarticulate when dealing with an artist . . .

While contempt for the snivelling, grovelling aspect of Irish religion, an association of piety with the peaty, is both legitimate and comic, the accusation of aesthetic envy is completely unwarranted and appears to derive from personal paranoia. It is inherently absurd to claim that Lough Derg's pilgrims are preoccupied with their philistinism and nothing whatever in the poem supports this initial outburst. Unexorcised painful memories of the start of Kavanagh's 1940 pilgrimage appear to be intruding at the outset of his literary pilgrimage. It is unfortunate that the reader should begin by distrusting the narrator.

For the first third of the poem its poet-narrator struggles to strike a balance between scorn and sympathy. His dominant impulse is to sneer yet he attempts to check it and remind himself and us that some of the pilgrims are 'sincere'. However, he finds it difficult to tell Lough Derg's 'story straight'. Humorous irreverence manifests itself in the choice of incongruous similes: pilgrims 'shooed through the chapel door . . . like hens to roost', or praying with outstretched arms 'like young police recruits being measured'. Veteran pilgrims watching newcomers arrive are described in burlesque fashion, smothering

> . . . the ridiculous cheer
> That breaks, like a hole in pants,
> Where the heroic armies advance.

A statue of St Patrick is mischievously depicted 'wearing an alb with no stitch dropped' but minus the shamrock he once clutched in his hand. 'Ireland's national apostle' is also deflated by being rhymed with 'the men's hostel'. Passages of whimsy about the moon's and sun's facetious attitudes to Lough Derg are embarrassingly *faux-naif*. The poet-narrator rails against 'the half-pilgrims . . . who are the true/Spirit of Ireland', trivialisers, uncommitted jokers, 'wanting some half-wish', not recognising that his own conversion from half-pilgrim to pilgrim is the real theme of his narrative.

Lough Derg records Kavanagh's wavering faith, not in God but in his co-religionists. However, the poem's special *animus* is directed against the middle classes. With the exception of 'a Castleblaney grocer', who is arbitrarily awarded the gift of mystical vision, the middle classes are excluded from the narrator's charity. They are the 'smug too-faithful' and their trials and tribulations are set to a callously cheerful tune to illustrate the vanity of human wishes:

> Solicitors praying for cushy jobs
> To be County Registrar or Coroner,
> Shopkeepers threatened with sharper rivals

Than any hook-nosed foreigner.
Mothers whose daughters are Final Medicals,
Too heavy-hipped for thinking,
Wives whose husbands have angina pectoris,
Wives whose husbands have taken to drinking.

The Irish middle classes are distrustful of aestheticism or sensuousness: love, flowers, light, 'to shopkeepers and small lawyers' are 'heresies up beauty's sleeve'. At one point the claustrophobic, intrusive piety of the pilgrims drives the poet homicidal:

This certainty in men,
This three-days too-goodness,
Too neighbourly cries
Temptation to murder
Mediocrities.

What provokes this fury of resentment is the sight of four methodical, middle-class men, who seem unruffled by the spiritual or physical stresses of the pilgrimage.

Interest in *Lough Derg* is diffused over a number of characters which, while it extends the social profile, also increases the risk of superficiality and fragmentation. In an attempt to counteract the poem's tendency towards pageantry and to introduce some 'plot' and characterisation, three pilgrims are singled out from the island congregation. Aggie Meegan, a beautiful young woman, and an anonymous monk, confess their shameful histories to Robert Fitzsimons, a young farmer with literary pretensions. Robert lusts after Aggie but when she confides her tale of 'birth, bastardy and murder' his puritanical Catholicism is affronted. Kavanagh is gesturing, somewhat perfunctorily, at the Irish Catholic bias against sexual sin which had led to Aggie's crime. In a later essay, entitled 'Sex and Christianity', he noted that 'somewhere in the 19th century' Ireland became infected with 'an anti-life heresy' disseminated throughout the society by priests trained in Maynooth.[31] In the poem Robert finally succeeds in overcoming his Jansenist brand of Christianity and being reconciled with Aggie. Since the narrator refers to 'three characters', Robert's other confidant is probably both the ex-monk, who sinned against his vow of chastity by having carnal knowledge of a young girl, and the monk who had yielded to 'the coquetry of art'. This narrative-within-a-narrative, whose farmer-pedant hero appears something of a self-portrait, further upsets the poem's already precarious balance: the three characters verge on the melodramatic instead of being representative and they engage a disproportionate amount of poetic attention. Kavanagh's lack of narrative control over these dramatis personae is signalled by the fact that he twice tries to lose them in the crowd only to have them bob up again a few paragraphs later. They resurface in the final lines of the poem as sadder and wiser pilgrims who have, somehow, extra-textually,

> found the key to the lock
> Of God's delight in disillusionment

Lough Derg splits at the seams because it tries to document too many aspects of Catholic Ireland, to accommodate 'all Ireland's Patricks':

> A shamrock in a politician's hat
> Yesterday. Today
> The sentimentality of an Urban Councillor
> Moving an address of welcome to the cardinal.

Unusually, for Kavanagh, the poem even includes a historical dimension, evidence of his expanding sympathy with the poor and downtrodden. The 'caravan' of pilgrims contains a servile farmer whose female ancestors were victims of the 'droit du Seigneur' of 'five generations of capitalist and lord'. (The anachronistic 'capitalist' points up Kavanagh's new socialist bias.)[32] Ruins of monastic cells on the island movingly recall ruined cottages, a history of evictions, famine, emigration:

So much alike is our historical
And spiritual pattern, a heap
Of stones anywhere is consecrated
By love's terrible need.

That these 'holy cells' are reminiscent of

. . . the place where Mickey Fehan lived
And the Reillys before they went to America in the
   Fifties . . .

also reveals a homesick imagination.

Despite Kavanagh's attempt to construct a national religious profile and his newspaper observation that

the majority of the pilgrims appeared to be of the business class . . . because farmers are busy at this time . . .

the imaginative bias in *Lough Derg* is predominantly rural. The fact that many rural images enter the poem as similes shows the poet assimilating new material in terms of the familiar. A pilgrim's face is 'sad as a flooded hayfield'; white houses pop up 'like mushrooms in September'; daybreak is viewed from the perspective of a poacher or a farmer whose cow is calving. A group of male pilgrims chatting recalls Sunday evening gatherings on a country road; indoors, 'holy-looking women . . . going in and out of the rooms' remind the poet of a country wake.

Prayer in *Lough Derg* is an expository device, a method of penetrating the Irish Catholic consciousness, divulging secret hopes and fears. A parody of a litany to 'Our Lady of Miraculous Succour' gently mocks at the materialist nature of an Irish mother's piety:

That my son Joseph may pass the Intermediate
We beseech thee hear us
That my daughter Eileen may do well at her music
We beseech thee hear us
That her aunt may remember us in her will
We beseech thee hear us

That there may be good weather for the hay
We beseech thee hear us
That my indigestion may be cured
We beseech thee hear us
O Mother of Perpetual Succour in temptation
Be you near us.[33]

Even today, Irish readers will recognise the unmistakably authentic tones of middle-class Catholic Ireland in this litany.

Kavanagh's most adventurous experiment in creating poetry out of the everyday experience of Irish Catholics is a series of four prayers, 'shaped like sonnets', in which humble characters articulate the intimate details of their lives and longings. A poor countryman requests that he may marry the woman he loves and so also come into possession of her farm; a country woman prays for a husband in order to escape the indignities of life in a farmhouse full of unwanted daughters; an unemployed builder's labourer asks for a job so that he can afford to rent a room and marry; an old farmer, who inevitably recalls Paddy Maguire, repents the lust that is draining his energy. These lowly sonneteers pray to figures of popular Catholic piety, St Anthony, St Anne and the Sacred Heart.

While adhering to the technical requirements of the sonnet, Kavanagh fundamentally subverts the form by substituting the 'banal beggary' of the Irish poor for the sophisticated utterance usual in English sonnet discourse. A 1942 reader would not have expected to encounter references to drains, half-boiled pots, inside shirts and a 'job in a builder's yard' within the decorous confines of a serious Shakespearian sonnet. Such flouting of traditional expectation establishes a correspondence between imaginative and material impoverishment and linguistic and emotional deprivation.

What Kavanagh communicates through these sonnets is not just a series of case histories, such as he presents in the Lough Derg section of 'Why Sorrow?', but dramatisations of a consciousness in which religious awareness permeates every-day life. Each of the suppliants confides in a religious mediator whose personal interest in his or her problems is taken for granted, who is assumed to be generally familiar with local conditions and to need reminding only of special circumstances. The sincere, trusting tones of the pilgrims prevent these sonnets from being read as comic parodies. The poet's imaginative sympathy elevates the prayers of the 'meanly poor' into sonnet form; to his even more caring God they are magnified into 'Homeric utterances'. Those aesthetic values which were paramount at the beginning of *Lough Derg* are now usurped by compassion. The poet forgets his own prickly pride in imagining the pains of others. Once again, as in *The Great Hunger*, Kavanagh emerges as the conscious champion of the poor and oppressed, though this time his sympathies also embrace the urban unemployed, who fantasise about eternal employment in a socialist heaven:

> . . . the Eternal factory where the boss
> Himself must punch the clock.

One of the most often quoted lines from *Lough Derg* encapsulates the numbing sensation of cultural severance consequent on Ireland's neutrality in the Second World War:

> All Ireland that froze for want of Europe.

Yet Kavanagh makes a poetic virtue out of de Valera's isolationist policy, defiantly flaunting the fact that he has elected to write about a remote island pilgrimage and about the common sufferings of common people in time of 'the breaking of nations';

> They must seem realer, Churchill, Stalin, Hitler,
> Than ideas in the contemplative cloister.
> The battles where ten thousand men die
> Are more significant than a peasant's emotional
>   problem,

> But wars will be merely dry bones in histories
> And these common people real living creatures in it
> On the unwritten spaces between the lines . . .

At the conclusion of his poem he deliberately juxtaposes his realist, interlinear narrative with contemporary newspaper reportage:

> All happened on Lough Derg as it is written
> In June nineteen forty two
> When the Germans were fighting outside Rostov . . .

For the remainder of his career Kavanagh was to fulminate against newsworthy definitions of the important, which exclude the normal, day-to-day lives of ordinary people. In *Lough Derg* he justifies his aesthetic choice of 'the common and banal' in biblical terms:

> Only God thinks of the dying sparrow
> In the middle of a war.

Only God and Kavanagh! The poet's concern for apparently insignificant people here arises from his Catholicism:

> A man's the centre of the world,
> A man is not (an) anonymous
> Member of the general public.
> The Communion of Saints
> Is a Communion of individuals.
> God the Father is the Father
> Of each one of us.

Kavanagh's awareness of the poem's failure is written into the text of *Lough Derg* and it is portrayed as a failure in charity, in Catholicism:

> Lough Derg overwhelmed the individual
>   imagination . . .

The Romantic analogy between the artist and God breaks down because the artist's sympathies and skills are inadequate to his creative task. Catholicism welcomes

> . . . all shapes of souls as a living theme
> In a novel refuses nothing.

The poet, by implication, is more selective and cannot cope with Lough Derg's teeming piety. 'God the poet' could construct from Kavanagh's narrative-within-a-narrative 'a reasonable document'; the human poet concedes that he has not succeeded in so doing. Realism is also threatened by cynicism and God is invoked, parenthetically, as the muse of truth:

> (O God of Truth
> Keep him who tells this story straight
> Let no cheap insincerity shape his mouth) . . .

Kavanagh's final verdict on his poem is that it is partly incapacitated by the nature of the subject and partly by personal prejudice; it is limited by 'the commonsense of a flamboyant bard'. He has found it impossible to document the spiritual in a realist mode: 'the rags of the commonplace' concealed the 'burning emotion' it was his mission to discover. The ego-rhythm of the lyric poet prevented him from rendering a fully impartial account, arriving at true vision, turning himself into a compassionate as well as an invisible God-author:

> . . . and the half untrue
> Of this story is his pride's rhythm . . .

Perhaps Kavanagh, one of his own harshest critics, was too hard on the poem. While *Lough Derg* is divided against itself and lacks the dramatic variety and the imaginative intensity and cohesiveness of *The Great Hunger*, it does succeed in embodying a peculiarly Irish Catholic ethos. A comparison of Kavanagh's poem, written in June 1942, with T. S. Eliot's more justly celebrated deployment of pilgrimage in 'Little Gidding', published in October 1942, will help to determine the positive nature of the Irish poet's achievement. It may seem inappropriate to juxtapose 'Little Gidding', whose labyrinthine spirituality is presented through a complexly

controlled and economically indirect rhetoric, with the unpublished and unrevised *Lough Derg*, where the poet in the
act of signposting a simple faith frequently loses his own
sense of direction. Moreover, the two poems are very different, not least because Eliot eschews the documentary mode
favoured by Kavanagh:

> You are not here to verify,
> Instruct yourself, or inform curiosity
> Or carry report . . .

Nevertheless, the fact that both poets write of pilgrimage in a
national and wartime context does allow some enlightening
points of comparison to emerge.

Eliot's pilgrimage is the solitary mental journey of the
rarefied spirit towards a state of being in which there is 'no
earth smell/Or smell of living things'. The pilgrim is obliged
to put off 'sense and notion'; his destination is a mystical
place that is 'England and nowhere' and a mystical time,
'Never and always'. Transcendence is arrived at through a
series of spiritual steps that involve renunciation of the
human and material. *Lough Derg* is a much more democratic
work than 'Little Gidding'; its pilgrims are ferried back and
forth by the boatful. It is a crowded poem, and the religion of
its 'prayer-locked multitude' is not remote from everyday
living: its characters speak in local accents, articulate mundane worries about jobs, marriage, a place to live, utter their
basic human fears of loneliness and poverty, indulge in
happy moments of chatter and relaxation. At the heart of
Kavanagh's poem is a vision of ordinary people participating
in a religious endurance test and a social occasion.

Unlike Eliot, Kavanagh does not seek to justify the ways of
God to men in time of war, nor is he interested in the place of
war in the divine economy. His God is an Irish God, created
in the popular image of a political fixer, a celestial county
councillor or TD, who has a ready grasp of the workings of
Irish life and wields considerable influence in the matter of
jobs and housing. *Lough Derg* also provides an early glimpse

of Kavanagh's feminine God, here soothing human distress as tenderly as a woman consoles a hysterically impotent lover.

The pilgrimage to Lough Derg is not a *via mystica* as is the route to Little Gidding but a combination of penance, prayer and religious blackmail. A useful corrective arising from the comparison of 'Little Gidding' with *Lough Derg* is that it underlines, despite critical propaganda to the contrary, just how slight is Kavanagh's emphasis on religious mysticism and how powerful his sense of Catholicism as an integral part of the Irish consciousness. In *Lough Derg* mystical vision is a miraculous and unearned gift, a surprise bonus bestowed on such an unlikely recipient as a Castleblaney grocer, and most of the six hundred-odd lines of the poem record the popular piety of dependence rather than the rarer religious gift of transcendence.

Lough Derg is a manifestation of the homogeneous religion of a country where Catholicism is a common birthright. Eliot's Little Gidding, by contrast, is an English spiritual shrine that represents an official yet elitist, Anglo-Catholic and royalist culture. Kavanagh, who is almost devoid of historical imagination, probes a contemporary reality, 'terrifyingly Today'; Eliot, the dissenter turned orthodox member of the Church of England, the returned East Coker exile, obsessed by the English Civil War, elevates a private cultural preoccupation into a national myth. Eliot's hortatory voice urges renunciation of the human; pilgrimage is for Kavanagh a means of coming to terms with his fellow countrymen. However much he may try to write as an outsider, Kavanagh is one of the pilgrims. He cannot achieve Eliot's detached, visionary clarity because he is struggling with his own tribal prejudices, trapped in a love-hate relationship, familial in its intensity. Perhaps *Lough Derg* is not a masterpiece because it is such a touchingly honest poem.

Kavanagh is a poet who writes best out of established affections and long associations, not out of instantaneous reaction to a transitory happening. Pilgrimage, which bore some superficial resemblance to parochial Catholicism, actually placed him in a strange and temporary communion of the faithful. His recognition of the utterly unexotic nature of Irish Catholicism and its inseparability from the comedy of quotidian Irish life is better evoked through his 'parish myth'. Though it was not until 1952 that Kavanagh articulated his conviction that his 'parish myth regarding literature' was contrary to 'the myth of Ireland as a spiritual entity' on which *Lough Derg* was based, he may have intuited the contradiction much earlier. This is possibly one of the reasons why he never attempted to rewrite or salvage any part of *Lough Derg*,[34] as he did in the cases of his two near contemporary, parish-based fictions, 'Why Sorrow?' and *Stony Grey Soil*.

By the close of 1942 Kavanagh was beginning to waver in his commitment to a socio-realist literary programme. 'Advent', a manifesto poem published on Christmas Eve 1942,[35] renounces the socio-analytic mode of *The Great Hunger* and *Lough Derg*. Originally entitled 'Renewal', it desiderates a reversion from poetry which offers 'a criticism of life' to poetry based on an uncritical appreciation of the wonders of the ordinary and everyday. Kavanagh's work had completely changed direction in the previous eighteen months and, after the failure of *Lough Derg*, it may have seemed that his recent excursion into judgmental, didactic realism was a misguided venture and that the way forward was the way back to that state of pre-lapsarian innocence his poetry had sometimes enjoyed 'ere Corkmen taught him to be wise'.

In 'Advent' the country Catholicism on which Kavanagh's imagination had been nurtured and the familiar domestic and outdoor scenes of his rural upbringing are intertwined to evoke, not a particular memory as in 'A Christmas Childhood', but a remembered mode of perception. Advent austerities, traditionally undertaken to make ready for Christ's coming at Christmas, here serve as a metaphoric preparation for a poetic renewal. Penitential Catholic rituals, distrusted in *Lough Derg*, are now invoked as an ascetic prelude to aesthetic

plenitude, a 'charm' to undo the evil spell of adult sophistication:

> We have tested and tasted too much, lover—
> Through a chink too wide there comes in no wonder.
> But here in this Advent-darkened room
> Where the dry black bread and the sugarless tea
> Of penance will charm back the luxury
> Of a child's soul, we'll return to Doom
> The knowledge that we stole but could not use.

The Edenic association of knowledge with doom announces a
return to Kavanagh's primitivist aesthetic. 'Wonder', 'astonishment', a 'spirit-shocking' awe at the ordinary, are now the
prerequisites of poetry. 'Advent', indeed, recalls those early
hortatory poems on the virtues of innocence, dialogues of self
and soul addressed 'To a Child', though the apostrophised
'lover' here is either an unsexed muse or an amenable alter-
ego. Fortunately, the disavowal of the analytic and the
sensuous, the 'tested and tasted', does not result in a return
to the vague abstractions so pervasive in Kavanagh's early
verse. Imagery in 'Advent' is precise and specific, from the
'dry black bread' and 'the sugarless tea' of the penitential diet
to the sights and sounds registered by the purged perception
in the second stanza.

Once its indoor rites of purification have been completed
the poem moves outdoors, reverting to 'childhood country'.
A black-slanting Ulster hill, reminiscent of Shancoduff,
whins, bog holes and cart tracks, conduct towards a second
coming, a poetic rebirth in a stable:

> And the newness that was in every stale thing
> When we looked at it as children: the
>   spirit-shocking
> Wonder in a black slanting Ulster hill
> Or the prophetic astonishment in the tedious
>   talking
> Of an old fool will awake for us and bring
> You and me to the yard gate to watch the whins

And the bog-holes, cart-tracks, old stables where
Time begins.

One of the techniques Kavanagh calls upon to indicate the restoration of a pristine and unclichéd attitude to experience is to establish a paradoxical connection between customarily opposed entities: 'penance' and 'luxury', 'newness in every stale thing', 'astonishment in the tedious', '*old* stables where *Time begins*'. Religious imagery is intrinsic to this poem, signifying a visionary as opposed to a common-sense perception of the world; it is these two kinds of perception that are opposed in its paradoxical conjunctions. Ordinary scenes and talk are now 'spirit-shocking' and 'prophetic', not subject for documentation or socio-aesthetic polemic; poetic renewal is inseparable from psychic renewal.

'Advent' is composed of two sonnets. Instead of following customary sonnet convention the first sonnet is divided into two halves, assigning equal importance both to self-abnegation and the consequent poetic renaissance. The epiphany of a visionary rebirth, the start of a fresh poetic era, is structurally as well as thematically pivotal in the poem. 'O after Christmas' launches a second sonnet, a new temporality.

What is promised for the future is a peopled poetry whose speech will not be exclusively rural. It may include the 'whispered argument of a churning' and the voices of lurching village boys, but it will not exclude the 'decent' accents of suburban gardeners. It will find human and natural images and a language:

Wherever life pours ordinary plenty.

Revitalisation of the vernacular is central to Kavanagh's new poetics, a reanimation of everyday talk resulting from a perception of the sacramentality of signs:

O after Christmas we'll have no need to go searching
For the difference that sets an old phrase burning—

Defamiliarisation will automatically result from this new visionary attentiveness to the mundane; there will be no need to interrogate or explicate, to ask

> The why of heart-breaking strangeness in dreeping
>   hedges
> Nor analyse God's breath in common statement.

'Advent' expresses a belief that poetry depends on the poet's attitude to the world. He need only bring a christened heart that watches and receives and the images and the words will be given him. Appropriately, it concludes with an unexpected organic image that relates Christ's birth with natural blossoming, a beauty emanating from winter austerity:

> And Christ comes with a January flower.

The certainty that a new poetic florescence will occur is signalled by the sudden change from future-tense to present-tense statement in this, the poem's closing line. Yet in 'Advent' the assertion of the poetic empowerment resulting from the cultivation of ingenuous spirituality is disingenuously expressed in the carefully crafted form of a double sonnet, each of whose final lines is connected by an allusion to the beginning of a new Christian dispensation.

While both *The Great Hunger* and *Lough Derg* represent a fall from the state of childlike imaginative grace espoused in 'Advent', the poem reads specifically like an early recantation of *The Great Hunger* in its rejection of 'pleasure, knowledge and the conscious hour', a trinity of values lauded in that poem. Instead of appearing as human virtues stifled or buried by clay as in *The Great Hunger*, these values are debased into 'clay-minted wages', material rather than spiritual rewards, mortal trash to be 'thrown in the dust-bin'. 'Advent' is an unflattering obituary on its recent analytic and documentary predecessors

> We have tested and tasted too much, lover . . .

and a salute to its spontaneous and incandescent successors.

Though it is not a poem about Catholicism *per se*, 'Advent' shows how Catholicism could play an imaginatively enabling role, providing not only aesthetic metaphors but transfiguring the world through theophany. It is one of a number of manifesto poems, written at different stages of his career, in which Kavanagh sets out to reorient his poetry away from documentary realism, topicality, satire or anger, and towards celebration, uncontaminated innocence, sacramental vision or transcendentalism. Such reorientation is usually accompanied as here by a return to 'childhood country'. His resolve to reform his poetics rarely succeeds and, certainly, 'Advent' does not serve as a reliable signpost pointing out the direction his writings will take for the remainder of the 1940s. Ahead lies a decade in which Kavanagh will not only continue his project of writing Catholic Ireland, but will gradually assume the role of embattled artist, vehement cultural critic and inveterate self-promoter. However, 'Advent' does represent a persistent transcendentalist aspiration in Kavanagh's poetics, an expressive goal he never quite loses sight of, even when he is most embroiled in satire and polemic.

6

Parochialism

Introduction

PATRICK Kavanagh's appropriation of parochialism as an honorific aesthetic category dates from 1952.[1] However, many of his forties' writings were parochial *avant la lettre*. The theme of the poet's relationship to his parish was, in fact, introduced, albeit negatively, in 'Inniskeen Road: July Evening' (1936). The poet of 'Inniskeen Road' was 'king and government and nation', a reluctant yet voluntary castaway from his community. Though by no means going so far as to affect a regal indifference to the doings and sayings of his neighbours, the transmission of their 'half-talk code' and 'wink-and-elbow language' formed no part of his poetic brief. By 1939 his 'mile of kingdom' was peopled. 'Christmas Eve Remembered', 'A Christmas Childhood' and 'The Long Garden' summoned up a 'poor parish' in Monaghan as an affectionately recollected, childhood context whose literary *raison d'être* was autobiographical. From as early as 'Art McCooey' (1941), though the autobiographical form was retained, parochialism had become a central, rather than an incidental theme. 'Art McCooey' dramatised an easy, unconscious bonding between poet and parish. The embryonic poet was depicted assimilating his neighbourhood as innocently and naturally ('Unlearnedly and unreasonably') as a baby in the womb nurtures itself on maternal blood. This manifesto poem was a conscious exploration of the unconscious processes of poetic gestation which postulated an affective and inevitable relationship between the adult poet and his youthful matrix: past warmth thawed the exiled writer's numbed fingers and released a poem that, in turn, reconstructed his home parish.

Kavanagh soon learned to turn his disadvantaged upbringing to advantage, to exploit the Revival's cult of the peasantry as a subversive literary strategy. He recognised early that his parochial experience was completely at odds with the dramatisations of rural Ireland presented by Ascendancy writers such as Synge. His perspective was that of the aborigine, the insider; Synge's that of the anthropologist, the visiting observer and recorder. In *The Great Hunger* Kavanagh turned Anglo–Irish literature inside out, making the hitherto almost invisible Catholic parish his centre and treating all external opinion on rural experience as peripheral, irrelevant or impertinent. While still assenting to the primacy of geographical inspiration in post-colonial Ireland, he asserted a new territoriality, that of the local place and the local community, reversing the customary assimilation of the parochial unit in a national literary generalisation. *The Great Hunger* takes its aesthetic stand on authenticity, insisting on the superior truth of the insider's understanding, estranging the outside observer from the peasant ethos, making rural Ireland inaccessible in the very process of revealing it.

On 18 September 1942, approximately five months after the publication of *The Great Hunger*, Kavanagh openly commenced hostilities against Synge for his inauthentic portrayal of the Irish peasant. Because of his near-classic status in Anglo–Irish literature as a dramatist of rural Ireland, Synge was the father figure who was to suffer most from Kavanagh's loy. His myopic misreading of this precursor as a social realist enabled Kavanagh to sharpen his own focus on parochial art. His essay, 'The Playboys of the Western World',[2] a perverse assault on the authenticity of Synge's conception of the 'playboy', shows how what Harold Bloom would characterise as a 'self-saving caricature' fostered Kavanagh's pride in his own superior knowledge of the small-farm world and pointed him towards an alternative rural narrative:

Nobody as far as I know has written about the Irish 'playboy' from the inside. Synge, who gave the idea a pseudo-classic permanence, was so fundamentally superficial that as a social document his play is worthless. We only see face values and if a man's face wears a smile we take it that he is happy.

The Irish talent for 'acting the cod' is very widespread. This talent is the child of poverty and oppression. It was of course the English conquerors that were responsible for the 'playboy'. They would not take us seriously and as a result we got a name for a certain kind of harum-scarum humour that I am glad to say we never really deserved . . .

Then follows the personal witness of the parochial writer, the insider:

I have known many 'playboys' intimately. One of them was a jolly devil-may-care fellow who sang and drank and made himself out to be the drollest fellow alive. But underneath was a bitter heart. I met him . . . in his own kitchen. To overhear that man and his wife discussing affairs of farm and state was a revelation. The talk was hard and to the point . . . Now suppose a town visitor or a writer with no inside knowledge of the country such as Synge, he would bring away a picture of a delightful character, a man who would be a grand companion in a tavern, but not a man who could be entrusted with anything like a serious job of work . . . I do not want to over-emphasise the cynical side of the 'playboy' but I cannot too strongly declare that practically all the acting of men of this description is done with a purpose. The laugh and the folly is the poor man's cloak of invisibility from his enemies and competitors. . . . My point is that there's no such thing as an authentic 'playboy'.

By emphasising the dichotomy between the viewpoint of the insider and the outsider, the visitor and the indigenous countryman, Kavanagh draws attention to an absence in Revival literature and confirms his own resolve to occupy this vacancy.

Despite his angry condemnation of the spiritual impoverishment of his parish in *The Great Hunger* Kavanagh did not lose faith in its literary adequacy. He satisfied the claims of national rhetoric and social commitment by co-opting the individual parish as a metaphor of national cultural destitution. Without denying Donaghmoyne's parochial distinctiveness he concluded his poem by converting it into a representative Irish parish, reversing the norm of Irish national discourse by articulating a suppressed local identity and joining the nation to it.

However, his conviction that Irish writing required a national signature was inimical to Kavanagh's incipient and unformulated notion of the legitimacy of a local art. Likewise, his adoption of the role of Irish social critic temporarily encouraged him to seek out exemplary fictions or locations and to undertake 'condition of Ireland' reportage and polemic. His concern with writing Catholic Ireland impelled him to embark on an imaginatively recalcitrant pilgrimage away from Inniskeen towards Lough Derg, to worship at a national shrine. By the mid-1940s he was retracing his steps, magnetically attracted back to the kindred points of heaven and home. A January 1949 poem, 'The Hero', informed his *Irish Times* readers that he had also abandoned his social preoccupations.[3] The kind of hero he now endorsed, 'was an egotist with an unsocial conscience . . . Wanting to be no one's but his own saviour'. In 'Father Mat' (1947), a poem salvaged from the abandoned 'Why Sorrow?', and in the novel, *Tarry Flynn* (1948), a reconstruction of the unpublished *Stony Grey Soil*, his theme is once again the poet's relationship to his parish. In both instances he is reimagining early discarded fictions in the light of his rediscovered, though as yet unnamed, parochial poetics. *Tarry Flynn* is 'Art McCooey' writ large.

Few and far between though they be, Kavanagh's forties' parochial writings constitute his entire parochial canon. His 1952 definition of parochialism and its desynonymisation from provincialism offer a retrospective identification and clarification of the nature of his own earlier literary originality rather than an assessment of his contemporary practice. Naming and elucidating his hitherto nameless poetics enabled him to deploy it as a concept in cultural discourse, to purvey it as an alternative to a, still prevalent, national or ethnic aesthetic. After 1952 Kavanagh concentrated on promoting parochialism as a literary ideal rather than practising it as a literary activity. Even those early fifties' lyrics which are locally based, 'Epic' and 'Innocence', are reflexive poems about the legitimacy and desirability of their own localisation rather than evocations of the parish as milieu.

The 'parochial mentality', as Kavanagh first defined it in May 1952, 'is never in any doubt about the social and artistic validity of his parish'. Such conviction as to the legitimacy of a parish-based art is contrasted with the aesthetic timidity and derivativeness which characterise the 'provincial' mentality:

> The provincial has no mind of his own; he does not trust what his eyes see until he has heard what the metropolis — towards which his eyes are turned — has to say on any subject.

Kavanagh concludes that all great civilisations are based on parochialism 'Greek, Israelite, English'.[4] Parochialism in the cultural domain, then, connotes that assured acceptance of local distinctiveness which allows civilisations to evolve independently; in the aesthetic sphere it signifies artistic integrity in the evocation of a local way of life. Parochialism is a realist art, trusting what the 'eyes see'. Authenticity of representation is the primary virtue of the parochial artist, whereas the provincial will distort or falsify his material to make it conform to the images and conventions sanctioned by a powerful cultural establishment. 'A provincial', according to Kavanagh, 'is always trying to live by other people's loves',[5] the corollary of which is that a parochial is one who is independent and courageous enough to value what an aesthetic, intellectual or commercial orthodoxy would dismiss as ugly, backward or insignificant. Parochial art cherishes a particular parish in and for itself. 'Real roots,' Kavanagh asserted, 'lie in our capacity for love and its abandon.'[6]

George Moore and James Joyce were nominated 'great Irish parishioners' because their evocation of Dublin life in *Hail and Farewell* and *Ulysses* was unaffected by the potential incomprehension of an English audience:

> They explained nothing. The public had either to come to them or stay in the dark. And the public did come. The English parochial recognizes courage in another man's parish.[7]

William Carleton was parochial because

> he recorded the lives of his own people with a fidelity that preserves for us the culture of pre-Famine Ireland[8]

but in so far as he kowtowed to the religion of the Protestant colonist he was provincial.[9]

Although he was no etymologist it would appear that Kavanagh valorised 'parochial', despite its existing pejorative aesthetic associations, instead of the more neutral aesthetic term, 'local', because it conjured up for him not merely a place but a community of people, a 'separate cultural entity'.[10] His parochial writer has a peopled imagination. The aesthetic and the social were connected in Kavanagh's first definition of parochialism and in later musings on his 'parish myth' he described it as being

> accompanied in one's consciousness by many others who are not present at all . . . As one goes on in the

country, knowing exactly who is down in the valley sowing turnips or levelling the potato drills and who is not, and what they are all thinking about.[11]

He is suggesting here a communal bonding that survives absence or exile, a definition of the parish myth that relates it to the poetic milieu of 'Art McCooey'.

The writer's parish may be urban or rural, Moore's and Joyce's Dublin, Carleton's south Tyrone countryside, his own Inniskeen. Yet Kavanagh's concept of parochialism undoubtedly originated in his rural Catholic upbringing where the parish was a homogeneous cultural and social unit, a community of people who not only lived in the same place but were bound together by a shared way of life and a shared religion. In a day's walk in any direction from his home the young poet would encounter, he tells us, the same way of life, even the same furniture, in every house he entered and the same husbandry and economy out of doors. The Catholic parish of his youth was a 'confident enclosure'.[12] Even Kavanagh's privileging of the term, parochial, is something of a parochialism since its primarily social and religious connotations for the rural Irish Catholic were at odds with the sophisticate's denigratory aesthetic application of the word. The parochial writer shares in a communal Catholic consciousness. Kavanagh's project of writing Catholic Ireland had become more narrowly concentrated on writing the local Catholic parish.

In his first definition of parochialism Kavanagh was cocking a snook at metropolitan artistic hegemony, taking advantage of Matthew Arnold's designation of 'provincial' as a pejorative term only to subvert its rationale. For Arnold the artist becomes provincial when he is too far from a 'supposed centre of correct information, correct judgment, correct taste', whereas, for Kavanagh, it is precisely such deference to an authoritative centre that turns the writer into a provincial. Ironically, distance from a metropolitan centre, far from guaranteeing the writer's parochialism, is more likely to ensure that he becomes provincial. The County Meath poet, Francis Ledwidge, for instance, whose youthful circumstances were similar to Kavanagh's own, did not write 'out of his Meathness'.[13] The disadvantage of coming from such an undereducated 'society and background' as Kavanagh himself did was that he accepted 'as the final word in painting and literature the stuff that was being produced in Dublin'.[14] The author of *The Green Fool* was still anxious that his peasantry perform the roles that Dublin or London demanded. He was still enthralled by the poetry of Padraic Colum, James Stephens, F. R. Higgins and Seumas O'Sullivan. However, instead of continuing to rest content with imitating past masters' voices, the peasant subject of the Revival began to answer back, to say otherwise, to declare his artistic independence by publishing counter-narratives of Irish country life.

In exalting the despised aesthetic category of parochialism Kavanagh did not dissociate it from those connotations of localism, unfashionableness and backwardness for which it was demeaned. Rather he transformed these very qualities into prized attributes. Parochialism privileges neglected or subservient areas of national life. The role of the parochial writer is to reveal and valorise an intimately known but artistically ignored and undervalued hinterland, to ignore literary stereotypes and express his own subculture, to turn his back on overseas or metropolitan aesthetic values and face inland:

> And you must go inland and be
> Lost in compassion's ecstasy . . .
> ('Prelude')

Inniskeen's cultural backwardness and rebarbativeness was the source of his own radical disruption of Irish literary continuity.

Parochialism was an anti-establishment, anti-canonical aesthetic. Though its affiliations were realist, it did not seek any connection with the mainstream of English literature. Neither did it, like so much other Revival and post-Revival Irish literature, seek any confluence with the dammed up mainstream of Gaelic literature. It was neither intellectually nor formally avant-garde. Its originality was dependent on the authenticity with which it rendered a local distinctiveness. Kavanagh invented his own parochial tradition, re-evaluating an undervalued writer in the case of William Carleton, re-reading recently or currently esteemed writers in the cases of George Moore and James Joyce. Carleton, Moore and Joyce, his three 'great Irish parishioners', he regarded as comic, realist and Catholic writers, who re-created the life of a local subculture. Carleton who 'had lived his whole youth . . . intimately with his people' evokes scenes 'out of deep, loving memory'.[15] *Ulysses*, Kavanagh read as a 'very funny book' and 'almost entirely a transcription of life',[16] and *Hail and Farewell*, was, for him, 'the companion of *Ulysses*' and 'in some ways a better picture of Dublin than Joyce's work'.[17] Catholicism was intrinsic to the art of these three writers. At his best Carleton was 'incapable of being anything but a Catholic';[18] 'Moore was a Catholic in all his points of view';[19] and Kavanagh's extremist Catholic aesthetic prompted the tendentious assertion that 'Almost the most outstanding quality in Joyce is his Catholicism or rather his anti-Protestantism'.[20]

Kavanagh explicitly opposed his 'parish myth regarding literature' to the Revivalist 'myth of Ireland as a spiritual entity'.[21] The Ireland he envisaged was not a homogeneous unity but a plurality of parishes, a collage of diverse regions. His realist aesthetic demanded that art have a 'local habitation'; to define Irish people 'racially in the lump'[22] was to substitute a simplified, abstract Ireland the poets had imagined for the complex, multi-cultural, living reality. The 'sole test' for the Irish writer was no longer metaphorical contact with the soil but actual attachment to a particular local community. Yeats's portrayal of Synge as a 'rooted man' was to Kavanagh a nonsense. Synge was an inauthentic country-man whose peasants were 'picturesque conventions' and their language an 'invented speech'.[23] The Ascendancy writer could not be parochial. Even if he lived all his life in the same place he was debarred by class and creed from an imaginative sympathy with or understanding of the local Catholic parishioner. Parochialism was a sectarian literary myth, a continuation of Kavanagh's Catholic challenge to the hegemony of the Protestant ascendancy in the Literary Revival. He was mounting a counter-Renaissance, a revolt of the peasants against the oppressions of misrepresentation.

Parochialism did not stop short at attempting to invalidate the Ascendancy-inspired Revival. It was a divisive aesthetic, fragmenting a national literary synthesis that had been designed to reconcile differences in religion, class, politics and language. More disruptive than its continued promotion of Catholicism as a literary orthodoxy was its perpetuation of Kavanagh's advocacy of a contemporary, realist art. Since Romantic Ireland was dead and gone, anti-Revivalist iconoclasm was part of the normal process of critical revaluation. However, Kavanagh's insistence on contemporaneity struck at a historicism that was endemic to the Irish literary establishment since the nineteenth century. Because Ireland shared a common language with the colonist, the cultural enterprise of separating Irish literature from mainstream English literature had concentrated on providing Irish writing with a distinctively Gaelic dimension by turning to Gaelic literature as a source. The Irish writer's painful sense of having inherited a 'gapped, discontinuous' tradition has been movingly articulated by Thomas Kinsella. Seeking to identify his poetic forebears he is conscious that for a hundred years before Yeats, 'there is almost total silence' and before that 'a great cultural blur'. He must exchange one language for another, his native English for eighteenth-century Irish:

Here, in all this, I recognise simultaneously a great inheritance and a great loss. The inheritance is mine, but only at two enormous removes—across a century's silence, and through an exchange of worlds.[24]

Irish poets since the nineteenth century attempted to bridge their 'gapped' tradition by translating or adapting Gaelic poetry, by adopting Gaelic poetic techniques and by treating of specifically Gaelic literary subjects, an endeavour to create a national poetics which became increasingly urgent in the years preceding Independence and in the self-consciously chauvinistic era that followed.

Kavanagh did not share the post-colonial insecurities of those fellow countrymen who were anxious to promote a separatist Irish culture. His soul did not fret in the shadow of the English language; it was revived Irish that seemed to him an 'acquired speech'. The Irish language he looked on as a quaint survival from the remote past, useful for explaining place-names but, otherwise, best left to its dying.[25] Not only was Kavanagh a monoglot, he was utterly bereft of historical consciousness. As a poet he was not haunted by Irish ancestral voices. Indeed he was most disrespectful about Gaelic poets,[26] excepting those Ulster poets who wrote of neighbouring fields and lanes and place-names, Art McCooey being a case in point.[27] He condemned the 'Irish mode', patented by Thomas MacDonagh and perpetuated by his own contemporaries, Robert Farren and Austin Clarke, because its preoccupation with resuscitating the dead art of Irish verse through translation and imitation focused attention on the craft and images of another age.[28] The whole cultural enterprise of establishing an ethnic poetics was anathema to Kavanagh. 'Irishness is a form of anti-art' is one of his most extreme and succinct pronouncements on the subject.[29]

From as early as 1942 Kavanagh was embattled with the neo-Gaels.[30] Even when he adhered to 'that formula for literature which laid all the stress on whether it was Irish or not',[31] his promotion of Catholicism as a criterion of Irishness laid the emphasis on sensibility rather than on language.

Parochialism, which legitimised ordinary, contemporary local life as literary material, was opposed both to the cult of ethnicity, which regarded Ireland 'racially, in the lump' and to the 'backward look' characteristic of such artistic separatism. From the early 1940s onwards Kavanagh insistently advocated a contemporary aesthetic:

> The idea of the writer or artist who is apart from the ordinary flood of living does not appeal to me. The true artist must be part of life as it is lived by the ordinary people — otherwise he is no more than a dilettante.
>
> (*The Irish Press*, 19 April 1943)

> Poet, musician, artist should be so excited by life that he would not dream of going elsewhere for a theme. This going back to the dead past is very common in literary circles, and it is disastrous . . .
>
> (*The Irish Press*, 15 October 1943)

The fact that his first six years as a professional writer coincided with the Second World War accentuated Kavanagh's defiant championship of 'seemingly petty events' and seemingly obscure people, the common fate and the humdrum situation, as artistic subjects:

> It is hard in the middle of a great war to think that the little doings of a simple man in some backward village may be in the long run of more importance than the names of Darlan or those others who fill the news.
>
> (*The Irish Press*, 31 December 1942)

In referring to parochialism as a parish 'myth' Kavanagh was mischievously setting it against the Yeatsian and Yeats-influenced obsession with Irish myth, and against the inherent presence of a past cultural narrative in national literary myth. Parochialism, which espouses the local, the unscholarly, the day to day, privileging lyrical opportunism above the national phantasmagoria of folklore, literary tradition and history, was germinant in Kavanagh's poetics almost from the start. His confidence in the inadequacies of everyday life as artistic subject matter challenged the once revolutionary aesthetic of the Literary and Gaelic Revivals, a nationalist revolt against the hegemony of an alien colonial culture which had since been tamed into a provincial convention. John Montague has complained that Kavanagh 'liberated' Irish poetry into ignorance.[32] Contemporary Irish poets usually find themselves compelled to choose between what Seamus Deane has described as 'a twentieth century day to day Kavanagh, and a mythological *oeuvre*-directed Yeats'.[33]

Very little of Kavanagh's own work is parochial: only a handful of lyric poems, *The Great Hunger* and *Tarry Flynn*. In the later 1940s his parochial writings were limited to adaptations of earlier unpublished work, as if rereading his previous poetry and fiction by the light of his, as yet unarticulated, new aesthetic he saw how it could be reshaped to accommodate his innovative vision. The lengthy narrative poem 'Why Sorrow?' was drastically pruned into the comparatively short and more parochial 'Father Mat', while in *Tarry Flynn*, a rewriting of *Stony Grey Soil*, he followed the example of his three Irish parishioners and made comic, realist prose his parochial mode. The remainder of the chapter is devoted to a consideration of these last two parochial works, focusing especially on *Tarry Flynn*; for it was in the more expansive medium of this affectionate, mellow novel that Kavanagh finally succeeded in re-creating his comprehensive insider's experience of day-to-day life in a small-farming neighbourhood as he had known it in the 1930s.

The Poet and the Parish

(i) From 'Why Sorrow?' to 'Father Mat'

'Why Sorrow?' is a long, sprawling, unfinished, narrative poem[34] centring on a vocational crisis in the life of its hero, Father Mat, a parish priest who is also a farmer and a poet. Father Mat is torn between his pastoral responsibility towards his devoted parishioners and the claims of his unbaptised poetic imagination. He reluctantly sacrifices poetry to priesthood and is still struggling to subdue his instinctive paganism when the poem peters out.

Two of Kavanagh's 'great Irish parishioners', George Moore and James Joyce, may have exerted a thematic influence on this crisis poem whose central conflict recalls Father Gogarty's vacillation between the antagonistic claims of priesthood and sensuality in *The Lake* (1905) and the rival attractions of priesthood and literature for Stephen Dedalus in *A Portrait of the Artist as a Young Man*. It is more likely that 'Why Sorrow?' was conceived independently of such models, for the dilemma of the poet-priest, hesitating between his pastoral and his poetic roles, is quintessentially Kavanaghish, a variation on the motif of artistic exile which recurs throughout his *oeuvre* from the concluding chapters of *The Green Fool* through the sonnet sequence, 'Temptation in Harvest', and the novel, *Tarry Flynn*, to the late essay, 'From Monaghan to the Grand Canal', and the even later '*Self-Portrait*'.

Peter Kavanagh claims that Father Mat is based on Canon Bernard Maguire,[35] parish priest of Inniskeen from 1915 to 1948. This priest was an intellectual who had been rector of the Irish College at Salamanca from 1898 to 1907 and must have suffered keenly in the culturally stunted parish of Inniskeen. He was probably the model for the rhetorically skilled parish priest of *Tarry Flynn*, in addition to lending his name to the anti-hero of *The Great Hunger*, and may, indeed, have suggested the possibility of using the persona of an elderly parish priest as a figure of rural alienation. Nevertheless, Father Mat is not so much a biographical or even dramatic character as a fictional alter-ego whose white hairs and sacerdotal garb but thinly disguise his similarity to his creator.

Though he is said to hail from Corofin, Co. Clare and to exercise his ministry in County Cavan these territorial fictions are not sustained in the poem and several of the place-names associated with Father Mat's youth and his priesthood—

Candlefort, Drumcatton, Dromore and Seola—are drawn from Inniskeen and its environs. When Kavanagh excerpted 'The Long Garden' from 'Why Sorrow?' he substituted first-person for third-person narration, thus identifying Father Mat's childhood experience with his own.

Like the solitary poet of 'Inniskeen Road: July Evening' the farmer-priest is one of the people yet also a man apart: 'So like mere earth and yet not one of us', as his parishioners express it. This difference they attribute to his priesthood, not suspecting that a more fundamental distinction between them is that Father Mat is a pagan poet. While he stands beside a cart talking about 'fairs:/The price of pigs and store-cattle' his vision is of Pegasus rather than of farm animals. Father Mat is portrayed as a role player, deceiving the parishioners who trust and revere him, and haunted by a guilty sense of fraudulence:

> I doubt
> But must not let them see
> That I am signing with a lie
> Their checks of holy constancy . . .

This continual pressure to conform to local mores and the strain of living a secret double life were problems with which Kavanagh himself had to contend, especially before he became a London-published poet. In its central debate between the pastoral and the aesthetic imperative 'Why Sorrow?' is, on one imaginative level, a dramatisation of its author's agonising indecision as to whether he should leave Inniskeen to become a professional writer. The awareness of pastoral responsibility which has been so dinned into Father Mat's consciousness that it expresses itself with insistent repetitiveness—

> But his people needed him,
> His people needed him,
> His people needed him . . .

—may well be a metaphor for Kavanagh's own sense of familial responsibility and also for that emotional attachment which bound him to his native place. By electing to remain in his parish rather than pursue his poetic calling the priest loses his imaginative vision and is reduced to the same level of realist perception as his parishioners:

> Now he was with his people, one of them.
> What they saw he saw too
> And nothing more; what they looked at
> And what to them was true was true
> For him. He was in the crowd
> A nobody who had been proud.

Father Mat's fate is probably an enactment of his creator's own fear that his literary gift would have been stifled had he not escaped from Inniskeen.

Unlike *The Great Hunger* and *Lough Derg*, where the commentator maintains a moral and judgmental distance from his characters despite his privileged access to their consciousness, 'Why Sorrow?' has recourse to free indirect style which allows the narrator to empathise uncritically with his hero. Through the fictional medium of 'Why Sorrow' Kavanagh was freed from the autobiographical inhibitions attendant on first-person lyricism. His choice of a priest-farmer-poet persona enabled him to express something of the ambivalence and complexity of his attitude towards his own people: love, understanding and compassion, seriously qualified by an awareness of educational superiority and imaginative difference. The Dromore people's hero-worship of their priest is possibly a misfit poet's fantasy of being honoured as a prophet in his own country.

Though the excerpt entitled 'The Long Garden' was published in December 1941, 'Why Sorrow?' was probably written earlier. A preoccupation with pagan aestheticism rather than social concerns suggests that it pre-dates *The Great Hunger*. For the same reason the Lough Derg sequence with which it concludes is more likely to have been based on

Kavanagh's first trip to Lough Derg in 1940 than on his second in 1942. The imaginatively frustrated, old, celibate farmer-poet, Father Mat, is the antithesis of the sexually frustrated, inarticulate old bachelor farmer, and the composition of 'Why Sorrow?' may have been the rite of self-exorcism which allowed Kavanagh to grant dramatic autonomy to Patrick Maguire. 'Why Sorrow?' probably marks the poet's transition from the short lyric with regular stanzas to the long narrative poem in which he experiments with a collage of poetic forms, blank verse paragraphs, free verse, irregularly and regularly rhymed sequences. It appears to anticipate the more accomplished technical virtuosity displayed in *The Great Hunger*. Since Kavanagh's development was somewhat erratic, *Lough Derg*, for instance being a considerably less impressive long poem than *The Great Hunger*, the strongest argument for an early dating remains thematic.

'Why Sorrow?' appears to pre-date both 'Art McCooey' and *The Great Hunger* because it denies the legitimacy of the local as poetic material. The fundamental issue in this poem is not a conflict between exile and rootedness or between pagan aestheticism and Christian philistinism. Its real theme is that poetry is divorced from the humdrum drama of ordinary everyday village life, that it is a solitary, isolated art, deriving from a singular love of natural beauty, and cannot accommodate the local community. Poetry is completely at odds with the Irish country poet's indigenous culture, with the small-farm milieu, with rural Catholicism. The poetics that informs 'Why Sorrow?' is not only unparochial but anti-parochial. Its anti-parochialism is all the more remarkable because, apart from the Lough Derg sequence, this is a parish-based poem whose priestly hero considers his neighbours primarily as parishioners.

In 'Why Sorrow?' poetry is a pagan art whose God is Apollo, whereas Catholicism abhors aestheticism, cultivates 'Sorrow', and its God is the crucified Christ. This opposition between poetry and Catholicism is introduced in the opening lines:

> It was the month of May. Father Mat walked among
> His cows that evening dreaming of a song
> That Christ had closed the window on.
>   Now the priest's pride
> Was a Roman poet hearing of the Crucified.
> Apollo's unbaptized pagan who can show
> To simple eyes what Christians never know . . .

The Great Hunger distinguishes between the penurious per-
versions of peasant religion and the creative plenitude and
generous vitality of Catholicism. It salutes Christ as the
incarnate *Logos*, a manifestation of the indivisibility of humanity, divinity and poetry. 'Why Sorrow?', on the contrary,
establishes a sharp dichotomy between the natural, the
libidinal, the poetic, and the repressive and religious. Its
Christ has condemned natural fertility by transforming a tree
into a cross and denied human carnality by his crucifixion:

> No earth-love was transfigured on that Hill
> All flattened out most prostrate, muddy-mouthed.

Mud, a recurring reductive image in this poem, corresponds
to the use of 'clay' in *The Great Hunger*, though it lacks the
symbolic resonance attaching to 'clay'. While the farmers of
The Great Hunger demean and desecrate a world that is
charged with the grandeur of God, the Christ of 'Why
Sorrow?' is associated with muddy abasement.

Delight in natural beauty and in bodily pleasure are clas-
sified as sinful by the Church which Father Mat serves. One
of his priestly duties is to administer the sacrament of
penance, to sit in the confession box listening 'with bowed
head':

> As the earth came in to be burned, every stalk
> That grew green in the heart to be uprooted,
> Every memory that surprised with an unChristly
>   pleasure

> The clod growing a daisy, the oily black stones in
>   the river
> Put away for ever.

In his role of confessor Father Mat instructs the faithful that

> All poetry in nature or in book
> Must be outcast this night . . .

Catholicism is here represented as both unnatural and philistine, an instance of an over-identification between narrator and character which results in a lack of dramatic realism, since the people of Dromore are unlikely to be afflicted with an undue attachment to poetry in any form. The most prominent sacrament in this poem is penance which is portrayed, not as a testimony to divine mercy, but as an instrument of unnatural repression. Likewise, it is the purgatorial-cum-philistine dimension of Lough Derg that is emphasised. On St Patrick's Purgatory

> . . . every leaf that is green is changed to fire
> And everything that makes art and literature
> Is a thing to be abhorred — impure desire.

Far from revealing the *Logos*, what Christianity offers in 'Why Sorrow?' is a late ascetic scripture superinscribed on an earlier, joyful secular testament:

> But the Gospel was printed over an older writing . . .

In vain does the priest-poet hope to

> . . . find in Charity's
> Illiterate book of pieties
> Apollo's writing in a Christian hand.

Poetry and Catholicism are irreconcilably opposed. When the priest, who prefers a coltsfoot blossom to the sacrament, renounces his paganism he sacrifices his visionary imagination. Once he is reconciled with the Church he is condemned to ordinary perception and sees

No hills beyond new-green; no raw flesh bleeding
No light astonishing as a knife drawn
In Shercock cattle-fair at dawn . . .

As a true disciple of the crucified Christ, Father Mat also surrenders his gift of joy:

Everywhere he went now grief was come or arriving . . .

Carnal pleasure is represented in 'Why Sorrow?' by 'Casey's house', an Irish village bower of bliss, framed in luxuriant summer flowers, inhabited by generations of fallen women, resounding with a laughter that modulates into the Romantic song of larks and nightingales. When he has repented of his paganism Father Mat becomes a killjoy and turns the bower of bliss into a squalid house of shame. Yet poetry, according to this poem, is incompatible with the Christian ideal of female virginity: its muse is the violated Venus:

As Father Mat walked home
Venus was in the Western sky
And through her broken maidenhead
He saw the womb of poetry . . .

Since the conflict between art and religion in 'Why Sorrow?' is so redolent of late nineteenth-century aestheticism it is appropriately anachronistic that the poem's antichrist, the priest's pagan tempter, should be a conflation of two favourite Romantic tropes, the diabolic rebel and the 'dancer'. This Salome figure's incongruity in a Cavan/Monaghan setting epitomises the perversity of the aesthetic which 'Why Sorrow?' strives to uphold. Father Mat's reconversion to Catholicism is treated as a regrettable capitulation to the pressures of pastoralism. As a pagan poet he felt 'unhomed'. It would appear that Kavanagh did not consciously recognise the imaginatively deleterious effects of such homelessness, so the plot of 'Why Sorrow?' equates homecoming with imaginative failure. It is not surprising that he found it impossible to finish this poem, for the rootless, non-indigenous aesthetic it endorses is completely at odds with the very real poetic strengths of the parochial imagination it attempts to quash.

What Kavanagh had created in the persona of Father Mat was, in fact, an incarnation of the parochialism he set out to reject in the poem, an embodiment of the Catholic, small-farm ethos. The priest is a kind of *genius loci*:

> He was a part of the place, as natural as
> The stones in grazing fields that are not seen
> By those who walk the ridges . . .

Catholicism and farming blend easily in his person. So his face, gait and conversation are those of a farmer — 'soft eyes', 'slow flat tread', talk of 'things growing and growthy' — but he is equally well adapted to the role of priest, his 'thick tongue' fitted for 'bargaining fair/Or for prayer'. The intimate relationship between Catholicism and the small farm is manifest in Father Mat's biography. Thrifty and ambitious parents had fashioned his priesthood out of the 'sour soil' of 'their six fields':

> In steely grass and green rushes
> Was woven the vestments of a priest . . .

Priesthood is here a type of farm produce. Moreover, the rural Catholic bias of Father Mat's imagination betrays itself in his choice of metaphor:

> He saw the daisies now and the white
> Confirmation dresses of the alder trees . . .

or

> The dripping branches on the carts going home
> Is a holy-water blessing this hour . . .

His youthful image of the Virgin Mary is a synthesis of his images of village girls, their laughter on the stiles in July, their cries of encouragement, their nimble-footed athleticism. The priest's parochial imagination is perhaps most obvious in his insider's knowledge of the 'homes and hearts' of his parishioners. On a 'sick call' to a local house he sees beyond what would be visible to any casual visitor to the secret squalor concealed behind closed doors or under beds:

> Within the house he knew every rag and stick
> The mean unmade bed behind the kitchen
> The sights they hurried to hide when he came in.
> His soft eyes pierced
> Into the secret rooms of their homes and hearts
> Where everything was topsy-turvy; an unwashed
>   shirt
> Kicked under the bed, and the chamber-pot
> That the woman forgot to empty,
> A stolen pitch-fork standing in a corner . . .

This is the kind of inside information that Kavanagh would soon pit against Revivalist misrepresentations of the realities of country life, and, in particular, against Synge's portrayal of the peasantry. Here, where rural realism is devalued, it enters the poem as part of the mean, ugly, impoverished small-farm milieu that the aspiring poet spurns. Kavanagh is re-creating the world he knows only to disown it as unworthy of poetic attention. Father Mat makes his way up 'that long lane in a pocket of the hills' to discharge the duties of the priestly ministry that is frustrating his poetry. In its attempted rejection of his Inniskeen background, 'Why Sorrow?' recalls 'Stony Grey Soil'. It is as if Kavanagh is anxious to dissociate himself from, to flaunt his superiority to, his country Catholic origins. He is writing against the grain of his genius at this point, refusing the parochial sympathies which his choice of pastoral persona compel, willing a pagan tragedy into a Catholic setting. When the poem peters out during Father Mat's pilgrimage to Lough Derg, its narrator still begrudges his hero's inevitable surrender to Catholicism and pastoralism.

Paganism in 'Why Sorrow?' is largely a sign of difference, a metaphorical transfiguration intended to signify the extra-ordinariness of ordinary phenomena by singling them out from their Catholic cutural context, saving them for poetry. In the passage excerpted as 'The Long Garden', the myth of the Hesperides is invoked to describe the imaginative riches of a country childhood instead of the Edenic myth used in 'A Christmas Childhood'. Trivial, commonplace, country happenings,

> The rattle of buckets, rolling of barrels under
> Downspouts, the leading-in of foals

are introduced as 'happenings dipped deep in pagan wonder', whereas in such poems as 'A Christmas Childhood' and 'Advent' wonder is christened.

By the mid-1940s Kavanagh recognised that the unfinished, unpublished 'Why Sorrow?' was a parochial poem *manqué*, that its strident paganism and devaluing of the comedy of country Catholicism had been misguided. Despite his efforts to control the poem by focusing on a single dramatic consciousness and a single crisis of conscience, his narrative plot had been almost overwhelmed by the deluge of familiar country images which came flooding in, an imaginative torrent partly released by exile and partly by the removal of certain inhibitions due to the use of a persona. He now set about revising 'Why Sorrow?' so as to achieve a more balanced tension between its pagan and its parochial dimensions.

Pages 11 to 14 are missing from the 27-page typescript of 'Why Sorrow?'. These were the pages which formed the basis of much of the new poem. Kavanagh tore out the heart of 'Why Sorrow?' to create 'Father Mat'. Where the original poem was sprawling and diffuse, the revised version is tautly structured in five parts. An abbreviation of the narrative time span from the priest's lifetime to an evening in his life makes for greater economy and concentration. Father Mat now walks into the poem on his way to the chapel to hear Saturday evening confessions and walks out of it at the end on his way home. The long flashbacks to his childhood and adolescence are omitted. The insistent anti-Catholicism

which dominated 'Why Sorrow?' is considerably more sub-
dued and the priest's parish milieu plays a more conspicuous
part.

Kavanagh's parochial poetics, while still lacking a name,
was almost fully evolved and he was consciously setting out
to convey something of the texture of Irish rural Catholicism.
In a 1945 article, entitled 'Sunday in the Country', he wrote:

> . . . to attempt to show the religious life of a people as
> something apart from the ordinary business of living is a
> false approach.[36]

and by way of illustrating how these two should be combined
in poetry he quoted the first twelve lines of 'Father Mat':

In a meadow
Beside the chapel three boys were playing football.
At the forge door an old man was leaning
Viewing a hunter-hoe. A man could hear
If he listened to the breeze the fall of wings—
How wistfully the sin-birds come home!

It was Confession Saturday, the first
Saturday in May; the May Devotions
Were spread like leaves to quieten
The excited armies of conscience.
The knife of penance fell so like a blade
Of grass that no one was afraid

Just what a reorientation in Kavanagh's approach to rural
material has occurred may be appreciated when we encounter lines from the revised 'Why Sorrow?' quoted as exemplary
Catholic verse.

The integration of the religious and the rural is revealed in
these opening lines through the juxtaposition of meadow,
football field and chapel: farming, Catholicism and sport
are being casually connected. In the second stanza popular
piety, the May devotions and the Catholic sacrament of
penance, are related to a country context through simile. This

figurative technique is later used to similar purpose when
Father Mat's priestly voice absolving his penitents is compared to 'a briar in the breeze'. Father Mat's role as farmer-
priest is also exploited in this poem to show the blending of
theological and agricultural concerns in the Catholic countryman's consciousness:

> 'They confess to the fields', he mused,
> 'They confess to the fields and the air and the sky',
> And forgiveness was the soft grass of his meadow
>   by the river;
> His thoughts were walking through it now . . .

Penance is the poem's sacramental centre and the natural is
sometimes related to the sinful through fantastic association
as in the hyphenated 'sin-birds' of the opening passage,
whose coming home to roost corresponds with the penitents'
arrival at the confessional. A similar fantastic association between natural and human sinfulness is introduced later:

> The trees
> Heard nothing stanger than the rain or the wind
> Or the birds—
> But deep in their roots they knew a seed had
> sinned . . .

In 1946 Kavanagh published a 38-line extract from 'Father
Mat' and this, like the twelve lines he had published the
previous year, is a parochial sequence which omits the titular
hero entirely. It begins with an image of the easy intercourse
between chapel and country life:

> Through the open door the hum of rosaries
> Came out and blended with the homing bees . . .[37]

The open chapel door is an image designed to remove any
barrier between the religious and the rural, while a further
interchange is effected by the transposition of 'hum' from
'bees' to 'rosaries', as well as by the near-echo of 'hum' in
'homing'. The extract, which concludes at the end of part III

of the finished poem (lines 58–95), is chapel-centred and focuses on the part played by Catholicism in parish life, alternating between religious and mundane images without any sense of hiatus.

Kavanagh is not solemn about his parochialism, but fully alert to the religio-human comedy. An intimate knowledge of farm life is summarily displayed in the sketch of the last-minute scramble to be in time for May devotions:

> Cows were milked earlier,
> The supper hurried,
> Hens shut in,
> Horses unyoked,
> And three men shaving before the same mirror.

The clipped lines capture the flurry and excitement that chapel-going brings into farm routine and the image of the shared shaving mirror contributes a humorously authentic touch. Late arrival in the chapel is turned into a miniature comedy: the embarrassment over-loud footsteps cause the latecomer is accentuated by assonance and Kavanagh playfully notes the congregation's unholy curiosity as to his identity:

> The trip of iron tips on tile
> Hesitated up the middle aisle,
> Heads that were bowed glanced up to see
> Who could this last arrival be . . .

The contradictory requests of two lovers to the Virgin Mary add a spice of comic irony to the May devotions:

> A secret lover is saying
> Three Hail Marys that she who knows
> The ways of women will bring
> Cathleen O'Hara (he names her) home to him.
> Ironic fate! Cathleen herself is saying
> Three Hail Marys to her who knows
> The ways of men to bring

Somebody else home to her—
'O may he love me.'
What is the Virgin Mary now to do?

The low key comic drama of Cathleen O'Hara rather than the passionate melodrama of Scarlett O'Hara—such is the stuff of parochialism.

The parish includes not only the living community but their dead who lie buried in the graveyard adjoining the chapel, a communion of the faithful poetically re-created through the verbal association of 'murmur' and 'memory':

Murmur of women's voices from the porch,
Memories of relations in the graveyard . . .

Earlier this same graveyard had served as a comic setting which again illustrated the casual mingling of the secular and the sacred, being a place where a goat nibbles a yew or chickens stray. On Kavanagh's Breughelesque village canvas even chickens are minor comic characters, depicted straggling home with 'anxious looks'; that they are the cobbler's chickens is his little in-joke.

Tension between parochialism and paganism, a plot retained from 'Why Sorrow?', centres as before on the person of Father Mat, though here he no longer enjoys his previous narrative ascendancy and the poem's attitude to paganism is altogether more ambivalent. The old priest enters the poem savouring the 'unbaptised beauty' of the countryside, 'the smell from ditches that were not Christian', yet once again he is an embodiment of his small-farm setting:

He was a part of the place,
Natural as a round stone in a grass field . . .

His wonder at ordinary sights, a flower opening, a stick carried down a stream, the 'undying difference in the corner of a field' is contrasted with his curate's competent, complacent Catholicism, rather than serving as an index of a pagan love of nature. When in the confessional he consigns his farm and its stock to the fires of purgatory it is a gesture to 'cool his mind' and no longer an embittered act of denial as in 'Why Sorrow?'. The tempter, who is once again a conflation of devil and dancer, is deployed as a narrative device to externalise the poem's pagan dimension, instead of internalising it in the priest's consciousness. As in 'Why Sorrow?' this tempter is equated with the Satan who tempted Christ during his forty days in the desert, but the condemnatory connotations of such an explicit biblical allusion are stronger here because of the absence of an anti-Catholic context. Moreover, the devil's offer of

> .'. . all that's music, poetry, art
> In things you can touch every day.

appears redundant in the parochial context of 'Father Mat' where such an aesthetic has already been attained under a Christian dispensation. Because 'Father Mat', unlike its predecessor, is not the vehicle for a vehemently anti-Christian polemic, it ends with a neatly balanced choice between

> The domestic Virgin and Her Child
> Or Venus with her ecstasy.

Such a stark choice had been refused a few stanzas previously:

> Why should poet in the twilight choose?

Despite the poem's apparent inconclusiveness it is imaginatively weighted away from paganism and towards the domestic alternative, an everyday religion for everybody.

'Father Mat' is an unsatisfactory poem, lacking a narrative *raison d'être*. It is hampered by its thematic dependence on 'Why Sorrow?', since the retention of parts of the original plot, while dispensing with the vocational crisis in the priest's life, deprives the narrative of point and purpose. It also fails to incorporate many parochial passages from the original poem. In a discarded draft Kavanagh had experimented with reconciling the secular and the sacred dimensions of small-farm life through the priest's visionary imagination:

> Into the moment that was gathered around him—
> A great world—Christ on His Cross
> And after Saint Peter as Pope
> The Martyrs, Saints, Crusaders all came
> Fitting easily in,
> Did not disturb the buttercups
> Or the woman who was kneading dough
> Or the man who was mending the gate, or his son
> Or the cat in the ruins of the straw . . .
>
> Christ was born in a stable here
> And Christendom spread
> Through this moment that filled a townland.
> And was spreading wider and wider over hedges,
>   over hills.

A discarded version of the conclusion is also unambiguously Catholic where the final text is ambivalent:

> In the Western sky
> The Star of the Sea,
> Mercy where merciless Venus had ruled
> Guide of the wanderer pray for me.

Venus is here ousted by the Virgin Mary and two phrases from one of the most popular Catholic hymns, and one of Kavanagh's own favourites, 'Hail Queen of Heaven', are interwoven with the poet's phrases to arrive at a poetry that obviously emanates from a Catholic consciousness. These rejected versions show Kavanagh groping his way from the original 'Why Sorrow?' towards a parochial poetry. Unfortunately, 'Father Mat', though it is a chapel-centred work which reveals an affectionate appreciation of the comedy of country Catholicism, still retains too many traces of its pagan genesis to be a fully achieved parochial poem.

The Poet and the Parish

(ii) Tarry Flynn

Tarry Flynn (1948), a portrait of the artist as a young farmer, is Kavanagh's affectionate, comic evocation of day-to-day life in an Irish country household and parish as he had known it in the 1930s. It is his most sustained achievement in the parochial mode, the culmination of years of piecemeal creation of his parish myth. The Inniskeen glimpsed in 'Christmas Eve Remembered', 'A Christmas Childhood', 'Art McCooey', *The Great Hunger*, 'Why Sorrow?' and 'Father Mat' is now fully revealed in all its ordinary sordidness and humour, even though it is here fictionally disguised as Dargan and situated in Co. Cavan. Prolonged absence and an emotional distancing from the instinctual life of his people had clarified Kavanagh's vision of a once familiar world, enabling him to realise its quotidian comedy without sentimentality or rancour. It was for its parochialism that he commended *Tarry Flynn* in later years, claiming that it was a true expression of the small-farming society of south Monaghan and 'not only the best but the only *authentic* account of life as it was lived in Ireland this century'.[38]

Tarry Flynn had a slow gestation. It is an extensively revised version, really a rewriting of *Stony Grey Soil*, the novel based on the Inniskeen dance-hall case, already referred to in chapter 3. Sympathetically reviewed by Frank O'Connor as a product of the new post-Independence realist school of Irish writing while still in manuscript, it was, nevertheless, rejected out of hand by Methuen in 1942.[39] Kavanagh reworked the novel throughout the 1940s, at first retaining the dance-hall plot and refusing to allow his literary hero to escape from his life as a subsistence farmer.[40] According to his biographer the novel went through ten drafts.[41] The principal reason why Kavanagh persisted with the ur-*Tarry Flynn* was because it was a fictionalisation of the small-farm world he knew so intimately and had close imaginative associations with such lyrics as 'Spraying the Potatoes' and 'Art McCooey', both of which are quoted from in early forties' drafts.[42] Indeed some of the names in the quoted version of 'Art McCooey' are the same as those of the characters in the novel:

> A hare is grazing in Callan's meadow,
> Minnie Dillon is prowling for dead branches.

In one of these drafts the hero, Martin Flynn, gives vent to an angry outburst which momentarily relates him to the narrator of *The Great Hunger*:

> Mothers have too much authority in the country. Women, the priests and the fields are the ruin of men. They make us blinkered horses in a plough . . . so that we never look up to watch the light on the hills.[43]

Excerpts from the ur-*Tarry Flynn* were published as 'Three Glimpses of Life' in *The Bell* in July 1944. These 'Three Glimpses' are three realist epiphanies of life in rural Ireland, observed by Tarry and his friend Eusebius 'as they went a threequarter mile journey to Cavan in the year nineteen hundred and thirty five'. Two were retained in a revised form in the published novel: a dramatisation of the family row that ensues when grown-up sons who work the family farm ask their father for pocket money on a Saturday night, and a view of a country cottage of ill fame. Though these 'glimpses' are comic their dark October evening setting connects them with the world of *The Great Hunger*, whereas *Tarry Flynn* is a summer novel. In June 1946 Kavanagh published a short story, 'One Summer Evening in the Month of June',[44] which is an off-cut from his unpublished novel. It concerns an amorous encounter between its country hero, Tarry K., and a young neighbour woman named May. Tarry, an absent-minded dreamer, is dominated by a fond but 'morale-sabotaging' mother, who knew without rising from her chair in the kitchen every movement of his body. That was because she had followed every move of his mind with an intense love since he was a baby.

The triangular relationship described here is very similar to the relationships portrayed in *Tarry Flynn* and Tarry's identification with his author is obviously hinted at in his abbreviated surname.

By 1947 Kavanagh was making a 'new novel' from his previous drafts and had completed it by September.[45] This time he filleted the dance-hall plot out of the narrative, dismissing it as a 'big lie', even though it was based on fact.[46] To the parochial writer it was a 'lie' in that it was an extraordinary and atypical event whereas he now wanted to dispense with plot and focus instead on 'telling what the people did in a peasant community'. His 'new novel', *Tarry Flynn*, 'a remarkable improvement on the foolish original', in its author's estimation,[47] is a plotless autobiographical fiction, describing Tarry Flynn's last months as a farmer-poet and concluding with his departure from the parish of Dargan in the summer of 1935. The only surviving remnant of the original dance-hall plot is a comic sequence on a concert-cum-dance in the village hall. Part of this new novel was serialised in *The Bell* as four 'picturisations' between May and September 1947[48] and it was published by the Pilot Press, London, in October 1948 and by the Devin-Adair Company, New York in 1949. Like many Irish novels of the 1930s and 1940s *Tarry Flynn* attained the notoriety of being banned in Ireland and its author was quite pleased by the attendant publicity.[49] In this case the Appeal Board lifted the ban after a few weeks.[50]

Tarry Flynn reworks the same ground as *The Green Fool*. A comic, autobiographical fiction as opposed to a comic, fictional autobiography, it, like *The Green Fool*, combines a portrait of the artist with a portrait of a region. However, *Tarry Flynn* is a more aesthetically coherent work than its early predecessor.

Whereas *The Green Fool* was composed of a series of disparate incidents with the narrator's role alternating between that of recorder and character, the poet-farmer of *Tarry Flynn* is the hero of a novel in the realist mode whose rural neighbourhood is his dramatic context. In *The Green Fool* a gallimaufry of colourful characters was summoned to entertain the reader with their 'quaint and bizarre' eccentricities. Now Kavanagh is intent on countering the baneful, provincial influence of stage-Irish and Literary Revival conventions and revealing 'real elementalism' as he himself had actually experienced it, a 'tawdry thing, resentful, mean and ungenerous'.[51] The family as a social unit had been largely ignored in *The Green Fool* and, despite its extended cast of characters, Kavanagh succeeded in conveying very little sense of community either. Characters were introduced to perform an amusing or instructive role and then despatched. In *Tarry Flynn*, on the contrary, where the same characters recur throughout, Tarry is involved in an intricate network of relationships with his mother and sisters and with the local community. Home truths and neighbourhood scandals intrude on his poetic dreams and rhapsodies. *Tarry Flynn* is also more concentrated in its time span than *The Green Fool*, a slow-paced, detailed evocation of Tarry's last few months on the farm rather than a biographical survey of thirty-odd years of a poet's life. It is, too, much more localised with Tarry making only one paragraph-long trip to a nearby town whereas the Green Fool indulged in chapter-long junkets to Dublin, the west of Ireland and London, in addition to numerous jaunts to places nearer home. The poet's departure from his parish, with which *Tarry Flynn* concludes, is all the more decisively climactic because of the novel's introverted rooted ness.

'To achieve the illusion of life is the most difficult thing of all', Kavanagh once remarked.[52] *Tarry Flynn* bases its claim to originality on authenticity of representation. As a realist writer Kavanagh believed that 'It is only in normality that you can have originality'.[53] His fictional strategy in *Tarry Flynn* is parochial, re-creating the comedy of day-to-day life in a small-farming community, the family squabbles and neighbourly tensions, the routine of farming and housekeeping chores, the small embarrassments, trivial triumphs, petty disasters, minor satisfactions, occasional happinesses, that characterise ordinary country experience. The narrative is mediated for the most part through the consciousness of the hero and its object is to present an insider's view of the claustrophobic world of family and parish in a rural backwater, where privacy is almost unattainable because the only spice life has to offer anyone is to spy on, gossip about, thwart and intrigue against others. Throughout the eight chapters the documentation of context and the interrelationships characteristic of the realist novel are deployed to display the inner workings of a closed rural society, to capture the small-farm ethos as Kavanagh had known it, the 'barbaric life of the Irish country poor'.[54] *Tarry Flynn* is a rather episodic and discontinuous novel, characterised by abrupt transitions between paragraphs. Kavanagh's model was Carleton's *Traits and Stories of the Irish Peasantry* and he was less interested in constructing a fluid narrative than in stringing together scenes and episodes that re-create a way of life.

This concern to expose the intimacies of small-farm life is evident from the outset of the novel which opens with a domestic morning scene, a glimpse of the country household as visitors never see it, the mother just out of bed and still barefoot, her daughter yawning and emptying the slops bucket, a hint of frowsty bedrooms aft. The kitchen setting is not described but is instead evoked through casual reference to a dresser, table and fan bellows, a hen and chickens pecking at crumbs on the floor, a man's cap lying among the newspapers on a window sill. Kavanagh is particularly good at catching the tensions of family life, with its niggling quarrels, point scoring, temporary truces and shifting alliances between mother, brother and sisters. In the first scene Tarry irritates his mother by dawdling about the kitchen instead of setting off for mass and the ensuing family friction, like the tiff in Carleton's 'Ned McKeown' which Kavanagh so much admired, captures the ambience of the Irish Catholic farmhouse.[55]

The Flynns are displayed both as a small-farming family and a part of a larger parish community through the device of opening the novel on the feast of Corpus Christi, a Catholic holiday of obligation which coincides with an important fairday in the neighbouring town, thereby compelling the faithful to satisfy the claims of both God and Mammon. The people of Dargan are first encountered on their way to mass or in the local chapel and the reader soon finds himself on first name terms with this crafty, opportunistic, inquisitive and acquisitive community where everybody knows everybody else's business and all are dedicated to besting or, at least, discomfiting their neighbours. In the chapel the social structure of the Catholic parish is revealed: the respectable people, the police, the stationmaster, the schoolteachers, the miller and the publican look down on the small farmers and jobbers like Tarry, his friend Eusebius Cassidy, and Charlie Trainor, a calf dealer. However, ultimate power and authority are vested in Fr Daly, the parish priest, who rules his community from the pulpit with sermons 'fit to scald the hair off a cannon-ball':[56]

> Rapscallions of hell, curmudgeons of the devil that are less civilised than the natives on the banks of the Congo. Like a lot of pigs that you were after throwing cayenne pepper among . . .

Such a performance delights his listeners, who, starved of melodrama and excitement in the drudgery of daily life, receive the sermon with 'a grain of humorous salt and peasant doubt', well able to distinguish between ecclesiastic rhetoric and prosaic reality. Once outside the chapel the priest's abusive sermon is forgotten under pressure from more urgent topics, such as 'the crops and the fair and their neighbours'.

The practice of Catholicism is a mark of conformity and normality in the country parish. Only those beyond the pale of respectability, bankrupt farmers like the Carlins or prostitutes like the Dillon women, dare to miss mass. The parish priest and his curate are regarded as authorities whom it is safest to placate because their assistance may be useful in a neighbourhood dispute and because they are quite capable of revenging themselves by doing 'a bad turn', if crossed. This attitude is typified by Tarry's mother who is afraid that his derogatory remarks about religion will come to the priests' notice:

> Not that she loved the priests—like a true mother she'd cut the Pope's throat for the sake of her son—but she felt the power of the priests and she didn't want to have their ill-will.

Tarry considers himself the priests' intellectual equal or superior, yet such is the supremacy of the clergy in his parochial world that he secretly longs for their admiration or approbation. He aspires to the honour of holding the collection box, fantasises about participating in the concert they have organised, would even be content, when all else fails, with the menial task of carrying buckets of water to make tea for the concert goers. To the clergy 'a little learning is a dangerous thing' in a peasant, to be discouraged or suppressed. This quotation the parish priest attributes to Shakespeare, much to Tarry's concealed amusement, but he is, nevertheless, invariably wrongfooted in all his dealings with priests, and disparaged as a village idiot. A visiting missioner patronisingly advises him to confine his reading to the *Messenger of the Sacred Heart*, a popular devotional journal which, *faute de mieux*, the print-hungry young poet already devours. These embarrassing encounters with the clergy contribute to the humour of *Tarry Flynn*. An early suggestion of an antagonism between the priests' God and the 'god of Poetry', reminiscent of 'Why Sorrow?', is not developed.

Throughout *Tarry Flynn* Kavanagh emphasises the integration of faith and farming in the pervasively Catholic but utterly unchristian parish of Dargan, where hating rather than loving one's neighbour is a fundamental tenet of small-farm religion. Emulating Carleton who had illustrated how 'the same breath that utters a Hail Mary suffices to shoo the chickens off the floor or the cat from the jug of cream',[57] he delights in showing how family prayer is interrupted by domestic cares:

> Holy Mary, Mother of God, pray for us . . . cat, down out of that and don't be trying to lift the lid of that can . . . sinners now and at the hour of our . . . Tarry, come down out of that . . . death, Amen.

or

> Thou O Lord wilt open my lips
> And my tongue shall announce Thy praise.
> 'Did you put in your bike, Mary?'

Religious allusions are part of the currency of common speech:

> 'I wonder what the devil's father them people wanted to know about the hen.'

> 'Hell won't be full till you're in it.'

> 'What in the Name of Father, Son and Holy Ghost had you to do with this Molly one?'

Tarry's sister, Mary, taunting her suitor about his elderliness, says

> Go home and buy yourself a blessed candle . . . it's the Last Sacraments you ought to be thinking of . . .

Tarry Flynn comes closest to the bleak vision of *The Great Hunger* in its opening chapters where the parishioners of Dargan, assembled in the village chapel at mass and mission, are portrayed as a congregation of the aged and sexually frustrated:

The parish was comprised of old unmarried men and women. From a mile radius from where Flynns lived Tarry could count only four houses in which there were married couples with children.

As in *The Great Hunger* clayey images are invoked to suggest spiritual and imaginative deprivation:

It was a squalid, grey-faced throng . . . Skin was the colour of clay, and clay was in their hair and clothes. The little tillage-fields went to Mass.

Such embittered observations are rare, however. That savage exposure of the drab dispiritedness of country living undertaken in *The Great Hunger* is explicitly abjured in *Tarry Flynn* where 'To lay bare the myth of living, to tear up the faith and show nothing but futility' is pronounced a sin. Even the dearth of libido in Dargan is treated comically when Fr Daly decides to forestall an outbreak of wild orgies of lust in the parish by inviting the Redemptorist Order who were 'specialists in sex sins' to hold a mission. The effect of this mission is to arouse the parishioners' dormant sexuality:

The crooked old men sat up and took notice when they heard of the Mission; they began to dream themselves violent young stallions who needed prayer and fasting to keep them on the narrow path . . . Men who had forgotten what they were born for came out of the confessional . . . 'ready to bull cows'.

Although the socialist editor of *The Bell*, Peadar O'Donnell, encouraged Kavanagh in his final revision of *Tarry Flynn*, his political views had no discernible influence on its mellow, parochial aesthetic. That the shift from the earnestly indignant rhetoric of *The Great Hunger* to a stance of comic detachment is a deliberate authorial strategy is twice confirmed within the novel. Comparing the preaching techniques of parish priest and missioner in chapter 2 Tarry decides that 'humour, the appearance of not being too in earnest' rather than emotive rhetoric is the 'real sign of sincerity'. Towards the conclusion of the novel Kavanagh demonstrates that parochial literature is composed in a light-hearted mood in which the trials and misfortunes of everyday appear merely 'funny'. The novel, on the whole, offers an alternative version of pastoral to *The Great Hunger*, comic rather than tragic, a summer narrative instead of the predominantly wintry poem, a youthful, cheerful and imaginative hero as opposed to the elderly, repressed and clay-bound Maguire. Its rustic chorus is not cowed and defeated but as fighting fit and mentally alert as it needs to be to survive the internecine strife that constitutes the norm of parish life.

The people of Dargan are red in tooth and claw, struggling not so much for survival as for a minimal social betterment. Money is hard to come by and Tarry's friend, Eusebius Cassidy, illustrates some of the shifts and stratagems necessary to accumulate it: keeping an undersized cut-price stallion at stud, stealing railway sleepers, 'storing' farm machinery for a neighbour threatened by the bailiffs, a case of doing good by stealth. In such an exploitative world it is unwise to leave a farm without a steward for a day. Small meannesses abound in a neighbourhood where every cigarette butt is counted. The women watch out that other women's fowl do not join theirs at feeding time and are careful to remove the kettle from the hob when a visitor is sighted lest they have to offer him tea. Gone are the ceilidhes and story-telling sessions, beloved of the folklorist. This is the grim, tight-fisted rural Ireland of the Depression years; the novel is set in 1935. Young men who slave on the family farm from dawn to darkness have to wheedle and threaten to be given sixpence by their parsimonious parents. Tarry's mother likes him to have a shilling in his pocket, provided he doesn't spend it. On the evening of the dance in the parochial hall he is short fourpence of the admission price and knows that not even his best friend will lend him these paltry few pence.

Possessiveness is one of the deepest instincts in the small-farmer's psyche and it is a deeply divisive passion, militating against any sense of community. Each family pursues its own advantage ruthlessly, and attempts to thwart others. Alliances between families are tactical and temporary. Farm tools like the graip or the slashing hook are turned into weapons to defend boundaries and rights of way. Battles are fought over the cutting of a bush on a fence common to two farms. A neighbour's purchase of a few acres (contemptuously referred to as 'land-grabbing') inflames festering dislike to murderous hatred. Occasionally, neighbours are depicted lending a helping hand, assisting at a calving or giving a can of milk to an impoverished family, but more usually they are locked in rivalry and mutual hostility.

The tension between the ingenuous, dreamy, nature-loving lyric poet, Tarry, a would-be worldling, and his worldly wise, hard-headed, and treacherous neighbours is encapsulated in his relationship with his mother. One of the great matriarchs of Irish literature, she epitomises the small-farming ethos: shrewd, vigilant about animals, crops, tools and neighbours' doings, thrifty to the point of meanness, endlessly calculating how to better her family and farm. Gossiping is for Mrs Flynn an intelligence gathering operation and she is careful not to disclose her own plans. To outsiders she rarely betrays her forceful character and usually acts the part of a soft, helpless and ingratiating female, but in private she is venomous about the neighbours she publicly flatters. Such hypocritical behaviour is shown to be characteristic of Dargan people, whose friendship is invariably untrustworthy. Tarry's closest friend, Eusebius, takes advantage of him whenever possible while Petey Meegan, who is seeking to marry Tarry's sister, secretly sides with the family which is plotting the Flynns' downfall.

Mrs Flynn is a fully realised dramatic character who dominates the novel as she does her own family. Kavanagh exploits her managerial and manipulative skills to assign her a controlling function in his fictional structure. Like Mrs Maguire she is a petty tyrant, a capable widow who runs the family farm, keeps a firm hold on the purse strings and is, therefore, in a position to dictate to her grown-up but financially dependent children. Though a tireless dictator and schemer, Mrs Flynn is a much more sympathetic figure than Mrs Maguire, energetic, vigorous and commonsensical, salty and malicious in her speech, possessed of a keen sense of drama. Life in the Flynn household hurtles from crisis to crisis as trivial happenings are elevated to momentous importance by a mother who likes to enliven routine with melodrama.

This propensity to counter the tedium of the daily round with exaggerated over-reactions to minor events, feuding, scandalmongering, the spreading of vicious rumour, is characteristic of Dargan's parishioners. The community's liking for dramatic scenes enacted with the express purpose of undermining a neighbour is illustrated in two amusing incidents. Joe Finnegan pretends to have been fatally wounded in a fight he provoked with Tarry and arranges all the public trappings of a mortal illness. So the priest is sent for, the doctor's car is observed driving up to the house, the wounded man's brother runs there 'at a gasping trot', and neighbours rush through the fields carrying such sickroom paraphernalia as a commode, a white quilt and a blessed candle. Later the Finnegans rehearse a courtroom scene to prepare their case for assault and battery against Tarry. This scene is set out as a comic playlet in the text, with Tarry and his friend, Eusebius as a concealed audience. Much of its humour derives from the disparity between the realist appearances and actions of the dramatis personae and the pompous courtroom roles they are assigned and from Tarry's presence at Petey Meegan's impersonation of him.

In Mrs Flynn's ceaseless obsession with farming chores, projects and improvements, we are shown the limited world of the ambitious subsistence farmer. The opening scene of the novel illustrates her preoccupation with the nitty-gritty of farm management, her mind running on hen and pig food, broken eggs, the straining of milk, calves getting a scour, a 'cow looking the bull', a broken wire paling tearing a cow's teats, the swapping of young cocks for pullets at the market, while all the time she issues a stream of orders, complaints and laments intended to manipulate her children into carrying out her wishes. The Carlins, bankrupt farmers whose land she attempts to purchase, are exploited by Mrs Flynn as dreadful examples to her own family of all the faults she most detests: laziness, thriftlessness, irreligion, failing to treat parents with due respect. In *Tarry Flynn* the mentally absorbing, energy-consuming nature of small-farm life is shown in a far more sympathetic light than in *The Great Hunger*. It is a full, rich, busy life, crammed with incident, never boring or predictable. While its rewards may appear financially meagre and its preoccupations trivial, farming has here all the bustle and excitement of running a thriving commercial enterprise. The tensions and rivalries endemic to parish and family life also ensure that there is rarely a dull moment.

Nowhere before or since in Irish fiction has the routine working life of the farmer been so vividly documented as in *Tarry Flynn*. We are shown Tarry engaged in various chores about the farm: cutting ragweeds and thistles, moulding the potatoes, greasing a cart, clearing a drain, driving a cow to the bull, trimming briars, spraying potatoes, making hay, cleaning the haggard. With the exception of the drain-cleaning episode these are not set pieces and are presented obliquely, the emphasis being on Tarry's thoughts and feelings as he gets on with the job in hand. Kavanagh deliberately does not dwell on the documentary aspect of his fiction. He wants agricultural detail to enter the novel unobtrusively as a normal part of farming experience. It is the sheer accumulation of casually proffered information that contributes to the book's authenticity as a country novel.

The drain-cleaning episode is the only expansive, leisurely treatment of farm labour, enabling the reader to get under the skin of the working farmer and share intimately in his experience. The drain in question is a stream which Tarry has to clean because it is choked with 'flaggers' and, typically, he undertakes the task with some reluctance because it is likely to benefit his neighbours' fields as well as his own:

> The heavy squares of flagger roots yielded very slowly to his strain. They carried a huge backside of oily mud that was sometimes a hundredweight. Bit by bit he dragged it up the bank and as he eventually landed it safely he was filled with deep satisfaction. The pool left behind by these sods was like a clear well.

Here farm labour is fully and sensuously described, the physical exertion involved in lifting the sodden weight of the flagger roots conveyed through words indicating heaviness and slowness. The syntax enacts the difficulty and the gratification Tarry experiences and turns an ordinary chore into a dramatic event. Nothing momentous happens to Tarry in the course of this day's work; he is visited by his mother and by Molly Brady, a girl who fancies him; he thinks, rests, reads, wipes the sweat off his face with muddy fingers, registers the hum from a wild bees' nest, is bitten by a 'cleg'. His shirt climbs up his back, his braces slip and he is uncomfortably aware that his boots have taken in water and pebbles. Through such a web of ordinary circumstance the texture of a farmer's day is re-created. Work is not unmitigated drudgery as in *The Great Hunger*; Tarry is young and healthy and relishes the sense of physical well-being that accompanies a good morning's work and a tasty dinner. The rewards of farming are manifest, too, when Tarry pauses to take pride in his flourishing crops or in such possessions as his small red cart, and when he savours the joy of ownership as he walks through his own fields.

In *Tarry Flynn* Kavanagh succeeds in conveying the feel of ordinary, everyday small-farm life despite having a poet as hero. Though Tarry has written some verses 'these poems did not jut out of his life to become noticeable or make him a stranger to the small-farmer community of which he was a child'. Tarry is still at least half a farmer, sharing to some extent in the aspirations, duplicities and meannesses of his fellow countrymen. He sometimes envisages a future as a contented Dargan parishioner, repeating the pattern of his father's life:

> He would be happy in that country, happily married with children, and would go to the forge with the horses and converse with the blacksmith, and wander over to the cross-roads of a Sunday afternoon and discuss the football team and politics. He would be among the old men with his hands in his trousers pockets dreaming about the past. Then he would walk slowly home for his tea and the children and wife would be there waiting for him and everything would be as it was in his father's life. How right his mother was! Why should a man seek crucifixion?

However, Tarry's 'difference' from his neighbours, which he attempts to conceal or suppress, is remarked and resented by them. He is still the scapegoat poet of *The Green Fool*, 'the butt of many an assembly', here singled out at crossroads and village hall as the fall-guy in a slapstick comedy designed to make him appear disreputable in the eyes of the clergy and the village hierarchy. The innocent and unworldly Tarry is no match for his country-cute neighbours. He unwittingly falls victim to the vicious machinations of local families whose customary envy has been exacerbated into overt hostility by Mrs Flynn's attempted purchase of a bankrupt's farm. As the novel draws to a close Tarry's troubles multiply: he is threatened with a law suit over an assault provoked by a neighbour, has been cheated out of the best part of the newly bought farm, and is held accountable for the pregnancy of a girl he never managed to lay.

Much of the comedy of *Tarry Flynn* derives from Tarry's amorous misadventures. He seeks to gain women's attention by declaiming a literary phrase, such as 'The birds of Angus', in a 'dramatically silly tone'. Local women, more accustomed to 'aphrodisiacal double-meaning, illiterate joking' and phrases like 'me hand on yer drawers' by way of sexual banter, think him 'a little touched'. Completely devoid of sexual experience himself Tarry is obsessed with the subject of young women's virginity. As a romantic idealist he spurns the readily accessible charms of a village slattern, Molly Brady, and prefers to worship a superior and less attainable madonna, Mary Reilly, the daughter of a rich local farmer whom he cannot aspire to marry. Mary Reilly, a convent school-educated girl, is sufficiently impressed by his poetry to overlook the guacheries of Tarry's mismanaged attempts at courtship. He overcompensates for his sense of social inferiority and for the patched, clownish attire his mother insists he wear by lecturing the unfortunate girl, prudishly refrains from touching her when clearly encouraged to do so, fantasises about her and contrives to meet her accidentally yet repels all her advances. In matters sexual Tarry is like a young Patrick Maguire and seems set for a life of celibacy. However, due to his comparative youth his romantic plight appears amusing. Tarry's life is not wretched, frustrated and hopeless like Patrick Maguire's; his failures as a lover are comic mishaps, embarrassing situations designed to make the reader smile.

Mrs Flynn is not as overtly opposed to her son's romantic adventures as Mrs Maguire. Though she prolongs the twenty-seven-year-old Tarry's adolescence by denying him any responsibility and ceaselessly harries him in an attempt to turn him into an efficient farmer, she is utterly devoted to what she perceives as his welfare. In a novel centred on Tarry's point of view the narrator momentarily enters his mother's consciousness to reveal her love for her errant son:

> She loved that son more than any mother ever loved a son. She hardly knew why. There was something so natural about him, so real and so innocent which yet looked like badness. He hated being in time for Mass. He had always slept soundly through the Rosary in the days when his father was alive to say that evening prayer.

And he was forever reading and dreaming to himself in the fields. It was a risk to let him out alone in a horse and cart. The heart was often out of her mouth that he'd turn the cart upside down in a gripe while he was dreaming or looking at the flowers. And then the shocking things that he sometimes said about religion and the priests . . . He was a queer son in some ways. There was a kink in him which she never had been able to fathom.

Here Tarry's shortcomings are deplored with affectionate indulgence. This warm, nurturing dimension of family life was absent in *The Great Hunger* which emphasised bondage instead of bonding.

It was a fine comic stroke to provide the enraptured lyric poet with such a hard-headed, earthy mother: the ensuing conflict between rhapsody and pragmatism is an unfailing source of humour in the novel. Tarry's dramatic announcement that 'The Holy Spirit is in the fields', for instance, is deliberately deflected by his mother who develops a sudden concern with a corn on her foot and with such household practicalities as feeding the hens and emptying the slops. After these deflationary tactics, designed to underline the inappropriateness of visionary insight in the Flynn *ménage*, she invites him to repeat his statement:

After a while she quietly asked
'what was that you said about the Holy something?'
'I said the Holy Spirit was in the fields.'
'Lord protect everyone's rearing,' she said with a twinkle that was half humorous and half terror in her eye. She knew there was no madness on her side of the house—that was one sure five—but— . . .

In Tarry and his mother Kavanagh succeeded in embodying the two contrary impulses in his own nature between celebration and denigration, ensuring a continual comic conflict between two value systems, the imaginative and the materialist, an extension of the mini-drama enacted in 'Shancoduff'.

The authenticity of Kavanagh's parochial comedy derives largely from his accurate rendering of local speech. In this he makes no concessions to non-local readers and foreigners may find the novel's dialogue almost impenetrable in places. Such is the price exacted by parochialism. The attempt to reproduce the local accent through spelling as 'the morrow' for 'tomorrow', 'the day' for 'today', 'go lang' for 'go along', 'bleddy' for 'bloody' may increase the foreigner's mystification. Kavanagh resorts to deliberate localisms like 'Take Carrol's factory to keep him in fags' or 'They'll do a turn like Mickey Grant said about the wife' and regional idiom is sometimes localised by the addition of a neighbour's name: 'Take off that good suit,' she advised her son, 'and not have everything on the one rack like the Carlins.' On rare occasions Kavanagh is self-conscious about his local language as when he reflects on the various interpretations of the word, 'hello':

> In country places a single word is inflected to mean a hundred things, so that only a recording of the sounds gives an idea of the speech of these people.

On the whole dialect arises with apparent spontaneity from the novel's dramatic context.

Kavanagh's country parish is prejudiced against unusual utterances. Predictability in speech and an abundant recourse to platitude indicate that a person is a safe, normal, reliable member of the community. So characters generally draw on a common currency of local clichés and learned responses such as 'Damn to the bother', 'I don't know the day or hour', 'They're all hard pleased and easy fitted', 'the God's honest truth', 'You'd forget your head only it's tied to you'. The repetition of 'That's the way' in the scene where the elderly bachelor, Petey Meegan, visits Flynn's house in the hopes of courting the daughter, Mary, shows the linguistic impoverishment that is as common in Irish country conversation as its more publicised opposite. Kavanagh's characters are terse by comparison with Synge's. This tight-fisted community is as grudging with words as with money and the long sentence is not its forte. Local invective at its liveliest is displayed in the bickering of Tarry's family, especially in his mother's flytings, but even she resorts to staple local speech as in the following exchange with her daughter, Bridie, who gives as good as she gets:

> 'Oh nobody can talk to you,' said Bridie with a pout, 'if a person only opens their mouth ye ait the face off them'. 'The divil thank ye and thump ye, Bridie, ye whipster, ye. Your face is scrubbed often enough and the damn to the much you're making of it. I could be twice married when I was your age'.
> 'A wonder ye didn't make a better bargain'.
> 'Arra what?' the mother was rising in her anger, 'arra what? Is it making little of your poor father—the Lord have mercy on him—ye are? My bad luck to ye into hell and out of it for a tinker that . . . Go out one of yez and bring in a lock of sticks for the fire . . . Oh a brazen tinker, if ever there was one. Oh a family of daughters is the last of the last. Half of the time painting and powdering and it would take a doctor's shop to keep them in medicine.'

Country language in *Tarry Flynn* is usually reductive and belittling, scabrous or scatological rather than lyrical or fanciful:

> She's not a girl nor a patch on a girl's backside . . .
> . . . they're like horse-dung, you never walk the road but you meet them. . . .
> . . . in and out like a dog pissing on snow . . .
> . . . Charlie Trainor that 'id lift a ha'penny out of a cow-dung with his teeth . . .
> I wouldn't marry her if her backside was studded with diamonds . . .

When Tarry is shy about chatting up Mary Reilly, his sister, by way of encouragement, remarks:

> 'Isn't she only a lump of dung like the rest of us
> ... Make a rush at it as if you were taking a dose of
> salts ...

The dialogue in the first chapter had to be cleaned up in deference to the publisher's squeamishness.[58]

Tarry Flynn is faithful to Inniskeen talk even when such language is neither colourful nor entertaining.[59] It uses such homely phrases as 'have you any cutting up in you at all?', 'what ... *are* you pouching for?', 'the whole bill of the races', 'the targer', 'teeming the pot', 'putting in your cutty', 'them and Christians differ', 'You'd think she was made in a foundry', which even people from another Irish parish may find incomprehensible. Such fidelity to local dialect was one of the qualities Kavanagh most relished in Carleton's *Traits and Stories*:

> in one of his lesser pieces Carleton gives the pronunci-
> ation of a word that I myself used in *Tarry Flynn* and
> which was the pronunciation I heard my mother use in
> certain circumstances; and which carried a subtle over-
> tone of comedy. The word was 'cure-ossity' for curiosity.
> It is a tiny example but it is by these tiny examples that
> the genuineness of dialogue can be tested. It is in such
> small things that a writer shows his courage ...[60]

Parochialism requires artistic courage, since the writer, by refusing to concede to the demands of mainstream English, risks forfeiting a large readership.

As a 'portrait of the artist' *Tarry Flynn* is manifestly autobio-graphical. Kavanagh actually sheds his fictional disguise by attributing to Tarry three of his own published poems, 'Anna Quinn', 'My Room'[61] and the poem with which the novel concludes, three stanzas of which had been quoted in the *Irish Press* in 1943.[62] Tarry the poet is also the devotee of schoolbook poetry encountered in *The Green Fool* and in several essays.

The theme of the poet in the parish, introduced in 'Inniskeen Road: July Evening', treated at biographical length in *The Green Fool* and fictionalised and dramatised in 'Why Sorrow?', is most fully and complexly explored in *Tarry Flynn*. In *The Green Fool* the newly fledged writer chronicled the external manifestations of his literary progress, his discovery of new books and authors, the publication of his poems, the patronage or fellowship of other writers. His account of his literary development in *Tarry Flynn* is altogether more introverted, reflecting that self-consciousness about his own imaginative processes which was to become a recurring theme in the late 1940s and early 1950s. Like 'Why Sorrow?' the novel dwells on the farmer-poet's secret double life and his problematic relations with his parish community, though it is a poetic 'kink' in his character rather than a poetic cult of paganism which separates Tarry from his neighbours, and his apartness is rendered comically rather than earnestly. What really distinguishes the portrayal of the two farmer-poets is that in *Tarry Flynn*, Kavanagh is specifically concerned with artistic genesis whereas paganism and a pagan love of nature served as a generalised sign of aestheticism in 'Why Sorrow?' In the novel, where Tarry's imaginative development is compressed into a few months, Kavanagh focuses on the origins of his creativity, his evolution from instinctive love of nature to articulate responsiveness, his discovery of his parochial poetics, his recognition of the importance of artistic detachment.

Tarry shares Father Mat's unconventional love of those common country sights usually ignored or dismissed as ugly by other nature-lovers. 'Every weed and stone and pebble and briar all along an ordinary headland' belong for him to 'the world of the imagination'. He is shown thrilling to the 'simple, fantastic beauty of ordinary things growing—marsh-marigolds, dandelions, thistles and grass':

He did not ask things to have a meaning or tell a story.
To be was the only story.

The rich profusion of vegetation excites him:

The lush nettles and docks and tufts of grass. Life pouring out in uncritical abundance.

Kavanagh's Romantic preoccupation with the dynamics of
the relationship between the poet and nature is rendered in
sexual imagery. It is even carried to the Hopkinesque extreme where the beholder receives an 'instress' from natural
phenomena, for when Tarry becomes impatient with 'the
flirtatious gamboling of birds and trees' they force themselves
on his notice and he finds himself 'caught in the stare' of
objects.

In *Tarry Flynn*, unlike 'Why Sorrow?', Kavanagh analyses
the emergent artist's self-liberation from an instinctual life,
(what he elsewhere refers to as 'a Mucker fog') and his
realisation of his separate identity as observer, namer and
recorder of the local scene. Naming, a source of multifarious
satisfactions to Kavanagh, is here presented as a first stage in
the translation of experience into language, a conscious
separation of the self from its surroundings. Early in the
novel we are told that Tarry 'hardly ever had an experience
that could be named', that

He could get no perspective on life, for life lay warm, too
warm, around him, and too close and nearly suffocating.
He was up to his neck in life and could not see it to enjoy
it. His whole conscious mind was strained in an effort to
drag himself up out of the belly of emotion.
Sometimes he would concentrate, saying to himself: 'I
am alive. Those are potatoes there, and that is a black-
thorn's root'.

However, the presentation of Tarry's emergence as an

artist does not follow a developmental model and sometimes reflects the author's aesthetic views rather than his character's progression from 'simple country body' to poet. While the narrator maintains a comic distance from his hero in the delineation of his social relations, free indirect style is occasionally used to blur the distinction between narrator and character when aesthetic affairs are under consideration. So we are surprised to read on page 28 with reference to the apparently immature comic hero:

> The land keeps a man silent for a generation or two and then the crust gives way. A poet is born or a prophet.

and immediately afterwards to note the unmistakable conflation of the narrator's and character's viewpoint:

> Even teeming the pot was very important in his life and in his imagination. Any incident, or any act, can carry within it the energy of the imagination.

The narrator's own viewpoint is not consistent. On occasion he endorses Tarry's nature lyricism, at other times he regards his younger self as a failed parochial poet whose relationship with nature insulates him from his neighbours:

> . . . he was not in love with his neighbours; their lives meant little to him, and though off his own bat he was a very fine thinker and observer he had only one pair of eyes and ears and one mind. Had he loved his neighbours he would have the eyes, ears and minds of all these, for love takes possession . . .
> He loved the fields and the birds and trees, stones and weeds and through these he could learn a great deal — but hardly enough. He saw the centre as a poet sees, but this introversion was leading to aridity. Men impacted themselves on him almost against his will

Like the nature-loving poet-priest of 'Why Sorrow?' Tarry regards 'human sympathies' as 'side-tracking activities'. The parochial aesthetic which Kavanagh now embraces, however, is a comic, dramatic aesthetic based on love of neighbour so that, whereas he fully endorsed Father Mat's alienation from his parish, he is critical of Tarry's failure to appreciate the ordinary social comedy of country life. His neighbours' conversation was 'fascinating talk for those who had the faith to see it as the expression of the divine gift of life' but 'Tarry listened bored'.

Towards the end of the novel Kavanagh definitively closes the aesthetic gap between his past and present selves and presents Tarry as a parochial writer engaged in making literature out of his local experience; writing *Tarry Flynn*. Where naming released the lyrical poet from a stifling emotional involvement with his environment, a humorous perspective enables the parochial writer to escape from 'the net of earthly intrigue'. Looking down from a height of amused detachment on his quarrels with his neighbours Tarry transposes unpleasant actuality into comic realist fiction:

> Looking down at his own misfortunes he thought them funny now. From this height he could even see himself losing his temper with the Finnegans and the Carlins and hating his neighbours and he moved the figures on the landscape, made them speak, and was filled with joy in his own power.

At this point, four lines from 'Why Sorrow?' are quoted, as if to connect the two fictional farmer-poets, Kavanagh's older and younger alter-ego, Father Mat and Tarry:

> The rattle of buckets, rolling of barrels under
> Down-spouts, the leading in of foals
> Were happenings caught in wonder
> The stones white with rain were living souls.

An apparently minor change in this version of the lines is significant. Ordinary country 'happenings' are now 'caught in wonder', not 'in pagan wonder'. The early association of country poetry and paganism has been dropped. The focus of Kavanagh's parochialism is the Catholic parish. As the above prose passage clearly demonstrates, his parochial aesthetic is also consciously comic.

It might seem that such comic detachment from one's parish should render physical exile unnecessary, yet *Tarry Flynn* also notes the writer's difficulty in remaining aloof from his material while it is still impinging on his daily life: the mounting pressure of local events threatens to disturb 'the magic of the fields' in Tarry's imagination. Nevertheless, his sudden departure from Dargan with a visiting uncle brings the novel to an unsatisfactorily abrupt conclusion.

The inexplicableness of his departure from Inniskeen was of obsessive imaginative importance to Kavanagh until the end of his career. In *Self-Portrait* (1964) he was still trying to rationalise it:

> I had no messianic impulse to leave. I was happy. I went against my will. A lot of our actions are like that. We miss the big emotional gesture and drift away . . .[63]

His most voluptuous poetic expression of the tug of love between affection and aesthetic commitment, Inniskeen and Dublin, in the 1940s, was the sonnet sequence, 'Temptation in Harvest'. Two parts of this sequence were published in 1945 and 1946,[64] the years just preceding his revision of *Tarry Flynn*, and a time when he was also revising 'Father Mat'. That the first part of this sonnet sequence was originally entitled 'The Monaghan Accent' reveals its intimate connection with Kavanagh's parochial poetics. In all three of these near-contemporary works, the motif of temptation is introduced to describe the hero's reluctant attraction away from his heartland. 'Father Mat' concludes indecisively: the choice between pagan art and parochial attachment is still present in the closing lines. *Tarry Flynn* ends decisively with the farmer-poet's exit from his parish. 'Temptation in Harvest', though it too ends with the poet's departure, is pervasively ambivalent. Here the poet is a returned native, surrendering to the erotic charms of the country which he had deserted six years previously. 'Surrender' is given both sexual and military connotations in this poem: it is both pleasurable and dishonourable. The harvest fields are irresistibly seductive, yet the aesthetic imperative demands that the poet does not succumb to their sexual temptation and his coital pleasure is both intensified and troubled by a sense of wrongdoing:

> Where can I look and not become a lover
> Terrified at each recurring spasm? . . .

However, his pursuit of culture is no less problematic than his love of nature. The Parnassian figure who lures the poet away from home and parish is also a temptress. Though he knows that 'only what we love is true/And not what loves us', he forsakes his rural love when art beckons. To follow art is a sin against life, against the instinctual, in this poem. The poet is placed in an impossible dilemma. Rural symphonies break down what the will asserts, yet the refusal to yield is not a heroic choice. Once again, as in 'Why Sorrow?' and 'Father Mat', the aesthetic tempter is a meretricious figure.

In the realist novel, *Tarry Flynn*, the role of successful tempter is assigned to Tarry's uncle. However, in this fictionalised version of the poet's departure from Inniskeen, the unexpectedness of Tarry's exit strains credulity. Though his uncle is referred to in the opening chapter of the novel and his arrival is prepared by several letters announcing his intention to visit, he is given only seven pages in which to influence Tarry to leave home. This *deus ex machina*, a circus ringmaster who arrives in a taxi for which he cannot afford to pay, is a comic deliverer. A nomad and worldly failure without wife, family, money or possessions, he is diametrically opposed to the small-farm ethos. Thomas à Kempis' *Imitation of Christ*, which preaches spirituality and denounces worldliness and materialism, is his bible and he is much given to aphorisms on detachment. His one achievement in life is that he has 'learned not to care' and in this he is an early exponent of an attitude which Kavanagh would adopt as an aesthetic credo from the mid-1950s.

Tarry's uncle is an authorial intrusion disguised as a character. In the person of this avuncular rascal the older Kavanagh is counselling and reassuring his younger self:

> A man without talent is nobody ... The only things worth having are talent and genius. The rest is trash.

and

> ... if you have anything worth while in you, any talent, you should deliver it. Nothing must turn you from that.

The author of *Tarry Flynn* is confident that a well-loved place is not lost to the imagination in exile, that

> The best way to love a country like this is from a range of not less than three hundred miles.

and that

> If it's as beautiful as you imagine, you can take it with you.

Unfortunately, the uncle in his role of returned native is also reductive of the parochial comedy so lovingly constructed in the novel and is to some extent an embodiment of a destructive streak in Kavanagh himself, a distrust of his own affectionate and celebratory instincts.

In the beginning of the novel Mrs Flynn had likened Tarry to his uncle Petey and at the end the two men are united against her. His uncle emboldens Tarry to break free of his maternal bonding, minimising his mother's personal suffering by generalising with male condescension on the tribulations of womanhood. As Tarry tears himself away from home the 'pain of roots dragging up' deliberately recalls the novel's long set-piece, the drain cleaning episode, and, indeed, the poem with which the novel concludes was anticipated in part in that episode. This concluding poem is an aesthetic justification of departure. Nothing in Tarry's farming life becomes him like the leaving of it: as he goes he is already visualising a scene that 'took shape as a song'. Small-farm life is distilled into poetry. Pain is metamorphosed into the myth of a lost paradise: 'fields that were part of no earthly estate'. Absence which makes the heart grow fonder fosters the creation of parochial art. Nevertheless, *Tarry Flynn* undeniably concludes too abruptly and the uncle who tempts Tarry away from home is too obviously a combination of authorial mouthpiece and flashing exit sign to function successfully as a character in a realist novel.

Tarry Flynn did not receive the immediate critical and popular acclaim that Kavanagh expected. He had difficulty in finding an American publisher for it; Devin-Adair of New York was the only press willing to take it in 1949. It was sold for the most part through their Catholic Book Club and, though it was marketed as a Catholic Book Club selection, sales were poor. Many club members found its portrayal of Irish country life grossly offensive.[65] Kavanagh made the mistake of publishing *Tarry Flynn* in England (1948) with a small, obscure company, the Pilot Press. It 'went broke immediately and the novel was remaindered at a shilling'.[66] Despite fairly favourable notices, it was not reissued until he had achieved a high critical reputation with his next volume of poems, *Come Dance with Kitty Stobling,* published by Longmans, Green and Co. in 1960. Even then, his editor at Longmans had trouble placing *Tarry Flynn* with another publisher, and Penguin was among those who declined it.[67] The book was finally brought out as a paperback by Four Square Books in 1962, and was reissued in hardback by MacGibbon and Kee in 1965. Since then it has been reissued several times, and Penguin has made amends for its earlier rejection.[68] In Ireland *Tarry Flynn* was adapted for the stage by P. J. O'Connor and first played to packed houses in the Abbey theatre in November 1966.

Why was *Tarry Flynn*, the most comprehensive and most sustained expression of Kavanagh's parochial poetics, so slow to gain a readership? Did such rural realism appear old-fashioned in 1948 coming from a country that had already produced *Ulysses, At Swim-Two-Birds, Murphy* and *Watt*? In spite of the example and exhortation of Seán O'Faoláin and Frank O'Connor in the 1940s, had Irish fiction bypassed realism on its way to the heart of Ireland? Would *Tarry Flynn* ever have been reissued if its author had not attained prestige as a poet?

The problematics surrounding the reception of *Tarry Flynn* are inseparable from the problematics of parochialism as a literary mode. It does not travel well. The use of dialect probably contributes in no small measure to its neglect. Even native speakers of English have to brave a language barrier in order to read parts of it and it is almost untranslatable into a foreign language. To overseas readers it probably appears indistinguishable from the outdated genre of stage-Irish comedy. So a transatlantic critic like Hugh Kenner, who in *A Colder Eye* displays contemptuous familiarity with Irish literature, does not discriminate between Kavanagh's representation of his native parish in *The Green Fool* and in *Tarry Flynn*. Kavanagh, he remarks, had only 'one story' to tell, 'and he told it twice, the second time in 1947, less lyrically, as *Tarry Flynn*'.[69] Perhaps only the Irish reader can distinguish between spurious stage-Irishry and the genuine parochial article. It may be one of parochialism's peculiar disadvantages that 'local individuality'[70] can only be fully appreciated by a local audience, sensitive to the subtlest nuances of mood and speech, and such an audience is necessarily small. Authenticity is a virtue that may well elude the scrutiny of literary critics. Of those other books which Kavanagh cited as examples of parochialism, *Hail and Farewell* and *Ulysses* are formally innovative and urban works, more attuned to a modern readership than *Tarry Flynn*, and esteemed for qualities other than comic realism. Kavanagh's fiction, though less uneven than Carleton's, comes closer to the genre of *Traits and Stories* than to either of these. Though Kavanagh constantly championed Carleton as a parochial writer, he knew that it was difficult to persuade potential readers of his merits.

Even in Ireland *Tarry Flynn* was hampered by the fact that its honesty made for uncomfortable comedy. Despite its swift unbanning it remained unpopular with Grundyites. Many squeamish Irish readers, like the Irish-American members of Devin-Adair's book club, would have preferred a more sentimentalised, less painful and less ugly version of Irish pastoral.[71] Or they would have preferred an exclusively country comedy rather than a blend of rural realism and a portrait of the artist. The stage adaptation of *Tarry Flynn,*[72] which was a box-office success in Ireland, comes close to the kind of Abbey kitchen comedy which Kavanagh loathed.

Tarry Flynn remains 'the best and most authentic account of life as it was lived' in rural Ireland in the first half of this century. Now that Irish readers' insecurities about their rural past are fast disappearing it is gradually being accorded the classic status it so richly deserves.

7

Muck and Anger:
Critic and Satirist, 1942–1956

... to bother
Ireland with muck and anger.
('The Paddiad')

Introduction

THE publication of *Tarry Flynn* in 1948 marked the close of
Patrick Kavanagh's pastoral and parochial period. The
countryside now became an imaginative hinterland to be
revisited momentarily, though often memorably. Kavanagh's
retrospective and rural fiction and poetry had been complemented since 1942 by a counter-literature; urban, often
topical, and increasingly aesthetic and critical in orientation.
This was published for the most part in newspapers and
magazines and presented in a journalistic mode, as if intended for immediate consumption only. It was opinionated
but volatile, and did not engage in sustained argumentation. The style was conversational, the tone relaxed, despite
occasional touches of solemnity or bombast, though, gradually 'the preacher's loose, immoderate tone' became more
dominant, as Kavanagh's stance became more dictatorial,
aggressive and intolerant.

Prose and poetry mingled casually and unselfconsciously
in this urban journalism. Not only did several of Kavanagh's
poems make their first appearance in an opinion column; on
occasion, they substituted for an article or book review. The
demarcation between his creative and his critical writings
diminished as the same preoccupations and attitudes, the

same words, and, above all, the same speaking voice were encountered in both. Throughout the later 1940s and early 1950s, as Kavanagh's poetry became increasingly implicated in his critical enterprise, it tended more towards satire than celebration, often serving as an extension or offshoot of his journalistic quarrels. Cultural criticism was frequently his poetic subject, and even those poems published separately from his journalism often seem designedly ephemeral, mere quips and cranks, squibs and jibes, intended to divert or discomfit contemporaries rather than amuse posterity.

Kavanagh's urban prose and verse record his increasing alienation from his cultural milieu. His early years in Dublin were pleasant and productive. He was happy to have escaped from the uncouth society of Inniskeen to a city which he regarded as a 'literary metropolis', 'full of writers and poets', whose work had 'the Irish quality' which he at that time esteemed.[1] The Pearl and the Palace bars were the haunts of Dublin's established and aspiring writers, and the Palace bar, where the editor of the *Irish Times*, Bertie Smyllie, presided over gatherings of writers and journalists, appeared to Kavanagh 'the most wonderful temple of art'.[2] The unschooled poet, fresh from the farm, was welcomed as a curiosity by Dublin's literary circles. In the long wake of the Revival, peasantry was still fashionable and Kavanagh was immediately assigned the role of ploughman poet-in-residence. (He features prominently in Alan Reeve's celebrated 1940 cartoon of the Palace bar, entitled 'Dublin Culture'.) In 1940 he was awarded the AE Memorial Prize of £100 for 'the best literary work either creative or scholarly by an Irish writer under 35', despite stiff competition from Brian O'Nolan whose *At Swim-Two-Birds* received special commendation.[3] He was soon reviewing for the *Irish Times* and writing occasional pieces for Dublin's three daily newspapers. By 1942 he had a regular twice-weekly column, 'City Commentary', in the *Irish Press*[4] and from February to June 1943 he contributed a column, 'The Literary Scene', to *The Standard*.[5] His *Irish Press* column shows that he used his press

card to attend numerous social functions and enjoyed hob-
nobbing with celebrities and the rich and titled. Among those
whose friendship he prized was John Betjeman, press attaché
at the British Embassy during Kavanagh's first years in
Dublin. These happy years were among Kavanagh's most
creative. The imaginative stimulus he gained from the close
companionship of such radical intellectuals as Frank O'Connor, Seán O'Faoláin and Peadar O'Donnell, and from his
association with *The Bell*, helped him to mature rapidly as a
poet. However, his literary work in his first years in Dublin
was rural in orientation, and by the time he began to take
cognisance of his urban surroundings in his poetry, he was
becoming disenchanted with Dublin as a cultural centre. The
saeva indignatio of 'Stony Grey Soil' and *The Great Hunger* was
now directed against the metropolis. Only in the 'City
Commentary' column he contributed to the *Irish Press* from
September 1942 to February 1944 do we catch a glimpse of an
eager and contented newcomer to town, enthusiastically exploring his new terrain.

A combination of circumstances contributed to Kavanagh's
disaffection and the consequent routeing of his literary talent
towards journalistic polemic and verse satire. One major
contributory factor was financial insecurity. The Civil List, a
British endowment which had helped both Yeats and Joyce,
had ceased to operate when the Free State was set up in 1922.
After Yeats's death the Irish Academy of Letters did not
attract sufficient funding to enable it to make awards to
writers in need. A promised Ministry of Fine Arts never
materialised and the Arts Council, established in 1951, concerned itself mainly with the performing and plastic arts
during Kavanagh's lifetime. The absence of state support for
the Irish literary artist was not compensated by corporate or
private patronage in the 1940s and 1950s. A poet had to
supplement his meagre literary earnings as best he could by
journalism or by finding non-literary employment. The difficulties of his situation were exacerbated by wartime paper
shortage, since newsprint was curtailed. There was fierce

competition for any position requiring communicative skills, such as a job with Radio Éireann or with the Irish News Agency, founded in 1950. Kavanagh was not employed by either of these state-funded enterprises and his early fifties' journalism and verse satire reflect his bitterness at this neglect and at the failure of his applications to the Advisory Committee on Cultural Relations, set up in 1947 to develop cultural relations between Ireland and other countries.

By upbringing and temperament Kavanagh was peculiarly unsuited to the precariousness of earning his living as a free-lance writer, the career which, *faute de mieux*, he was compelled to adopt, since he had no wish to emulate his own Maguire. Despite his escape to the city he retained the Irish small-farmer's obsession with material prosperity, his post-Famine fear of going hungry. For all his visionary raptures, Kavanagh was never to shed his belief in the importance of financial security. *Ars gratia artis* was not a theory to which he subscribed; rather he inclined to the contrary opinion that literary success should be reflected in the author's bank balance. He had witnessed too much of the indignity and degradation associated with poverty in his youth to relish the prospect of a hand-to-mouth bohemian existence. Poverty, as Kavanagh defined it, is 'anxiety about what's going to happen next week'.[6] His ambition was to find a well-paid job, preferably a sinecure, which would leave him the leisure to write. When, despite strenuous efforts, he failed to find non-literary employment, he became embittered against Dublin's wealthy middle class who had denied him salary or patronage and against those state institutions which refused to recognise and remunerate his genius. Kavanagh was forthright, at times wry, about his aspirations to a respectable, middle-class life-style, 'domesticity, wife, house, car'. His preoccupation with financial matters is evident, not only in his diatribes against Ireland's philistine bourgeoisie, but in the numerous allusions to money in his writings, one of his most succinct comments on the plight of genius being that 'Posterity has not printed its banknotes yet.'[7] Monetary metaphors recur throughout his poetry in unexpected and unlikely contexts, as when common sense is dismissed as

> a bank will refuse a post
> Dated cheque of the Holy Ghost.
> ('To Hell with Commonsense')

By 1944 he had become too engrossed in his own pecuniary problems to heed 'the cries of the most numerous and the most poor', who had elicited his imaginative compassion in both *The Great Hunger* and *Lough Derg*.

Kavanagh's disillusionment with Dublin as a cultural metropolis may also be attributable to his own increasing sophistication. The conversation in the Pearl and Palace bars probably seemed mentally stimulating initially to one more accustomed to the 'half-talk code' and 'wink and elbow language' of the country crossroads or McNello's pub, but, as his own imaginative and verbal powers rapidly developed, Kavanagh became bored with the 'tiresome drivel' of Dublin's literati.[8] His low opinion of Dublin's intellectual life was shared by Seán O'Faoláin who, in 1941, found it remarkably 'weak for a capital':

> Politics, journalism, conversation, are generally tawdry, and sometimes far worse . . . There is none of that which Whitman called the compost of literature—the daily bandying about of opinion by critics, journalists, connoisseurs, boulevardiers. There is merely tittie-tattle and gossip.[9]

In the case of Kavanagh's relationship with literary Dublin the disillusionment was mutual since he, disappointingly, failed to conform to the Revival peasant model. He was found to have serious artistic aspirations and to be utterly lacking in such stereotypical peasant skills as fluency in the Gaelic language and a repertoire of folksongs and folktales. Moreover, the subversiveness of his *Great Hunger* did not go unremarked. His poetry was badly received in neo-Gaelic circles as 'crude and non-Gaelic'.[10]

A literary movement has been defined as 'two or three writers who live in the same place and cordially detest one another'.[11] The fact that Dublin was a small city whose writers were all known to each other, where there was a multiplicity of literary talents and a scarcity of literary opportunities, fostered an atmosphere of mutual rivalry and envy. O'Faoláin not only agreed with Shaw that 'a certain flippant, futile derision and belittlement' was 'peculiar to Dublin' but thought that even Shaw's description did not fully convey that city's endemic begrudgery:

> . . . no sooner does any man attempt, or achieve, here, anything fine than the rats begin to emerge from the sewers, bringing with them a skunk-like stench of envy and hatred . . .[12]

To Cyril Connolly the Palace bar in 1941 appeared as 'warm and friendly as an alligator tank' and its occupants had acquired a 'leathery look' from 'a long process of mutual mastication'.[13] Kavanagh's growing tendency to equate criticism with destructiveness throughout the 1940s may well have been influenced by the prevalent literary climate. As he became more intimately involved in Dublin's daily spite he resorted to 'dangerous arrogance' and abusiveness as a defensive and offensive stance.[14] His bellicose strategy, learned on the playing fields of Inniskeen, might be summarised in the Monaghan phrase, 'Gut yer man'; forthright attack with no holds barred. Perhaps, he too early savoured the notoriety resulting from abusive journalism, when a passing insult to the Boy Scout movement in the course of a review of Maurice Walsh's *The Hill is Mine* in June 1940 provoked a six-week controversy in the letters page of the *Irish Times*.[15] As the years passed Kavanagh's cultural criticism in prose and verse became increasingly excoriating, and foe and erstwhile friend alike suffered the lash of his contempt.

Compelled to earn a hazardous living as a free-lance

journalist, Kavanagh became ever more righteously angry and isolated, nurturing his grievances and cultivating his sense of his own uniqueness. His scornful self-differentiation from his fellow writers was complemented by a parallel concern with the projection and promotion of a personal image both in life and in literature from the mid-1940s. Kavanagh's urban self-images will be the subject of the next chapter. This chapter considers his creation of a literature of alienation, his uncompromising antagonism towards his urban milieu, his savage criticism of his ideological opponents, his ruthless, often gratuitous or cruel repudiation of all ties or loyalties in the pursuit of a lonely individuality.

Kavanagh's difficulties in obtaining both journalistic and non-literary employment were compounded by his dissidence from the prevailing cultural ethos. His *Standard* column, 'The Literary Scene' was discontinued after only five months in 1943, because instead of restricting himself to book reviewing he used it as a critical forum. His later role as film critic for *The Standard* effectively muzzled his cultural criticism for that weekly, though he occasionally seized the opportunity to state his aesthetic opinions in his column, 'Round the Cinemas', which ran from 22 February 1946 to 8 July 1949. Some of his most extreme attacks on Irish writers and Irish culture were published in *The Bell*, *Irish Writing* and *Poetry* (Chicago). However, it was not until the end of 1949 that he was granted a regular platform from which to air his views: first, in the new monthly journal, *Envoy* (December 1949 to July 1951), and after its demise, in his own journal, *Kavanagh's Weekly*, for the thirteen heady weeks of its short-lived existence, from 12 April to 5 July 1952.

In his prose journalism Kavanagh addresses his public directly, defining his critical position and identifying the objects of his ideological scorn; in his satiric verse he ridicules literary Dublin through a series of fantasies and dramatic fictions designed to expose the absurdities and pretensions of his 'environment'.[16] Though these two activities are frequently conjoined in his writings in the 1940s and early 1950s, his verse satires will be studied separately from his critical prose.

First Impressions of Dublin

Kavanagh served his apprenticeship as an urban writer in the twice-weekly column entitled 'City Commentary', which he contributed to the *Irish Press* from 14 September 1942 to 8 February 1944 under the pen-name, Piers Plowman. His avowed object in 'City Commentary' was 'to give a country-man's impression of city life for the benefit of [his] friends in the country'.[17] What Kavanagh produced was an informal chat column, a record of his experiences and reflections written in a casual, friendly manner. Every now and then he broke into poetry, usually brief occasional pieces, 'light verses for the times that are in it'.[18] 'City Commentary' contains no distinguished urban prose or verse and, as a guide to life in wartime Dublin, it is singularly unenlightening, but it played a part in Kavanagh's development analogous to that played earlier by *The Green Fool*. It compelled him to communicate his impressions of city life in a direct, accessible style. Since coming to Dublin he had been so imaginatively obsessed with the countryside from which he had exiled himself that his new surroundings were not adverted to in his poetry. While he contrived to include a good deal of rural material even in 'City Commentary', he also revealed a lively curiosity about his urban milieu.

He roamed the streets as a roving reporter commenting on whatever encounter or spectacle took his fancy. From the beginning he saw himself as a diarist rather than a journalist. He was never interested in the merely topical, 'the day's loud lying', as he dismissed it in one poem of the period, or in sensational happenings.[19] His model diarist was Pepys who wrote an 'intimate personal record of seemingly petty events'.[20] Kavanagh watched children playing on the street, praised the vivacity of Moore Street traders, eavesdropped on women in a restaurant, chatted to a jeweller in his shop and to a gardener in the Botanic Gardens. He listened, disappointed, to the clichés of the 'gin and bitter blondes' stepping off the Belfast train at Amiens Street station and caught 'the accents of all Ireland' at an *Ard Fheis*.[21] He also interviewed low-paid workers about their lives and work, wages and prospects, and was particularly moved by the ordinary tragedy of a respectable clerk trying to keep up appearances on three pounds a week, unable to afford to date a woman or marry.[22] However, such sociological reportage was perfunctory and he flitted from topic to topic in his column, never allowing himself to become more than momentarily perturbed by the grim, frustrated lives of Maguire's urban cousins. It would appear that he considered it his function to entertain, not to trouble his readers, and, accordingly, he reverted to the contented, good-natured tones of *The Green Fool*. He comes across as a writer who identifies with the city's underdogs but is, on the whole, cheerful and easily pleased, chuffed at his promotion to regular newspaper columnist for one of Ireland's three national dailies. The *Irish Press* would not have been hospitable to social or cultural criticism in any case. Founded by de Valera, it was an organ of Fianna Fáil opinion. As such, it should have been anathema to Kavanagh, but his principles were subordinated to financial expediency in the early 1940s. As his 1944 poem, 'Pegasus', puts it, his soul was 'for sale' to any interested party.

The reason why 'City Commentary' contains so little memorable writing is probably because Kavanagh was familiarising himself with his subject rather than engaging with it in imaginative depth. He proclaims his aesthetic faith in the importance of ordinary life for the artist:

> The idea of the writer or artist who is apart from the ordinary flood of living does not appeal to me. The true artist must be part of life as it is lived by the ordinary

people—otherwise he is no more than a dilettante.
(19 April 1943)

and declares his preference for contemporary realism as
opposed to the 'going back to the dead past . . . very common in literary circles'.[23] However, he is conscious of the
ephemerality of his own enterprise, recognising that a 'net of
trifles' is necessary to catch a mood, but aware that the trifles
themselves are no substitute for the mood he is 'trying to
catch'.[24] The writer, for whom *Ulysses* was a second favourite
bedside book,[25] knows that he has failed to make the
imaginative breakthrough from city journalist to city poet:

> If only imagination could get free we would see things as
> they really are, and all the people coming and going the
> streets would unfold from the bud of silence . . . (20
> October 1943)

The snippets of verse included in 'City Commentary',
sometimes to round off a column, are, with very few exceptions, mere jingles, negligible as poetry, yet the writing of
these light-hearted, occasional pieces extended Kavanagh's
poetic range. Though many of the poems are more rural in
their imagery than the accompanying prose, he does make
some attempt to accommodate his urban experiences in
rhyme. Dublin place-names begin to crop up unobtrusively in
these odds and ends of verse—Inchicore, Grafton Street,
O'Connell Bridge, Abbey Street, Amiens Street, the Botanic
gardens, Mount Street bridge—a sure sign of Kavanagh's
affectionate annexation of urban territory. There are verses
recording his reactions to such diverse events as a film,
a beauty contest, a camogie match, a boxing tournament,
lunching in a restaurant, meeting the Belfast train. He is
nostalgic for pre-war Dublin,

> . . . midnight lighted streets,
> Cigarettes, tea, sugar and gas always on,
> Buses coming at a quarter to one . . .

These urban rhymes are little more than versified journalism and, indeed, he once experimented with writing his entire column in doggerel.[26] Although hardly to be dignified with the name of poetry, his 'City Commentary' verses show Kavanagh experimenting with a humorous, impromptu, conversational style and a contemporary idiom, allowing his personality free play, or fashioning a poetic persona which can cope with the trivia of the urban reporter's experience. He is in a carefree, holiday mood, writing a sonnet about a boxing match in response to a dare, waxing humorously satiric about a radio verse play, yawning his way through 'Gone with the Wind', or composing a comic Valentine verse. The often playful treatment of everyday concerns results in a continuation and extension of the flexible rhyming that had characterised *The Great Hunger* and *Lough Derg*: 'fighters' is rhymed with 'first nighters'; 'Rotunda' with 'Monday' and 'understand a'; 'bridge' with 'grudge'; 'monotonous' with 'botanist'; 'Finn McCool' with 'National School'.

'City Commentary' reveals Kavanagh in a transitional phase, the countryman turning city dweller, nostalgia yielding to the excitement of novelty, urban images and experiences nudging their way into print to join AE-influenced rhapsodies and rural reminiscences. He is no longer imaginatively locked in the past. His poetry is changing and adapting itself, however awkwardly and superficially, to his changed circumstances. He is taking it along with him rather than letting it stagnate in the countryside. Another significant development is that he no longer equates poetry with profundity, with the tragic destiny or the epiphanic moment. He is experimenting with verse that is 'an entertainment only' and not 'a profound and holy faith'.[27]

Unacknowledged Legislator: The Poet as Cultural Critic

Despite some sharp, iconoclastic criticism of the Revival and of such well established writers as Synge, Kavanagh's sporadic, early articles on and reviews of Irish literature are

relatively benign. He was generally better disposed towards contemporary Irish fiction writers than poets, though, in *The Green Fool*, even his comments on the poets are favourable. A survey of 'Fifty Years of Irish Literature' in 1945 succeeds in maintaining an appearance of critical balance by enthusiastically praising the fictions of Daniel Corkery, Lord Dunsany, Frank O'Connor, Seán O'Faoláin, Liam O'Flaherty, Peadar O'Donnell and Francis MacManus, while only qualifiedly approving Yeats and returning rather negative verdicts on such contemporary poets as W. R. Rodgers, Donagh MacDonagh, Robert Farren and Austin Clarke. Irishness was still an aesthetic criterion for Kavanagh at this point, so Colum's 'The Drover' is cited as an example of 'exclusively Irish literature'; Frank O'Connor is commended as an 'Irish Catholic writer'; F. R. Higgins has 'a queer, native quality, a bit artificial, perhaps—at least sometimes'.[28]

Two years later Kavanagh's opinion of the state of the arts in Ireland took a drastic turn for the worse and from then on his literary and cultural criticism was preponderantly defamatory. From 1947 he launched a series of fierce guerrilla attacks on individual Irish writers; on Irish literary journals and anthologies of verse; on the Abbey theatre, its players and its patrons; on the Gaelic language revival movement; on Dublin's artistic and intellectual pretensions; on Irish journalism. He was soon embattled with almost every established Irish writer, except Peadar O'Donnell, who as editor of *The Bell* from 1946 provided him with a public forum in which to air his increasingly unpopular views, and Brian O'Nolan, a fellow satirist, whose droll deflation of Irish cultural complacencies he admired. Kavanagh berated those with money, power and position in the new Irish Republic, as if inviting ostracism and unemployment. The insults that others muttered into their pints among friends, or reserved for use against specific enemies in Dublin's internecine faction fights, he fearlessly printed, and aimed at all-comers. His image of the poetic genius by 1949 was of one who created around himself an antagonism.[29] Unfortunately, it was easier and speedier to dissociate himself from others' achievements, standards and tastes, through published criticism than to create the literature that would implicitly testify to his artistic uniqueness. So much of Kavanagh's verbal energy was channelled into the demolition of rival talents and aesthetic models, and the articulation of his emancipation from his cultural matrix, that little was spared for the positive act of expressing his individualistic, new art. His importance as a critic of the Romantic, nationalist ethos which was furnishing Irish poetasters with a subject and a style, and of the opposing school of social realism which was performing a similar service for Irish fiction writers, almost eclipses his poetic achievement for a decade from 1947. The voice that sounds most persistently and most vehemently throughout these years is his 'angry foghorn', warning with monotonous regularity of the unhealthy smog that enveloped Dublin life and letters.

Kavanagh's first full scale assaults on contemporary Irish writers, an essay on the recently deceased F. R. Higgins, closely followed by one on his absent friend, Frank O'Connor, were so ruthless that they raised an outcry of protest. In November 1947 Higgins, whom he had praised, albeit with some reservations, in 1945, was vociferously denounced as an insincere Protestant who posed as a droll, 'gallivanting Irishman'; his life and his work were both declared inauthentic, because 'based on an illusion in which he pretended to believe—Ireland'. Higgins's crime was to have substituted the literary Ireland invented by Synge for the actualities of his own experience, to have cast himself in the role of 'playboy'.[30] The following month, Kavanagh mounted an equally devastating attack on O'Connor in an essay in *The Bell*, entitled 'Coloured Balloons'. This essay, which demonstrated a close familiarity with O'Connor's *oeuvre*, again applied the criterion of authenticity. In particular, it impugned the realism rested. O'Connor's fiction, though technically skilful, was found to be more subtly false than Higgins's verse, quasi-realist, 'very nearly on the earth' but 'about an inch from the top of the grass'. Criticism of O'Connor's lack of realism was reiterated throughout the essay in rural metaphors, despite the fact that most of O'Connor's stories were set in urban or small-town Ireland. The author of *Tarry Flynn* considered that O'Connor should 'have thrown in a few spadefuls of the earth's healthy reality—roots, stones, worms, dung' into his fiction. Responding to this essay in the next issue of *The Bell* O'Faoláin pointed out that Kavanagh's central weakness as an evaluative critic was his narcissism, accusing him of 'roaring contentedly at his own face in the mirror of everything he read(s)'. The 'good critic', O'Faoláin concluded,

> has to recognise a great number of categories. Mr Kavanagh's trouble is that he only admires and knows one.

O'Faoláin had accurately diagnosed that Kavanagh's criticism was really an exercise in aesthetic self-definition and self-justification. His charge that the O'Connor essay is narcissistic is a fair comment and it is also true that, instead of offering a judicious analysis of the work of fellow writers, most of Kavanagh's impressionistic appraisals are only enlightening as regards his own aesthetic values.

Kavanagh evidently repented his devastating attack on O'Connor and his subsequent surveys of the Irish literary scene usually include a flattering reference to him. However, the general tenor of his criticism of Irish writing continued to be derogatory and he was particularly disdainful of his fellow poets. In an essay on 'Poetry in Ireland Today' (*The Bell*, April 1948) he invoked the metaphor of death to describe that absence of vitality he deplored in Irish poetry:

> The poems being written are like perfectly laid-out corpses on a slab. They are perfectly shaped and perfectly dead.

Such an extreme metaphor allowed him to categorise and to condemn, simplistically, vehemently and subjectively, without any necessity to resort to aesthetic issues or analytic niceties: 'Death has neither a high nor low standard.' Recent anthologies of Irish verse were consigned to the pyre, the *Irish Times* anthology,[31] which included some of his poetry, as well as *Contemporary Irish Poetry*, edited by Robert Greacen and Valentin Iremonger, which did not.[32] Such anthologies endorsed a collectivist and ethnic approach to literature which the individualistic Kavanagh had begun to spurn. Vitality in 'Poetry in Ireland Today' is associated with contemporaneity in subject matter and speech, with coming 'out into the living day'. Yeats, whom Kavanagh always ambivalently admired, was, on this occasion, commended for his poetic vitality, and he even conceded that a few poems by a few contemporaries were 'genuinely alive': some of the work of W. R. Rodgers, Valentin Iremonger, Donagh MacDonagh, Geoffrey Taylor, Peter Wells and John Hewitt escaped the morgue.

In a January 1950 letter to *The Bell* Kavanagh also applied the metaphor of death to the Gaelic language, envisaging it as a 'corpse . . . propped up with pillows', being ministered and deferred to as if it were a living authority, because it was mistakenly identified with nationhood. Irish writers, Kavanagh asserted, should 'realise and express . . . the fact that language is not particularly a badge of nationhood', that 'The language a man speaks has very little to do with his outlook and character.' The promotion of the Gaelic language he construed as hostile to the interests of Ireland's English-speaking writers, who were decentred by being designated 'Anglo–Irish' rather than Irish. Kavanagh himself spoke of the Irish language as the 'old language' and consistently referred to it as 'Gaelic' in this letter, thereby divorcing it from modern Irish life and literature.

Acknowledging the death of Gaelic had another significant repercussion for contemporary Irish literature, adverted to in 'Poetry in Ireland Today'. It highlighted the artificiality of the

'Celtic Mode' or 'Note', first instituted as an artistic criterion in Thomas MacDonagh's *Literature in Ireland Today* (1916), and currently advocated by MacDonagh's former pupil, Austin Clarke, and by Robert Farren. So virulent was Kavanagh's review of Farren's *The Course of Irish Verse* (1948), which adopts the 'Irish mode' as a literary criterion, that the *Irish Times* refused to publish it. Both MacDonagh and Farren refer to an 'Irish' rather than a 'Celtic' mode (indeed, MacDonagh employs the term 'Celtic' pejoratively), so Kavanagh's use of 'Celtic', like his use of 'Gaelic', is polemically loaded.

When in August 1949 he was invited to review the 'Poetic Situation in Ireland since the death of Yeats' for *Poetry* (Chicago), instead of puffing his fellow authors, or boosting Ireland's claims to literary pre-eminence, Kavanagh, predictably, seized the opportunity to engage in negative propaganda and to undermine Dublin's artistic pretensions. His first moves were to demolish the image of Dublin as a literary metropolis and to undermine the concept of the Literary Revival:

> The metropolis of literary Ireland is London, with occasional glances towards America and even Paris. For a few years during what has come to be called the Irish Revival, but which might better be called the Time of Yeats, a centre had been established in Dublin which made its own standards. Today we are living on this past, an unhealthy food, the principal diet of journalists.

The new Irish Republic was denounced as the continuator of the Ireland from which Joyce had fled:

> Nets are still flung to catch the soul as it is born here. One greatly fears that the new-won political freedom is not going to improve matters. On the contrary, there is a danger that with the outside world no longer challenging we may become still more insular, more subject to the inside tyrannies of Church and State.

By 1949 most of Kavanagh's battle-lines were drawn. As a vehement critic of the new 'grocers' Republic' his target was similar to O'Faoláin's, though his style of attack was very different, a series of swift, would-be knock-out punches rather than elegant or subtle argumentation. As an abusive critic of fellow Irish artists and writers he had no peer. Obsessed by aesthetic values and utterly fearless in assessing others by his own criteria, it would appear that what most frequently spurred him into formulating his poetics was the attempt to articulate his dissatisfaction with, or very occasionally his meagre approval of, the work of his contemporaries. He habitually arraigned the same writers, sometimes merely to reiterate an already well rehearsed objection, but sometimes, too, to tease out his own aesthetic position, as if he could only think adversarially, or by the Arnoldian method of citing 'touchstones'.

The invitation to contribute a regular feature to *Envoy*, the new monthly review of literature and art, inaugurated by John Ryan in December 1949, provided Kavanagh with the stimulus and the opportunity to engage in a series of aggressive avowals of his poetics and his cultural views. *Envoy*, which prided itself on being young and 'vital',[33] welcomed his iconoclastic opinions, and, short of libel, he was free to be as absolutist and intemperate as he pleased in his critique of the arts in Ireland. The result was a monthly 'Diary', which to the unsympathetic reader may appear unbearably arrogant and judgmental, in which named persons and institutions were unsystematically, but repeatedly and ruthlessly, reviled. The first 'Diary' began by exalting love as a literary virtue:

> Before sitting down to write a man should make an Act of Deep Love. For outside Love is barrenness.

However, it soon became clear that this was a 'Deep Love' which would express itself through chastisement, and that the writer did not intend to spare the rod. The subtitle of Kavanagh's first 'Diary', 'Being some Reflections on the 50th Anniversary of Irish Literature', was itself a calculated affront

to the historicist pretensions of both the Gaelic and Anglo–
Irish literary camps, a declaration not of love but of war. It
also indicated the historical era with which he himself was to
be most concerned, Revivalist and post-Revivalist Ireland.

Kavanagh's aesthetic in *Envoy* was uncompromisingly elitist, cruel in its disparagement of all that fell below its
Olympian standards, intellectually despotic. For him, 'Comparative criticism is criticism without standards' and 'no
genuine writer as a critic was ever anything but absolute in
his destructiveness'.[34] Scarcely any notable Irish writer of the
previous fifty years 'scaped whipping in 'Diary'. Padraic
Colum, Douglas Hyde, Francis Ledwidge, J. M. Synge, James
Stephens, Sean O'Casey, Elizabeth Bowen, even, on occasion, James Joyce and W. B. Yeats, were summarily castig-
ated. His contemporaries fared no better: Austin Clarke and
Robert Farren, in particular, were regularly denounced. As a
literary critic Kavanagh appeared an autocrat who would 'bear
. . . no brother near the throne', though his ire against Irish
writers was rather, he claimed, a reaction against the indiscrim-
inate overpraise lavished on poetasters and literary hacks in a
society which seemed incapable of distinguishing between
good and bad. In the whole world there were, he said, only
about twenty creative artists worthy of the name, whereas

> In Ireland we never come to a last judgement. There are
> always a score of great poets, painters, novelists. (Nov-
> ember 1950)

Kavanagh who held that 'To praise everybody is to blame
everybody' took the precaution of praising hardly anybody,
and even those few, who, like Yeats, escaped the general
damnation, were only guardedly and selectively commended.

Austin Clarke and Robert Farren were singled out for
special vilification, not only for their perpetuation of the ideal
of a distinctively ethnic verse, but for their co-founding of the
Lyric Theatre Company and the Dublin Verse-Speaking
Society, and for their influential cultural positions in Radio

Éireann. The aim of the Lyric Theatre Company was to revive the Yeatsian ideal of verse-drama at the Abbey and members of the Verse-Speaking Society regularly broadcast choral and dramatic poetry on Radio Éireann. Kavanagh was critically myopic on the subject of painting and music, abhorred the Abbey theatre, and heartily loathed verse-speakers and actors. In his opinion 'Actors are loved because they are unoriginal', because they 'stick to their script' (January 1950). 'Off stage, without the parts which make them heroes, they feel embittered and resentful in company' (September 1950). Actors are projected as authors' mouthpieces, who receive the public acclaim which rightfully belongs to the writer. Verse-speakers are an even more detestable species, since their performance distorts the relationship between poetry and its audience:

> The worse the verse, the better it lends itself to this superimposed chant. Verse-speakers should have meaningless patter specially written for them upon which they can exploit their ludicrous virtuosity to their heart's pleasure. (May 1950)

Kavanagh's dislike of Radio Éireann may not have been entirely disinterested since it had refused his application for employment.[35] However, the national radio station's populist bias also offended his elitist cultural views, and it galled him that the education of the nation's poetic sensibilities should be entrusted to his ideological arch-enemy, Austin Clarke.[36]

Though most of his own income derived from journalism, journalists were among Kavanagh's favourite *bêtes noires*. Newspaper journalists he despised as debasers of language, purveyors of 'vulgar slang words' such as 'teenage' and abbreviations such as 'congrats'. Popular papers pandered to the lowest common denominator of taste, being 'written by the office-boy for office-boys' in accordance with 'Northcliffe's theory and practice' (May 1951). Newspapers substituted facts for truths and conferred importance on the trivial and ephemeral. In one of his most scathing observations on newspaper ethics Kavanagh compared rival papers' 'holier than thou' attitudes to the 'moralizing' of 'fag-puffing ladies-in-waiting on O'Connell Street at 1 a.m.' (January 1950).

In *Envoy* the diarist, who had appointed himself literary *defensor fidei* in several articles in *The Standard*, and who regarded Catholicism as inseparable from 'parochialism' for the Irish writer, acknowledged his alienation from Ireland's official religious ideology:

> The Catholic intellectual's problem is the problem of freedom of expression. This is particularly a problem in Ireland where some members of the Hierarchy exercise or attempt to exercise control over the written word. But more so than bishops in this censorship is the Catholic conscience which makes cowards of us all. It also makes cowards of us in the political and social fields. (December 1950)

The hypocritical Irish alliance between God and Mammon was repugnant to many writers in de Valera's theocracy, where philistinism masquerading as piety invoked the Censorship Act of 1929 or the more subtle blacklisting strategy of the whisper over the phone or dinner table to stifle authors critical of the status quo, branding them as unorthodox or unsafe.[37] Prior to 1949 Kavanagh had been guarded in his unenthusiasm for official Irish Catholicism, since one of his few patrons was the Archbishop of Dublin, John Charles McQuaid, who was probably instrumental in his obtaining the post of film critic with the *Standard*. However, his connections with the *Standard* had been severed in July 1949, and he was, therefore, more openly censorious about ecclesiastical and pietistic meddling in the arts. Nevertheless, he made a show of flourishing his own credentials to orthodoxy in *Envoy* by comparing Rome's festive Catholicism with the 'long-faced hypocrisy' and 'barbarous piety' which were 'to be found everywhere in Ireland' (December 1950).[38]

Kavanagh's cultural criticism was never as disinterested as O'Faoláin's. He was conducting a personal as well as a social crusade. His prose criticism and verse satires explicitly or implicitly reveal not only an unwavering faith in the poet's superior vision and socially redemptive mission, but an unassailable conviction as to his own poetic exceptionality. He arrogantly and unashamedly demanded the kind of enlightened private and state patronage that would reward his genius and set him free from financial cares to dedicate himself to his poetic vocation. His denial of others' artistic merits was a proclamation of his own, and he virulently denounced the jumped-up peasant middle class which refused to accept him at his personal aesthetic valuation and withheld the financial security he craved, and felt to be his just desert.

Dublin, in Kavanagh's view, was 'not an adult society' and lacked a 'clearly defined cultured class'. It was a new cultural entity, 'still in the melting-pot' (May 1950). In a less temperate 'Diary' he savaged Ireland as a land ruled by Firbolgs, 'where publicans, race-track touts and dispensers of trivia' were 'in authority', where money meant 'success, journalism, literature, or Show Business art' (November 1950). He deliberately set out to raise post-colonial hackles by invidious comparisons between attitudes to the arts in Ireland and England (November 1950), and this was to become one of his favourite ploys. London was portrayed as an El Dorado where the tight-fisted, mercenary morality that prevailed in middle-class Dublin was unknown. However, as Hubert Butler wisely remarked in his obituary on *Envoy*,[39] which folded after twenty months, Kavanagh's quarrel with Dublin and with Ireland was a lover's quarrel:

> Would a man who was not inextricably involved in a small society bother to insult it in such detail?

His 'Diaries', Butler observed, 'were meant for speech, not print'; they were 'at their best . . . paradoxical challenges flung out to stimulate thought'. Certainly, Kavanagh either determined to achieve an effect of improvisation or did not bother to organise his polemical 'Diaries' in essay form, taking advantage of their title to turn out a series of loosely connected or random jottings. Sustained rational argument was not his forte and he appears to have cultivated the tone of rash, impulsive speech in both prose and verse from the early 1940s. Nuances or qualifications which would have lessened the impact of his forceful pronouncements were disregarded. Whether Kavanagh's views were merely intended as a series of 'paradoxical challenges' is more debatable. His cultural criticism may indeed have appeared immoderate and ill considered, but Butler's unkind comparison of his critical mind to 'a monkey house at feeding time' is excessively severe. It would be more accurate as well as more charitable to consider these 'Diaries' as a series of interim reports from a writer 'wandering between two worlds', making occasional nostalgic returns to Inniskeen, but for the most part, desperately attempting to confront the urban, middle-class society and the literary context into which he had migrated.

Butler criticised *Envoy* and Kavanagh for pursuing the wrong targets:

> . . . it was bad management that all the violence went on in the guardroom behind the lines, while the Philistines looked on and laughed.

With hindsight it is easier to understand that Kavanagh was at least as much obsessed with literary criticism as with goading hostile philistines into reluctant patronage or with improving their artistic discernment. While busily engaged in bludgeoning other Irish writers, he was also trying to rationalise his own belligerence and, thereby, to formulate a poetics.

Kavanagh's demolition attempt on the Irish Literary Revival had been accompanied by a definitive rejection of an ethnic aesthetic since 1947. His 'Diary' of June 1950 exposes the primary 'falseness . . . in this idea of Ireland as a spiritual entity', eliminates 'the adjective "Irish" from the body of poetry written during this century in Ireland' and transcends national boundaries by greeting Auden, Dylan Thomas,

Moravia, Sartre and Pound as Irish poets, that is as poets who delight a man born in Ireland. To the end of his career Kavanagh vehemently reiterated his denunciation of ethnicity as an artistic criterion. In his later forties' essays and in 'Diary' he attempted to enunciate an alternative poetics. While he advocated contemporaneity in image and idiom in defiance of the thematic and technical retrospectiveness of the 'Celtic mode', he was neither altogether comfortable with the social realism of the *Bell* school, nor with the modernist foregrounding of experimental technique. Though he admired *Ulysses* for its rendition of the comedy of ordinary urban living, he distrusted Joyce's formal cleverness.[40] He attacked O'Connor for not being sufficiently realist in 'Coloured Balloons', yet responded to O'Faoláin's critique of this essay by stating:

> What I seek and love when I find it is the whiskey of the imagination, not the bread and butter of 'reality'.[41]

This appears disingenuous, a cop-out or evasion, but it may result from Kavanagh's sense that O'Connor was purveying 'emotional entertainment' rather than spiritual guidance. Realism in *The Great Hunger* had been conducted *sub specie aeternitatis* and in *Tarry Flynn* Kavanagh had managed to see-saw between realism and imaginative intoxication by having a farmer-poet as hero. Parochialism, though it trusts what the 'eye sees', also attempts to evoke a mentality which juxtaposes the earthly and the eternal.

Kavanagh could not conceive of art as solely mimetic or critical of the status quo. The poet was for him a prophet, the spiritual leader of his people. What distinguished 'perfect description' and 'competent' versifying from genuine poetry was an inspirational quality which he compared to light or flame or life; poetry was vatic:

> When Wordsworth or any genuine poet is ostensibly writing about—say—a daffodil, his real message is a transcendent one.[42]

What Kavanagh espouses and articulates piecemeal in *Envoy* is a high Romantic poetics, a poetics that is both expressive[43] and transcendental. In his 'Diary' of May 1950, for instance, he asserts:

> Poetry is not an 'art' only, but something more, a philosophy, a statement of life, a religion. Pictures and music fit perfectly into the bourgeois scheme, but ideas are dangerous . . .

Explicating the reason for his dislike of verse-speaking he struggles to distinguish between poetic technique as imaginative expression and literary craftsmanship:

> I do not quite agree that the sound of a poem is part of its meaning; it's true, music comes from an inner excitement, thought tensions. It is this inner music which throws a shadow of itself in the shape of the outer form. To say that sound is an important part of the verse is disastrous, the nearest to a simple definition I can get is —Poetry is statement, something said. (May 1950)

The expressive bias of his aesthetic is evident in his comment on Yeats in the first issue of *Envoy*:

> It is the pressure of a fine mind which gives to many of his slight poems their impact.
> You influence people not by what is conscious in your work but by the buried unconscious. The poems are hints of the deeper man.

The previous year he had declared that

> . . . poetry is not so much in words as in the attitude. It is a twist in the mind which can be recognised in any medium.[44]

Kavanagh subscribed to the high Romantic doctrine of the poet's oracular powers:

A poet must be . . . vitalizing the spirit of man in some way. He must have dug deep beneath the poverty-stricken crust of our time and uncovered new veins of uranium, the uranium of faith and hope, a transcendent purpose.[45]

Not content with serving as an 'unacknowledged legislator' he forthrightly affirmed that the poet was a social benefactor who deserved to be publicly subsidised:

He demands a living, and in most ages and societies he has been granted it. There is an instinct in mankind which recognises the priestly nature of the poet's function. This instinct has never been strong in Ireland, for Ireland is a particularly cynical and materialistic country — for all its boastings about religion.

When *Envoy* folded after the July 1951 issue Kavanagh found himself deprived of the pulpit to which he had become accustomed. He was a silenced poet-priest, eager to exercise his ministry to the Irish people, to preach to the unconverted. By April 1952 he had persuaded his brother, Peter, to finance 'a journal of literature and politics' named *Kavanagh's Weekly*. This eight-page journal was almost exclusively a fraternal venture. Most of it was written by Patrick under a variety of pseudonyms; Peter contributed a series of articles either anonymously or under the pen-name, John L. Flanagan, in addition to organising the layout, printing and distribution. Each number, except the last, contained an editorial on the state of the nation, feature articles, a gossip column called 'Graftonia', a theatre and radio column, a page of literary criticism, and a satiric anthology of press cuttings under the headline, 'The Old Foolishness'. The paper also offered mock competitions, parodying the vogue for crossword and fashion competitions in the Irish Sunday newspapers. Apart from his brother's weekly article or two, a few humorous pieces by Myles na gCopaleen, an essay on literature by Paul Rocquet, some features on the arts in Northern Ireland contributed by Gerard Keenan and one poem, signed N. Caffrey, Patrick Kavanagh wrote the entire journal for thirteen weeks. Any unsolicited contributions received apparently fell below the editor's Olympian standards and even some of Myles na gCopaleen's offerings were discarded as merely jocose and, therefore, incompatible with the *Weekly*'s mission to alert the Irish nation to its political and cultural plight. A *Kavanagh's Monthly* would have been a more feasible proposition in the circumstances. As it was, there could be no let-up in the supply of copy and the journal was a tremendous drain on Patrick's creative energy. That the Kavanaghs' funds ran out after only thirteen weeks was a welcome release from a treadmill of their own devising.[46]

Kavanagh's Weekly was probably modelled on *The Irish Statesman*, to whose format it bears a certain resemblance. The comparability of the two journals is actually adverted to in the eleventh number. In his capacity as literary father figure AE had provided his protégé with a role model of the poet as a synthesis of the contemplative and the socially committed, the artist as sage. The two most influential Irish poets of Kavanagh's youth, AE and Yeats, had invoked the authority of the artist as statesman and spiritual leader, and it was their mantle, though not their manner, that Kavanagh now assumed. Another of the young Kavanagh's mentors, Seán O'Faoláin, as founder editor of *The Bell*, had successfully stepped into the breach to fulfil the function of Irish artist-critic immediately after Yeats's death. By 1952 O'Faoláin appeared to Kavanagh less a collaborator than a challenging rival. So the *Weekly* relegates him to punditry's second division as a petty-minded chairman of radio debates. He is accused of acting as lay Archbishop of Dublin, a role which Kavanagh himself clearly coveted.[47]

Kavanagh's Weekly captures the *zeitgeist* of a particularly depressing period in Irish history. The country's post-war economic boom was over and its spirits, like its finances, slumped. The atmosphere of apathy and pessimism was almost palpable. Kavanagh's first iconoclastic editorial, entitled 'Victory of Mediocrity', presented Ireland's thirty-odd years of political independence as an era of decline into mindless mediocrity and ineffectual materialism. Ireland was only nominally Christian; its people were really committed neither to God nor to Mammon but only to a safe, unprofitable materialism, more concerned with pay and pension than with productivity. Free of any editorial restraint for the first time in his career, Kavanagh launched into a frontal assault on the status quo:

> All the mouthpieces of public opinion are controlled by men whose only qualification is their inability to think. Being stupid and illiterate is the mark of respectability and responsibility.
> The basis of this point of view is a fundamental lack of belief in God . . . Can any of these people who presume to be our leaders and voices be hurt in any way except through the pocket?

Kavanagh's ideological position had not changed since his *Envoy* days, and 'merit' and 'mediocrity' still constitute the two poles of his critical vocabulary. However, his critical base was broader, political now, as well as cultural. In so far as *Kavanagh's Weekly* is a 'journal of politics' it is vehemently opposed to the Fianna Fáil Party and it dubs Éamon de Valera the patron saint of Ireland's mediocracy.[48] Mediocrities 'control all thought by shutting out from the sources of money anyone who might look like exposing them'. Whereas the Soviet state sent its dissidents to Siberia, in Ireland the nonconformist is 'starved into silence' or forced to emigrate to Birmingham by a bourgeoisie which controls all patronage and cannot appreciate creative innovation 'at a range of less than forty years'. For the Irish intellectual the choice is between becoming 'a sort of despairing saint', satisfied with having 'neither house, nor wife nor good clothes', or joining in 'the jungle fight' as Kavanagh is doing here.[49]

In one memorable metaphor Kavanagh compares Ireland's

stagnant social and economic state to the ambience at a country wake. Its people are like insincere mourners mouthing platitudes to each other while the shrewd businessman-undertaker walks about on padded feet lest he disturb the atmosphere of mindless and simulated goodwill. A wake is a period when nothing serious is discussed and nobody is angry or destructive. The satirist thinks that the wake has been unduly protracted and that it is high time the Irish buried the corpse of 1916, the Gaelic language and the national inferiority complex, and turned their attention to the business of living.[50]

In *Kavanagh's Weekly* the place-name of Crohan, a parish where only one marriage took place in the previous year, becomes synonymous with the moribund state of rural Irish society. In the editorial in which he introduces the subject (3 May 1952), Kavanagh focuses, not on the actualities of life in Crohan, about whose location he is unsure, but on the antics of the bungling and complacent Irish bureaucracy which permits such a disquieting state of affairs to become a commonplace in Ireland's green and pleasant land. This shift away from the particularities of *The Great Hunger* towards general issues, a swing from parochial evocation to social analysis, is typical of the change in Kavanagh's literary focus in the late 1940s and early 1950s.

In what is probably the best known passage in *Kavanagh's Weekly* the poet distinguishes between parochialism and provincialism.[51] Kavanagh's poetry and fiction may be parochial but his social and cultural criticism might well be termed provincial in its continual invocation of English mores and standards. It was, in fact, a form of Irish parochialism, a self-congratulatory introspectiveness, that stimulated the Anglophilia which is so marked a feature of *Kavanagh's Weekly*. In the first issue alone the editor attributes Irish emigration to an attraction towards England's 'enthusiasm for life', states that, unlike Ireland, England has a 'reflective and thoughtful minority' and makes the further polemical point that 'the level of awareness here is much lower than it is in England as anyone who compares the popular newspapers of both countries will see or anyone who compares the entertainment sent out by the Irish and British radios'. In his last editorial Kavanagh is still harping on Ireland's cultural inferiority to England. Here Gaelic literature is dismissed in a provocative assertion calculated to cause apoplexy in neo-Gaelic circles: 'Ireland had no literature till it turned to the English language and found an audience outside the country.'

'The Old Foolishness' column, a selection of press cuttings designed to expose those shibboleths of national life to which Kavanagh voices a more direct opposition in the editorials, even today retains some of its satiric cutting edge, since the chauvinistic pomposities and philistine platitudes it ridicules are still, to a declining extent, a recognisable feature of Irish public discourse. In 1952 the Young Ireland rhetoric, which had been considered old-fashioned in Yeats's youth, still flourished on the platform and among journalists, a liking for such words as 'forefathers', 'bards', 'valiant', 'deeds' and for such tropes as 'spiritual and national emancipation', the 'stirring of old banners', the 'sealmark of nationhood', the 'upsurge of national spirit'. On one occasion de Valera was caught in the act of placing the well-being of the Irish people fourth on his list of priorities, the three more important considerations being freedom, the restoration of the Irish language and the unification of the country.[52] De Valera's wife and the Fianna Fáil Minister of Lands are among those who earn a place in the column for regarding nationalist sentiment as a mark of literary merit, the object of their ill-judged flattery being the deservedly obscure poetess, Ethna Carberry.[53] Even lower literary standards were achieved by the Sligo Vocational Education Committee which opined that the only two periodicals worth reading in Ireland were *Our Boys* and *Ireland's Own*.[54] There are several instances of the uncritical adulation of Irish writers, the most inflated being Daniel Corkery's lengthy list of younger writers in Gaelic, 'the least of whom is of significance to this land'.[55] 'The Old

Foolishness' testifies to a national mania for talent spotting, based on the notion that the country is full of untapped potential. Publicity is given not only to lists of writers but to beauty contests, fashion contests, screen tests and a competition to write a radio play. Talent is so abundant that a plane-load of Irish artists is sent to an all-star gala in England. Occasionally 'The Old Foolishness' simply sees the funny side of some innocuous public pronouncement, such as the Minister of Health's acknowledgment that Ireland is short of accommodation for its numerous mental defectives.[56] 'The Old Foolishness' was doubly barbed in that it impaled not only the original perpetrator of some nonsensical sentiment but also the newspapers which so insulted their readers' honesty and intelligence.

Literary, theatre and radio criticism in *Kavanagh's Weekly* is predictably truculent. Kavanagh's splenetic scorn for his fellow poets, in particular, helped to create or perpetuate an atmosphere of 'acrimony and insult', an 'ingrown, discouraging' literary climate in which 'a poem was to be kicked, not examined', an ambience which impelled young poets like John Montague to flee this 'poisoned land' in the early 1950s. Kavanagh's 'baffled fury' was, to Montague, that of 'a man flailing between two faded worlds, the country he had left and the literary Dublin he never found'.[57] Yet, in his favour it must be said that posterity would endorse many of the literary judgments which his contemporaries found so gratuitously offensive. Most of the poems of Donagh MacDonagh, F. R. Higgins, Robert Farren and W. R. Rodgers are no longer read, even in Ireland. Austin Clarke has his advocates, true, but few critics today would champion his lyrical dramas. While to the cynical observer it might have appeared that Kavanagh's preference for contemporary fiction writers was self interested since they offered no challenge to his poetic supremacy, it is also the case that the work of O'Flaherty, O'Connor and O'Faoláin has proved more enduring than that of any of the above-mentioned poets, excepting only Clarke.

Kavanagh's project of arousing a cautious, conservative, chauvinist society to a sense of the relationship between its spiritual and economic malaise was quixotic and, inevitably, doomed. His messianic sense of his own role as saviour of the Irish people was so at odds with Dublin society's perception of him as to verge on the megalomanic. He had a few disciples and cronies but was, on the whole, regarded as an eccentric bogman. Moreover, Catholic Dublin was already well equipped with conscience keepers and enjoyed a theological certitude about the means of ultimate salvation. Indeed, only a miracle or some divine assistance could have enabled such an ill-conceived enterprise as *Kavanagh's Weekly* to succeed. What earthly hope was there for a badly promoted weekly journal in a market where the lively and well-promoted monthly, *Envoy*, had failed and where even such a well-established monthly as *The Bell* had experienced financial difficulties. At sixpence a copy *Kavanagh's Weekly* was cheaper than *Envoy* or *The Bell* which sold at two shillings and one shilling and sixpence respectively, but since it was produced for the most part by only two writers it lacked the variety and range of either monthly, and tended towards a shrill monotone. Circulation was curtailed because the brothers did not manage to secure the services of the usual Irish distributors, Easons, and were compelled to establish their own limited distribution network.[58] Since the Kavanaghs set about systematically biting any hands that might have fed them the journal attracted only two advertisers.[59] 'Morality' was defined by Patrick as 'the courage to say what you believe to be true even though it cuts across your own best interests'.[60] Between them the brothers alienated numerous sectors of Irish society, while endearing themselves to almost no one. Their ire was directed at the moneyed middle class, the Fianna Fáil Party, the Civil Service in general and the Department of External Affairs in particular, the Tourist Board, Radio Eireann, the Arts Advisory Council, the Arts Council, the Cultural Relations Committee, the Abbey

Theatre, the Institute of Higher Studies, the Folklore Commission, the *Sunday Press*, the National Film Institute, Bord na Mona and the Gaeltacht Services, *Comhdháil Náisiúnta na Gaedhilge*, even the army and navy. Careless of the consequences, they savaged Irish society thoroughly and relentlessly for thirteen weeks. *Kavanagh's Weekly* quickly earned a reputation for 'destructiveness' and 'bitterness'. Patrick might argue that Irish society was so adolescent that it could not distinguish 'moral indignation from bitterness', but in a rare flash of insight he acknowledged that although his weekly was on the side of the angels, 'Even an angel cannot afford to be estranging too many people.'[61] The brothers had optimistically ordered a print run of three thousand copies to begin with, but *Kavanagh's Weekly* attracted few buyers. Its collapse after only thirteen weeks left Patrick Kavanagh unemployed and virtually unemployable. He was now at the mercy of the society he had indicted and was soon to suffer the kind of public pillorying he had so often inflicted on others.

The Poet as Satirist, 1944–1954

Disenchantment with Dublin as a cultural capital is the basis of Kavanagh's satiric verse. His satiric poetics is the negative contrary of his myth of exile, a myth which was to prove an enabling creative source until the mid-1950s. In the sonnet sequence, 'Temptation in Harvest' (1945–46), the country is a seductive, erotic presence, while the city is represented merely as an aesthetic locus, a cultural metropolis where 'art, music, letters are the real things'. The quasi-religious rather than emotional or sensual nature of Dublin's attraction is powerfully conveyed in the lines:

> The air was drugged with Egypt. Could I go
> Over the field to the City of the Kings . . .

an image which evokes the narcotic, comforting warmth of a familiar land and the reluctance to set out for the destination towards which faith impels. Exodus is undertaken at the call of duty, not of inclination, and the city appears an alien and undesirable, though noble and inevitable, goal. In Kavanagh's satires Dublin is no longer the 'City of the Kings'; it is an anti-Byzantium, a city of the failed imagination, the domain of frustrated, would-be artists. His satiric enterprise is, to a large extent, the public deconstruction of a naif, personal urban image, such stuff as youthful rustic dreams were made on. Although the mirage of the artistic metropolis never entirely vanished from his horizons, London was substituted for Dublin from the later 1940s.

In Kavanagh's satires, as in 'Temptation in Harvest', Dublin is regarded exclusively as a cultural capital. It is a city with an inflated sense of its own aesthetic importance, still basking in the reflected glory of the Revival, populated almost exclusively by artistic cliques, and preoccupied with literary chit-chat and the promotion of inferior native artists. The variety of ordinary urban life which had excited his interest in 'City Commentary' no longer impinges: shop windows, children's street games, impoverished waitresses and shabby clerks, Moore Street traders chaffing their customers. Now the streets that lead from his suburban apartment to the centre of town are allegorical routes from creativity to 'Frustration's holy well'; public houses are meeting places of the literati; the theatre is a Joycean 'nighttown', Dante's Inferno or a scene from Bunyan's *Pilgrim's Progress*; Dubliners are merely the artist's philistine public.

That Kavanagh should have become more imaginatively obsessed by literary Dublin than by any other aspect of that city is not altogether surprising given the circumstances of his life there. Apart from such distractions as flirtation and betting on horses, his Dublin experience was limited by the fact that he was a professional writer, his mornings spent hunched over a typewriter, his afternoons and evenings trading anecdote and abuse with other writers or literary fellow travellers. Even his brother, Peter, with whom he shared an apartment until 1946, was a schoolteacher with intellectual and literary aspirations, engaged in writing a PhD thesis on the Abbey theatre. The best environment for the artist, in Kavanagh's view, was 'the normally unhappy domestic one'.[62] However, his own familiarity with the lives of ordinary, non-literary people was retrospective and rural, and his fictional re-creations of family and neighbourhood are always set in the south Monaghan of his youth. For virtually all his time in Dublin he lived a 'most disorganized sort of life', without wife, children or domestic context.[63]

The 'social conscience', manifest in *The Great Hunger* and *Lough Derg*, was short lived and after 1944, as he became increasingly involved in Dublin's artistic circles, Kavanagh developed an aesthetic conscience instead, gradually arrogating to himself, as we have seen, the office of national arbiter in matters cultural. 1944 to 1954 was his satiric decade, the majority of his satiric verses being concentrated between 1948 and 1952. These verses contribute to his critique of the Irish literary establishment and of Ireland's cultural xenophobia. In 'City Commentary' he had experimented with snippets of verse criticism. Now his activities as poet and critic regularly overlapped, and rhymed and prose critiques rubbed shoulders in his journalism, especially in his *Envoy* 'Diary'. On one occasion the verse-playlet, later entitled 'Adventures in a Bohemian Journal', was substituted for his usual prose 'Diary' and an *Irish Times* review of Austin Clarke's *The Viscount of Blarney and Other Plays* was also cast in the form of a verse-drama. Kavanagh was at his most programmatically destructive of Irish aesthetic models and attitudes in his prose journalism; his satires complement his prose polemics. Rather than pursue an intellectual argument they evoke a milieu. They focus on the contemporary cultural scene, ridiculing Dublin's post-Revival literary pretensions, the new Irish middle class's cult of the arts, the journalistic flattery of mediocre native talent; they mock at the prevalence of nepotism and undiscriminating patronage, the advancement of ignorant, pushy peasants to positions of power and patronage, the 'poisonous fellowship' of Dublin's literary pubs. Collectively, they conjure up an image of a conservative, self-congratulatory provincial society, backward looking, intolerant of artistic sincerity or singularity.

Kavanagh's satiric poems are introvertedly local. Most were published in Dublin journals and, because they are addressed to an Irish and mainly Dublin readership, they exude that very coterie mentality which they purport to lampoon. The techniques of visual and verbal distortion which he favours—defamiliarising images, caricature, ventriloquism and parody—are calculated to amuse or infuriate a knowing local audience. Sometimes verging on the hysterical in their tone and often naively absolutist in their condemnation of Dublin's artistic shortcomings, his satires testify to an acute sense of alienation and personal spleen, rather than reflecting on the state of the arts in Dublin. If Kavanagh's dream of an intellectually rarefied Dublin were ever to be realised, as Myles na gCopaleen pointed out in a 'Counter-Diary' in *Envoy*, 'The town would be the despair of Joyce if he were still in it and would in any event be generally uninhabitable.'[64] His contempt for his urban milieu may be construed as the hurt, and consequently hostile, reaction of a poet who felt that the uniqueness of his own genius was unacknowledged, even unrecognised, and that the sacrifices he had made in the cause of art had gone unremarked and unrewarded.

Kavanagh's satiric art is usually self-referential; he is his own hero. The role he assigns himself is that of outsider in the complacent society he ridicules. Sometimes his pose is that of the rural naif appalled by urban artistic mores. Sometimes he figures as an internal exile, disbarred from membership of the literary establishment. He plays the part of the decentred satiric positive, marginalised because he represents a threat to the cosy cultural status quo. In the topsy-turvy world of satire where evil usurps good he appears disreputable and disruptive; in a society that thrives on hypocrisy he represents awkward, ugly, uncomfortable truth. Since inferior aesthetic standards triumph, he is inevitably a loser. Occasionally, the satirist effaces himself sufficiently to act as eavesdropper or audience, or even to remain in the wings and allow his satiric dupes to condemn themselves.

In his verse denunciations of literary Dublin, one of Kavanagh's satiric predecessors was Swift. Swift, exiled to Dublin from literary London, was a fellow sufferer and he admired 'the immediacy and exciting volatility' of spirit which produced the lines:

> In exile with a steady heart
> He spent his life's declining part
> Where folly, pride and faction sway
> Remote from St. John, Pope and Gay.

Parodying Swift, Kavanagh projected himself as a poet 'in exile with an unsteady heart'.[65] In his satiric verses he sometimes adopted the Swiftian octosyllabic couplet and he drew on *Gulliver's Travels* for metaphors of cultural alienation. Exaggerating his own superior moral and aesthetic stature he cast himself in the role of Gulliver and diminished his fellow Dubliners to Lilliputians. 'Pygmy' became a favourite term of abuse: Dublin was a 'pygmy town', Irish Revival writing a 'pygmy literature', and Dubliners, resentful and fearful of the gigantic talent in their midst, wished to 'Pin [him]/To the ground like Gulliver'.[66]

In appointing himself Dublin's aesthetic conscience Kavanagh's models were Alexander Pope and W. B. Yeats. Pope, whose 'whole life was spent in furthering the good fight against folly,[67] offered a supreme justification for commitment to a satiric aesthetic, and also for the deployment of the self as a satiric positive. The parallel between Pope's Grub street and neo-Revivalist Dublin is the basis of his most successful literary satire, 'The Paddiad'. A more recent satiric exemplar was Yeats, who had contended with the daily spite of the same 'unmannerly town'. Though, as a founding father of the Literary Revival, Yeats was Kavanagh's principal antagonist, he aspired to the older poet's moral stature, invoking him nostalgically as the scourge of untalented writers and uneducated audiences:

> When Yeats was at the head the mediocracy squirmed
> . . . [68]

Dublin's earnest cultural pretensions in the wake of the Literary Revival probably deserved some deflation, yet by arrogating to himself the moral and artistic authority of a Swift, a Pope or a Yeats, Kavanagh was substituting a borrowed critical hauteur for personal literary achievement.

A swing towards disillusionment and satire is discernible in the arrangement of Kavanagh's second volume of poems, *A Soul for Sale* (1947). This collection, which contains the nostalgic or celebratory rural lyrics of his early Dublin years, 'A Christmas Childhood', 'The Long Garden', 'Art McCooey', 'Spraying the Potatoes', opens with the whining, self-pitying 'Pegasus' and concludes with four poems voicing a variety of disenchantments, rural, cultural, urban and national: 'Stony Grey Soil', 'Memory of Brother Michael', 'A Wreath for Tom Moore's Statue' and *The Great Hunger*.

'Memory of Brother Michael' was a favourite with anthologists in Kavanagh's lifetime. The title is deliberately misleading, encouraging the reader to expect an elegy for this annalist, one of the four masters, in a year when their achievement was being honoured.[69] Instead the poem satirises the Irish cult of the past: both Brother Michael's historiography and the contemporary celebration of it exemplify a 'backward look' endemic in Irish life, a perpetual neglect of living artists because of a preoccupation with the glories of a bygone era. Though historically inaccurate, this is the most incisive and most artistically accomplished of Kavanagh's statements on an obsessive theme:

> It would never be spring, always autumn
> After a harvest always lost,
> When Drake was winning seas for England

We sailed in puddles of the past
Chasing the ghost of Brendan's mast . . .

Culture is always something that was,
Something pedants can measure,
Skull of bard, thigh of chief,
Depth of dried-up river.
Shall we be thus forever?
Shall we be thus forever?

The falling rhythms and repetitive texture of the verses create an appropriately mournful tone, yet the poem is subversively melodic, an obituary notice on Irish culture. He later repudiated 'Memory of Brother Michael', not only for its ahistoricism ('If a thing is untrue it cannot be good poetry'), but because of 'how appallingly' it 'accepts the myth of Ireland as a spiritual entity'.[70]

'A Wreath for Tom Moore's Statue', which dates from the same year, inveighs against Ireland's backward looking culture with a more cynical particularity.[71] For Joyce, Moore's 'droll statue' symbolised Irish inertia and paralysis: 'sloth of the body and of the soul' creeping 'over it like unseen vermin'. For Kavanagh, though he alludes to Stephen Dedalus's scathing metaphor, the statue was a monument to the mercenary caution of the Irish bourgeoisie:

The cowardice of Ireland is in his statue,
No poet's honoured when they wreathe this stone,
An old shopkeeper who has dealt in the
        marrow-bone
Of his neighbours looks at you.
Dim-eyed, degenerate, he is admiring his god,
The bank-manager who pays his monthly
        confession . . .

These opening lines and the dismissive statement in the last stanza, 'The sense is over-sense', recall Yeats's lofty disdain for the Catholic middle class's huckstering attitudes and craven lack of idealism in 'September 1913'. Kavanagh, who was apparently unaware that Moore's father was a Catholic shopkeeper, draws on more specifically Catholic imagery than Yeats, conflating confession with banking, condemning the venial as well as the venal nature of middle-class transgressions, the reduction of the seven deadly sins to the monotonous tedium of the 'seven-deadened'.

In 'A Wreath for Tom Moore's Statue' Ireland honours the dead poet because he is amenable to public exploitation whereas the living poet is less manipulable, unpredictable and given to wild oscillations of mood (probably a self-referential description), his impoverished apparel testifying to contemporary Ireland's neglect of its writers. The point is clinched memorably by rhyming two vividly colloquial, sartorial images:

> For the dead will wear the cap of any racket
> The corpse will not put his elbow through his jacket . . .

Poetry is vital, unruly, subversive; Irish patrons of the arts prefer to crown the safely dead

> Whose white blood cannot blot the respectable page.

The mercenariness, charlatanism and mediocrity of Dublin's middle-class culture were to be derided by Kavanagh for the next decade. A significant difference at this stage is that he is still hopeful about constructing an alternative city of the imagination and abjures urban satire in the name of prelapsarian innocence and irrationality:

> But hope! the poet comes again to build
> A new city high above lust and logic,
> The trucks of language overflow and magic
> At every turn of the living road is spilled . . .

'Pegasus', the title poem of *A Soul for Sale* and given pride of place in the collection, ushers in a more personalised form of satire, introducing what was to be a recurring theme in Kavanagh's writing for the ensuing decade, the relentless struggle to turn his talent to commercial profit. Here the poet's futile effort to market his genius (the poem was originally titled 'A Glut on the Market'),[72] is mediated through the transparent metaphor of the attempt to sell an unsaleable horse:

> My soul was an old horse
> Offered for sale in twenty fairs.

'Church and State and meanest trade' refuse him patronage or employment; he is pronounced unfit for 'high-paid work in towns' and, finally, ignored. Ultimately, he decides to stop 'haggling with the world' and as a consequence discovers imaginative freedom. The choice of horse trading as a narrative metaphor in 'Pegasus' is unfortunate, implying that the poet was ready to sell his soul to the first bidder and that it was only because he had failed to qualify as a work horse that he sprouted the wings of a Pegasus.

'Pegasus' and 'A Wreath for Tom Moore's Statue' both finish on an upbeat; societal shortcomings and personal disappointments are overtaken by the joy of poetic creativity. The satires which follow *Tarry Flynn* are more embittered, and attempt to 'turn/The laugh against the cynic's leer of power'.[73] Dublin's artistic inadequacies are now remorselessly exposed. The satirist's stance is that of an isolated outsider, conscious of the corrupt state of the arts, yet powerless to change it. His poetic gifts no longer compensate for his disaffection.

Kavanagh often resorted to a dramatic technique when travestying Dublin's literary milieu, compelling his characters to condemn themselves out of their own mouths in verse-dramas or dramatic monologues, or through passages of dialogue within a poem. His satiric dramas are plotless and peripatetic with a minimal interaction between their ventriloquial characters. He often apportions himself a leading role, availing of the dramatic opportunity not only to mimic the various voices of Irish literary convention and bourgeois philistinism but to record his reaction to their views. 'Bardic Dust', 'The Wake of the Books' and 'Adventures in the

Bohemian Jungle' are all cast in the form of verse-playlets. The last will suffice to introduce the introverted, inbred world of these satires.

'Adventures in the Bohemian Jungle' (*Envoy*, April 1950) focuses on the razzmatazz surrounding Irish theatre, its institutionalisation as the cultural charity most favoured by the establishment and as the happy hunting ground of both the pious and the philandering middle class. No mean showman himself Kav- anagh was always bitterly critical of Irish society's attraction to the histrionic:

> I often wonder if Ireland is not utterly inferior, an ex-hibitionistic society whose natural gods are actors.[74]

The fact that the Abbey theatre was one of the showcases of the Literary Revival exacerbated his scorn for this institution, and it would appear that its foyer and bar provide the disguised setting here. In this playlet, in which the author is, transparently, his own hero, a 'simple man arrived in town . . . A true believer in the mystical/Power of poets' is given a conducted tour of 'the world of art'. Poetry, commerce, 'Acting, Painting, Music', catholicism, journalism and tourism are all implicated in the invective.

Jungle imagery had been drawn on in the short earlier poem, 'Jungle',[75] where the area Kavanagh called his 'Pembrokeshire', near his Ballsbridge flat, was defamiliarised into a primitive terrain inhabited by predatory beasts and partially evolved humans. By depicting the city as far less civilised than the countryside he had left behind he was revenging Dublin's patronising characterisation of him as a 'ploughman poet'. The jungle metaphor, foregrounded in the title of his satiric drama, also suggests vulnerability; the 'simple countryman' is an innocent abroad in a dangerous world.

What passes for culture in Dublin, according to this satire, is really show business; the rich, Catholic film-star, Sheila O'Mulligan, is the inevitable idol of a city where the beauty competition is closely allied to the theatre and support for the arts affords an opportunity for licentiousness. His stint as film critic for the *Standard* had prejudiced Kavanagh against the cinema as an art form ('Through *Gone with the Wind* I yawned my way') and Sheila O'Mulligan is depicted as a synthetic jungle beast:

> . . . the stuffed tiger of Desire
> With nylon fur and wire-recorded roar
> The flashing fangs like Instinct's, yet quite safe . . .

The perversion of intellectual and aesthetic standards, arising from the journalistic confusion of celebrity with genius, is ironically demonstrated by the newspaper interview in which Sheila O'Mulligan is asked to select 'America's outstanding mind'. Journalism is discredited as amoral, offering a model of unprincipled expediency:

> See life as newspapers show it
> Without a moral judgement,
> The bank Integrity
> Holds but a beggar's lodgement.
>
> Truth's what's in power to-day
> The lie's what's in the breadline
> So take your Gospel straight
> From the morning headline . . .

The Catholic Church's support for the arts is ridiculed when the Catholic Cultural League rewards artistic endeavour with chalices and rosary beads, the repeated figure 'two gross' being a heavy-handed pun on the vulgarity of such patronage. The Catholic Cultural League is a fictional disguise for the Catholic Stage Guild of Ireland. Kavanagh was appalled by this alliance between church and stage and twice attacked it elsewhere in *Envoy*.[76]

Film-star Sheila's father, Count O'Mulligan, his presumably papal title at odds with his plebian surname, is a caricature of the *nouveau riche*, Catholic, philistine middle class:

God nicely in His place, card-indexed,
His stomach comfortable on golf dreams
The Bishop calling round to have dinner to discuss
With him the problem of the city's poor . . .

Count O'Mulligan is portrayed as the kind of patron who pays a poet starvation wages while making a munificent public donation to the Catholic Cultural League. 'Benign, bountiful—evil', he resembles the devil of 'The Paddiad', but the equation of misguided patronage with evil on this occasion seems melodramatic, and in 'Adventures in the Bohemian Jungle', as a whole, Kavanagh does not succeed in making a credible moral issue out of middle-class Dublin's failure to include him among its favoured charities.

Since the satiric focus in 'Adventures in the Bohemian Jungle' is on theatrical patrons and hangers-on, Irish drama almost escapes censure, though not quite. Its literary basis and remoteness from contemporary actuality are succinctly criticised through the introduction of a procession of players in medieval costume *en route* to perform a verse-play. This gibe at Austin Clarke's Lyric Theatre Company summarises much of the criticism levelled at his drama in the earlier 'Bardic Dust'.[77]

The naif hero of 'Adventures in the Bohemian Jungle', an uncorrupted poet from 'the mythical land of Simple Country', plays the role of Dublin's moral and aesthetic conscience. His attitude to the theatre is puritanical. Moral condemnation of the sexual promiscuity of theatre goers is gestured at through a series of literary parallels between bohemian Dublin and 'the nighttown scenes in *Ulysses* or Dante's Hell or something out of John Bunyan'. Later, moral disgust at the spectacle of middle-class Dublin on the spree is translated into nausea. Artistic Dublin finally appears to the country poet as a hell in which an unholy trinity of 'Patrons, players, playboys' worships the second-rate. The 'countryman's' righteous recoil from urban mores appears an overreaction, his satiric zeal excessive, though Kavanagh does manage to conjure up a recognisably Irish philistinism in which partying, profiteering and piety mingle.

The play's last impassioned speech denounces urban culture as moribund and expresses the satiric positives of vital intensity, originality and clarity in a succession of rural images:

> I dreamt of sin and it was fire
> A May-time-in-the-fields desire,
> Violent, exciting, new,
> Whin-blossoms burning up the dew;
> Sudden death and sudden birth
> Among the hierarchies of the earth;
> Kings that ruled with absolute power
> If 'twas only for an hour;
> Trees were green, mountains sheer
> And God dramatically clear.
> But here in this nondescript land
> Everything is secondhand:
> Nothing ardently growing
> Nothing coming, nothing going,
> Tepid fevers, nothing hot,
> None alive enough to rot;
> Nothing clearly defined . . .

Though this speech begins vividly and offers a vehement indictment of the stale, derivative nature of urban corruption, its longing for the 'clear' and 'clearly defined' betrays a simplistic, moral extremism. In his recourse to octosyllabic couplets for satiric purposes Kavanagh may well have been modelling his verse on Swift's, and the urinating contest with which the playlet concludes suggests the scatological influence of Swift or Pope. This final lunge into indecorum, in which the countryman chooses to fraternise with 'Crumlin gurriers' in preference to Dublin's middle-class theatre goers, was undoubtedly intended as an affront to bourgeois sensibilities; however, it comes across as an adolescently boorish act of defiance.

'The Christmas Mummers', a verse drama consisting of a series of dramatic monologues, illustrates the localised texture and appeal of Kavanagh's satires. Since it was printed in the English journal, *Nimbus*, (edited by an admirer, David Wright),[78] it had to be accompanied by a set of explanatory notes, without which some of its references would have been inaccessible to non-Irish readers. The very mumming routines which provide the poem's structural framework needed explanation because 'the custom of mummers or rhymers going round before Christmas performing in rural kitchens' was current only in a few parts of Ireland in 1954. Even with the aid of explanatory notes, much of the poem would still have been lost on a non-native audience since the verses are 'crude loud homespun', their satire of Irish modes of achieving fame and fortune, full of cultural nuances comprehensible only to one who had lived in Ireland. This is necessarily the case, since Kavanagh is ridiculing a peculiarly Irish gogetter mentality which manipulates national sentiment in its scramble to the top. A rather incoherent introductory 'Apology' apart, however, this is one of his most controlled and most zestful satires. Mummery provided a flexible structural framework, allowed for diversity in personae and subject matter, imparted a light-hearted, festive air to the proceedings and ensured the maintenance of a lively pace.

Kavanagh was particularly incensed by Dublin's air of literary self-importance, all the more so because he himself had once been deluded by it. Dublin's pub culture is the target of two *Envoy* flytings, 'Tale of two Cities' and 'A Sonnet Sequence for the Defeated'.[79] The wittiest line in 'Tale of Two Cities' is the title (a later addition). Perhaps the inclusion of actual names in the original version gave a certain *frisson* to its Dublin readers.

> How was Harry Kernoff and Seamus O'Sullivan
>   and Smyllie
> And Gogarty, the greatest Dubliner of them all?

the satiric butt originally inquired and his hearer was 'back in the Pearl' bar as he listened. This is a satire that reeks of the coterie mentality it affects to despise.

'A Sonnet Sequence for the Defeated' (renamed 'The Defeated') derides the self-congratulatory insularity of those who considered Dublin the equal of London or Paris as an artistic capital, and Ireland as

> the last preserve
> Of Eden in a world of savage states . . .

Kavanagh's satiric technique in this sonnet sequence is to mimic the smug, condescending attitude and tone of a Dublin man of letters realistically, while simultaneously undercutting his opinions by situating him in an Orwellian satiric fantasy in which Dublin appears a pigsty, its poets, pigs, and its literary pubs, troughs. The Dubliner's delusions of grandeur are ridiculed through his pigheaded refusal to concede the existence of other superior cultures whose inhabitants live in houses rather than sties. The most amusing sonnet is the second with its image of the mystical, rejected and abusive Kavanagh as a pig with 'skyward turned snout', missing out on the finest sows, and damning each hog he meets 'straight to his face'.

A defamiliarising image which recurs in the urban satires is the portrayal of Dublin as hell. Hell in Kavanagh's satiric eschatology is a place dedicated to the worship of second rate art, where mediocrity reigns supreme and artists adhere to a safe predictable convention. The rhetorical intention in resorting to infernal imagery is to stress the gravity of the sin but a risk, which Kavanagh seldom avoids, is that the punishment may seem ludicrously disproportionate to the offence. Recourse to infernal and celestial imagery in the concluding sonnet of 'The Defeated', for instance, makes the disillusioned poet sound as if he has regressed into the yearning, youthful idealist of *Ploughman and Other Poems*:

> O God, I cried, these treats are not the treats
> That Heaven offers in the Golden Cup.
> And I heard the demon's terrifying yell:
> There is no place as perfect as our hell.

The diabolic intervention, meant to convey righteous moral condemnation of Dublin's literary complacency, is merely hysterically melodramatic, and heaven's 'Golden Cup' appears a vague substitute for a satiric positive. This terrifying demon is a far cry from the bland, smooth-talking devil of 'The Paddiad', the most sinisterly credible of Kavanagh's diabolic creations. Without the controlling and deflationary discipline of humour, his indignation at inadequate artistic standards tends to run amok in sentimentalism and rant.

'The Paddiad' is the most accomplished of Kavanagh's satires on literary Dublin. Since Pope was one of his exemplars in the sphere of aesthetic morality it is not surprising that 'The Paddiad' owes much of its moral definition and authority to his epyllion on eighteenth-century literary London, *The Dunciad*. The substitution of Irish Paddies for Pope's dunces and of a Dublin literary pub for Grub street is an entertaining invention. Dublin Mediocrity replaces London Dullness as Kavanagh's satiric target:

> In the corner of a Dublin pub
> This party opens—blub-a-blub
> Paddy Whiskey, Rum and Gin
> Paddy Three sheets in the wind;
> Paddy of the Celtic Mist,
> Paddy Connemara West,
> Chestertonian Paddy Frog
> Croaking nightly in the bog.
> All the Paddies having fun
> Since Yeats handed in his gun.
> Every man completely blind
> To the truth about his mind.

The combination of a predominantly trochaic metre and seven-syllabled lines, as compared with Pope's slower paced heroic couplets, brings a comic zest to Kavanagh's verses.

A post-Romantic rather than a neo-classical vice, Mediocrity is characterised by a lack of originality and individuality, an espousal of literary conventions, traditions, schools. It is personified as a devil, zealous to promote the emphasis on ethnicity in Irish letters, presiding over a powerful coterie of *echt*-Irish writers who judge literature by such extra-literary criteria as its piety, Gaelic dimension, regionalism. Not only is the chauvinist attitude that literature should express a national or regional identity vilified as satanically inspired but the folly of the 'Irish mode' is exposed through comic exaggeration when the devil projects a series of anthologies subdividing Irish poetry at county level:

> How many poems, Mist, can you spare
> For my new anthology of Clare? . . .
> But they must definitely be Clare;
> Some lyrics in your recent volume
> Were influenced by Roscommon . . .

Under the diabolical system of patronage 'the fusty, safe and dim' flourish and true genius is left to starve. Irish Paddies enjoy one distinct advantage over Pope's dunces: in Ireland it pays to be dull. The Dublin literary establishment is projected as a business cooperative, preoccupied with marketing and advertising strategies, overseas sales, window display, tourist propaganda; oblivious to standards of excellence. Artistic integrity is identified with dissent from this cultural conspiracy.

Local response to 'The Paddiad' focused less on issues than on personalities, in particular on the identity of the maligned Paddies. Three were privately named by Kavanagh as Maurice Walsh or M. J. McManus, Austin Clarke and Robert Farren.[80] Publicly he hinted that the poem was set in the Pearl bar when, reporting on the state of Irish letters in *Poetry*

(Chicago) in August 1949, the month in which 'The Paddiad' was published, he mentioned that there was a good deal of 'low literary life' in Dublin, instancing the Pearl bar with

> Paddy Drunk and Paddy Sober
> Slobbering over their pints of porter.

Poetry (Chicago) had earlier rejected 'The Paddiad' possibly because its appeal was too provincial, since it concerned a 'local row' rather than a theme of universal interest. The poem was published instead in *Horizon*, where part of *The Great Hunger* had originally appeared, a symbolic gesture because the change from Paddy Maguire to Paddy Conscience as poetic hero signals the reorientation of Kavanagh's poetry from life to literature, from social conscience to literary conscience, and from disinterested indictment to enlightened self-interest.

It is typical of the self-righteous and self-inflationary bias of much of Kavanagh's literary criticism that 'The Paddiad' should resemble a morality play in which the devil Mediocrity and his literary minions are confronted by Paddy Conscience, a personification of the aesthetic conscience who bears a striking similarity to Paddy Kavanagh. As usual the bias of Kavanagh's satire is anti-bourgeois, so the devil, 'bland and mellow', 'saintly', 'quiet-voiced', monkish, embodies the middle-class virtue of sanctimonious gentility, while Paddy Conscience is anti-genteel, 'drunken', 'dirty' dishevelled, 'condemnatory and uncivil', bothering his auditors 'with muck and anger'. The creation of a compound Conscience, a conflation of Yeats, Joyce, O'Casey and himself, invests Kavanagh with the literary superiority of three of the most eminent Irish twentieth-century writers.[81] He chose three writers who lived or died in exile to buttress his argument that to be ostracised by Dublin's poetasters is a mark of excellence. As well as deriding prevailing literary standards in Dublin 'The Paddiad' makes a vice of amiable clubability and a virtue of surly singularity.

While Pope had furnished a precedent for the author's casting himself in the role of satiric positive, it is unfortunate, though inevitable, that 'The Paddiad' should be so self-referential: unfortunate, because Kavanagh who aped Pope's arrogant dismissiveness towards contemporary hacks, his strong antipathy of good to bad, lacked his master's aesthetic credibility as a poetic arbiter; inevitable, because of the intimate connection between his destruction of existing models and the achievement of his unique literary identity. No poem of the period better illustrates this dual thrust in Kavanagh's writing.

Poetry's refusal of 'The Paddiad' was probably a considerable blow to Kavanagh's confidence as a satirist. He did not run the risk of any further rejection of his new poetic material and published most of his other satires in Dublin journals. As a result these poems and playlets are often carelessly executed, diffuse or localised, sometimes all three, whereas in 'The Paddiad' he succeeds in presenting his criticism of literary Dublin in a controlled and amusing dramatic narrative, sustaining his fantastic invention, drawing intelligently on literary allusion, and aiming at specific satiric targets.

'Irish Stew', published in *The Bell*,[82] is the most nakedly self-interested of all the satires, based on a purely personal gripe about the reluctance of the Advisory Committee on Cultural Relations to sponsor the poet as an overseas representative of Irish culture. Within its limits it is an entertaining piece in which a politician's rhetorical patter is realistically imitated and simultaneously ridiculed through the use of rhyming couplets. The politician invokes national shibboleths and then, while paying lip-service to the poet's genius, quashes his aspirations to middle-class comfort:

> Luxury would ruin your sublime
> Imagination in no time
>
> And domesticity, wife, house, car,
> We want you always as you are.

> Such things don't fit into the scheme
> Of one who dreams the poet's dream.

He proceeds by justifying the nepotistical appointment as Irish cultural emissary of an inferior poet who happens to be his own cousin. The mimicry is astute, capturing the insinuating reasonableness of the politician's tone, and the couplets prove a perfect vehicle for conveying bland insensitivity and glibness. It is one of Kavanagh's better satires. But what a come-down that the author of *The Great Hunger* should now be serving up 'Irish Stew' or, far worse, 'A Pathetic Ballad of a Big Dinner'.[83]

By the later 1950s Kavanagh himself was less than happy with his satiric verse. A number of satires were included in what was virtually a mini-collection of his poems in *Nimbus* (winter 1956), and Kavanagh's friend, Anthony Cronin, in a eulogistic introductory essay, claimed that the satires contributed to 'the dialectic of innocence and experience' which was the mainspring of his work.[84] However, no satires were collected in *Recent Poems* (1958), and only two, 'The Paddiad' and 'House Party',[85] were preserved in his 1960 collection, *Come Dance with Kitty Stobling*. Why a poet, usually so quick to detect cant in himself as well as in others, should have been so impressed by 'House Party' is puzzling. The sprightly 'Who Killed James Joyce' would have been a better choice as a literary satire. An entertaining inquisition on the burgeoning Joyce industry, this poem is a lively parody of 'Who Killed Cock Robin', which sustains the question and answer format of the original. 'House Party' depends on a heavy-handed ironic contrast between the comfortable circumstances of the Catholic Church's middle-class critics and the impoverished conditions in which old country priests carry out their ministry. Its conclusion is highly sentimental:

> In far off parishes of Cork and Kerry
> Old priests walked homeless in the winter air
> As Seamus poured another pale dry sherry.

Did parish priests ever walk homeless in the Ireland of the 1950s?

In an allegorical dialogue of 1952, 'The Road to Hate',[86] Kavanagh admitted that hostility was fast becoming a way of life for him, hatred an all-consuming passion. In this poem the city that beckons is no longer the 'City of the Kings', the aesthetic goal of 'Temptation in Harvest', but 'the very city of Hate', probably the same city seen from another perspective. Although the poet here states his determination to persist in the hostilities in which he had been engaged since the mid-1940s and asserts that the 'road to hate' is a route to sanctity, he was usually less defiantly confident about his satiric project after 1950.

Kavanagh gradually came to acknowledge that by transforming Dublin into a 'City of Hate' he was destroying, not the city, but himself. Like Samson's, his massacre of the Philistines was proving suicidal. Unease about his satiric enterprise, indeed, became one of his poetic themes. In 'Leave Them Alone'[87] he apparently recognises that he is expending imaginative energy on ephemeral trivia and counsels himself to leave his victims to time's oblivion:

> There's nothing happening that you hate
> That's really worthwhile slamming;
> Be patient. If you only wait
> You'll see time gently damning
>
> Newspaper bedlamites who raised
> Each day the devil's howl
> Versifiers who had seized
> The poet's begging bowl
>
> The whole hysterical passing-show
> The hour apotheosised
> Into a cul-de-sac will go
> And be not even despised.

Here journalists and poetasters are satirised in the very act of satiric renunciation, and rant, apparently abjured, is outrageously indulged. The hysteria attributed to the 'passing-show' is the poet's own and his rhetoric is ludicrously inflated, as is evident from the description of journalists as 'newspaper bedlamites', their writings as 'the devil's howl' and public praise as 'apotheosis'. This is satire disguised as anti-satire; the ultimate condemnation is to state that the target is beneath contempt. However, in 'Auditors In' and 'Prelude', which will be discussed in chapter 9, Kavanagh's repentance of his satiric poetics is genuine.

Yeats considered that 'to be choked with hate/May well be of all evil chances chief' and, certainly, Kavanagh's satires are among his least memorable poems. Yet, to exclude them from his canon, is to simplify the poet. He was not only, at various stages, a champion of the underprivileged, an affectionate portraitist of the Irish parish, a transcendentalist; he was also a combative, self-serving, vituperative versifier, a poet much given to 'muck and anger'. The satires, most of which appeared in *The Irish Times*, *The Bell* or *Envoy*, are expressions of his antagonistic dialogue with Dublin, prolongations of café and public-house quarrels, literary retaliations for real life insults, afterthoughts and delayed repartees, compensatory ego-boosting fantasies. While some of Kavanagh's verse satire pierces the pious, patriotic and Gaelic guises cloaking the opportunistic greed of Ireland's upwardly mobile smallfarmer class, his moral indignation sometimes appears that of a bourgeois *manqué*. A peasant who hasn't made it to middleclass bliss is reviling successful parvenus, naively nurturing the conviction that financial reward and public esteem should be commensurate with literary talent. One suspects that his gripe against Dublin had less to do with its status as a literary metropolis than with its failure as a meritocracy. For disinterested verse satire of contemporary Ireland in the 1950s one has to turn to three collections by Kavanagh's detested rival, Austin Clarke: *Ancient Lights* (1955), *Too Great a Vine* (1957) and *The Horse-Eaters* (1960).

Dublin's 'great hatred, little room' maimed Kavanagh almost from the start. The protracted exile from Ireland chosen by such contemporaries as Samuel Beckett, Brian Coffey and Denis Devlin might have proved a wiser course. Instead Kavanagh opted for internal exile and became an embattled writer, channelling much of his creative energy into asserting the artist's importance in society and challenging Ireland's official ideologies. It was a brave but foolhardy decision. What we hear in Kavanagh's satire and cultural criticism is a violent tearing of the nets of nationalism, philistinism, censorious Catholicism. A poet is attempting, without leaving Dublin, to achieve 'flight in the light'.

8
Urban Self-Images

Introduction

THE self was Patrick Kavanagh's dominant image from the
outset of his literary career. *The Great Hunger* and *Lough
Derg* were digressions in an *oeuvre* that was really a prolonged
autobiography written in different styles, a continuing narrative of the poet's imagined life. Despite his advocacy of
parochial art Kavanagh's own evocations of his parish usually
served as a backdrop to automythology, with Inniskeen re-
created in loving detail as the context of his discovery,
recovery or invention of himself as country poet. The most
parochial of his poems and fictions, 'Why Sorrow' and
'Father Mat', 'Art McCooey' and *Tarry Flynn*, were also self-
dramatisations and those recollections of his native village or
records of his visits there, which proliferate in his writings
after 1950, are unashamedly biographical. Inniskeen is significant because Kavanagh once lived there: 'Gods make their
own importance'.

Possibly because it was such a supreme achievement for
one from his educationally and culturally deprived background to arrive at the status of London-published author,
Kavanagh was never to lose a sense of the miraculousness of
his own talent, a respectful awe towards himself as poet, a
Romantic conviction as to his own bardic singularity and
specialness. Although he was from the beginning a self-
conscious poet, self-identification did not become a pressing
concern until after he had taken up residence in Dublin; the
label 'poet' was distinction enough for him in his Inniskeen
days. The move to Dublin, a city over-populated with established and aspiring writers, was a shock to his self-esteem.

Previous visits to the capital before he took up permanent residence there probably bolstered his sense of cultural superiority on his return to Inniskeen. By the early 1940s Kavanagh recognised that his status was that of a mere private in what he, later, sardonically termed, 'the standing army of Irish poets', many of whom were billeted in Dublin.[1] After an initial period of adjustment to urban life his self-differentiation from the rank and file of the city's pen-pushers came to be of paramount importance. He set about defining himself in opposition to his context, in scorn of his audience imagining a man.

Satire and criticism were for him a rhetoric of dissociation from Dublin's literary establishment, a negative expression of his gradual emancipation from existing Irish literary conventions and models, a defiant assertion of individuality and independence. Poetic satire, in particular, was primarily an egocentric activity, a literary strategy of self-identification and self-creation, self-promotion and self-justification. In his satiric portrayal of Dublin he is a dominant, if disruptive, presence, an unacknowledged legislator. Self-righteousness is elevated into a moral and cultural positive; rejection by the establishment into an expression of inverted superiority. The *poète maudit*, who pursues his unpopular and unprofitable course through the satires, maintains his lonely integrity at the expense of others' inferiority, their bad faith, stupidity and opportunism. By degrading and discrediting other writers he asserts the superiority of his own talent, by herding them into cliques and coteries he proclaims his own uniqueness, by disparaging Dublin's cultural standards he accounts for his failure to achieve fame or even acceptance. The satires are public gestures of alienation, disavowals of Dublin's 'poisonous fellowship',[2] celebrations of his own ostracism. They may be regarded as a mode of expressing individuality through nonconformity.

The negative aggression of the satires is the obverse of Kavanagh's imaginative obsession with the construction of a persona and a personal poetics and their self-idealisation is only one of a number of self-projections in which he was engaged for a decade from the mid-1940s. Dublin in his poetry is a Kavanagh-centred city. Whether in his public role of poet-about-town or his private role of inspired contemplative, he is his own cultural hero. The external drama of his day-to-day activities and the interior events of his creative imagination provide his fictional plots. Every Dublin lyric is 'a song of myself'. It was typical of his contemporary preoccupation with subjective realism and modes of self-revelation that he should have entitled his *Envoy* column, 'Diary', emphasising the public intimacy of his journalism.[3] Even his solitary communings with the god of the imagination attained a kind of public privacy by being made the subject of his art.

In his everyday life, instinctive, emotional, intellectual and behavioural stances were cultivated and exaggerated to project and sustain a readily identifiable persona. This public persona was a deliberate expression of dissent from Dublin's bourgeois values and literary orthodoxies, an embodiment and extension of his cultural criticism, an acting out of his radicalism. He was constructing a self-image that would serve as a literary image, transforming himself into a kind of living poem so that the author and his poet-hero, though not identical, were not discontinuous either.

By the end of the 1940s Kavanagh had elevated the cult of selfhood into an aesthetic principle. His new-found conviction, formulated in his *Envoy* 'Diary' and in *Kavanagh's Weekly*, is that 'the only valid thing any man has to offer the world is his own personality' and that the art most likely to endure is 'that little unfashionable kind which is unlike everything else, personality'.[4] The personal dimension in realist art is now acknowledged and applauded: 'It is by making as accurate a statement about the subject as possible that the artist's personality comes across.' Kavanagh believes that a work of art, whatever its theme, should express the unique identity of the artist, so that 'all portraits must be self-portraits' as well as 'likenesses'. Picasso's portraits of Dora

Maar are considered exemplary because they are 'so accurately like Mme Maar on the one hand and so definitely like Picasso on the other'.[5] Jean Cocteau's commendation of the subjective element in painting is quoted approvingly:

> For me those painters who have imprinted themselves on their canvasses are painters I love, because their hearts, their souls, their very guts are contained in the colours and shapes they've bequeathed to us . . . For a true painter landscapes and models are only occasions for talking about himself.[6]

In literature, Kavanagh pronounces 'the external story' to be 'of no value except as the frame for a man's own reality' and his favourite books and authors are re-evaluated according to the new critical touchstone of personality. *Moby Dick* is perceived to be 'only incidentally about the sea and fundamentally about the soul' and *Ulysses* to be 'only incidentally about Dublin and fundamentally the history of a soul'.[7] Proust is complimented for courageously defying fictional norms so as to express a personal reality.[8] The author of *Hail and Farewell* is eulogised because he 'had a personality and a rare capacity for seeing not only others but himself'[9] and Yeats, despite his underestimation of Moore's personality, is commended for his 'sincere mind'.[10] Sincerity, rather than realism, is Kavanagh's aesthetic criterion from the mid-1940s. A writer must to his own self be true, a test that the 'gallivanting' F. R. Higgins conspicuously failed. The falsity in Synge's portrayal of rural life is attributed in *Kavanagh's Weekly* to 'the basic insincerity upon which he built', 'the lie in his own heart', the fact that he 'never asked himself the fundamental question: "Where do I stand in relation to these people?"'[11] 'Truth is personality' is Kavanagh's most succinct summation of his new aesthetic philosophy.[12]

He frequently identifies personality in art not only with honesty and sincerity but with artistic courage. So, in what reads like an apologia for his own personal and literary subversiveness and the extremism of his critical polemic, he asserts in the last number of *Envoy*:

> To have the courage of being yourself is to be truthful. You will be an iconoclast and considered a maker of wild statements, but every personality in movement is iconoclastic.

His quest for a personal poetics reinforced Kavanagh's instinctive recoil from prevailing Irish literary conventions and techniques, the phantasmagoria of myths and legends and native pieties. His Romantic, personal aesthetic is now scornfully contrasted with the ethnic aesthetic which had dominated Irish poetry for half a century. The cult of nationality in literature is pronounced the refuge of writers who lack a distinctive personality:

> The average man requires a ready-made cloak with the clear pattern of his nation on it, for this gives the nonentity a distinction.[13]

Its self-referentiality doubly isolated Kavanagh's poetry from its Irish literary context since, as Samuel Beckett remarked, 'the device common to the poets of the Revival and after was a flight from self-awareness' and 'self-perception' was not for them 'an accredited theme'.[14] Kavanagh, on the contrary, always perceived himself as a singular and exceptional individual, never as a representative countryman or Irishman or as the heir to a separatist cultural tradition. Even in the pre-Dublin poem, 'Dictator's Genealogy', he proclaimed his independence and uniqueness: '"I am", as Napoleon said, "my own ancestors."'

In his *Envoy* 'Diary' Kavanagh addresses the problem of revealing himself 'without self-pity or loss of dignity' and concludes that 'the best medium for releasing our private selves, the heart's cry, is verse which can give nobility to intimacy'.[15] The cultivation of personality in poetry demanded not only the creation of an identifiable persona but the development of an individual style. The fact that contemporary Irish culture was the target of his satires, and his own life in Dublin was increasingly becoming the subject of his poetry and fiction, encouraged Kavanagh to modernise his imagery and idiom. He had admired the up-to-date tone of W. H. Auden's verse since 1941 and in the penultimate issue of *Envoy* he substituted an essay in praise of Auden for his usual 'Diary'. The whole thrust of Kavanagh's own urban poetry from his first brief experiments in 'City Commentary' is towards occasional verse and an informal and relaxed demotic utterance.

He deliberately cultivated effects of spontaneity, learning how to deliver his lines with colloquial ease, to incorporate jargon and slang, to indulge in mood swings and changes of pace and tone, to introduce outrageous or off-rhymes for deflationary or comic effect. The flexibility and playfulness, characteristic of his lighter verse, persists into his serious poetry, undercutting the pomp and solemnity of Romantic afflatus. An endearing trait of the Kavanagh poem becomes its reconciliation of gaiety and gravity, mystical 'flight into the light' and throw-away flippancy. Even in his confessional verse he achieves a stylistic unburdening. Kavanagh had inherited a Wordsworthian conception of the poet as a man speaking to men rather than a singer or symbolist. When he occasionally breaks into song—matching a new lyric to an old tune or resorting to refrains, lilting rhythms and insistent rhyme—he usually does so to obtain an effect of tonal nonchalance, lyrical insouciance. His realist phase is over and there is no longer any attempt to emulate the detail and particularity of 'The Great Hunger' and *Tarry Flynn*. His Dublin poems are less crowded with images and altogether less 'thingy' than the confessional verse of his American contemporaries.

Kavanagh's celebrations of self, his cult of distinctive personality, his impassioned belief in individualism, his use of poetry primarily for self-projection, self-analysis and self-affirmation, his introspective concern with his own creative processes, reveal him as a latter-day Romantic, though one who fortunately often combines the egotistical sublime with the ridiculous. Chapters 8 and 9 focus on two contrary aspects of his self-fictionalising in his Dublin poems. In this chapter I discuss the persona of the extroverted and flamboyant public performer, the poet of Dublin's streets and bars who is usually cast in the literary role of aesthetic hero or frustrated lover or entertaining clown. In chapter 9 I turn to Kavanagh's self-portrayal as an introverted, contemplative or reflexive poet, a 'spirit that lives alone', anxious to withdraw from urban entanglements and nurture his imaginative life.

Poet-about-Town

> O I had a future
> A future.
>
> Gods of the imagination bring back to life
> The personality of those streets,
> Not any streets
> But the streets of nineteen forty.
>
> Give the quarter-seeing eyes I looked out of
> The animal-remembering mind
> The fog through which I walked towards the
>   mirage
> That was my future
>
> The women I was to meet
> They were nowhere within sight.
>
> And then the pathos of the blind soul,
> How without knowing stands in its own kingdom.
>
> Bring me a small detail
> How I felt about money,
> Not frantic as later,
> There was the future.
>
> Show me the stretcher-bed I slept on
> In a room on Drumcondra road.
> Let John Betjeman call for me in a car.

It is summer and the eerie beat
Of madness in Europe trembles the
Wings of the butterflies along the canal.

O I had a future.

'I Had a Future', which appeared in the first number of
Kavanagh's Weekly, is the disenchanted poet's retrospective
portrait of himself as he was the year after his arrival in
Dublin, a time when misplaced optimism cancelled out
current hardship. Hindsight no longer prompts an indulgent,
affectionate attitude towards youthful insouciance, as it did
in 'Art McCooey', and the recovery of past time in this poem
is not conducted with apparent spontaneity but deliberately
contrived; twelve-year-old images are being consciously summoned to fuel and stoke present-day bitterness. Futurity
mediated through the past tense expresses the irony of
youthful promise as viewed from the disillusioned perspective of middle age. The sardonic opening and closing line, 'O I
had a future', frames this portrait of the fecklessly cheerful
newcomer to the Dublin scene and the tone of self-mockery is
sustained throughout by jaundiced repetition of the phrase,
'a future'. The vague, chrysalid stage, from which the Dublin
poet has now cynically emerged, is evoked through visual
metaphor; he was 'quarter-seeing', 'blind', fogbound, his
goal a 'mirage', the women who were to frustrate or foster
him 'nowhere within sight'. As in 'Art McCooey' Kavanagh
depicts himself in a pre-conscious phase: 'animal-remember-
ing', unaware of his imaginative powers, not recognising that
the streets of Dublin were now his literary 'kingdom' as
'Inniskeen Road' had been formerly.

Gradually, more precise recollections are summoned up.
Naming is a sure sign that Kavanagh's retrospective imagination is stirring and so there is no need to continue the series of
imperatives—'bring back to life', 'give', 'bring me', 'show
me', 'let'—in order to coerce recollection. Imaginative recovery of the past is rhetorically signalled by a transition to
the present tense in the final stanza. This change of tense

enacts the movement from willed recollection to repossession of and by the past. The mood becomes one of surrender to the music of what happened. A strange, insistent wartime rhythm ('eerie beat') now resonates through the Dublin scene. Self-absorption and self-pity yield momentarily to an external image of fragile beauty. The recently exiled country poet, alert to the *rus in urbe* beauty of the butterflies along the canal, is revealed as a European poet with a heightened consciousness of the vulnerability of the beautiful in wartime. In the context of war, futurity takes on tragic connotations which undermine the limited self-irony of the concluding refrain, 'O I had a future'.

The poem illustrates how the imagination, stimulated into activity by the conscious manipulation of memory, finally triumphs over easy, formulaic contrasts between innocence and experience. A fine lyric is bred from the tension between the imposed viewpoint characteristic of the Dublin satires and the subversiveness of the engaged imagination. How significant, too, that the escape from self-preoccupation into celebration should take the form of a canal epiphany.

On moving to Dublin Kavanagh may have cherished some hopes that as a London-published writer with two books to his credit he would be cosseted and indulged by an art-loving public. However, in *The Green Fool* he admitted that during his frequent visits to Dublin before 1939 he was merely regarded as a colourful character, fit subject for a lurid paragraph in a Sunday newspaper. As early as 1938 he was already entertaining the notion of exploiting his idiosyncratic country image, resenting the fact that in Dublin, as in Inniskeen, he was more celebrated as an oddity than as a poet, and yet alert to the publicity value of his own otherness.

The state of myopic contentment recalled in 'I had a Future' was of short duration for, once installed in Dublin, Kavanagh set about attracting that notoriety and immediate identifiability to which he had grown accustomed in his native village. He was soon launched on the career of iconoclasm discussed in the last chapter: anti-bourgeois, disparaging Irish theatre, journalism and radio, baiting public institutions and person- alities and ridiculing national shibboleths, belittling estab- lished literary reputations and inveighing against such gener- ally esteemed cultural movements as the Literary Renais- sance and the Gaelic language revival. There was, usually, an air of daredevil exhibitionism about his critiques, a provocat- ive imbalance and insolence in his polemicism, that seemed calculated to invite retaliation and stir up a public dogfight. As he became more and more engrossed in the internecine cultural conflicts, which he did so much to initiate and perpetuate, it seemed as if local notoriety rather than fame were Kavanagh's spur.

By the mid-1940s he had evolved that inescapably ob- trusive public persona which was to become a recurring image in his writings for the next decade. He had turned himself into a Dublin character, readily identifiable by the man in the street, a folk-hero whose larger-than-life antics were designed to stimulate interest in his literary produc- tions. In the mornings he usually stayed indoors and wrote, but in the afternoons and evenings he was on public display in the city centre, a flamboyantly staged personality, a stroll- ing player entertaining a local audience in street, café or public house.

Capitalising on the image of 'peasant poet', which had piqued him at first, he accentuated his appearance of farmer- about-town, flaunting his rustic uncouthness, drawing atten- tion to his large physique and ungainliness, and priding himself on the curtness and acerbity of his Monaghan speech. He made no apparent effort to curb the peasant trait which he characterised as 'insultability' and was given to wildly unpre- dictable mood swings from banter and dry irony to sudden anger and cutting repartee. By parading himself as an abrasive, ill-kempt, boorish, no-nonsense north-country poet, Kavanagh was proclaiming his difference from Dublin's middle class, many of whom were first generation urbanites successfully adapting to city ways, and also from his more orthodoxly educated and genteel fellow poets.[16] His personal image was an exhibitionistic and sustained expression of dissent from Irish urban and literary values. It was an incarnation of his scorn for what was in his estimation a materialist and philistine citizenry and a derivative and effete literary establishment. He was a guerrilla at the edge of the complacent Irish cultural scene, a permanent outsider and subversive. His exaggerated country persona, indicative of his refusal to change, adapt or conform to urban mores, was presented as a living symbol of his honesty, incorruptibility and authenticity. That he should have clashed with Brendan Behan was inevitable: it was a classic Irish confrontation between 'Culchie' and 'Dub', between two would-be folk heroes, both exploiting their respective demotic backgrounds to project an image of primitive vigour and originality.

So extreme was Kavanagh's display of rural uncouthness that he seemed a stage-countryman and his histrionics attracted the malicious attentions of journalists and fellow writers. Despite the grotesquerie of its caricature, Larry Morrow's account of an interview with the poet in 1948 gives some idea of the kind of colourful figure he cut on the Dublin scene by the late 1940s.[17] His ostentatiously countrified air prompted Morrow to satirise him through rural images: 'great root-like' hands, 'enormous, mountainous shoulders, tufts of oily, black hair like scraps of fleece caught on barbed wire'. One of his favourite tropes is the comparison of Kavanagh to a horse: spectacles like blinkers, 'scobed nostrils', equine teeth, an imaginary jingle of harness when the poet tosses his head. Morrow also drew attention to the stagy rusticity of Kavanagh's attire, mischievously comparing him to the picture of a countryman on a pre-war seedsman's catalogue, an outdated marketing image of the rural. He mocked at the poet's oversized appearance and manner: he was constructed on the 'heroic' scale, his voice and movements magnified to Brobdignagian disproportions, his opinions so outrageous that it was impossible to adopt a neutral attitude towards him. Kavanagh's larger-than-life persona seemed to dwarf his extremely small creative output, in Morrow's view, although, as the author of *The Great Hunger*, his literary reputation was secure.

Morrow was unaware that the persona Kavanagh had so assiduously cultivated was about to be transposed into his dominant literary image. In 1947 he had put the finishing touches to his self-portrait as rural poet in *Tarry Flynn* and for the next eight years most of his poetry and fiction was to be devoted to the promotion of himself as urban poet. Whereas in his satiric verses he was sometimes content to pose as a disillusioned spectator or audience, in a series of urban self-portraits, published between 1946 and 1955, he takes the centre-stage.

Kavanagh believed that 'the poet is a poet outside his writing', that 'he creates an oral tradition', 'does something to people'. A corollary of his expressive aesthetic that poetry is the product of a poetic mind was that 'a man may be a poet in prose as well as in verse, or in talking to the people':

> To narrow the poetic spirit down to its expression in verse is equivalent to narrowing religion down to something that happens on Sundays.

A poet, in Kavanagh's opinion, is recognisable by his 'powers of insight and imagination', whatever the occasion:

> If I happened to meet a poet . . . I would expect him to reveal his powers of insight and imagination even if he talked of poultry farming, ground rents or any other commonplace subject.[18]

In his own case he ensured that the poet would be immediately recognisable to the onlooker by effecting a *rapprochement* between his public and poetic self-images. Public persona and autobiographical first person became interdependent modes of self-expression.

The eponymous hero of the short story, 'The Lay of the Crooked Knight' (1946),[19] a tall, graceless, unkempt and impoverished poet, is the first of Kavanagh's urban self-dramatisations. Anachronistic imagery of knights, castles and crusades is introduced for purposes of transparent fictional disguise, and the unnamed urban setting is identifiable as the Dublin of the satires. In this didactic romance the Crooked Knight's lady-love succeeds in transforming him into a suave, fashionable and rich young man, and he is just about to propose marriage to her when he discovers to his chagrin that he has been ousted by another suitor. Immediately he reverts to his former gaucherie and the story concludes with the knight back where he had started and looking forward to his next adventure.

Failure in love was to be a recurring feature in Kavanagh's self-portrayal for the next decade and, undoubtedly, many of his tales of unrequited love have an autobiographical basis. Whatever the degree of sublimation involved it is significant that, in this instance, he turns his love story into a moral fable about artistic authenticity. The knight is presented as a lone crusader who sees it as his vocation to contend with the infidels 'Untruth and Charlatanism', and to become rich. The lady diverts him from the first part of his quest in order to aid him in the second, and thus the story illustrates that crusading in the cause of truth and amassing wealth are incompatible pursuits. The fable's central concern, however, is with the artist's image as an expression of his unique selfhood. By metamorphosing from frog into handsome and socially acceptable prince at his lady's bidding the poet surrenders his individuality. Dishevelled appearance, clumsy gait, eccentric behaviour and poverty are now regarded as outward signs of aesthetic integrity. For the first time Kavanagh is deploying his personal image as a symbol of authenticity in opposition to spurious urban values and, in particular, to false images of the literary. Unkemptness and physical and social maladroitness are represented as macho attributes, distinguishing the true poet from the literary dilettante, who is dandified and effeminate. The knight's gentrification involves a move towards effeteness, learning to sip sherry, use a cigarette holder and substitute 'sweet, affected talk' for his own unpolished idiom and accent. Such surrender of his individual voice, of course, points to the close connection between social and artistic compromise and it is significant that the knight's efforts to conform to the norms of polite bourgeois society result in 'a whole series of evasions' of the truth.

Nonconformity with urban society's expectations gives the poet a licence to be rude, aggressive and abrasive in his conduct. Indeed, authenticity demands boorishness in this story: the knight's 'rough edges' were 'actually the grip on the wheels of his destiny'. Honesty was to be one of Kavanagh's most prized moral and literary virtues in the decade ahead and already it is being associated with discourtesy, angularity and social alienation. When Knight Kavanagh suddenly sees the error of his gracious ways, his conversion is signalled by an *outré* display of contempt for the mores of urban café society:

> . . . he rose from the table, gave one huge roar. He cursed everything and everybody. He spat on the floor . . . He was real again . . .

Kavanagh is rather pleased at the Crooked Knight's exhibition of himself as a country bull among the tinkling urban china and interprets the spectators' reaction as one of envy at such uninhibited behaviour.

The fable concludes with a sudden lunge into moral and religious metaphor in which the city, where rich women and arty men amuse themselves, is viewed as a hell inhabited by damned souls. According to this eschatological poetics only the aesthetically committed are saved. The artistic elect are alienated and anti-social; the true poet is ostracised by the literary coteries: he offends against contemporary taste and his genius goes unrecognised. It is, perhaps, unfortunate that the incarnation of aesthetic uprightness should be dubbed 'crooked'. Kavanagh's customary term for the difference that sets the poet apart from his more socially adjusted and more

pragmatic fellow men was the word 'kink', which is sometimes explicitly associated with moral and aesthetic honesty,
a 'kink of rectitude'.

As in his rural self-portraits Kavanagh is still a social misfit,
misunderstood, mistrusted and maltreated by more worldly-
wise contemporaries. One notable difference is that he tends
to treat the antics of his urban persona more seriously. He is
self-righteous rather than self-mocking, too immersed in his
quarrel with Dublin to achieve that comic perspective on his
trials and tribulations which he so successfully adopts in
Tarry Flynn.

The persona created in the 'Lay' reappears as an aesthetic
hero in 'Adventures in the Bohemian Jungle' and 'The
Paddiad'. The hero of the former who, like the knight,
succeeds in escaping from Dublin's cultural hell, celebrates
his deliverance by engaging in a urinating contest, a performance even more calculated to *epater la bourgeoisie* than the
knight's roaring and spitting. 'The Paddiad' resembles the
'Lay' in that its central satiric conflict between artistic mediocrity and the literary conscience is embodied in contrasting
personal images. The devil Mediocrity is depicted as socially
assured, bland, saintly and smooth, whereas Paddy Conscience is a disruptive presence, a social nonconformist,
exhibited in 'bedraggled pose' with 'drunken talk and dirty
clothes', an outsider to Dublin's polite literary cliques. Paddy
Conscience is clearly another manifestation of Knight Kavanagh, still tilting at charlatanism; gentility and social success
retain their infernal associations; and literary authenticity is
expressed through 'condemnatory and uncivil' behaviour.

The self-portrait in the posthumously published autobiographical fiction, *By Night Unstarred*, complements that presented in the 'Lay'. The principal character's name was
changed from Michael to Patrick by the novel's editor, thus
removing any vestige of fictional disguise and emphasising
that the author is once again his own hero.[20] On this occasion
his self-image does not acquire symbolic status. His lack of
social skills, ignorance of how to dress, behave, conduct a

courtship, win friends or influence people, no longer testifies to uncorrupted originality but simply to a disabling lack of *savoir-faire*. Once again the hero is provided with a girlfriend who mothers him and takes his worldly education in hand. Unlike the unnamed lady in the 'Lay', Margaret is unsuccessful in advancing his fortunes because she is unable to teach him social tact and check his tendency to crass verbal outrage. However inopportune the occasion he cannot resist stating his unflatteringly honest opinion on any artistic subject.

Part two of *By Night Unstarred*, which focuses on Patrick's efforts to obtain employment, reveals him as unemployable, especially in the kind of public relations post he covets. The hours he spends canvassing influential persons are nullified by a moment's abrasive candour. He is too proud and too unself-disciplined to thrive in an insecure, *nouveau riche* society and his insulting behaviour is not calculated to endear him to Dublin's wealthy parvenus. That 'kink' in his character, which passed as a sign of rectitude in the 'Lay', is now presented as a self-destructive tendency to turn unpredictably on potential benefactors, 'firing on the ships that were coming to rescue him'. His self-esteem and his contempt for Dublin's ruling class are too pronounced to allow him to play the part of sycophant.

One of the most intimate and unflattering self-portraits occurs in Patrick's interview with the bishop in the second part of *By Night Unstarred*. In the bishop's presence the scourge of Dublin's drawing-rooms is reduced to childish defencelessness. His propensity for sharp, malicious character assassination is checked by an atavistic respect for the authority of the church and a simple trusting faith in the goodness of churchmen. The bishop's paternalistic attitude exposes Patrick's dependency, his longing for a powerful patron. His reactions as the bishop writes a letter on his behalf—fidgeting, picking his ear and nose, sweating and mopping his brow with a dirty handkerchief—are not such as to inspire confidence in the prospects of this would-be publicity director. Patrick's obvious error, however, is that he vacillates over accepting a hand-out of three pounds from the bishop. Acceptance would relegate him from the ranks of the about-to-be-employed to the role of beggar; refusal would antagonise the donor. By hesitating over the offer Patrick manages to make both mistakes and he exits from the episcopal palace at a half-walk, half-run, completely demoralised by the encounter. The episode displays the writer's mastery of the comedy of embarrassment.

It is clear from *By Night Unstarred* that Kavanagh was not fully committed to self-righteous satire and retained his capacity for self-irony and self-ridicule. He is far more engaging in the role of comic anti-hero than in that of aesthetic hero. His attitude towards poverty and joblessness is less idealistic and less priggish here than it was in the 'Lay'. Then he had associated wealth and social success with artistic compromise; now he is anxious to come in from the cold and join the ranks of the middle classes. Then he had portrayed himself as one who, though he could easily acquire gentility and fortune, had nobly chosen otherwise; now he reveals himself as insecure and socially maladjusted, unable to control his antagonistic outbursts. Perhaps it was because its self-portraiture was so devastatingly accurate that Kavanagh never completed or published *By Night Unstarred*. It exposed anxieties, insecurities and an eager innocence at odds with the crusty, cantankerous, arrogant persona he publicly affected.

Failure as poet and as lover were conjoined by Kavanagh, as I noted, in the early poem, 'Sanctity':

> To be a poet and not know the trade,
> To be a lover and repel all women . . .[21]

Later these 'twin ironies' were reduced to one, as failure in love became a concomitant of aesthetic integrity. The dramatisation of himself as a poet irresistibly attractive to women yet always unsuccessful in love was to be a recurring pose in Kavanagh's urban self-portraits. His 'dark-haired Miriam' always runs away.[22] What women find attractive about the poet are his poverty and his unconventionality. The tamed and affluent knight is deserted by his lady in the 'Lay' and in the poem, 'Auditors In', where Kavanagh again aspires to the trappings of urban middle-class life — 'A car, a big suburban house' — he wryly stipulates that such acquisitions should be 'half-secret' lest he lose

> The wild attraction of the poor
> But proud, the fanatic lure
> For women of the poet's way . . .

Yet in the same poem he blames his bachelor state on his poverty, characterising himself as

> A lonely lecher whom the fates
> By a financial trick castrates . . .

The recurrent personal myth of the poet-hero unsuccessful in love, yet irresistibly attractive to women, is conflated with the classical Narcissus myth in 'Narcissus and the Women':

> Many women circled the prison of Reflection
> Where he lay among the flashing mirrors
> Hoping somewhere to find some door of Action
> By which he might be rescued from his errors.

This compressed lyric is grammatically ambiguous since the subject of 'hoping' may be either the speaker or the 'many women'. So one reading portrays the speaker as desirous of breaking out of the prison of narcissism to join his lady admirers. The other endorses the total self-preoccupation which appears regrettable to the women. Capitalisation reinforces the traditional opposition between action and reflection and the pun on the latter renders self-regard synonymous with contemplation. Since the quatrain was originally published along with the manifesto poem, 'Intimate Parnassus',[23] the preferred reading may be that narcissistic non-involvement with women is a form of aesthetic detachment, a necessary withdrawal from 'the disturbances in human hearts' into a Parnassian hall of mirrors. Alternatively, the poem's ambiguity may express an unresolved ambivalence on the poet's part towards the conflicting claims of self-love and self-surrender to heterosexual love.

The women, whom Kavanagh designates 'poet's girls', are usually 'well-bred' convent girls, 'wrapped in middle-class felicities',[24] his social superiors and his opposites in elegance, self-assurance and *savoir-faire*. Even Tarry Flynn is made to fall in love with the convent-educated daughter of a local big farmer. The beloved is often cast in a semi-maternal role like the unnamed lady of the 'Lay' or Margaret in *By Night Unstarred*. Both women act *in loco parentis*, teaching the poet how to walk and talk, what to wear, how to conduct himself in company. They reward him when he is good, remonstrate with him when he misbehaves. The Knight tells his lady sensational stories about his exploits, 'such as he always tried to bring home to his mother'. Woman draws out the childish, conformist element in the poet's character, encouraging his approval-seeking tendencies, exerting an undue formative influence. She may, therefore, be an obstacle to his achievement of poetic integrity and maturity. Woman in the 'Lay' is a temptress who subverts the poet's otherness and makes an ordinary man of him. But the maternal woman may also fulfil the positive function of ministering to the poet's vulnerable ego. In 'God in Woman', for instance, woman is represented as a *magna mater*, a supreme udder, nourishing and sustaining the poet. Kavanagh's feminine ideal, never overtly alluded to in his poetry, was a beautiful, rich patron-cum-wife or mistress who would support him financially in the style to which he would have liked to become accustomed.[25] His middle-class women rarely serve as muses and, although in 'Question to Life' he expostulates:

> Surely you would not ask me to have known
> Only the passion of primrose banks in May . . .

as a poet he is a lover of the meadows and the woods and of this green earth rather than a laureate of human passion. The

'Lay', among other things, expresses an instinctive recoil from the surrender of selfhood involved in the relationship with a woman; similarly, the flirtatious poet of 'If Ever You Go To Dublin Town' is ultimately revealed as a loner, happy in his solitary dedication to his art.

Several poems on the subject of unrequited love were composed as songs, their musical rhythms reducing passion to sad or comic sentiment. 'On Raglan Road', the most popular of these songs, is almost contemporaneous with the 'Lay'. Its Irish popularity may be partially due to the fact that it is based on that very well-known Irish air, 'The Dawning of the Day', and that it was recorded by the late Luke Kelly of 'The Dubliners', yet it is also intrinsically attractive as a lyric, one of those sweetest songs that tell of saddest thought. The Dublin setting, viewed in retrospect as lost love's domain, is pervaded with that nostalgic magic which Kavanagh once reserved for the Inniskeen landscape. Raglan Road, trans-formed by love, becomes 'the enchanted way' just as the lost fields of home once seemed 'part of no earthly estate'. The poet's defensively arrogant posturing as an angel who has wooed an unworthy 'creature made of clay' tends to be overlooked by an uncritical, late-night Irish audience, absorbed in the lovely intricacies of internal rhyme, the interlacing of assonance and alliteration, and the pleasures of melodious and localised sentiment.

By contrast the poet appears as a comically unsuccessful lover in 'Cyrano de Bergerac' and 'The Rowley Mile' (1954), published together as 'Two Sentimental Songs'.[26] These two variations on a theme are formally related, both, as originally published, consisting of four stanzas of eight alternately rhyming lines. The unfortunate omission of the final twelve lines of 'Cyrano de Bergerac' from *Collected Poems* and *Complete Poems* obscures this formal and thematic relationship and the two poems are not paired in either collection.[27]

In 'Cyrano de Bergerac', Kavanagh identifies with Ros-tand's tongue-tied poet-lover whose big nose so often proved a romantic impediment. Cyrano's nose reminded him of his own disabilities which his lady loves had attempted to overcome in the 'Lay' and *By Night Unstarred*; for him it was 'a symbol of the price by which every gift is bought'.[28] His 'Cyrano de Bergerac' is organised as a three-act comedy with a coda. Its bashful, middle-aged poet misinterprets a young girl's obtrusive avoidance of him as a sign that she loves him, devises various ruses to initiate a conversation but fails through fear of losing face and, when finally introduced, discovers that she had mistaken his lechery for priestly concern. The twelve omitted lines read:

> She told me I was subtle, her
> Love distress to note;
> She *was* in love and worried
> About someone who was not.
>
> And she always thought when looking at
> My loving priestly face
> That I was one who surely
> Could give her love-advice . . .
> And from the mirror, going out
> The lecher looked at me
> And grinned before resuming
> His priestly dignity.

Without these lines the poem's ironic point, a rueful contrast between Kavanagh's public image and private self, is lost to the reader. His public persona, unlike that projected in the 'Lay' and in his late forties' poems, is now outwardly respectable, celibate clergyman rather than lecherous bachelor; disreputableness has been internalised. The older poet has also recovered his capacity for self-ridicule.

Its companion piece, 'The Rowley Mile', reads like an alternative version of 'Cyrano de Bergerac'. Once again the poet as comic romantic hero mistakenly assumes that a young girl he meets on the street is in love with him but this time he dispenses with the formality of an introduction and proceeds straight to the point. The loss of dignity he had feared in the previous poem now ensues when the surprised girl repulses his advances. The anti-hero's 'gathered courage' is ironically paralleled by the girl's reaction as 'she gathered herself into a ball'. It is a situation which allows Kavanagh to indulge in that comedy of embarrassment for which he had shown such talent in *Tarry Flynn* and *By Night Unstarred*. His efforts to cover up his mistake are described with excruciating specificity. In the end his tone turns sour as he blames the girl's flirtatious smile on the code of sexual conduct taught her by her 'old gummy Granny'. The racing image, drawn on in the title and setting, is not fully exploited until this indignant final stanza in which the stern realities of courtship and marriage for a young girl are implicitly compared to that gruelling test for young horses, the Newmarket April classic over one mile.

'The heart of a song singing it . . . is not caring', Kavanagh wrote in *Self-Portrait*. 'The Rowley Mile' fails this test of detachment. In a more buoyant mood the frustrated Casanova of 'A Ballad'[29] consoles himself with an uncharacteristically optimistic monetary metaphor:

For wealth is potential not the readies at call . . .

Significantly, the most tender love poem of the 1940s is also the least self-regarding. 'Bluebells for Love' (1945),[30] which pre-dates Kavanagh's assumption of his abrasive urban literary persona, is formally and thematically tentative, its narrative hypothetical, its subject the desirability of obliquity in affairs of the heart. Unusually for Kavanagh, it is a love poem which combines love of natural beauty with personal relationship. The title hints at the strategy of indirection adopted in this piece, presenting a covert responsiveness to natural loveliness as a metaphor for undeclared passion. Scene and stance are elaborated, while the emotional pact between the two lovers remains unstated until the end:

We will be interested in the grass,
In an old bucket-hoop, in the ivy that weaves

Green incongruity among dead leaves,
We will put on surprise at carts that pass—
Only sometimes looking sideways at the bluebells
   in the plantation
And never frighten them with too wild an
   exclamation . . .

We will have other loves—or so they'll think;
The primrose or the ferns or the briars,
Or even the rusty paling wires,
Or the violets on the sunless sorrel bank.
Only as an aside the bluebells in the plantation
Will mean a thing to our dark contemplation.

We'll know love little by little, glance by glance.
Ah, the clay under these roots is so brown!
I caught an angel smiling in a chance
Look through the tree-trunks of the plantation
As you and I walked slowly to the station.

Here love has a mutuality, a delicacy, and an intimacy rare in
Kavanagh's depiction of heterosexual relations, and the
poem's metaphoric strategy is such as to protect the lovers'
privacy. The narrator is wary of self-consciousness, knowing
that it results in 'virtue's naturalness' giving way to a studied
'pose', a 'mere facade'. Such emotional and technical restraint
soon disappeared as the poet became increasingly exhibitionistic and strident, translating the personal into public statement, too often content with 'mere facade'.

'The Hero' (originally entitled 'Dublin'), is a case in point.[31]
Though it is not written in the first person, it is a shameless
piece of self-apotheosis, a laureate fantasy in which a reluctant poet has greatness thrust upon him by an admiring
Dublin bourgeoisie. Intellectual and moral ascendancy are
rendered in images of gigantic physique. The Dublin poet
sees himself as Gulliver in Lilliput, 'trapped in a pygmy

town', or perhaps, more accurately, as Paddy in Wonderland who has drunk out of the wrong bottle:

> Vainly on all fours
> He tried the small doors . . .

This poet-hero dwarfs Dublin's legislators and businessmen, towering over them like an allegorisation of Morality or a Lord Bishop of Misrule, a motley-clad alternative to Archbishop McQuaid, with the city's conscience in his keeping. The entire piece is a *jeu d'esprit*, of course, in which self-adulation is licensed by laughter, yet enjoyment of Kavanagh's high jinks involves some collusion with his inflated self-representation. To the end it is an egregiously arrogant poem and the pity that the one-time satirist feels for the 'insincere city' arises less from compassion than from insufferable condescension.

Such megalomaniac tendencies were partially mocked in his *Envoy* 'Diary' for May 1951 where, fantasising about his posthumous reputation, Kavanagh entitled his future biography, to be written by his friend and fellow writer, Anthony Cronin, *He Was God*. 'Portrait of the Artist', a poem about biography and the artist, originally appeared, untitled, in this context. The poem contrasts two kinds of artist. The first, who lives in impoverished obscurity elicits only a dismissive seventeen-word obituary; the second, jocosely named Reilly, who lives the sensational and adventurous life that the public expects of the 'great artist', is the subject of an enthusiastic biography. This is a self-pitying and self-justifying poem in which, by associating publicity and notoriety with theatre and film, sex and syphilis, Kavanagh manages to identify with the poor, underrated writer, the cliché garret-artist.

Entitling his fictitious biography *He Was God* is Kavanagh's jokey acknowledgment of his own messianic fantasies. As in his Monaghan days he still envisaged himself as something of a 'street-corner Christ', though now he tended to associate suffering with artistic incorruptibility:

The world today is full of Pilates, asking the question which is always cynical: 'What is Truth?' And every man who has in him something of Christ will reply 'I am' before he is led off—to starvation.[32]

He was always attracted by the role of pundit and public saviour, the mystic with a message, an Irish Walt Whitman smelting 'in passion the commonplaces of life'.[33] In his poetry he liked to fantasise about being offered the role of 'prophet and saviour', ostentatiously declining it in 'The Gift' and 'No Social Conscience', assuming it after a show of reluctance in 'The Hero', and considering it a 'question to speculate upon in lieu of an answer' in 'After Forty Years of Age'. His 'Jim Larkin' is created in the image of the poet he yearned to become, a leader of the common people, inspiring them with an imaginative faith despite their materialism and indifference. It is typical of the self-aggrandising tendency of Kavanagh's verse at this period that two of his self-portraits were entitled 'The Hero'.[34]

In 'Spring Day' and 'Irish poets open your eyes' Kavanagh assumes the role of aesthetic leader.[35] Both poems wear their seriousness lightly, setting dogmatism to a lively tune. Rhyming couplets and emphatic rhythms formally enact these poems' anti-intellectual and anti-literary bias, their advocacy of an appreciation of ordinariness as a prerequisite for poetry. The first is presented as a popular Irish song, the 'Come all ye', a form whose rhetoric invites communal assent, presupposes that singer and audience share a common ideology or that the singer's message will be endorsed by his audience. Kavanagh exploits the form to lead an aesthetic revolt against modernism, philosophy and contemporary psychology. His pose is that of the carefree comic hero, kicking the traces of intellectual respectability and solemnity, treating bookishness as an aberration from the human norm of sexual and sensuous enjoyment. He leads his poet-followers a merry dance from culture back to nature:

O Come all ye gallant poets—to know it doesn't
   matter
Is Imagination's message—break out but do not
   scatter.
Ordinary things wear lovely wings—the peacock's
   body's common.
O Come all ye youthful poets and try to be more
   human.

   Similar advice is delivered in a similarly hortatory yet ostensibly light-hearted manner in 'Irish poets open your eyes'.
Here Kavanagh resorts to the subversive strategy of parody
to countermand Yeats's final instructions to Irish poets in
'Under Ben Bulben' and substitute his own poetic counsel:

Irish poets open your eyes,
Even Cabra can surprise;
Try the dog tracks now and then—
Shelbourne Park and crooked men . . .

Be ordinary,
Be saving up to marry.
Kiss her in the alleyway,
Part—'Same time, same place' and go.

Learn repose on Boredom's bed,
Deep, anonymous, unread
And the god of Literature
Will touch a moment to endure.

Yeatsian artifice, the concern with craftsmanship and with
the phantasmagoria of Irish subject matter in 'Under Ben
Bulben', is here shrugged off in favour of a cult of common
humanity. The everyday experiences of ordinary people are
pronounced the stuff of poetry. In *Envoy*, where this poem
first appeared, Kavanagh had expressed reservations about
the durability of Yeats's poetry because of its lack of
humanity:

> He does not evoke pity, passion or anger, and for all his
> burden of his native country in his work no poet could be
> more outside what we may call the Irish consciousness,
> and this is because he is too detached, too careful, too
> prudent to be human.

Instead of being excommunicated for his lack of Catholicism,
Yeats is now excluded from communion with his race because of the dearth of self-revelation in his verse:

> He was constantly autobiographical, but it was all writ-
> ing on the veil of Public Importance . . .[36]

Wilful though such a reading of Yeats may be, it reveals how
much store Kavanagh set by personal images and banal
situations as poetic materials in the early 1950s and his
opposition of an aesthetic of 'simplicity' to the Yeatsian
'embroidered coat'. Yeats's experiments with popular forms
such as the ballad, he dismissed as sounding an 'artificial
note'. Kavanagh creatively misread Yeats so as to emphasise
the essential difference between them; Yeats's mythological
mandarin verse is being contrasted with his own preference
for the 'careless Muses' and the common touch. For all his
cult of the quotidian, however, Kavanagh's poetry from the
early 1940s onwards is obsessed with aesthetic issues and, a
few romantic or comic love poems apart, it rarely separates
the man from the poet as subject. Ordinariness is preached
more than it is practised, or it is represented as a novel and,
therefore, extraordinary poetic theme, as it is in 'Spring Day'
and 'Irish poets open your eyes'.

Though the self is usually the indulged hero of his autobiographical verse, Kavanagh is occasionally excoriating about
his own public image and pretensions, notably in 'Bank
Holiday', the only one of these self-portraits in which he
refers to himself by name.[37] Here the private poet rounds on
his public alter-ego with as much venomous disdain as he
ever lavished on his enemies. His susceptibility to women,
elsewhere indulged as an amiable weakness, is now bitterly

derided, especially his excessive gratitude for meagre sexual favours:

> There he comes your alter ego
> Past the Waterloo and Searson's
> With a silly gaping mouth
> Sucking smiles from every slut,
> Sure that this is Heaven's high manna—
> God is good to Patrick Kavanagh,
> Building like a rejected lover
> Dust into an ivory tower.

His failure to acquire male friends is also scathingly satirised and, with unerring self-perception, Kavanagh admits that his public-house exhibitionism was motivated by a craving for affection. His public persona has sold the private man short, trading the 'essence of his heart' for 'a porter-perfumed fart'; the octosyllabic couplet with its deflationary rhyme underscores his degradation. This bank holiday reckoning takes account only of the seven lean years since his 'City Commentary' column. The present imaginative ascendancy of the urban is evident from the metaphoric use of rural imagery as opposed to the realistic foregrounding of the Dublin scene.

Parading his public failings as familial personifications in the final stanza makes the point that these faults are intimately, though not inextricably, associated with the self:

> Knock him to the ground for he
> Is your sister Vanity,
> Is your brother Clown
> Exhibited for a sneering town.
> He's your son who's named Tomorrow,
> Kill him, kill Remorse, your mother,
> Be the father of your fate
> On this nineteen-fifty date.

The metaphor of kinship suggests that self-reform will be difficult despite the zeal for self-improvement and the optimism displayed in this final mustering of imperatives.

Not surprisingly, the best and best known of Kavanagh's Dublin self-portraits, 'If Ever You Go To Dublin Town' (1953),[38] is the most lenient of these personal sketches since a half-playful affection for his material is the characteristic tone of most of Kavanagh's better poems. Here he sets about immortalising himself as a 'character', transforming life into legend. The poem is structured around a series of interviews with posterity; its medium, hearsay, anecdote and opinion:

> If ever you go to Dublin town
> In a hundred years or so
> Inquire for me in Baggot Street
> And what I was like to know.
> O he was a queer one
> Fol dol the di do,
> He was a queer one
> I tell you.

Different Dubliners are asked to sum up the impressions of Patrick Kavanagh handed down to them and their contrary verdicts project the poet as a multi-faceted personality, still a talking point a hundred years after his lifetime. The series of rigged interviews is an ingenious device for accentuating certain aspects of his personal image, both shaping and controlling popular memory.

As this is a relatively late portrait Kavanagh is content to sketch in rapidly the salient features of the persona he had cultivated in life and in literature since the mid-1940s. The image projected here still resembles that of the Crooked Knight with his eccentric mien, dishevelled appearance, attractiveness to women and macho arrogance. While the soberly programmatic 'Lay' made a virtue out of unkempt-ness and angularity, these once vaunted attributes are now partially deprecated by the playful tone. Neither is the antagonism he aroused in other men proposed as a mark of authenticity as it was in the 'Lay' and 'The Paddiad'. Here, on the contrary, Kavanagh is on the defensive and takes two stanzas to cope with it, the first pleading for a fair hearing, the second glossing the unflattering verdict. It is characteristic of his peculiar honesty that he does not balk at including uncomplimentary opinions in the legend he is perpetuating. Honesty also prompts his wistful admission of loss of confidence in the permanence of the personality he had so assiduously promoted:

> If ever you go to Dublin town
> In a hundred years or so
> Sniff for my personality,
> Is it vanity's vapour now?

With this repetition of the opening two lines the poem is redirected from posterity's assessment of his life to its evaluation of his poetry. He is unperturbed by, even gleeful about, academic criticism that he has never achieved his potential. In the end, however, he turns from external opinion to self-appraisal and from light-hearted hypothesis to serious statement. The private poet rather than the public persona finally stands revealed, the solitary, totally committed and fulfilled artist hidden behind the gossip-worthy exterior:

> He knew that posterity has no use
> For anything but the soul,
> The lines that speak the passionate heart,
> The spirit that lives alone.
> O he was a lone one
> Fol dol the di do
> Yet he lived happily
> I tell you.

He is confident that even if he is forgotten as a 'character' he will survive as a poet by popular franchise, which indeed he has.

In choosing a ballad as his biographical medium Kavanagh has appropriated a form ideally suited to the metamorphosis of life into legend. He has transformed himself into a folk hero and folk poet. Yet the effect of the ballad's combination of rhythmic stress and verbal slightness is to play down such heroics. Repetitive phrasing, alliteration and assonance weave a near-weightless texture, and the short lines and half-stanza, half-refrain format elicit a minimal utterance. Much of this slight verbal expenditure, especially in the refrain, is invested in relaxing the reader, making light of what is, in fact, being emphasised. The refrain also contributes to the creation of the Kavanagh legend. It is delivered with that mixture of rueful admiration and knowingness by which the Dubliner conveys that the man under discussion qualifies as a 'character' and it concludes with the 'I tell you' which clinches his opinion and brooks no contradiction. This refrain with its nonsense line also manages to suggest that the poet has passed from folk memory into folk repertoire.

By this stage Kavanagh is in full control of his own image and has learned how to create a mood in which it may be affectionately received so that the colossal vanity of his enterprise is overlooked. The reader no longer resists or resents the poet's vision of a Kavanagh-centred Dublin as in the satires and some of the other self-portraits and happily colludes with the poem's narcissism because folksong imparts an acceptable nonchalance to self-promotion.

If the ballad 'If Ever you go to Dublin Town' represents one sort of high point for Kavanagh's poetic self-creation, his libel action, almost a year later, represents quite another. Kavanagh went to court to protect his self-image, claiming that he had been libelled in an article, 'Profile: Mr Patrick Kavanagh', printed in a national weekly, *The Leader*, on 11 October 1952. The 'Profile' was anonymous and its authorship remained a closely guarded secret. It is now time to reveal that the author was, as has long been surmised, the poet and diplomat, Valentin Iremonger, who was assisted in his labours by a fellow civil servant, Paddy Lynch. Their warts-and-all portrait, which extolled the poet's literary achievement in *The Great Hunger* and a handful of lyrics and sympathised with his failure to obtain state patronage, also mocked at his public image, ridiculed his fantasies, aspirations and self-aggrandising criticism and deplored his absorption in satire and anger. The 'Profile' was based on a close acquaintance with Kavanagh's poetry and journalism, which was alluded to or quoted from with devastating effect, and, unkindest cut of all, its appraisal of the poet's works and pomps was wickedly amusing. Published a few months after the demise of *Kavanagh's Weekly*, the 'Profile' was particularly scathing about this fraternal venture. Peter Kavanagh's attack on Irish embassies in the first issue had, undoubtedly, piqued Valentin Iremonger, a distinguished member of the then Department of External Affairs. While it was far more appreciative of Kavanagh's 'intense personal vision' and 'verbal genius' than Morrow's earlier portrait, the 'Profile' was ultimately more patronising both in its general tone and in its urbane overview of the poet's *oeuvre* and opinions. It was possibly its air of knowingness, the shrewdness of its critical assessment and its condescending humour, that goaded Kavanagh into taking a suit for libel.

This libel action, which opened in the High Court on 3 February 1954, was the high point of Kavanagh's career as self-publicist, a courtroom drama which became a runaway box-office success. For seven days he played the part of a much maligned writer before a crowded court. Under skilful cross-examination he proved an artful dodger, parrying or evading the most probing questions and endearing himself to his supporters by his witticisms and disconcerting repartee.[39] It was a virtuoso performance which alternately had his audience in bursts of laughter or contrasting attentive silence. The newspapers gave the case extensive coverage and such media attention ensured that the poet's achievements and opinions reached a wider readership than ever before. While Kavanagh failed in his immediate objective in that the court decided that he had not been libelled, this was the climax of his career of histrionic self-promotion, his most notorious exhibition of the writer as public persona.[40]

9

Counter-Urban Self-Images

Introduction

BY THE end of his first decade in Dublin Kavanagh was disturbed at the direction his writing was taking. Since 1944 he had been devoting himself increasingly to poems on public themes, to satire, cultural criticism and to self-portraits in prose and verse. Both his satiric poems and his self-dramatisations were a public poetry in which the line between life and literature was often blurred. The satiric poems were retaliatory, a continuation of public-house and journalistic quarrels; the self-dramatisations were extensions of his flamboyant, real life role-playing, scripted versions of the street theatre which he daily enacted. Now he was assailed with doubts that controversy and exhibitionism were stifling, or distracting him from, the exercise of his real creative gifts. In his own rural metaphor he was neglecting to 'dig and ditch [his] authentic land'.[1] While still expending much of his time and talent on rhetoric and role playing he struggled to check the satiric, aggressive and extroverted bent of his writing and to channel his literary energies from the 'quarrel with others' into poetry.

As he set about taking himself 'in hand' from 1950 onwards his poetry displays a new introversion. In 'Auditors In', whose subject, as its title suggests, is a reckoning up of liabilities and assets both personal and poetic, he distinguishes between verse as 'entertainment' and verse as 'profound and holy faith', verse which belongs in the public domain and 'inner history'. Though rhetoric and exhibitionism remained conspicuous features of his prose and poetry, he now began to promote the myth of the two Kavanaghs, the public persona and the private poet, the gulf between them being as wide as that between the two Brownings in Henry James's

'The Private Life'. His self-portrait in 'Bank Holiday' dramatises this dual identity, the *angst*-ridden poet 'sitting in' his
'room alone', his public *alter ego* sauntering the streets and
performing in bars. 'If Ever You Go To Dublin Town' is a
deliberate attempt to perpetuate the myth of a public and
private self: the *flâneur*, flirt, and gruff, macho drinking man,
and the private poet, solitary, celibate, spiritual, dedicated to
his art. This private poet is the subject of many of his early
1950s' poems. The self is still centre stage but the spotlight is
turned more often on inner drama, on auto-analysis, the
exploration of the psychological origins of his verse, the
relationship between memory and imagination. Usually self-
regarding his poetry now becomes reflexive.

Despite his apparent absorption in the cut and thrust of
literary and social criticism in the late 1940s and early 1950s
Kavanagh never quite succeeded in suppressing his aesthetic
aversion to argument and debate. He had attempted to
exculpate himself from the censoriousness he knew was
forthcoming by opening his *Envoy* 'Diary' with an act of
humility and love. So it is not altogether surprising to find
that, after thirteen weeks of vituperative condemnation of
Irish writers and Irish institutions, he concluded *Kavanagh's
Weekly* with a poem[2] which began

> Yet having said all this he feels
> That he should go down on his knees and pray
> For forgiveness for his pride . . .

This immediate dismissal of his editorial role as a manifestation of pride reveals Kavanagh's serious misgivings about his
engrossment in journalistic polemics. Private conscience here
takes over from public conscience and the sudden swerve
from controversy to interiority is typical of the imaginative
reorientation which was taking place in his work from 1950
onwards. It is significant, too, that the swing from polemical
rhetoric to confessionalism should take the form of a transition from prose into poetry since poetry rather than prose
was to become the medium of the private self.

Sometimes, after over ten years spent struggling to make his mark as a writer in Dublin, what Kavanagh confesses to is a sense of failure, not just a dearth of external success symbols—'the scarlet Jag/House in Foxrock and wife and kids'—which is only 'failure of a kind', but creative failure. 'Bank Holiday', in which he taunts his public self about his ineffectual philandering and exhibitionism, portrays the private man more sombrely as a talent in decline:

> Sitting in my room alone
> Conscious of a season gone.
> Ultimate failure straggling up
> Through the barren daydream crop.

'Barren' and 'unfruitful' are adjectives which recur in connection with his work in these years. 'I Had a Future' is the sardonic refrain of one who considers himself *passé*, and in 'To be Dead' he confronts the Romantic fear of drying up or stagnating as a poet:

> To know that growth has stopped,
> That whatever is done is the end;
> Correct the proofs over and over,
> Rewrite old poems again and again . . .

Verse which focuses on 'inner history' tells of 'the failure of man's mission'. So 'Auditors In' begins by taking failure for granted; the only question is whether he should conduct an in-depth analysis of the sad fact:

> Should it be my job to mention
> Precisely how I chanced to fail . . .

Yet Kavanagh is not one to wallow in self-pity for long, and over and over again he rallies his poetic forces; 'to stop believing/In the masterpieces [he] will begin tomorrow' is 'to be dead'.

His attempt to rededicate himself to the 'profound and holy faith' of poetry after years of frittering his talent resulted in an imaginative renunciation of Dublin, which he now regarded as an environment uncongenial to his genius. Sometimes he sought refuge from the din of towns and cities by cultivating a Parnassian aloofness from the doings of mere mortals, or he escaped from the publicity-seeking antics of his Dublin persona and the superficiality of his commerce with 'pleasure, knowledge and the conscious hour' by retreating into the privacy of his subconscious. Sometimes his anti-urban bias led him to identify Inniskeen as his creative homeland, his innocent, pre-urban paradise.

The central tenet of his new aesthetic faith is that poetry originates in a 'pure positive' and that it may be attained only by the purging of all negative feelings, anger, aggression, ill-will, hatred, destructiveness, pride, all the emotions that had motivated his satires. The true poet must nurture the aesthetic virtues of detachment, repose, praise, universal benevolence, the worship of the good. The poet's 'heaven' is the 'generous impulse', contentment 'with feeding praise to the good'. In Kavanagh's new poetics his expressive terminology is often Christian because creative and religious states are conflated. Creativity is exalted into a mystical state and thus separated from satire, narcissism and rhetoric. His muse is the Christian God seeking to incarnate himself in the Word of the poem, so in 'To be Dead' he acknowledges that orthodox religion, bereft of its expressive dimension, is not his 'kind of truth'.

The involuntary nature of inspiration is rendered in Christian mystical terms in 'Having Confessed':

> Lie at the heart of the emotion, time
> Has its own work to do. We must not anticipate
> Or awaken for a moment. God cannot catch us
> Unless we stay in the unconscious room
> Of our hearts. We must be nothing,
> Nothing that God may make us something . . .

The speaker here is the Romantic poet awaiting the divine visitation of his muse. In order to prepare himself for the coming of the Word he must purge himself of all interference from the consciousness, enter into a passive state of pure emotion, surrender all sense of selfhood. The creative event cannot be anticipated or hurried or forced.

Despite the many modern touches in his 1950s' verse, Kavanagh is a born-again Romantic, reliving nineteenth-century aesthetic dilemmas in a contemporary Irish context: the relationship between innocence and experience, between the transcendental and the actual, the 'placeless Heaven' and the local habitation, imagination and memory. Yet he is also his own man, a quirky, humorous, unpredictably predictable individualist. By the 1950s he was evolving a voice to express his own distinctiveness as opposed to merely projecting an idiosyncratic persona, a staged uniqueness.

Away, away . . .

Although it is not the first of his introspective poems, 'Auditors In' introduces a new confessionalism into Kavanagh's verse and enacts his poetic reorientation from rhetoric and role playing to expressive transcendentalism. Originally subtitled 'Speculations on a Theme',[3] that theme is the self as man and poet, but mostly as poet. The subtitle points to the new informality of Kavanagh's approach in part I, a thinking aloud rather than making anything, as Matthew Arnold had accused the nineteenth-century Romantics of doing. Kavanagh is usually a 'maker', very conscious of poetic structure in his serious verse, as may be discerned from his fondness for the sonnet and his tendency to favour regular stanzas and rhyme schemes. Now that he is intent on communicating personality through verse, revealing an 'inner history' of aspirations, anxieties, hesitations, enthusiasms and neuroses, he experiments with stanzas of varying length to reinforce the impression of spontaneity conveyed by the shifting moods and tones of the 'I', while the use of couplets, chiefly octosyllabic throughout part I, contributes an underlying sense of personal and formal cohesion.

At the beginning he is self-conscious about his new, intimate confessional approach which dispenses with his

customary distancing devices, allegory, fantasy, role playing
or the recollection of a younger self:

> The problem that confronts me here
> Is to be eloquent yet sincere;
> Let myself rip and not go phoney
> In an inflated testimony . . .

This introductory emphasis on the aesthetic problem involved in talking honestly, directly and unpretentiously
about the self is not merely a rhetorical ploy to disarm
criticism; it illustrates the new familiarity between author and
reader. We are being made privy to the difficulties of the
confessional mode itself.

Yet these apparently reader-conscious opening lines also
form part of the poem's dialogue of self and soul, since in
'Auditors In' Kavanagh is both addresser and addressee,
auditor and audited, and his readers are eavesdroppers on a
private auto-analysis. The punning title takes account both of
the element of stocktaking and of the readers' role as
listeners-in. We are given the impresssion that the poem is
being composed spontaneously and that we are assisting at
its unfolding. 'Write down here: he knew what he wanted',
Kavanagh orders, and proceeds to carry out his own instruc-
tion, itemising his middle-class aspirations.

Tonal shifts prevent confessional outpouring from becoming boringly self indulgent; the poet is perplexed, assured,
playful, reproachful, self-admonitory, self-accusing, self-
dismayed and self-reassuring by turns. Soul baring is conducted with racy flexibility and humour; the couplets, often
jauntily feminine in their rhyming, undercut confessional
seriousness and the style is relaxed and demotic, freely
resorting to colloquialisms such as 'Let myself rip', 'Should it
be my job to mention', 'to get down to the factual', 'You
never catch on', 'You must take yourself in hand'. This blend
of the solemn and the self-mocking, abstraction and vernacular, is distinctively Kavanaghish, the voice that had emerged
in the journalism is now being heard in the verse. His poetry

sometimes suffered formally from being tossed into a journalistic context but it also gained in communicative ease and thematic adaptability, while the blurring of the line between literature and life in his satiric and self-dramatising poems contributed an immediacy and contemporaneity to both image and idiom. He is now instantly recognisable from his utterance without the necessity for the externals of self-portraiture.

Failure in personal relationships is, as usual, presented comically here, with the sexually irresistible poet unable to capitalise on his charms. He is Rasputin, priestly confidant of upper-class ladies, a wild west hero with unerring sexual aim, a wolf who is whistled at; yet, underneath it all, this magnetic hero is the victim of his own catholicism and idealism, confounding sex and sin, a pauper, too, unable to afford a wife and children. Sexual failure is now compensated for by a love that is neither *agape* nor *eros*, an affection for the ordinary and familiar: a girl retracing the poet's former mass-going footsteps from the Inniskeen townland of Ednamo; dandelions, his favourite weeds, growing by Willie Hughes's. Such ordinary material is pronounced 'equally valid' for 'urban epic, peasant ballad', for the art of a Joyce or a Kavanagh. (How he must have relished the fact that the name of his Inniskeen neighbour, Willie Hughes, cropped up in *Ulysses*!) In part II of 'Auditors In' he will measure himself against his famous predecessor, here he is content with a cryptic connection.

Kavanagh would return to the subject of the poetic legitimacy of ordinary subject matter in 'Epic', where a 'local row', which might seem suited only to a peasant ballad by the Bard of Callanberg,[4] is shown to be potentially Homeric. What engages him now is the identification of 'intense love' as a creative source. Love is a transcendent and transforming power, immortalising the transitory, proving 'youth's eternity'. The recollection of emotion is here distinguished from its poetic recreation:

Not mere memory but the Real
Poised in the poet's commonweal

Capitalisation emphasises the distinction between poetic fact
and remembered fact. Such desynonymisation of imagination
and memory is an idea elaborated in several other poems on
the creative process at this period, notably 'Kerr's Ass' and
'On Reading a Book on Common Wild Flowers'. Recognising
that he is still capable of feeling intense love reassures the
poet that he is still capable of writing poetry and he admon-
ishes himself to set about the work he has been neglecting, as
Mrs Flynn might have nagged Tarry:

And you must take yourself in hand
And dig and ditch your authentic land.

The 'authentic land' which he must reclaim and cultivate is
more a 'commonweal' than a commonwealth, a state of
balanced, unruffled ('Poised') contentment, undisturbed by
ill-will and aggression. His 'mile of kingdom' is not a physical
but a metaphysical realm. Authenticity, an aesthetic preoccupation in the later 1940s, is here associated with love
rather than with a proclamation of unique personality
through agressive self-differentiation from others. 'Only
what we love is true', Kavanagh had written in 'Temptation
in Harvest'.

By the end of part I the poet has restored his self-
confidence through versifying his problems. Poetry is seen as
auto-therapeutic, an antidote to the alienation and vengeful-
ness of satires such as 'Jungle' ('the looney ghosts that goad/
The savages of Pembroke Road'). The connection between
composure and composition at the conclusion of part I
anticipates the conclusion of part II. Part I ends with a retreat
from self-analysis into grateful prayer.

A silent interval in the text prepares for the rhetorical
transition from part I's confessionalism to the poetic expressiveness of part II. A formal change from near-doggerel

slackness to sonnet strictness parallels the thematic move
from the dimension of the potentially literary to the plane of
aesthetic experience. This sequence of three sonnets travels
the traditional tripartite mystical route from detachment
through trance to transcendental contemplation.

In the first (and weakest) of these sonnets the poet divests
himself of all worldly attachments, his audience-consciousness ('the props of a reputation') and the larger-than-life
persona that the entertainment of such an audience demanded. Humility ('I at the bottom will start') replaces his
histrionic high jinks as Gulliver in Lilliput. The writer is here
a private person who belongs in a 'little room' rather than in
street theatre, who needs a 'quiet corner' for contemplation,
whose subject is the ordinary, not the stupendous.

The second sonnet, which depicts Kavanagh in full flight
from Dublin, enacts his imaginative reorientation towards
rural subject matter:

> Away, away on wings like Joyce's
> Mother Earth is putting my brand new clothes in
>   order
> Praying, she says, that I no more ignore her
> Yellow buttons she found in fields at bargain prices.
> Kelly's Big Bush for a button-hole. Surprises
> In every pocket—the stream at Connolly's corner,
> Myself at Annavackey on the Armagh border,
> Or calm and collected in a calving crisis.
> Not sad at all as I float away, away
> With Mother keeping me to the vernacular.
> I have a home to return to now. O blessing
> For the return in Departure. Somewhere to stay
> Doesn't matter. What is distressing
> Is waking eagerly to go nowhere in particular.

Joycean allusiveness, as well as giving a comic buoyancy to
Romantic trance, evokes economically, through correspondence and contrast, some of the salient features of Kavanagh's
new poetics. The most obvious parallel is between two Irish

writers exiling themselves from Dublin. However, the conflation of Joyce's character with Stephen Dedalus's also suggests
an implicit parallel between two self-portraitists making
literature out of their personal and aesthetic experience. In
addition, Kavanagh playfully parodies the realism of *Portrait
of the Artist*, in which Stephen's urban mother puts his 'new
second-hand clothes in order', to underscore the expressiveness of the personification in which his earth mother packs
'brand new' rural images in his imaginative luggage. The
homely maternal gesture of secreting surprises in the packing
captures the delightful unexpectedness of remembered
country images. It is significant that the memories Kavanagh
takes with him are specific and localised epiphanies from his
Inniskeen youth, nothing urban. That recollection of himself
'calm and collected' in a calving crisis prefigures the fusion of
emotion and tranquillity at the birth of a poem.

Still echoing Stephen's Dublin mother, Kavanagh's earth
mother prays 'she says' that he may 'no more ignore her',
thereby anticipating his return to rural subjects and images
and to the Monaghan vernacular. Home is Inniskeen. The
allusion to Stephen's mother's prayer reminds the reader that
exile may result in love. Stephen left Dublin in order
to encounter 'the reality of experience' imaginatively and
Kavanagh invokes Joyce, the most celebrated Irish benefici-
ary of the 'blessing' of 'the return in Departure', to emphasise
the innovativeness of his own poetics. By advocating a
spiritual and imaginative liberation, not a physical removal
from Dublin, Kavanagh is reorientating a native imagination
nurtured on the Joycean myth of artistic exile. To the writer
who believes in aesthetic transcendence 'somewhere to stay'
is unimportant; what does matter is having an imaginative
home to which one has right of access at any time, and what
is to be avoided is the kind of disorientation which the
imaginatively displaced Kavanagh had recently suffered in
his attempt to transform himself into a Dublin writer.

Obtrusive and specific Joycean analogies tend to obscure
this sonnet's Romantic lineage, an ancestry of which the poet

may or may not have been conscious. For the image of flight, which primarily alludes to Stephen's shaking 'the wings of an exultant and terrible youth', derives from the traditional Romantic motif of the bird as a symbol of imaginative and lyrical transcendence. Likewise, the repeated 'away', which echoes Stephen's words, also recalls Keats's projected flight on the viewless wings of poesy and his desperately willed attempt to escape the weariness, the fever and the fret of contemporary circumstance.

In the final sonnet of the sequence, aerial, imaginative journeying is succeeded by a non-spatial image of arrival. The 'placeless heaven' is Kavanagh's most abstract and most complex exposition of his new poetics:

> From the sour soil of a town where all roots canker
> I turn away to where the Self reposes
> The placeless Heaven that's under all our noses
> Where we're shut off from all the barren anger,
> No time for self-pitying melodrama,
> A million Instincts know no other uses
> Than all day long to feed and charm the Muses
> Till they become pure positive. O hunger
> Where all have mouths of desire and none
> Is willing to be eaten! I am so glad
> To come so accidentally upon
> My Self at the end of a tortuous road
> And have learned with surprise that God
> Unworshipped withers to the Futile One.

The concept of a 'placeless Heaven', a positive creative state rather than an actual location, indicates a change of aesthetic focus from realism to expressive transcendentalism. Poetry, as it is envisaged in this sonnet, is no longer an affair of reactions, the product of anger or self-pity as so much of his recent verse had been. The proper aesthetic condition is now one of 'repose', a state in which the imagination is unperturbed by actual circumstance. Creativity demands a calm benevolence, the elimination of all negative impulses. Divine worship and the cultivation of the muses are almost inseparable here. God is the creating Word, his opposite the figure of futility. Futility was a generic term of abuse in the satiric writings, applied, for instance, to Dublin's frivolity, vanity, triviality and lack of artistic commitment in 'The Lay of the Crooked Knight'. Here, too, its withered condition relates it to Dublin's 'canker' and to the 'barren anger' of the satires. Now that Kavanagh is renouncing satire and reorientating his poetry towards a 'pure positive' the Futile One is projected as a subjective negative, a personification of the poet's neglect of the life-enhancing virtues. The opposite of nurturing the muses is creative starvation and frustration: 'hunger' and 'mouths of desire'. Despite his protestations of equanimity in this sonnet it is clear that Kavanagh has still not purged himself of his rancour against Dublin and that, try as he may to summon up a 'placeless Heaven', his creative paradise has an anti-urban dimension. Fertility is implicitly associated with the rural and sterility explicitly with the urban.

The self still looms large in Kavanagh's new aesthetic. It is twice capitalised in this sonnet and the separation of 'My Self' into two capitalised units futher stresses this self-importance. The journey towards creative transcendence is made to coincide unexpectedly with a circuitous journey towards self-discovery. The true self is now indistinguishable from the poet.

'Auditors In' is a Romantic crisis lyric, its first part a confession of the writer's disabilities, its second an exposition of imaginative purification and renewal. The whole poem demonstrates the autobiographical intimacy characteristic of Kavanagh's poetry from the 1950s onwards. The obverse of his public satiric obsession with the inadequacies of his milieu is an introspective, reflexive verse, preoccupied with the discovery and elucidation of his poetics and with the exploration of his imaginative processes.

The creative matrix envisaged in 'Auditors In' has latent feminine connotations made explicit in the independent sonnet, 'God in Woman', which succeeded 'Auditors In' in the next issue of *The Bell* (November 1951):

> Surely my God is feminine, for Heaven
> Is the generous impulse, is contented
> With feeding praise to the good. And all
> Of these that I have known have come from women.
> While men the poet's tragic light resented,
> The spirit that is Woman caressed his soul.

The 'spirit that is Woman' is a supportive, cosseting figure, soothing and pampering the wounded male ego into that 'pure positive' conducive to poetic composition. Kavanagh's female deity is a *magna mater*, a nurturing presence, the vulnerable and insecure poet's enabling muse.

Kavanagh's supreme celebration of the eternal feminine was the anti-elegiac 'In Memory of My Mother', inspired by her death in 1945.[5] An idealised portrait, as much an expressive as a memorial image, it anticipates his shift from realism into creative metaphor in poems like 'Auditors In':

> I do not think of you lying in the wet clay
> Of a Monaghan graveyard; I see
> You walking down a lane among the poplars
> On your way to the station, or happily
>
> Going to second Mass on a summer Sunday—
> You meet me and you say:
> 'Don't forget to see about the cattle—'
> Among your earthiest words the angels stray.
>
> And I think of you walking along a headland
> Of green oats in June,
> So full of repose, so rich with life—
> And I see us meeting at the end of a town
>
> On a fair day by accident, after
> The bargains are all made and we can walk
> Together through the shops and stalls and markets
> Free in the oriental streets of thought.

Imaginative reality here challenges realism and the poet's dead mother lives in the present tense of his thought and vision and as his primary audience. Recollected images are, as in 'Auditors In',

> Not mere memory but the Real
> Poised in the poet's commonweal . . .

This poem is no requiem, for imagination counters death's quiescence. The mother is 'not lying'; she is ceaselessly active, on her 'way', 'walking' to the station or along a headland or through the streets of a town or 'going' to mass. In her person the conflicting aesthetic positives of 'repose' and energy are reconciled as in her words the contrary categories of realism and transcendentalism merge. This Monaghan muse is equally at ease in countryside or town, field or fair, mass or market. Mother and poet, mutually transforming a local town into Araby, are liberated from realism into a metaphorical relationship with the actual.

The final scene, too, despite the appropriate change of setting from summer to autumn and from daylight to moonlight, is poised in an eternal imaginative now:

> O you are not lying in the wet clay,
> For it is a harvest evening now and we
> Are piling up the ricks against the moonlight
> And you smile up at us—eternally.

Here the roles of mother and son are complementary, creating a harmony of contemplation and activity. The mother, preserved for ever as a sustaining and supportive presence smiling in eternal benison on her son's labours, represents the continuous nurturing love without which Kavanagh feels himself poetically disabled. Holding 'in mind/All that has loved [him] or been kind' keeps satire at bay.

Given his dissatisfaction with the defensive arrogance and spleen of so much of his city poetry it was predictable that Kavanagh would attempt to revert to country tropes. This 'need to go back' which he recognised as a 'recurrent motif' in his writings by the early 1950s, he identified as a pre-natal impulse. His relationship with Inniskeen was umbilical. It was his motherland:

> The mother is the roots. The mother is the thing which gives us a world of our own.

Maternal bonding was the source of his poetics in which creativity was dependent on love. His discovery of the 'placeless Heaven' was a return to the 'warm womb':

> Far have I travelled from the warm womb
> Far have I travelled from home[6]

So the reversion to rural themes in the early 1950s is not merely a programmatic escape from disabling urban distractions and negative emotions; it is a positive exploration of his own primal creative urges. Kavanagh's project is no longer, as it was in the late 1930s and early 1940s, the evocation of Inniskeen. His Inniskeen-based poetry is now reflexive, a dramatisation of his poetics. 'Ante-Natal Dream' enacts his involuntary and inevitable bonding with the motherland.[7] 'Innocence' and 'Epic' are further Romantic crisis lyrics in which, more economically than in 'Auditors In', he signposts his aesthetic deviations and reorientates his verse. 'Innocence' and 'Epic' celebrate a homecoming.[8]

The state of passivity depicted in 'Ante-Natal Dream' is not one of waiting for particular inspiration as in 'Having Confessed'. It is rather a highly sensuous representation of the pre-imaginative phase, described in 'Art McCooey', when the potential poet unconsciously registers the sights and sounds of his environment and

> poetry is shaped
> Awkwardly but alive in the unmeasured womb.

As its Freudian title promises, 'Ante-Natal Dream' makes the point that such pre-poetic experience not only provides the embryonic poet with subject matter but actually determines the kind of poet he will become. The ante-natal poet is portrayed as a country lad, drowsed with the warmth of summer, dozing against a haystack. He is a passive presence, not even a lazy looker-on at life, wishing only to remain unconscious and unaware. The flora and fauna of the surrounding hayfield, on the contrary, are active agents which force themselves on his notice. Their attentions are intrusive and unwelcome yet they compel the indifferent youth to register them visually and aurally:

> I only know that I was there
> With hayseed in my hair
> Lying on the shady side
> Of a haycock in July.
>
> A crowd was pressing round
> My body on the ground
> Prising the lids of my eyes—
> Open and you'll be wise
>
> The sky that roared with bees,
> The row of poplar trees
> Along the stream struck deep
> And would not let me sleep.

The personification of insects, trees and weeds as an importunate 'crowd' works well here, suggesting that the future poet is at the mercy of his surroundings, that, whatever his reluctance, he cannot escape the impress of the environment on his consciousness. At no point is he in control, and in every stanza after the first, plants and insects take the initiative. Their imaginative impact is reinforced by the poem's insistent music: in each stanza rhyming couplets set up a double pattern of echoes which further resonate through internal rhyme, assonance and alliteration. By the end of the poem the sounds and rhythms of the external scene are being internalised, transmuted into a country song, and it is a deterministic song which stresses that Kavanagh, wherever he resides, cannot be otherwise than a country poet:

> For we are all you'll know
> No matter where you go—

Every insect, weed
Kept singing in my head.

The realistic image, 'hayseed in my hair', introduced in the
first stanza, has taken on metaphoric connotations by the
time it is reiterated in the concluding line: the country seed
lodged in the poet's head will bear its crop by and by.

In 'Innocence', on the contrary, Inniskeen subject matter is
presented as an inspired choice rather than an ineluctable
theme. The poem is one of a group of short lyrics and
sonnets, including 'God in Woman', 'Epic' and 'On Looking
into E. V. Rieu's Homer', published in *The Bell* in November
1951, the month after 'Auditors In', and elaborating on some
of the aesthetic issues introduced in that poem. 'Innocence'
enacts the imaginative return to Inniskeen mooted in the
penultimate sonnet of 'Auditors In'. A poem about thematic
reorientation, it proceeds, by way of an allusive dialogue with
Kavanagh's earlier poetry of rural disenchantment, to an
affirmation and celebration of the renewal of his bucolic idyll
and the recovery of original innocence:

> They laughed at one I loved —
> The triangular hill that hung
> Under the Big Forth. They said
> That I was bounded by the whitethorn hedges
> Of the little farm and did not know the world.
> But I knew that love's doorway to life
> Is the same doorway everywhere.
>
> Ashamed of what I loved
> I flung her from me and called her a ditch
> Although she was smiling at me with violets.
>
> But now I am back in her briary arms
> The dew of an Indian Summer morning lies
> On bleached potato-stalks —
> What age am I?
>
> I do not know what age I am

I am no mortal age;
I know nothing of women,
Nothing of cities,
I cannot die
Unless I walk outside these whitethorn hedges.

The critics confounded in the first stanza would appear to have no objective status and to be merely externalisations of the poet's own misgivings. Throughout the 1930s and 1940s Kavanagh was generally categorised as a rural poet and no opprobrium attached to him on that score; it was with himself that the label 'peasant poet' rankled. If 'love's doorway to life is the same doorway everywhere' then his failure to transform himself into a Dublin poet is due to the local limitations of his affections at this period. Instead of pursuing the urban implication of his affective dogma, however, he chooses to focus on the abandonment of his Inniskeen muse as an act of infidelity, a crime against love, and various lyrical treacheries are recalled that they may be repented. There are several allusions to 'Stony Grey Soil', the poem which most conspicuously opposed the celebratory tone of Kavanagh's early rural poetry and prepared the way for the harsh denunciations of *The Great Hunger*. In particular, the personification of the country as a seductive woman looks back to her portrayal as a scheming, flattering, obsessive female in 'Stony Grey Soil'. Then he had protested that she had 'flung a ditch' on his 'vision'; now he acknowledges the charms he had previously denied. In 'Plough' (1938), another rejection poem, the plough, like the land, was depicted as a clinging lover preventing the poet's departure. Then he churlishly spurned her sexual ploys:

Plough take your thin arms
From around my middle . . .

Now those 'clinging arms' are attributed to the countryside and he is happy to be restored to their 'briary' embrace. This slightly ironic sensuous image of a return to rural dalliance is reminiscent of the sexual surrender to country pleasures indulged in 'Temptation in Harvest':

> Where can I look and not become a lover
> Terrified at each recurring spasm?

Then aesthetic commitment summoned the poet back to the city; now he is content to know 'nothing of cities'. He is ready, too, to forego the knowledge of women other than his rural muse, whereas in 'Stony Grey Soil' he had complained bitterly about such deprivation. In setting the scene of his reconciliation among 'bleached potato-stalks' Kavanagh is, doubtless, placating the joyless ghost of Patrick Maguire in his 'bleached white' potato fields.

The poem's pivotal image, the 'whitethorn hedges', appears in all four stanzas with different connotations: as a metaphor for limitation, as a rejected or reinstated muse, and finally as the boundary of an Eden, a state of primal innocence in which the poet is protected from fatal contact with experience. Rural positives are subtly associated through assonance which links the 'whitethorn hedges' with 'the triangular hill', the 'doorway to life', the ditch 'smiling with violets', the 'briary arms', the dew that 'lies' on the potato stalks and that blessed state in which the poet 'cannot die'. The poet's rural love affair is not just sensuously evoked; it is musically consummated through the assonating of 'I' with each of these well-loved images.

Imaginative return to Inniskeen is projected as the assured route to literary immortality for Kavanagh. There is no necessary contradiction between the 'placeless heaven' of 'Auditors In' and his choice of Inniskeen as omphalos: the first describes a creative condition, the second an executive decision regarding theme and/or metaphor. That the small farm should provide a pre-sexual as well as a pre-urban protective enclosure turns it into a regressive, womb-like refuge. By insulating himself from experience Kavanagh is closing the 'doorway to life'. His refusal of mortality is really a refusal to grow up. The polarisation of his aesthetic attitudes into negative and positive, hatred and love, urban and rural, satire and celebration is an impediment to poetic maturity and the risk of imaginative stunting inherent in his rejection of the marriage of contraries is apparent in 'Innocence'.

Although any explicit reference to his failure as an urban writer is suppressed in 'Epic' it is significant that in this defence of local art Kavanagh turns the calendar back to the fateful year of 1938 when Europe was on the brink of war and he himself was on the verge of making what, with hindsight, appeared a disastrous decision to leave Inniskeen for Dublin. Imaginative backtracking to 1938 allows him access to a state of benevolence without the necessity of composing his current quarrel with Dublin. His return to Inniskeen material at this period involved a temporal and spatial partitioning of his concerns, cordoning off his celebratory and reflexive poetry from the satire and rhetoric with which he was contemporaneously engaged.

While it is also an expression of his new rural poetics, 'Epic' is, at once, less defensively personal and more doctrinaire than either 'Ante-Natal Dream' or 'Innocence'. It is also more localised. There is no parochial allusion in 'Ante-Natal Dream' while only one place-name is mentioned in 'Innocence' and its rural paradise is unpeopled. By contrast, 'Epic' is set in the small-farm world of *Tarry Flynn* with its neighbourly rivalries and feuds and it draws on common local surnames and on the names of obscure townlands:

> I have lived in important places, times
> When great events were decided: who owned
> That half a rood of rock, a no-man's land
> Surrounded by our pitchfork-armed claims.
> I heard the Duffys shouting 'Damn your soul'
> And old McCabe stripped to the waist, seen
> Step the plot defying blue cast-steel—
> 'Here is the march along these iron stones'
> That was the year of the Munich bother. Which
> Was most important? I inclined

> To lose my faith in Ballyrush and Gortin
> Till Homer's ghost came whispering to my mind
> He said: I made the Iliad from such
> A local row. Gods make their own importance.

'Epic' is a tactical triumph, encouraging the reader to indulge a disdainful smile at the simple annals of the poor only to wipe the supercilious grin off his face in the closing line. Whether or not we come to this poem prejudiced against an art that deals with 'the common and banal', we are manipulated into colluding with the poet's apparent loss of faith in it. Kavanagh's rhetorical strategy is to begin by emphasising the seeming perversity of choosing the local world as text. The apparent misapplication of the inflationary diction 'important', 'great', and the deflationary 'bother' underscores the irrationality of choosing to write about a 'local row' in the context of the Second World War. The Duffys and McCabe appear to belong in mock-heroic rather than in epic. A bathetic reading of the opening lines is ensured by the pejorative terminology, 'half a rood of rock, a no-man's land', yet the wary reader will notice that this comic terrain alludes explicitly to the battleground of the First World War. The 'local row' is itself a mini comic drama: its participants are in deadly earnest but the ironic context insists that we view their swaggering bravado with amused condescension. As in 'Shancoduff' the farmer-poet is 'shaken' in his imaginative faith. However, 'Shancoduff' belongs to the pre-Dublin debate about the viability of being a country poet, whereas 'Epic' is the product of a new-found conviction that heeding the cattle drovers was a bad artistic and financial decision. Now the local poet dramatises his conversion from loss of confidence to aesthetic faith in rural subject matter by dialoguing instead with a universally acclaimed precursor. E. V. Rieu's Homer may whisper rather than speak out loud and bold yet he authoritatively proclaims that nothing whatever is by imagination debarred, that a literary classic may originate in an insignificant episode of village life.

In 'Innocence' the poet's personal deviation from and return to his rural sources is his theme; in 'Epic' his personal artistic dilemma is situated in a European literary context. That universalisation of the local which is his subject is reflected in the poem's structural movement from specific instance to doctrinaire pronouncement. The literary joke involved in entitling a sonnet, 'Epic', also has a serious relevance in the light of his belief in the potential global significance of petty happenings.

An easy commerce between playfulness and solemnity characterises Kavanagh's finest lyrics and 'Epic's' companion-piece, 'On Looking into E. V. Rieu's Homer', despite its ludic title is a serious meditation on the poet's claim to the status of exceptional individual.[9] 'Innocence' concluded by asserting the poet's immortality, 'Epic' by deifying him; now both conclusions are interrelated and explained. For Wordsworth, the poet was a man who differed from other men in degree but not in kind; for Kavanagh, the poet apparently differs in kind, being half divine. (Predictably his divinity derives from the distaff side.) What elevates him above ordinary mortals is a god-like vision which transcends temporal successiveness and death, and perceives past and present as coexisting in an eternal now:

> In stubble fields the ghosts of corn are
> The important spirits the imagination heeds.
> Nothing dies; there are no empty
> Spaces in the cleanest-reaped fields.

This recalls the imagination's triumph over realism and death in 'In Memory of My Mother'. Kavanagh's differentiation between poetic imagination and ordinary perception is neo-Romantic: a variation on Coleridge's distinction between perception and imagination in his definition of the primary and secondary imagination.

The poet not only sees 'the immortal in things mortal'; he creates immortal material. Hector's death and Priam's mourning are a present-tense occurrence at each reading of the *Iliad*. Nevertheless, Kavanagh presents his empathy with Priam as a special imaginative event, an illustration of his own divinity, 'no human weakness':

> It was no human weakness when you flung
> Your body prostrate on a cabbage drill—
> Heart-broken with Priam for Hector ravaged;
> You did not know why you cried,
> This was the night he died—
> Most wonderful-horrible
> October evening among those cabbages.
>
> The intensity that radiated from
> The Far Field Rock—you afterwards denied—
> Was the half-god seeing his half-brothers
> Joking on the fabulous mountain-side.

As in 'Epic' Kavanagh escapes momentarily from the insularities of the Anglo–Irish literary tradition to engage in a high Romantic reading of classical literature, discovering in the *Iliad*, as he had in *Gulliver's Travels*, monuments of his own magnificence. Whereas in the satires his superiority to his fellows is moral; here it is grounded in a neo-Romantic aesthetic. In keeping with the local reorientation of his poetry at this period his intimations of immortality have a rural setting. He re-enters his small-farm world confidently, risking the bathos of indulging tragic emotion among cabbage drills and the mock heroics of transferring Olympus to Inniskeen, relishing the self-ironies as well as the self-apotheosis of his Romantic classicism.

Deification in 'Intimate Parnassus' is a metaphor for aesthetic detachment.[10] Parnassus was a favourite image of Kavanagh's from the mid-1940s onwards and he has been severely criticised for resorting to this old-fashioned literary trope whose nineteenth-century overtones are at odds with the contemporary idiom of his fifties' verse. In Kavanagh's defence it must be said that, like Hopkins, he invested

Parnassianism with his own specialised meaning. It became for him an image of aesthetic transcendence, a metaphor for the separation of the mind which creates from the man who suffers. Initially Parnassus had both local and aesthetic connotations. In 'Temptation in Harvest' it was anti-rural and connected with the city where 'art, music, letters are the real things', a city not quite separable from Dublin. When Dublin proved an artistically hostile environment Parnassus was internalised; and in *Tarry Flynn* it was a state of emotional detachment conducive to creativity. Tarry, the writer, escaped from the 'net of earthly intrigue', in which Tarry, the man, was enmeshed, by entering 'Parnassus, the constant point above time' where he was sufficiently distanced from his misfortunes to translate them into fictions. The Parnassus of 'Intimate Parnassus' is partly a refuge, partly a height of condescension, and, ostensibly, a state of creative detachment:

> Men are what they are, and what do
> Is their own business. If they praise
> The gods or jeer at them, the gods can not
> Be moved, involved or hurt. Serenely
> The citizens of Parnassus look on
> As Homer tells us, and never laugh
> When any mortal has joined the party.
> What happens in the small towns—
> Hate, love, envy—is not
> The concern of the gods. The poet poor,
> Or pushed around, or to be hanged, retains
> His full reality; and his authority
> Is bogus if the sonorous beat is broken
> By disturbances in human hearts—his own
> Is detached, experimental, subject matter
> For ironic analysis, even for pity
> As for some stranger's private problem . . .

Here, as in the concluding sonnet of 'Auditors In', three years previously, Kavanagh's theme is still the reorientation of his poetry away from the audience-consciousness and retaliatory rhetoric that had literally bedevilled his recent satiric verse. Yet that self-deification which is now presented as a state of aloofness from small-town cultural politics is also a vengeful metaphor, a triumphalist image of his arrogant superiority to his opponents. Parnassus offers a compensatory dignity of elevation to 'the poet poor,/Or pushed around', even permitting him to score sexually over his begrudgers in the final (unquoted) stanza. The Parnassus of this lyric, unlike the Olympus of 'On Looking into E. V. Rieu's Homer' and 'Freedom', is a solemn elevation, whose citizens 'never laugh'. 'Intimate Parnassus' has a good deal in common with a satire published in the same issue of *The Bell*, the laureate fantasy, 'The Hero', in which a gigantic Kavanagh dwarfs Dublin's Lilliputian and insincere citizenry. Following on the failure of *Kavanagh's Weekly*, the libel in *The Leader* and the 'trial', he was, despite his claims to the contrary, too 'moved, involved or hurt' to achieve dispassionate objectivity, a disinterested perspective on Dublin's intrigues.

The poem's thematic progression betrays the conflict between the poet's stated aesthetic of detachment and his insuperable pain and rage. Though he is still possessed by the 'barren anger' and self-pity he had exorcised in 'Auditors In', his 'main purpose' is to attain to an uninvolved, controlled, Olympian perspective on life:

> to be
> Passive, observing with a steady eye.

'Intimate Parnassus' is a doctrinaire poem vitiated by the human prejudices it attempts to invalidate and deny.

Throughout the 1950s Parnassus continued to be invoked as a literary trope. In 'Dear Folks' it retains its paradoxical connotations of detachment and defensiveness, a peculiar blend of disengagement and defiance:

> The main thing is to continue,
> To walk Parnassus right into the sunset

Detached in love where pygmies cannot pin you
To the ground like Gulliver . . .

Once again the image of the mountain and the giant come together in a metaphor of condescension. In the second 'Canal sonnet', on the other hand, Parnassus is associated with a poetry of reposeful contentment. Unusually, it is sited among 'islands'; life is being viewed horizontally and not from a peak of self-aggrandisement. The Parnassian mode is here warm, summery, sensuous and serene. A less egotistical Kavanagh is willing to share his poetic paradise. Perhaps the most remarkable change since 'Intimate Parnassus' is that Parnassus is now located at the heart of Dublin.

Parnassianism often occurs in a context of abstract theorising in Kavanagh's poetry; his more exciting verse has a local habitation. Two short poems, 'Kerr's Ass' and 'On Reading a Book on Common Wild Flowers', describe his creative process from its origin in specific memories to the climactic evocation of an alternative imaginative world. 'On Reading a Book on Common Wild Flowers' was published along with 'Intimate Parnassus'.

A distancing of rural material is indicated by the title; memories of Inniskeen flowers are now culled from the pages of a book:

> O the prickly sow thistle that grew in the hollow
> of the Near Field
> I used it as a high jump coming home in the
> evening—
> A hurdle race over the puce blossoms of the sow
> thistles . . .

Remembrance in this poem is a therapeutic strategy: recollected images crowd out contemporary anxieties and pressures. The 'ravening passion', so inimical to the 'pure moment', is not glossed; however, since this poem's companion-pieces were 'Intimate Parnassus' and 'The Hero', it presumably refers to an obsessive involvement in the 'Hate,

love, envy' of 'small towns'. As in 'Auditors In' the return to
rural images is a rite of creative purification and renewal. The
poem's rhetoric is celebratory ('Let me not moralize or have
remorse') and the long opening lines of the first two stanzas
mime the spontaneous overflow of happy youthful memories:

> O the greater fleabane that grew at the back of the
>   potato pit:
> I often trampled through it looking for rabbit
>   burrows!
> The burnet saxifrage was there in profusion
> And the autumn gentian—
> I knew them all by eyesight long before I knew
>   their names.
> We were in love before we were introduced.

The printed page paradoxically releases memories of an
instinctive, pre-verbal relationship with local flora and the
transfer of romantic cliché to a love affair with nature is a
distinctively Kavanaghish touch. That the object of his affections should be *common* wild flowers is also typical of his
attraction to the ordinary and banal. What the poet recalls
about these flowers is likewise unremarkable: their colour,
texture, location, his own unsentimental attitude to them,
jumping over or trampling them. Despite that leap into the
past at the beginning of the poem he is again intent on
distinguishing between memory and imagination. Memory's
function is to detach the mind from quotidian anxieties;
naming is a pre-imaginative ritual:

>   for these names
> Purify a corner of my mind;
> I jump over them and rub them with my hands,
> And a free moment appears brand new and spacious
> Where I may live beyond the reach of desire.

When the poem turns a mental corner in this, the last stanza,
the past habitual actions of jumping over and trampling are

transmuted into a rhythmic alternation of withdrawal and caress, a deliberate frictioning of the memory to achieve imaginative ecstasy. This imaginative state is a 'brand new' time and space, a transcendental alternative to and refuge from the fever and fret of everyday. The adjective, 'brand new', had been applied to the poet's imaginative luggage in 'Auditors In' and the escape from desire here also recalls the creative 'repose' achieved at the conclusion of that poem. Unlike the second part of 'Auditors In', which offers a generalised metaphoric account of imaginative transcendence, 'On Reading A Book on Common Wild Flowers' illustrates a specific application of aesthetic strategy.

A similar but more subtle and individualised approach to the same subject occurs in one of the most anthologised of Kavanagh's poems, 'Kerr's Ass', an affectionate, lyrical affirmation of the relationship between memory, exile and imagination. This poem pre-dates and, I think, surpasses part II of 'Auditors In'. When first published it appeared in the prose context of a contrast between the slow amble of the ass and cart of Kavanagh's Inniskeen days and the speed of modern air travel, a change of pace which rendered the term 'exile' 'melodramatic'.[11] In his poem the poet traffics mentally between London and Inniskeen, exile and home, reverting to the leisurely pace, foreshortened focus and redundant idiom of his youth:

> We borrowed the loan of Kerr's big ass
> To go to Dundalk with butter,
> Brought him home the evening before the market
> An exile that night in Mucker.
>
> We heeled up the cart before the door,
> We took the harness inside—
> The straw-stuffed straddle, the broken breeching
> With bits of bull-wire tied;
>
> The winkers that had no choke-band,
> The collar and the reins . . .

In Ealing Broadway, London Town
I name their several names

Until a world comes to life—
Morning, the silent bog,
And the god of imagination waking
In a Mucker fog.

Though the connection between homesickness and remembrance is implicit, the London-based poet avoids designating himself an exile, preferring to apply this 'melodramatic' term comically to the ass's overnight stay a few miles from home.

This poem is one of Kavanagh's understated testaments to the significance of ordinary subject matter. A deliberately trivial event is recalled with affectionate particularity and the rural narrative concludes with a slow-motion sequence, a naming of parts of the ass's harness and their individual flaws. Such trifling recollections, however, culminate in imaginative vision, a transition signalled by the change from night-time chronicle to morning epiphany. Naming is the key to this imaginative liberation. In itemising the harness parts the poet performs a mnemonic pre-imaginative ritual, summoning up specific images from the past and transforming a catalogue into an alliterative litany. Naming, which at first plays an unobtrusive role in the narrative with the mention of the local place-names, Mucker and Dundalk, and the personal name, Kerr, is foregrounded in the third stanza. Here a line devoted to London place-names is followed by a line on the act of naming itself in which the word appears as both verb and noun. The imagination's dependence on naming is emphasised syntactically by making the 'until' clause, which expresses imaginative vision, subordinate to the clause on naming. The world that comes to life at the end of the poem is one in which the first awakening of the creative imagination from a Mucker fog and its present arousal from memories of a Mucker twilight coalesce in the present tense. The muse is portrayed as a creative divinity and the imaginative process is evoked as a movement from unconsciousness to conscious awareness: a coming to life, a transition from evening to morning, from silence to sound, from sleep to waking, from fog to visibility.

When Kavanagh returned to the mnemonics of naming and its power to stimulate his imagination in 'On Reading a Book on Common Wild Flowers' in 1954 he did so with a sense of desperation foreign to the easy, affectionate mood of 'Kerr's Ass'. By 1954 he was conscious of an ever present threat to his creative equilibrium. This year, which he apostrophised in the sonnet, 'Nineteen Fifty-Four', was probably the worst year of his life when he was broken in spirit after the failure of his libel suit, financially straitened and, unknown to himself, ill with lung cancer. In what is one of the most intimate of his confessional poems he makes the year a scapegoat for his lost equanimity, his disorientation and sense of fragmentation, his feelings of friendlessness and rejection. One image of alienation looks back to one of his earliest sonnets, 'Inniskeen Road: July Evening', as once again his isolation is highlighted by contrast with the communal delights represented by dancers. Now his position has worsened in that he is a middle-aged insomniac listening to the 'homing' revellers.

The most distressing aspect of his plight is his inability to turn it to creative use, to 'organise a perspective' on it, 'patter' his way out of it, find an appropriate formulation or 'formula' to contain it. Such revelations of creative disability are not as artless as might appear. 'Nineteen Fifty-Four' is a Romantic dejection lyric and, like those of his Romantic predecessors, Kavanagh's articulation of his sense of psychological and poetic disintegration is actually a controlled performance. The structural discipline of the Petrarchan sonnet gives an unacknowledged and unobtrusive shapeliness and coherence to his account of 'hellish scatter'.

The most remarkable poem to come out of this unfortunate year, and a lasting testimony to Kavanagh's poetic resilience, is 'Prelude', first published the following February.[12] In 1954 it was Kavanagh's Christmas gift to the then Taoiseach, John A. Costello, who, as counsel for the defence, had cross-examined him in his libel case.[13] It is the plaintiff's private self-analysis, a poetic complement and corrective to the admissions and evasions elicited in the courtroom, possibly also a consequence and continuation of that trial of his image and opinions.

'Prelude' is, like 'Auditors In', a poem in two parts, though these structural divisions are not numbered. The first part pursues a principle of randomness to illustrate the 'hellish scatter' resulting from an infernal poetics; the second moves purposefully towards a creative resolution, a secure haven/heaven of love and nurture. The presence of a third-person interlocutor in the opening lines is a dramatic device to enliven or disguise the intimacy of what is, in fact, a confessional monologue, or a dialogue of self and soul. The witty and allusive vernacular voice cajoling the poet into renewed productivity (another poem . . . 'a book') gradually modulates into the self-exhortatory tones of the poet himself, as so often in these years redirecting his poetry from satire and criticism.

Nevertheless, it is Apollo the archer and not Apollo the lyricist who presides over the first part of this poem where satire is bitterly indulged before being revoked. *The Irish Times* wisely omitted the first six ranting lines of stanza three, possibly because of their apparent anti-religious or actual anti-journalistic bias, and should also have dispensed with the feeble anti-academic satire which completes the stanza. As is usual in his satiric writings Kavanagh is his own aesthetic hero, here projecting himself as the honest, incorruptible poet:

> You have not got the countenance
> To hold the angle of pretence . . .
> You have not got a chance with fraud
> And might as well be true to God . . .

His enemies are denounced as charlatans: 'bogus priests', knaves who have 'made pretence into a science', 'Card-sharpers of the art committees', misappropriators of public funds to whom sincerity seems 'eccentric'. 'Humourosity', the 'comic spirit', characterises Kavanagh, the true poet, ('Though sadness for a little claimed/The precedence'), so his villains either 'counterfeit' humour or are dull, serious look-ing, grave faced. A concept of comedy as tragedy tran-scended, adumbrated in *Tarry Flynn* and most notoriously invoked in his repudiation of *The Great Hunger*, is here associated with the lyrical transcendence of personal ad-versity:

> . . . art's a kind of fun;
> . . . all true poems laugh inwardly
> Out of grief-born intensity . . .
>
> Dullness alone can get you beat
> And so can humour's counterfeit.
> You have not got a chance with fraud
> And might as well be true to God.
>
> Then link your laughter out of doors
> In sunlight past the sick-faced whores . . .

At this point the poems fails to distinguish between satire, in which humour is synonymous with sneering contempt, and the 'fun' integral to true art. They are connected by a 'then' which indicates logical progression: 'Then link your laughter out-of-doors'. This is an external and derisive laughter to which the poet is merely linked or loosely attached, extrinsic rather than intrinsic. For all its parade of honesty and 'humourosity' this section of 'Prelude' lacks the undeceived self-perception and affectionate playfulness of the corresponding section of 'Auditors In'.

The poem is half-way through before satire is finally renounced as sterile and unproductive and, interestingly, its renunciation still involves the invocation of rural imagery:

> But satire is unfruitful prayer,
> Only wild shoots of pity there,
> And you must go inland and be
> Lost in compassion's ecstasy,
> Where suffering soars in summer air—
> The millstone has become a star.

The equation of poetry and prayer arises from the religious expressiveness so central to Kavanagh's poetics. His route away from the satiric leads 'inland', towards interiority and towards Monaghan simultaneously. The 'inland' poet is not concerned with metropolitan criticism. Momentarily he is a 'parochial'. 'Compassion', conspicuously absent from the satires and even from Kavanagh's self-engrossed positive poetics, which regards 'disturbances in human hearts' as 'things aside from the main purpose', is now pronounced an aesthetic virtue. The satirist in this poem is a spectator for whom the 'walk past' suffices; the true poet empathises with others' sufferings. Kavanagh, who once found 'a star-lovely art/In a dark sod', now discovers that human sympathy is imaginatively liberating. At this turning point in the poem the negative is converted into 'pure positive' and that benevolent psychic state essential to creativity in 'Auditors In' has been attained.

Yet just at this point the poem changes tack, and the phrase, 'Count then your blessings', which promises a litany of sufferings transcended and fellow victims emphathised with, instead introduces a *non-sequitur*, a succession of enabling human sympathisers and local epiphanies. The self is at the centre of this poetic universe, waited upon by a salvation army of women, midwives to the creative event, or singled out for metaphysical favours by natural scenes and images. The poet of 'Prelude', like the poet of 'On Looking into E. V. Rieu's Homer', is conscious of 'the immortal in things mortal', rural and ordinary. 'God is in the bits and pieces of Everyday' as he was in *The Great Hunger*: 'bits of road' are transfigured into 'eternal lanes of joy', trees are invested with mystery, waters are inspirational. The litany that culminates in the creation of an alternative world recalls 'Kerr's Ass', and the economy of salvaging beneficent or mystical experiences as a preparation for creativity anticipates the bird's activity in 'Canal Bank Walk': 'gathering materials for the nest for the Word'. The beatification of the ordinary is so Wordsworthian that at one point the collocation of word and image echoes 'The Daffodils':

> Collect the river and the stream
> That flashed upon a pensive theme . . .

Love in 'Prelude' translates as being loved rather than loving: the poet needs human and natural support to withstand the threat of financial insecurity. Impoverishment in Dublin had proved a satiric goad and as early as 'Shancoduff' the label 'poor' had 'shaken' the affectionate imagination. Now love is opposed to materialism. Resolution in the face of destitution inevitably reminds the reader of Wordsworth's 'Resolution and Independence'; however, the conscious allusion at the beginning of the final stanza is to Blake. The beast into which the poet metamorphoses himself combines the contrary qualities of Blake's lamb and tiger, gentle yet incandescently intense. Blake's dark primeval forest is transfigured into a Parnassian forest, a place of serene detachment. Belatedly, Kavanagh recognises that the poetic misdirection of his Dublin years was due to his frustrated and mistaken search for patrons and providers. His promised land was a paternalist or materialist heaven. Now loving supporters seem more essential to creativity than powerful backers. The affirmative and authoritative conclusion,

> Ignore power's schismatic sect
> Lovers alone lovers protect

while it enshrines the holiness of the heart's affections and excommunicates the unhelpful middle classes, also betrays the poet's continued vulnerability. His association of love with protection reveals a persistent insecurity, a transfer of his dependency from the privileged indifferent to nurturing sympathisers.

Formally, 'Prelude', with its octosyllabic couplets arranged in stanzas of irregular length, is reminiscent of part I of 'Auditors In'. It recalls the earlier poem, too, in the intimacy of its self-analysis and in its flexible command of a variety of tones and moods from the coaxing and cajoling to the condemnatory, the consolatory and the celebratory. Demotic language, 'a better bet', 'get you beat', 'card-sharpers', 'gear', 'Count . . . your blessings', and images from the boxing ring, the betting shop, the fairground or race track and the charity hostel jostle with allusions to Greek mythology, Joyce's *A Portrait of the Artist* and Blake's 'The Tyger'. Abstractions, straight or allegorised, and religious and mystical vocabulary, are interspersed with snippets of verbal fun: the mischievous rhyming of 'middle-age departure' and 'archer', 'missions' and 'kitchens', 'comic veil' and 'travail', the play with literary allusions, the lively portrayal of the untrustworthiness of the Arts Council, the twinning of 'kiss and kitchens'. Kavanagh is capable of veering suddenly from the sublime to the ridiculous, the impish to the solemn, platitude to parody. A poetics which invests 'the bits and pieces of Everyday' with transcendental importance must have access to the vernacular of street and pub and newspaper, the clichés and slang of everyday conversation, as well as to the aggrandising diction of myth, literature and religion. Platitude has its 'part in the larger legend' because it is a verbal expression of the commonplace. Kavanagh can reinvigorate a cliché such as 'Count your blessings' by drawing on both its aggregative and beatific properties. The poem's syntax, on the contrary, shows little flexibility. Verbal exuberance is contained within a controlling rhetoric, a series of imperatives and exhortations, since Kavanagh is here taking himself 'in hand', making a supreme effort to reorientate his poetics or to clear the way for potential future poetry.

'Prelude' is more a Wordsworthian than a Paterian title. Kavanagh thought that poetry should aspire to statement rather than to music and his 'Prelude', like Wordsworth's, is intended as a prefatory poem, a work of auto-therapy, a confession of past failures and a discovery of human and aesthetic values. It is peculiarly fitting that this phase of his career should close on such a Wordsworthian note for throughout the first half of the 1950s Kavanagh was at his most quintessentially Romantic, an introverted rural exile, retreating from 'the din of towns and cities' and 'greetings where no kindness is' to explore his own creative processes and to talk directly about his poetic difficulties, disabilities and search for new directions.

10
From the Grand Canal

Introduction

(i) The Grand Canal

PATRICK Kavanagh underwent surgery for lung cancer in the Rialto Hospital, Dublin, in March 1955. This unexpected and potentially fatal illness, the most 'spirit-shocking' event he had experienced since his traumatic departure from Inniskeen, is completely overshadowed in all published autobiographical accounts by the expressive drama of his convalescence on the banks of Dublin's Grand Canal between Baggot and Leeson Street bridges in July of the same year. Kavanagh convalesced in Dublin's Hibernian Hotel, with his sister in Longford, and back in Dublin he sat or lay in the hot July sun in St Stephen's Green, as well as reclining by the Canal. However, it was the banks of the Grand Canal that he singled out as the site of the climactic epiphanic experience of his life, the locus of his ultimate aesthetic revelation.

That the Canal scene should have made such a profound psychic impression on Kavanagh is understandable. Those solitary, leisurely, warm hours, recumbent on its grassy banks, recalled happy, lazy days in summer fields. In his weakened physical condition the poet was content to surrender himself to the 'static pleasures of looking and listening'.[1] For once he was free from journalistic pressures. Having just escaped the final deadline, he was happy to be alive. *Sub specie aeternitatis*, the quarrelsomeness and bitterness of the past fifteen years must have seemed an expensive waste of spirit. It was as if the psychic cancer Kavanagh had so long struggled to eradicate had been removed along with his diseased lung. His brush with death had undermined his messianic pretensions; illness had humbled his arrogance. The 'positive world' he had aspired to 'make' in 'Prelude' now acquired a local habitation and a name.

By 1959 Kavanagh had conceived his supreme fiction: that he had been born or reborn as a poet on the banks of Dublin's Grand Canal in July 1955. It was a fiction that relegated his former city persona to pre-natal status, enabling him to remain in Dublin while exiting from the bardic role he had created for himself there as a self-centred, embittered, cantankerous and power-hungry public performer. Prior to this, Kavanagh's automythology had been retrospective or regressive, its focal concern his exile from or projected return to Inniskeen. This personal myth was Edenic and anti-urban, presenting the poet's years in Dublin as a postlapsarian period, a prolonged fall from imaginative grace. While Inniskeen was still endowed with literary significance as the place of his previous poetic birth or aborted delivery, his native village was assigned a subordinate and chronologically remote position in his new schema; this earlier stillbirth or short-lived incarnation had occurred 'thirty years ago'.[2] While not oblivious of his rural past, his self-fictionalising was now forward looking, concerned with starting afresh, with inventing a destination and a destiny.

Kavanagh represented his Canal convalescence as a watershed in his career; henceforward the current of his poetry would flow in a different direction. The Canal scene became for him consecrated ground, its waters sacramental, washing away the old sinful Adam and baptising the poet into a new celebratory mode. In this natural hermitage at the heart of the city, a rural retreat from urban fever and fret, he also found an image of his return to the aesthetic values of his youth.

Although Kavanagh published only two sonnets celebrating the imaginative importance of the Canal scene, he set about publicising his new personal myth in a series of autobiographical narratives published between 1959 and 1964. It is given special prominence in the three key prose manifestos of his last literary phase: 'From Monaghan to the Grand Canal', an essay published in 1959,[3] *Self-Portrait*, a television programme, transmitted in 1962 and published in 1964,[4] and the 'Author's Note' prefacing his *Collected Poems* of 1964.[5] In these three manifestos the autobiographical genre is deployed to invest the narrative of the poet's life with plot and purposefulness. The symbolic significance of the Canal is established in 'From Monaghan to the Grand Canal', reiterated in *Self-Portrait*, and briefly affirmed in 'Author's Note'.

'From Monaghan to the Grand Canal' begins:

> I have been thinking of making my grove on the banks of the Grand Canal near Baggot Street Bridge where in recent days I rediscovered my roots. My hegira was to the Grand Canal bank where again I saw the beauty of water and green grass and the magic of light. It was the same emotion as I had known when I stood on a sharp slope in Monaghan, where I imaginatively stand now, looking across to Slieve Gullion and South Armagh.

Here Shancoduff and the Grand Canal are descriptively and emotionally conflated, though the imaginative predominance of the Canal setting is indicated by the fact that those features singled out for praise in the Canal sonnets—water, greenness and 'fantastic light'—are superimposed on the black hills.

The essay presents the poet's life in Dublin parenthetically as a prolonged hiatus, a misguided postponement of that imaginative conjunction between Shancoduff and the Canal bank with which it begins. His literary career after 1939 is summarised through flashback and thereby subordinated to the controlling narrative of the Canal epiphany. Memories of Dublin are actually introduced as an irritating interruption of present ecstasy: 'But something disturbs my imagination'. Past bitterness is now contained within a benign frame, yet it still exerts a destabilising influence. Kavanagh's quarrel with Dublin's literary and bourgeois citizenry is demoted rather than resolved. In the teleological narrative of 'From Monaghan to the Grand Canal' his many aberrations are attributed to the false aesthetic attractions of the Literary Revival, whose artistic emphasis on peasantry, regionalism and nationalism proved almost irresistibly seductive to the Irish country poet.

Journey and hegira are recurrent metaphors in 'From Monaghan to the Grand Canal'. The journey is one of literature's best established and most accessible allegorical structures for making sense of life's perplexities and discerning pattern and design in the apparent confusion and disorder of daily existence. In Kavanagh's tale of his life's itinerary the Canal serves both as a goal and a starting point. It offers a myth of closure, a happy ending that outwits the inconclusiveness of autobiography. After a series of deviations and detours, the poet has at last arrived at his final resting place. He is spiritually saved; inerrant. He has been gathered into the artifice of eternity, an immutable aesthetic state in which he will sing of what is passing or to come.

The word, hegira, endows Kavanagh's arrival at the Grand Canal with religious significance. It invites comparison with Mohammed's migration from Mecca to Medina, which also occurred in July. Kavanagh identified with this prophet who had incurred the hostility of the merchant class in Mecca. In addition to its connotations of a retreat from the capital, hegira also signified the start of a new dispensation, since the Muslim era was dated from 16 July 622, the date of Mohammed's migration.

It is appropriate that the title of 'From Monaghan to the Grand Canal' should comprise two place-names grammatically connected by an implicit journey image. Naming in this essay confers an objective, public status on private, mental or imaginative states. True, places and place-names had featured in Kavanagh's poetry since 'Inniskeen Road: July Evening', landscape had become a reflexive metaphor as early as 'Monaghan Hills' (1936), and after 1939 Dublin and Inniskeen were customary imaginative antipodes, representing the polarised attractions of satire or celebration. In 'From Monaghan to the Grand Canal', however, Kavanagh set about redrawing his aesthetic map and changing his sign-posts. The principal places and place-names on his new meta-terrain—Shancoduff and Monaghan, Dublin and the Grand Canal—are distanced from each other chronologically rather than spatially. Everything he had published between his arrival in Dublin and his Canal convalescence is now discounted, whether its setting or its subject was Inniskeen and whether its mood was nostalgic, angry or celebratory. Shancoduff, a place-name now inseparable from his favourite early poem of the same name, represents his primitive aesthetic. So, in 'From Monaghan to the Grand Canal' Shancoduff is detached from its geographical location in County Monaghan and Monaghan is made synonymous with the baneful influence of the Literary Revival. Thus the essay concludes:

> It was a long journey for me from my Monaghan with my mind filled with the importance-of-writing-and-thinking-and-feeling-like-an-Irishman to the banks of the Grand Canal in nineteen fifty five . . .

That repeated 'my' emphasises the association of 'Monaghan' with a particular state of mind. In this scenario Dublin signifies polemicism and satire and the Grand Canal is detached from it as Shancoduff is from Monaghan.

In 'From Monaghan to the Grand Canal' the rurality of the Canal scene is evoked as an image of the psychological circularity of Kavanagh's autobiographical journey, though Inniskeen is now fixed as its *terminus a quo* and the Canal as its *terminus ad quem*. Such circularity is also one of the themes of *Self-Portrait* where the autobiographer writes:

> Curious this, how I had started off with the right simplicity, indifferent to crude reason and then ploughed my way through complexities and anger, hatred and ill-will towards the faults of man, and came back to where I started.

Again 'Shancoduff' is cited as representative of his early

poetics. The choice of ploughing as a metaphor for difficult progress suggests that he had never really reneged on his agricultural past; the stony grey soil had been internalised. On this occasion, Kavanagh also quotes from 'To a Child' (1931) to illustrate that he had found his way even earlier than 'Shancoduff'.

The Canal epiphany, however, disposes of the need to return to Inniskeen. Exile is displaced as an enabling myth, allowing the poet to celebrate the here and now, or to greet the future optimistically. The post-operative poet is grateful to have been given a second chance, a new lease of life. In one of his earliest published reports on his convalescence Kavanagh describes how he lay on the Canal bank 'in an ante-natal roll'[6] and he was quick to capitalise on the symbolic significance of this foetal posture. 'Birth' was the title he chose for a 1958 confessional sonnet recording his past entrapment in a cycle of failures and broken promises of reform and his belated and unexpected liberation through 'angelic grace'.[7] In *Self-Portrait* Kavanagh reverts to the pre-conscious imagery of 'Art McCooey' and 'Ante-Natal Dream' to establish his new myth of origin:

> That a poet is born, not made, is well known. But this does not mean that he was a poet the day he was physically born. For many a good-looking year I wrought hard at versing but I would say that, as a poet, I was born in or about nineteen-fifty-five, the place of my birth being the banks of the Grand Canal.

The two metaphors of origin and destination associated with the Grand Canal are combined in a 1961 essay:

> It was however a long journey and a dark travail from the little fields of Monaghan . . . to that July afternoon on the Grand Canal beside Baggot Street Dublin.
>
> (*X*, August 1961)

In the 'Author's Note' which prefaces *Collected Poems* the automythological narrative deliberately peters out with the poet's arrival at the Canal.

(ii) Comedy

Kavanagh's Canal poetics, which is his ultimate poetics, is comic. His definition of the comic is, to some extent, idiosyncratically individualistic, however, and, as a whole, considerably more inclusive than any standard textbook definition. Comedy is, for Kavanagh, a polysemantic term, signifying and unifying all his final aesthetic positives and serving as the antonym of such antipathetical literary values as satire, self-pity and Irishness. Although the supremacy of comedy is the pervasive underlying theme of his post-1955 poetics, the subject is never systematically or fully explicated on any occasion. Rather it surfaces so frequently and in such a variety of contexts that it gradually becomes apparent that all the poet's aesthetic positives originate in a common comic matrix.

The comic, on Kavanagh's definition of it, is invested with its customary attributes and concomitants. It is connected with laughter, humour, entertainment, verbal fun, high spirits; and contrasted with sadness, solemnity, dullness, boringness, respectability, pedantry. 'The main feature about a poet', according to Kavanagh, 'is his humourosity'[8] and 'Laughter is the most poetic thing in life . . .'.[9] He himself is 'always in danger of bursting out laughing',[10] even at his own misfortunes. The poet is an entertaining companion: 'Any touch of boringness and you are in the wrong shop'.[11] Judged by this criterion literary Dublin is found wanting; the conversation on which it prided itself being 'tiresome drivel . . . No humour at all'.[12] Dullness is a valuable 'cultural asset'; the comic poet, who foregoes solemnity, respectability and pedantry and resorts instead to 'uproarious laughter', outrageous rhymes and contemporary slang, is regarded as undereducated and socially disruptive:

> People who are unsure of themselves cannot afford to break out into uproarious laughter or use a piece of slang. You may find a small number of readers who cotton on to the technique but large numbers of people

will look at you with contempt and say what a pity it is that he lacks schooling.[13]

The 'Irish school' cultivated 'dreadful sadness and lack of comedy',[14] whereas Kavanagh finds the tragic scenes in *Juno and the Paycock* embarrassing, endurable only because of 'the laughs in Captain Boyle'.[15] Yet comedy does not deny or exclude the darker side of life. *Waiting for Godot*, for instance, is 'a great comedy' in which Beckett 'has put despair and futility on the stage for us to laugh at them. And we do laugh.'[16]

In 'From Monaghan to the Grand Canal' comedy is a youthful mode, demanding gaiety and vigour:

> To write lively verse or prose, to be involved with Comedy requires enormous physical and mental power. Energy, as Blake remarked, is eternal delight. The more energy is in a poem or prose work the more comic it is.

That Kavanagh should have insisted on an energetic poetics is in keeping with his proclamation that he has returned to his youthful aesthetic, or that he is a born-again poet. Gaiety and exuberance, the imaginative attributes he associates with youth, may be discovered or recovered in old age:

> When, after a lifetime of struggle, we produce the quintessence of ourselves, it will be something gay and young.
>
> ('From Monaghan to the Grand Canal')

Iconoclastic attitudes towards established pieties, disrespectful speech, impatience with pomposity, a cult of incorrectness—these are the youthful qualities Kavanagh now cultivates. Poets are to be judged by the criterion of mental age.[17] Yet for all his relish of zest and irreverence, Kavanagh is unwilling to relinquish imaginative authority. By resorting to his favourite image of aesthetic elevation, he manages to combine 'gay youthfulness' and 'authority' as two of the 'marks of the poet'.[18]

Comedy, as Kavanagh conceives of it, is distinguished from satire, both because it is a non-rhetorical art and because its attitude towards subject matter is affectionate, not contemptuous. The 'purely written word' is 'written for an abstract audience, written for the writer'. *Moby Dick*, for instance, 'teaches nothing; it is poised in the pure air of the imagination'.[19] Comedy is also motivated by love of its material rather than by dislike or superiority. The 'right kind' of laughter is 'loving laughter'.[20] *Moby Dick* again exemplifies the connection between affection and comedy: 'Melville loved everything on that ship' and his novel is 'a tremendous comedy, borne along to its end on the wings of its author's outgiving faith in his characters'.[21]

Self-absorption, which involves a lack of detachment and of charity, is likewise inimical to comedy. Three of the commandments of Kavanagh's comic poetics enunciated in 'From Monaghan to the Grand Canal' involve self-transcendence:

> Without self-pity to look at things . . .
> Not to be self-righteous.
> . . . to avoid taking oneself sickly seriously.

The poet-persona he had so zealously cultivated in life and in literature for the previous decade, purpose-built to appear obtrusively and obnoxiously different and abrasive enough to snag against everything and everybody, has become redundant. Kavanagh is not advocating an impersonal art in which the author is as invisible as Joyce's manicured God. On the contrary, comic art expresses the writer's personality and his values and may, therefore, provoke an antagonistic reaction from its audience:

> A work that is inspired by the comic spirit has much to contend with, for a work that is inspired by the comic

spirit has a sense of values, of courage and rectitude—
and these qualities are hated immemorially.[22]

In his consideration of the relationship between comedy and
self-projection Kavanagh is attempting to retain the notion of
a personalised art while avoiding the 'self-pitying melodrama' and retaliatory rhetoric that had vitiated so much of
his previous Dublin poetry. His comic theory is fashioned to
accommodate his own peculiar aesthetic requirements.

Kavanagh adapted the literary tradition which connected
comedy with the portrayal of low life, extending it to embrace
his cult of the ordinary and the objectively unimportant as the
most appropriate artistic subjects. Comedy's sphere is, for
him, private rather than public experience, not 'subjects of
public importance' but 'casual, insignificant little things,
things you would be ashamed to talk of publicly'.[23]

A significant consequence of this separation of the comic
realm from the realm of *res publica* is that comedy is not
merely a private art, it is also a socially irresponsible art.
Tragedy, as its contrary, is presented as a literature of witness
or commitment, a didactic, socially concerned art. In 'Author's
Note' *The Great Hunger*, which was 'concerned with the woes
of the poor', represents such engaged literature; that it
should have attracted the unwelcome attentions of the police
only testifies to the 'kinetic vulgarity' of its discourse:

> A true poet is selfish and implacable. A poet merely
> states the position and does not care whether his words
> change anything or not.

While *The Great Hunger* was, undoubtedly, a socially committed work and, therefore, at odds with his irresponsible comic
poetics, it was also Kavanagh's most substantial and most
acclaimed poem, so that its rejection had a tactical shock
value. In designating *The Great Hunger* tragic, he emphasises
his new allegiance to comedy:

> 'The Great Hunger' is tragedy and Tragedy is under-
> developed Comedy, not fully born.

Such provocative subversion of the hierarchy of literary modes can hardly fail to startle even the most inattentive reader into registering the change in Kavanagh's poetics. The maieutic image indicates that what differentiates tragedy from comedy is a failure of authorial detachment. Elsewhere, he observes that a 'tragic' work is one that 'has not been detached from the author's personal life', and, again, *The Great Hunger* serves as a negative exemplar. It has 'some remarkable things in it, but free it hardly is, for there's no laughter in it'.[24]

The fundamental distinction between the customary textbook definitions of comedy and tragedy and Kavanagh's approach to these literary modes is that his aesthetic is expressive and not concerned with generic norms. He describes a work in terms of the authorial attitude that, in his opinion, informs it, not in the context of literary conventions and traditions. This emphasis on the expressive, on states of consciousness conducive to literary composition, rather than on the referential aspects of literature or on craftsmanship or generic criteria, pervades his entire comic poetics.

Kavanagh repeatedly stresses the unimportance of subject matter:

> Stupid poets and artists think that by taking subjects of public importance it will help their work to survive.
>
> *(Self-Portrait)*

> The material itself has no special value; it is what our imagination and our love does to it . . .

> The world that matters is the world that we have created . . .

> I am not suggesting that being true to life in a realist way is the highest function of a writer . . .
>
> ('From Monaghan to the Grand Canal')

A corollary of this refusal to attach any special significance to the artist's material is that nothing is excluded from artistic treatment; everything is turned into potential subject matter. What is significant to the expressive aesthetician is not the material, but the artist's 'point of view'. A poet with his 'point of view' is 'a man poised with a torch' to whom the material and the mundane serve only as so much combustible matter: 'All his life's activities are towards the final fusion of all crudeness into a pure flame'.[25] 'Light' and 'heat' are two recurrent images in Kavanagh's comic poetics to illuminate the importance of the poet's way of seeing and relating to the world. The urban scene is suddenly irradiated during the Canal epiphany in 'From Monaghan to the Grand Canal':

The light was a surprise over roofs and around gables

and 'Fantastic light looks through the eyes of bridges' in one of the Canal sonnets.[26] 'Heat' is an expression of sexual attraction towards unprepossessing phenomena in 'The Hospital'. Indeed the poems inspired by this sense of the radiant beauty of ordinary things are characterised as 'poems to the new light'.[27]

Poetic technique is also defined expressively by Kavanagh. He regards it as the product of a particular kind of imagination or of the capacity to enter into a particular kind of mental state:

Real technique is a spiritual quality, a condition of mind, or an ability to invoke a particular condition of mind . . . Technique is a method of being sincere. Technique is a method of getting at life. The slippery surface of the *cliché*-phrase and -emotion causes a light skidding blow.
('From Monaghan to the Grand Canal')

Here language and emotion are conjoined through hyphenation and technique is presented as a comic stance as well as a means of conveying such a stance. Its 'purpose', he points out elsewhere, is 'to enable us to detach our experience from ourselves and see it as a thing apart'.[28]

In 'Author's Note' Kavanagh states his belief that poetry is 'a mystical thing, and a dangerous thing' rather than a well-crafted artifact. ('Technique' is used pejoratively on this occasion, as a synonym for craft.) The sense in which poetry is 'a dangerous thing' is glossed in 'From Monaghan to the Grand Canal', where we are told that the poet awakens 'a disruptive, anarchic mentality' in his hearers or readers and that 'if we pursue him far enough we will be inclined to agree with Plato that the poet is a menace'. Coupling the 'dangerous' with the 'mystical' appears less paradoxical if the danger is seen as poetic effect and the mysticism as poetic origin.

On the vexed question as to whether Kavanagh is a mystical poet in a religious sense the answer would seem to be that he sometimes is, but most often is not. Kavanagh writes as a religious mystic when he represents the poet as one who enjoys a direct, unmediated knowledge of the divine: who knows 'the will of God' ('Canal Bank Walk'), has 'learned something of the nature of God's mind' ('Miss Universe') or encounters 'the One and the Endless, the Mind that has baulked/The profoundest of mortals . . . breathing His love by a cut-away bog' ('The One'). He is also a mystical poet in the more generalised sense that he believes in the spiritual apprehension of truths inaccessible to rational understanding or common sense, in 'arguments that cannot be proven', and he often relies on spiritual intuition, as opposed to information or cerebration, as a means of acquiring knowledge.

> And I have a feeling
> That through the hole in reason's ceiling
> We can fly to knowledge
> Without ever going to college.

This is how he articulates his anti-rational stance in the comic doggerel of the post-Canal poem, 'To Hell with Commonsense'. However, as 'To Hell with Commonsense' itself demonstrates, Kavanagh found it difficult to allow his championship of intuitive knowledge to triumph over his antagonistic impulse to teach. His advocacy of poetic mysticism in his

Canal poetics was an attempt to counter, if not to oust, the dogmatist in himself.

In 'Auden and the Creative Mind'[29] he had already confronted the problem of reconciling a religious and a comic poetics. There literary secularism was distrusted:

> But is this world of the poet, this world of sensation not likely to wear itself out, like all earth-turned emotions, if there are no reinforcements of hope and faith coming up from the silences to refertilize the wasteland?

On the other hand, though 'religious passion and purpose' were necessary, those who attempted 'the prophetic, the didactic, the responsible' failed as artists because their work was 'not earthed' and did 'not come alive'. Kavanagh was too much in love with this green world of eye and ear to settle for a purely transcendental art. Moreover, religious or philosophical commitment was incompatible with comedy, so Dante and Blake failed as comic poets in Kavanagh's estimation. Shakespeare and Cervantes were more successful because they were less consciously, more obliquely, religious: they 'lived on the capital of Christianity' or 'within it'.

Although he described the poet as a 'theologian' in 'From Monaghan to the Grand Canal', Kavanagh was not 'steel'd in the school of old Aquinas' and his relationship to Christianity was closer to Shakespeare's or Cervantes' than to Dante's. He drew liberally and unselfconsciously on Roman Catholic beliefs, symbology and terminology, with the ease of one who takes his religious culture for granted. Christianity was a potent source of moral metaphor in his satiric phase. The relationship between poetry and the divine in his comic poetics is expressive rather than ethical. God is described as a comic creator: 'the gay, imaginative God who made the grass and the trees and the flowers'. This creative divinity is also encountered in several post-Canal poems. The mystical experience most frequently described in Kavanagh's poetry is the mental state in which poetry originates, a state often portrayed through Christian imagery as, for instance, in the 'placeless Heaven' of 'Auditors In'. Kavanagh's mysticism is more reflexive than religious.

'Author's Note', which refers to poetry as a 'mystical thing', illustrates the kind of nature mysticism which may result in poetic creation. Arrival at the Canal is presented as a metaphor for the attainment of the psychological state of repose conducive to composition:

> But I lost my Messianic compulsion. I sat on the bank of the Grand Canal in the summer of 1955 and let the waters lap idly on the shores of my mind. My purpose in life was to have no purpose.

Canal water lapping replaces the lake water of Innisfree. It is also preferred to the 'river and the stream' of *Prelude* because it is unruffled, 'stilly'. The Canal poet's own tranquillity is indicated through imagery of stasis and physical rest. His pilgrimage is over; he sits still and yields to mental passivity. The expressive aesthetic Kavanagh describes here is quietist: the comic poet surrenders all conscious control, allows himself to be inspired. The Canal bank on which the waters lap becomes a metaphor for the quiescent mind's inertia and indifference to the impact of otherness. It is, simultaneously, a metaphor of poetic metaphysicality, of the interaction between the external scene and the poet's mind, a connection that is unforced, unlaboured, occurring 'idly'. Perception is inactive and involuntary. 'To let experience enter the soul' is one of Kavanagh's comic precepts in 'From Monaghan to the Grand Canal'; here no conscious effort is made to register the scene.

The Canal poet is solitary, private, uncommitted, at ease. He has abdicated his public roles of prophet, guru, leader of his people, social saviour and martyr. In keeping with such disinterestedness he abdicates responsibility for his *Collected Poems*. He is 'too indifferent, too lazy to eliminate, change or collect'. Here *The Great Hunger* epitomises a discarded

'Messianic' poetics. In *Self-Portrait*, too, it is faulted for its lack of serenity:

> There are some queer and terrible things in *The Great Hunger*, but it lacks the nobility and repose of poetry.

However, the self-cancelling syntax of 'My purpose in life was to have no purpose' betrays the writer's incorrigible sense of engagement. He is still the crusading Crooked Knight, though now his adversary is the enemy within: his own susceptibility to social pressures, and, in particular, his sacrifice of autonomous creation to rhetoric. Here involuntariness is willed into being.

So inveterate was Kavanagh's adversariousness and so ingrained his animosity towards the Literary Revival that, despite his claim to be a born-again poet, he uses his current advocacy of comedy to pursue his vendetta against Revival and neo-Revival poetry. By discounting the importance of poetic subject matter he disallows the validity of Irishness and regionalism as aesthetic criteria:

> Irishness is a form of anti-art. A way of posing as a poet without actually being one . . . I have no belief in the virtue of a place.
>
> (*Self-Portrait*)

Similarly he draws on his expressive definition of literary technique to discredit the 'Irish mode', which prided itself on imitating the craftsmanship of the Gaelic poets:

> On the road of my hegira I began to reflect with astonishment how poor as technicians the Irish school of poets and novelists have been . . . Lack of technique gives us shallowness: Colum's
>
> > O men from the fields
> > Softly come through

> Mary will fold him
> In a mantle of blue.

A charming sentiment undoubtedly, but all on the surface.

('From Monaghan to the Grand Canal')

Many facets of his comic expressiveness would have seemed familiar to readers acquainted with Kavanagh's poetry and criticism, since it was really a continuation of his recent aesthetic thinking and not, as he liked to represent it, a new discovery or a rediscovery of an early aesthetic. His comic poetics may have been born on the banks of the Grand Canal but he had been gestating it for many years. The cultivation of artistic detachment was implicit in his renunciations of satire, was explicitly advocated in 'Intimate Parnassus' (1954), and was expressly connected with comedy in *Tarry Flynn* (1948):

> The net of earthly intrigue could not catch him here. He was on a level with the horizon—and it was a level on which there was laughter. Looking down on his own misfortunes he thought them funny now. From this height he could even see himself losing his temper with the Finnegans and the Carlins and hating his neighbours and he moved the figures on the landscape, made them speak, and was filled with joy in his own power.

Repose, too, had been a feature of Kavanagh's expressive aesthetic for some time. The creative 'Heaven' of 'Auditors In' (1951) was a state in which 'the self reposes'; the poet of 'Having Confessed' (1952) admonished himself to 'Lie at the heart of the emotion', while in 'Intimate Parnassus' he asserted that the citizens of Parnassus look 'serenely' on the human spectacle for 'gods can not/Be moved, involved or hurt'. The paradoxical combination of repose and energy was present as early as 'In Memory of My Mother' (1945), which also, like the second Canal sonnet, juxtaposed the 'greeny' with the 'stilly' in a context of death. A quietist approach to creativity was voiced in 'Having Confessed'. Self-transcendence was the subject of 'Intimate Parnassus', where the poet's own emotional crises were merely 'subject matter' and his 'main purpose' was 'to be/Passive, observing with a steady eye'. Kavanagh had already publicly extirpated his 'social conscience' in 1949. He had extolled the literary benefits of neighbourly love in *Tarry Flynn*, and in 'Prelude' (February 1955), had counselled himself to 'be/Lost in compassion's ecstasy'.

Most aspects of Kavanagh's comic poetics had been anticipated in the essay, 'Auden and the Creative Mind' (1951). Even the use of fire as an expressive image had been included. There 'the great poets' were 'those who burn in the smithy of their souls the raw material of life' and critics who dismissed their 'material' as 'rubbish' were like men who

> would judge a fire not by its heat or by the fact that it was alight at all but by the largeness, the importance and the respectability of the lumps of unburnable stone or wet wood that were piled up in the grate.

As Kavanagh illustrated from the work of Auden, Shakespeare and Dickens *inter alia*, 'almost any kind of the crude material of life' could 'be burned'. The analogy between conflagration and comic creation in this essay was extended to include such similarities as consuming energy, the stimulation of the drab, an entertaining performance, an orgy of sensation and an activity that never gives the spectator a respite from excitement. In poetry 'at its purest all the didacticism' was 'burned away'. Great literature was equated with comic literature:

Shakespeare, like all great writers, only wrote Comedy.

If Kavanagh did indeed enjoy an aesthetic epiphany on the banks of the Grand Canal, what was revealed to him was not a new poetics but a reinforcement of an existing poetics. The essay 'Auden and the Creative Mind', his most extended meditation on the connection between comedy and creativity, pre-dates his Canal epiphany by four years, and pre-dates the first formulation of his Canal poetics by eight years.

That Kavanagh should have chosen 'Shancoduff' as his exemplary early comic lyric is understandable. Though narrated in the first person it was self-effacing, 'outgiving' in its affections, transfiguring an unattractive landscape and a humble farming chore through loving imagination, contrasting with materialist and common-sense values. Those 'black hills' were his first Parnassus or Olympus; already the young farmer-poet going about his ordinary tasks was imaginatively scaling the heights, transforming drumlins into Alps. The 'black hills' of Shancoduff also personified that central comic characteristic so often associated with imagery of height in Kavanagh's aesthetic: uninvolvement, detachment; they were 'incurious'. As we have seen in chapter 1, however, 'Shancoduff' was a once-off among Kavanagh's thirties' poems.

One of his earliest post-operative lyrics, 'Leaves of Grass', an autobiographical sonnet, published in December 1956[30] and not republished in Kavanagh's lifetime, provides an altogether different account of his poetic progress than that recorded in his three key prose manifestos. Though I referred to this poem in chapter 2, I quote it in full here, since its dismissal of his early poetry as slight, stupid, and lacking in context or comic perspective, is completely at odds with his descriptions of his literary progress as circular, a return to a primitive aesthetic:

When I was growing up and for many years after
I was led to believe that poems were thin

Dreary, irrelevant, well out of the draught of
   laughter
With headquarters the size of the head of a pin.
I do not wonder now that my mother moaned
To see her beloved son an idiot boy;
He could not see what was before his eyes, the
   ground
Tumultuous with living, infinite as Cleopatra's
   variety.
He hit upon the secret door that leads to the
   heaven
Of human satisfaction, a purpose, and did not
   know it;
An army of grass blades were at his call, million
   on million
Kept saying to him, we nearly made Whitman a
   poet.
Years after in Dublin in summer past midnight
   o'clock
They called to him vainly from kerbstones on
   Bachelor's Walk.

The poet's claim that his early poetics blinded him to the drama and glamour of such ordinary, everyday phenomena as grass, is fair comment. The 'fool', an inflationary self-image in the 1930s, is here transformed into a Wordsworthian idiot boy whose mother was right to fret over his welfare, rather than a saintly Dostoyevskean idiot. Common earth, formerly disregarded, is personified as a beautiful Cleopatra—custom cannot stale her infinite variety.

   In borrowing Whitman's title Kavanagh is, like the American poet, conflating the literary and the natural, the printed page and the teeming organic life of the earth, the world and the book. Poetry is not a closeted art; literature can be made of what is most commonplace, plentiful, taken for granted. As he had done with the epic, Kavanagh gestures towards the vast sprawl of Whitman's poem within the restricted confines of a sonnet. Unlike Homer, Whitman is arrogantly dismissed as a precursor. Kavanagh draws on the military metaphor latent in the banal phrase, 'blades of grass', to indicate the enormous potential inherent in the use of ordinary phenomena as poetic material. He has countless eager would-be recruits at his command, ready to be mobilised, marshalled into lines, ranked into rhythm and rhyme.

This Shakespearian sonnet concludes with a non-epiphany by the Liffey on a summer's night instead of an expressive revelation by the Grand Canal on a sunny July day. The poet of the concluding couplet is still a failed Dublin poet, deaf to the seductive tones of the 'leafy-with-love' grass on the pavement. His rural and urban worlds meet as in the Canal sonnets or in 'October', but he ignores what is before his eyes. The place-name, 'Bachelor's Walk', probably alludes comically to his unloved state. He is solicited on all sides by grasses calling like night-town ladies, but out of a mistaken avoidance of the sensuous, he passes up the opportunity to become a poet.

To acquiesce in Kavanagh's Canal myth involves not only colluding with a mistakenly inflated estimate of such early poems as 'To a Child'; it also results in a false simplification of the erratic course of his literary development as we know it. Consciously or unconsciously suppressed in this version of events are such early forties' lyrics as 'Spraying the Potatoes', 'A Christmas Childhood', 'The Long Garden' and 'Art McCooey', with their recognition of the poetic possibilities of Inniskeen simplicities, and also 'Advent', his earliest public recantation of *The Great Hunger*. *Tarry Flynn*, which may be read as a comic, alternative text to the tragic *Great Hunger*, and which offers a meta-commentary on rural lyricism and on creative and comic detachment, is also disregarded. Overlooked, too, are those poems, mostly concentrated in the early 1950s, which focus on the interplay of memory and imagination or on the theme of imaginative return to Inniskeen: 'Kerr's Ass', 'Epic', 'Innocence' and 'On Reading a Book on Common Wild Flowers'. Most blatantly ignored are such recent manifesto poems as 'Having Confessed', 'Intimate Parnassus', 'Auditors In' and 'Prelude', which advocate states of passivity, Parnassian detachment, love and benevolence, as essential to creativity. Kavanagh was never as wholly committed to 'anger, hatred and ill-will' as he claims in *Self-Portrait*. His satires were interspersed with more searching confessional poems and with serenely celebratory lyrics. Though he here pronounces 'the comic spirit' to be 'the ultimate in sophistication', he had, in fact, aspired towards comedy for most of his career, and especially from *Tarry Flynn* onwards. A knowledge of *Tarry Flynn* and the many expressive poems that followed it reveals that Kavanagh's comic Canal poetics was not, as he represented it, a new departure or a recovery of an early mode, but a continuation of his recent aesthetic philosophy.

Kavanagh's claim that he underwent an aesthetic conversion after his operation for lung cancer has a certain validity, however. A positive creative state, that combined comic detachment with 'unthinking joy', was an expressive ideal which he had sighted and lost sight of over and over again, and which he had pursued with intermittent ardour throughout the 1940s and early 1950s. Such an aesthetic ideal was finally sustained in the poems he wrote in the later 1950s. For a few years after his Canal convalescence, between 1956 and 1959, he published some of his finest lyrics. His myth of rebirth and his promulgation of a 'new' comic aesthetic were rationalisations after the event, designed both to account for and to emphasise this post-Canal poetry.

'Not caring', a colloquial phrase he appropriated in the early 1960s, encapsulates the mood of his Canal aesthetic. The importance of 'not caring' is established in *Self-Portrait* where, in addition to being represented as 'the very heart of the matter of human contentment', and defined as 'having the courage of one's feelings' and 'a sense of values and feeling of confidence', it is also given poetic primacy:

> The heart of a song singing it, or a poem writing it, is not caring.

Kavanagh extends the usual definition of 'not caring' to identify it with personal, social and artistic control: 'A man who cares is not the master.'

'Not caring' is a deceptively simple phrase that neatly sums up a complex cluster of comic attitudes. It suggests an emotional, mental and imaginative detachment that enables the poet to remain indifferent to criticism and immune to hatred or hostility, and, simultaneously, absolves him from all responsibility as spokesman or orator:

> A poet merely states the position and does not care whether his words change anything or not.
>
> ('Author's Note')

'Not caring' also excludes self-absorption: self-pity, self-righteousness, self-justification, 'taking oneself sickly seriously'.[31] It liberates the poet's originality, freeing him from social or artistic conventions, from adherence to established literary formulae. 'Not caring' may, therefore, be disruptive as well as disinterested, subversive of accepted social and aesthetic codes.

Its synonym, 'carefree', which dispenses with concern, pomp, solemnity and anxiety, indicates a relaxed, easygoing, cheerful, poetic stance. It suggests a poetry that does not stand on ceremony and avoids drawing attention to its own artifice, a poetry that talks intimately and unselfconsciously about 'casual, insignificant little things'[32] in a seemingly improvised and uncontrived manner. Closely connected with this is the interpretation of 'not caring' as 'carelessness'. The choice of carelessness as a poetic strategy points towards the deliberate cultivation of a slapdash and slap-happy technique: such devices as frequent recourse to colloquialism and doggerel, 'getting out of . . . respectability' by a 'judicious use of slang and of outrageous rhyming'.[33] The aim, as Kavanagh stated it in *Self-Portrait*, is to 'arrive at complete casualness, at being able to play a true note on a dead slack string'.

The adoption of a casual stance or a demotic idiom in Kavanagh's poetry was, of course, nothing new. He had in the past sometimes assumed a jaunty persona, as in 'If Ever You Go To Dublin Town', and the tendency of his Dublin verses from 'City Commentary' onwards was to resort to argot and jargon. Even poor Paddy Maguire occasionally 'said/Whatever came into his head/And inconsequently sang', and God in 'God in Woman' disguised herself 'in some fantastically ordinary incog'.

Nevertheless, 'not caring' has attitudinal, material and technical implications for Kavanagh's post-Canal poetry and helps to account both for its triumphs and disasters. While he did not always succeed in avoiding audience-consciousness and didacticism or self-projection and self-promotion, he did develop a markedly casual poetic style. Unfortunately, the aesthetic of 'not caring', which generated some of his best late poems, also encouraged the trivialisation of his talent. It provided a tone of voice and a manner that enabled him to chit-chat inconsequentially and play games with rhyme when he had nothing to say. On a more positive note, 'not caring' liberated the poet from an exemplary role and gave him a 'fantastically ordinary' medium through which to express the human comedy of his own life and perverse personality.

The poems discussed in the second part of this chapter are written in Kavanagh's post-Canal comic vein. This section focuses on the spate of poems he published between winter 1956 and October 1959. Fifteen of them were collected along with five earlier uncollected pieces, in a limited edition entitled *Recent Poems*, printed by Peter Kavanagh on his hand press in 1958. A commercial edition of Kavanagh's poetry, his first since *A Soul for Sale* (1947), was published in London in 1960 under the title, *Come Dance with Kitty Stobling*.[34]

Thirty-five poems were collected, including eighteen post-1955 lyrics and most of the best of his earlier uncollected poems.

Poems, 1956–1960

By July 1957 Kavanagh felt that he had discovered a 'new mood' in his poetry.[35] He was 'writing verse in a new style',[36] 'a new kind of poems with new words'.[37] A short spate of these 'noo pomes'[38] appeared between 1956 and 1959. Though this late fifties' poetry does not make a complete thematic or stylistic break with his previous verse, it does represent a fresh departure. The outlook and mood are different. His 'noo pomes' are utterly celebratory, scarcely troubled by any *arrière-pensées* of pain, bitterness or hostility. The anger and self-pity he had been trying to eradicate from his poetry since 'Auditors In' has been extirpated or subordinated. The comic poet is not only completely reconciled with life, with 'The way it happened, and the way it is'; he is euphoric, exuberant, maniacally delighted to be alive. When not simply giving vent to a sense of exhilaration, he writes love poems and hymns to the world: to canal and street, as well as to summer lane and cut-away bog.

Prior to this, Kavanagh's celebratory poetry was usually retrospective and rural. His new lyrics are present-tense salutations, greeting the here and now, or hailing the future with optimism. Whether set in 'colourful country' or 'the edge of a town', their tone is equally happy and buoyant. When they recall the past it is to involve it in a present joy. Everything, from 'Steps up to houses' to a 'bright stick', is bathed in a glow of love and rapture. Beatitude is no longer coaxed into existence as in 'Auditors In' or 'Prelude'. It is unearned and all-pervasive.

His love-affair with life provides Kavanagh with an 'unworn world' to praise and bless. This new poetry exudes a sense of plenty, of infinite riches:

> O wealthy me! O happy state
> With an inexhaustible theme

I'll die in harness
I'll die in harness
With my scheme.

('Is')

The discovery that 'A created splendour' can be made out of
anything, out of the 'residual',[39] even 'out of the frowsy, the
secondhand',[40] turns everything into poetic material. There is
no fear that the supply will run out. An imagination plagued
by poverty, by the anxiety about what is going to happen
next week, is temporarily appeased. Romantic 'dejection', the
fear that the poetic sources are drying up, will recur, but it
post-dates the 1960 collection, *Come Dance with Kitty Stobling*.

Most of Kavanagh's post-Canal lyrics, in addition to being
celebrations of his brave new world, are poems about poetry:
credos, manifestos, poetic stocktakings, announcements of
future schemes and programmes, acts of imaginative preparation, reflexive glimpses of 'the Muse at her toilet'. The
present actualities in which these poems delight also furnish
images for poetry. Their joy in the present is in large measure
due to the knowledge that it will provide poetic 'life and food
for future years'. The futurity to which they look forward so
confidently is a literary future tense in which a present
poetics will be translated into poems. If 'To be dead is to stop
believing in/The masterpieces we will begin tomorrow'; to be
alive is to start believing in them and stating one's conviction.
Kavanagh's late fities' lyrics are rarely self-contained; they are
preludes, poems to the next poem. Their muse is always
preparing 'to inform'. Even repose is a stance that makes
further poetry possible:

So be reposed and praise, praise, praise . . .

The God who presides over these poems is the 'God of
poetry'.[41] Sometimes he acts as an exemplary image of
Kavanagh's new aesthetic ideal: loving, creative, attentive to
the 'Everydays of nature', caressing his world into continued

productivity. At other times God is an enabling muse, forgiving past failures, lending his authority or support to certain creative stances, willing the poet to 'wallow in the habitual, the banal', 'to grow with nature again' like the 'leafy-with-love' Canal banks.

Though all of Kavanagh's late fifties' lyrics are narrated in the first person, they differ as to the role assigned to the poet persona. Some propose a self-effacing aesthetic as opposed to the flaunting of personality in his recent poetry; one, 'The Self-slaved', advocates a programme of unselving. Others project self-images which are at least as exaggerated, extravagant and arrogant as any of his former poses. The unself-centred lyrics celebrate states of contentment, passivity and repose; the 'songs of myself' are full of movement, adventure and travel. The self as loving spectator of the world plays the part of anonymous cataloguer of the scene; the 'I' is 'not important', 'the namer, not the beloved'. In the exuberant self-centred lyrics, the irrationality that Kavanagh had espoused since his earliest poems is turned into an excited pursuit of the wild, the violent, the zany. The figure in the scene is frequently a solitary in his quiescent moods; the more self-congratulatory and crazy persona is highly audience conscious. Love is usually love of phenomena rather than love of neighbour in these poems, but it serves to keep insecurity and aggressiveness at bay. In poems which include a notional human audience, comic detachment is often translated into cocking a snook, being provocatively outrageous. Conflict between these opposing personal roles is not an explicit subject; such tension occurs between lyrics, usually, rather than within them. However, in some lyrics the 'I' figure veers unexpectedly from one role to another; in some he advocates one mode while practising its contrary.

These 'noo pomes' are distinguished by their combination of certitude and nonchalance. Their mood is one of imaginative engagement; their manner debonair, devil-may-care, or skittishly flamboyant. They succeed in being simultaneously full hearted and light hearted, devoted and detached. At this stage in his career Kavanagh was obsessed with technique as never before, with finding modes of expression that would seem spontaneous and uncontrived. He was trying to circumvent the preacher in himself, the pundit within; to offset his tendency to the axiomatic and the abstract by stressing the importance of not being earnest, or rather of not appearing to be earnest. The uninhibited, vernacular, spoken style which he had been cultivating for years in his journalism, and in such early fifties' poems as 'Auditors In' ('Let myself rip'), allows him to lighten his verse without foregoing his project of enlightening the reader. He is consciously adopting the attitude of claiming while apparently disclaiming, that he had resorted to as early as 'Inniskeen Road: July Evening'.

Kavanagh's cult of 'not caring' is everywhere manifest in his late fifties' poems. Improvisatory techniques are exploited to convey an air of immediacy and lack of restraint. The speaker takes us into his confidence, shares his epiphanies and his elations, but celebration is counterpointed with playfulness, solemnity with levity. In keeping with their openness to 'ordinary plenty', these poems admit any word or phrase, however slangy or vulgar. Sudden flippancies in language, image or tone momentarily threaten Romantic afflatus. At its most serious this poetry often teeters on the verge of laughter. Poetic diction or decorum is flouted through rhyme and phrasing. Rhyme, which is frequently off-chime, brings together 'person' and 'arsing', 'thighs' and 'wise', 'purse' and 'verse', 'of' and 'love'. Cliché is coupled with abstraction; an amorous poeticism powered by a surge of lust:

> . . . all that
> was part and parcel of
> The wild breast of love . . .

What we frequently encounter in these late fifties' poems is a poetry about literature conducted in an anti-literary style:

> Therefore I say to hell
> With all reasonable
> Poems . . .

Yet for all its cult of casualness this verse has 'a shapely form'. Many of the late fifties' lyrics are sonnets; the remainder are, for the most part, written in couplets. All are rhymed. Their air of impromptu utterance and unrehearsed immediacy is the product of an art that conceals art. Kavanagh wanted his poetry to embrace all aspects of life with passion and gaiety, but also to reciprocate the grace of living with poetic grace:

> I will have love, have love
> From anything made of
> And a life with a shapely form
> With gaiety and charm
> And capable of receiving
> With grace the grace of living . . .

Although he did not recognise it as the start of a new poetic phase, one of the earliest of Kavanagh's post-Canal poems is, significantly, entitled 'The Hospital'. This is a doctrinaire poem that establishes a direct connection between the poetics it preaches and the poet's recent experience of being a lung-cancer patient in Dublin's Rialto hospital. Like so many of his late fifties' poems it is a sonnet. Published in winter 1956[42] it was extensively revised for republication in *Come Dance with Kitty Stobling*, so as to attune it more precisely to the poet's late fifties' affective aesthetic. This sonnet bears out Kavanagh's sense that his poetry was recircling towards 'Shancoduff': its themes are the poet's unconventional love for an aesthetically unattractive terrain and the interaction between love and creativity. But it reveals, too, some of the ways in which he had shifted his ground since that early poem. Not only has he transplanted his affections from the country; he has arrived at a clear recognition that no particular virtue attaches to one place rather than another, that the act of loving is more important than the love object. 'Epic', though it had proclaimed the subordination of subject matter to authorship, emphasised the legitimacy of rural parochialism;

and the more tentative 'Shancoduff' also ostensibly confined itself to a meditation on the literary validity of an impoverished country place. 'The Hospital' is more comprehensive: embracing urban and rural, indoor and outdoor subjects, and people as well as places, debarring nothing. Like the revised 'Shancoduff', and unlike 'Epic', it roots imagination in love rather than in artistic conviction, 'faith'. However, 'The Hospital' is more self-consciously and forthrightly programmatic than 'Shancoduff', more upfront, more assured. What was implicit in 'Shancoduff' is here made explicit; where the earlier poem moved from unquestioning confidence to interrogative ambivalence, 'The Hospital' proceeds by way of particular certitudes to general truths. To put it in Kavanagh's terms, 'Shancoduff' hints; 'The Hospital' has taken 'the hint'.[43] Its strategy is to state, not to dramatise. This is not to deny that it, too, is a very fine poem, merely to say that it is a very different poem.

In the opening quatrain, the hospital's aesthetic defects are stridently emphasised, not metaphorically transformed or disguised as were the unprepossessing aspects of the hill farm:

> A year ago I fell in love with the functional ward
> Of a chest hospital: square cubicles in a row
> Plain concrete, wash basins—an art lover's woe,
> Not counting how the fellow in the next bed
>   snored.

The phrase, 'an art lover's woe', is perhaps over-explicit, but it shows the poet taking a radical aesthetic stance, breaking ranks with orthodox art-lovers, making art out of anti-art. He is centralising what is normally disregarded or debarred, situating a 'functional' hospital ward among the Petrarchan 'sonnet's pretty rooms'. This quatrain is as innovatively bathetic as the title 'The Love Song of J. Alfred Prufrock'; Kavanagh is capitalising on the sonnet's origins as a love song. As in 'Epic' a comic deflationary technique is here a technical strategy to prepare for the subversion of an aesthetic orthodoxy; for a poetics which warmly welcomes the 'plain concrete' and does not exclude even the rhythms of 'snoring' from its musicality.

The comic and colloquial catalogue of love-objects in the first quatrain is followed by a rhetorical grand swell of abstract summation:

> But nothing whatever is by love debarred,
> The common and banal her heat can know ...

'Heat' is an economical reminder of the sensual nature of this love, succinctly suggesting a relationship that is, at once, lustful and intense. In keeping with this mood of warm expansiveness, the concluding lines of the octet conduct onwards and outwards, checked by, but overstepping, finite limits:

> The corridor led to a stairway, and below
> Was the inexhaustible adventure of a gravelled yard.

A 'gravelled yard', a gritty, commonplace site, a coming down to earth emphasised by the choice of such a homely monosyllable. Yet that deliberate reductiveness, the movement towards closure, is countered by a sense of amplitude, of infinity even, and a feeling of exhilaration, exuberance, 'inexhaustible adventure'. So the octet reaches a paradoxical conclusion, infinite riches in a little room. As in 'Shancoduff', Kavanagh is displaying the imaginative plenitude that can accrue from scant resources. Here the interlacing rhymes of the Petrarchan octet enact the theme of enfolding rebarbative phenomena in the embrace of love.

Love is central to this sonnet: referred to three times in both the octet and the sestet. The sestet breaks out of the hospital confines of 'ward' and 'yard', a rhymed enclosure, and its short catalogue bridges the divide between Dublin's Rialto and a country scene, between well-loved places of the recent and more remote past:

> This is what love does to things: the Rialto Bridge,
> The main gate that was bent by a heavy lorry,

The seat at the back of a shed that was a suntrap.

The opening phrase of the sestet is not referentially precise, but it gestures back towards the transformation of limitation into exciting potential in the octet, and forward to an inventory of ordinary, extra-hospital paraphernalia that can be so transformed. Is it merely fanciful to see that lorry bringing about the kind of 'kink' which poetic perception involves for Kavanagh? The 'suntrap', as well as catching the ensnaring attraction of ordinary things, recalls the 'heat' of line 6, giving a similar glow and radiance to both recent urban, and remote rural, experience. Kavanagh captures in a colloquialism the paradoxically extensive nature of intimate sensuous love that Donne teasingly engages with in planetary images in 'The Sunne Rising' or 'The good-morrow', encapsulating the universe, making a little space 'an everywhere'.

Summary notation of images is justified as an emotional and poetic strategy in the final quatrain. For the second time the sonnet swells from the vernacular of ordinary circumstance to the abstract language of rhetorical declamation, a densely dogmatic conclusion:

Naming these things is the love-act and its pledge;
For we must record love's mystery without claptrap,
Snatch out of time the passionate transitory.

Here the intimate relationship between love and the literary is enunciated. Poetry, in which the world enters into the word, is a love-act, a linguo-sexual rite of intercourse, a declaration of commitment in the present and for the future. That 'naming' is declared to be the poet's role stresses the sign and the signified, excludes self-referentiality. The use of 'naming' as the objective correlative of affection recalls the Imagists' fusion of description and reaction within the instantaneous complex of the image as a 'dry, hard' antidote to Romantic subjectivism. While retaining an overtly confessional frame, Kavanagh is advocating an anti-confessional or, at least, an only obliquely or implicitly confessional, poetic mode. The image is not for Kavanagh, as for Imagists like T. E. Hulme, a rejection of Romantic mystery and infinity. Instead 'naming' becomes a means of recording a love that passes all understanding.

No longer is it sufficient to perceive 'the immortal in things mortal'; such epiphanies must be preserved. 'Recording' is now the poet's function. Death is often a spectral presence at the festivities of these post-convalescence poems. Here it is latent in the choice of setting, and in the concluding line transitoriness is as powerful a poetic pressure as love. This line witnesses to a desperate urge to seize and save rather than savour experience. So 'The Hospital' arrives by a rather unconventional route at a traditional sonnet theme, the poet-lover's defiance of mutability. Assonance underscores the connection between sonneteering brevity and intimations of mortality: 'Snatch . . . the passionate transitory'. This assonantal finale also echoes much of the poem's earlier vowel music ('debarred', 'banal', 'gravelled yard', 'Rialto', 'back', 'suntrap'), implicating the entire sonnet in a love act that is a creative challenge to death.

'Naming' is also an anti-rhetorical imperative, dispensing with 'claptrap', with that audience-consciousness, which his journalism and his obsession with his own idiosyncratic persona had encouraged Kavanagh to indulge. The substitution of 'naming' for passionate statement will promote spareness, conciseness, economy of utterance. The tendency of the 'noo pomes' is towards brevity and concentration: narratives and manifestos in sonnet form, short-lined couplets, lists or inventories instead of detailed description and complicated syntax. Simplicity is now a rhetorical goal.[44]

The poems that followed on 'The Hospital' are those that Kavanagh identified as his 'new kind of poem'.[45] In 'Is' the minimalist aesthetic advocated in 'The Hospital' is restated and illustrated. Here Kavanagh is once again reorientating his poetics, turning from a personal to an impersonal art, focusing on objects, on the other, rather than on subjective reactions. Commentary, analysis and narrative plot are excluded from poetry and the emphasis is on the image. Once again what he is promoting is a poetry of 'naming', recording 'for the future'. It is assumed that the poet's emotional response is inherent in his choice of image and that the named object will contain and communicate the emotional charge that went to its selection. 'Mere notice' is enough; naming will 'take care of love'. It is not that Kavanagh has abdicated his role of sage but that didacticism is expressed in a new way. The emphasis is now on the visual rather than the ideological; the function of seer is subsumed in that of spectator:

> The only true teaching
> Subsists in watching . . .

What he is promoting is not voyeurism, but detachment, when he writes:

> To look on is enough
> In the business of love.

No longer self-obsessed, the poet is alert to the world around him, to colour, form, light, animals, girls, architecture. As in 'The Hospital' the common and banal are again projected as the subject matter of poetry—'The everydays of nature' or 'The life of a street'. The choice of ordinary subjects and the apparent absence of personal involvement help to create that easy relaxed air which Kavanagh now cultivates. Poetic statement is to take the casual form of a 'remark', a 'mention'. Contemplation is to be translated into direct, unadorned observation: lists and catalogues of associated items, such as 'deer running in a park' and 'water' or

> Girls in red blouses,
> Steps up to houses,
> Sunlight round gables . . .

Because he believes that the symbolic properties of the image are constant and familiar, its metaphoric dimension may also be taken for granted. Kavanagh is too saturated in Christian symbolism to engage in innocent seeing or to promote a purely denotative art. Water, for instance, is 'Always virginal,/Always original,/It washes out Original Sin'.

One of the distinctive features of this later fifties' poetry is that it tends to be written in the present tense. Here the present tense is foregrounded in the title, 'Is'. The monosyllabic, third-person, present-tense form of the verb exemplifies brevity, objectivity, impersonality, immediacy, vitality and essentiality. Mortality, seldom absent from these late fifties' poems, on this occasion is countered and almost overwhelmed by the celebration of present and future poetic vigour. The future tense finally usurps the present tense of title and poem:

> I'll die in harness with my scheme.

It is typical of Kavanagh's new vernacular approach that Pegasus, given pride of place in *A Soul for Sale*, is here slipped in between the shafts of a common idiom.

This poem, however, does not practise the poetics it preaches. Its 'business' is not watching or naming. It consists of a series of assertions, artistic axioms and imperatives, and ends on a note of aesthetic self-congratulation. It is a programmatic poem, projecting a 'scheme'. Kavanagh is identifying a new orthodoxy, what 'The important thing is'; he is more concerned with 'ought' than 'Is'. Ordinary things are valued not in and for themselves but as images, items in a newly discovered poetic cornucopia, the stuff of which a plotless epic may be made.

Short-lined couplets, catalogues, plain speaking, an easy, informal manner, combine to make the poem appear improvised, structurally unorganised and stylistically slapdash, thus distracting attention from its highly patterned interweaving of rhyme, assonance and alliteration, and above all from its dogmatism.

'To Hell with Commonsense', first published along with 'Is', was one of Kavanagh's own favourites, because it caught his new buoyant mood as well as promulgating his new carefree stance. The vigorous colloquial title and irreverent opening couplets get the poem off to an ebullient start:

> More kicks than pence
> We get from commonsense
> Above its door is writ
> All hope abandon. It
> Is a bank will refuse a post
> Dated cheque of the Holy Ghost.

As a dogmatist Kavanagh thrives on subversion, seeking a status quo to overthrow. Didacticism is here thinly disguised as anti-establishment rebelliousness. By associating 'commonsense' with distrust of the Holy Ghost and with Dante's *Inferno* the poet places his own cult of the casual on the side of the angels. Kavanagh here champions 'unpremeditated art' — 'nothing thought out'; intuition and inspiration are substituted for education and cerebration. His ideal poem is weightless, airborne, a mystical 'flight in the light', apparently innocent of artistry. Again his practice does not measure up to his preaching. 'To Hell with Commonsense' is the product of a 'concerned' writer imparting secular wisdom. Doggerel vehemence, an impudent stance, the play of rhyme against enjambment ('a post/Dated cheque of the Holy Ghost'), disrespectful diction ('to hell with', 'the final Wake Up'), do succeed in creating an effect of feckless exuberance. The celestial/infernal dichotomy so often earnestly resorted to in the satires is now carried off with an air of zestful insouciance. Nevertheless, the poem comes uncomfortably close to the poet's satiric terrain; its promotion of a casual creed is too dependent on the demotion of other writers.

The objective aesthetic, implicit in 'The Hospital' and 'Is', is explicitly endorsed in 'The Self-slaved',[46] where the self is portrayed as 'sticky', clinging, an impediment to liberation and aspiration:

> To love and adventure,
> To go on the grand tour

> A man must be free
> From self-necessity

This represents a complete reversal of the aesthetic of self-projection which Kavanagh had cultivated from the mid-1940s. The 'me' is here merely 'sufficient for the day', not for the future or the eternal. In this matter Kavanagh's poetry again refused to obey his poetics; the self proved almost impossible to dislodge. One of the most egregiously self-righteous of his poems, 'Dear Folks', dates from the late 1950s:[47] an epistolary sonnet informing his Irish readers that Gulliver has made a come-back to town, is still fighting fit, and intends 'to walk Parnassus into the sunset', like some contemporary matinee idol. Anger and satire, indulged in 'Dear Folks', are repudiated in 'The Self-slaved'. Yet, despite all its advocacy of self-transcendence, it is rhetorically self-absorbed, and includes a series of self-exhortations to self-lessness. Where George Herbert's 'Discipline' is addressed to God—

> Throw away thy rod
> Throw away thy wrath:
> O my God,
> Take the gentle path . . .

—Kavanagh's parody of these lines apostrophises the self:

> Throw away thy sloth
> Self, carry off my wrath . . .

'Wings' and Prometheanism are high Romantic images of transcendence and in spite of its concern to shed identity and abjure confessionalism ('No self, no self-exposure') 'The Self-slaved' is a poem in the confessional mode.

'The Self-slaved', like 'The Hospital' and 'Is', is powered by a new energy and confidence, the sense of having discovered an *'inexhaustible'* poetic resource. 'Song at Fifty'[48] is genially triumphalist, a song of gratitude for unexpected, and undeserved, good fortune. Jauntily and ostentatiously self-confident, it reverses the personal and poetic situation of 'Auditors

In'. The poet's credit-rating has improved remarkably since that earlier stock-taking. He has finally made good and revels in an atmosphere of approbation. Instead of lamenting his impecunious bachelorhood, as in 'Auditors In', he brags about his amorous triumphs as a surrogate husband, much sought-after by 'other fellows' wives'. Irony is almost absent from this show of bravado, and past improvidence serves only to highlight present achievement. Success is evaluated in monetary metaphors. In this rags to riches autobiography the poet portrays himself as an 'unthrifty' idler, 'arsing' about for years and finding to his astonishment that his 'undisciplined' and 'spendthrift' ways have yielded substantial dividends:

> A bankbook writ in verse
> And borrowers of purity
> Offering substantial security.
> To him who just strayed
> Through a lifetime without a trade,
> Him, him the ne'er —
> Do-well a millionaire.

The poem celebrates the rewards of 'not caring'. Kavanagh's cult of casualness also manifests itself in his choice of short-lined doggerel couplets; colloquialisms like 'part and parcel of' and 'arsing'; half-rhymes and near rhymes with their air of having been tossed off rather than 'thought-out': void/child, of/love, gold/world, up/clap, person/arsing. The final rhyme — '. . . ne'er/Do-well a millionaire' — appropriately caps a negative with a resounding positive, while cheekily splitting a colloquialism to bring the poem to an apparently improvisatory and amateurish conclusion.

Kavanagh had spent six months in America in 1956 and journeying or globetrotting are the images he most frequently uses to indicate energy, ebullience and optimism in his later fifties' verse: 'inexhaustible adventure', 'the grand tour', 'to walk Parnassus'. In 'Song at Fifty' the 'Crooked Knight' is transformed into a combination of fairy-tale romance hero and modern international celebrity:

So I take my cloak of gold
And I stride across the world
A knight of chivalry
Seeking some devilry
The winter trees rise up
And wave me on, a clap
Of falling rock declares
Enthusiasm; flares
Announce a reception committee
For me entering a city.

Such a fantastic ego trip is the subject of the title poem of
the 1960 collection, 'Come Dance with Kitty Stobling',[49] a
sonnet celebrating the poet's self-delighting ludic energy, *élan*
and comic verve. It begins with a vehement abrogation of the
heroic role, a triply reiterated negative reinforced by the
homonym, 'know':

No, no, no, I know I was not important as I moved
Through the colourful country, I was but a single
Item in the picture, the namer not the beloved.

As in other contemporary poems, the role of namer focuses
poetic attention on the external world rather than on the self,
but here an abrupt shift of stance at the beginning of the second quatrain creates an impression of personal volatility. By
line 5 the poet has found an antidote to mundane tedium, a hil-
arious alternative to his sober, self-effacing, country excursion:

Once upon a time
I had a myth that was a lie but it served:
Trees walking across the crests of hills and my rhyme
Cavorting on mile-high stilts and the unnerved
Crowds looking up with terror in their rational faces.
O dance with Kitty Stobling I outrageously
Cried out-of-sense to them, while their timorous paces
Stumbled behind Jove's page boy paging me.

The phrase, 'Once upon a time' is an appropriate introduction to this fantasy world. The circus artiste, stunts-person,

public performer, who disports himself here, has much in common with the self-images projected in the Dublin poems of the earlier 1950s. What is now emphasised is the zany audacity of his performance, the abandonment of common sense in favour of comic absurdity, the combination of high jinks and high risk adventure. Nevertheless, this new myth of superiority recalls Kavanagh's satiric representation of Dublin as Lilliput. ('Once upon a time' points to an awareness of such regressiveness.) Exaggeratedly long stilts become a measure of the distance between the carefree strides of the exalted poet and the faltering pace of his followers. His cavorting muse is flaunted as an image of 'unsolemn' hauteur, the poet towering above the inferior throng, a spectacle terrifying to the rational and respectable. Once again, as in 'Intimate Parnassus', he is commingling with the gods. In his antic or self-inflationary moods the poet tends to consort with pagan deities; in his more quietist or 'outgiving' verse he invokes the Christian God. Here 'paging' is a pun that associates readership with servitude, furnishing the arrogant, daring Olympian with a timid retinue. In the concluding couplet the high-spirited poet-persona finally comes down to earth only to fling a last taunt at his prosaic followers as he dismounts:

> I had a very pleasant journey, thank you sincerely
> For giving me my madness back, or nearly.

The original title, 'High Journey', possibly alluded to Yeats's 'High Talk', where Malachi Stilt-Jack stalking on 'timber-toes' is a figure of the poet. Indeed the sonnet is full of Yeatsian overtones. The phrase, 'Come dance', echoes Yeats, and the Yeatsian association of poetry with dance is quite unusual for Kavanagh, who had previously used the dance as an image of a common revelry from which his poetic uncommonness excluded him. A 'myth that was a lie but served' reminds one of those 'metaphors for poetry' that Yeats derived from his wife's automatic writing. Kavanagh normally prided himself on avoiding Yeatsian masks and his creation of the Kitty Stobling figure is a new departure in his verse. Experimentation with imparting a mood of gaiety seems to have drawn him temporarily closer to the poetic universe of late Yeats. Kitty Stobling is the expressive poet's Crazy Jane, representative of the 'outrageous' and the 'out of sense': the muse as a manic, lunatic Terpsichore. However, bawdiness plays no part in this poetic fantasy; Kavanagh is more interested in literary stances than in sexual positions. Body is customarily sacrificed to pleasure soul in his verse.

'Come Dance with Kitty Stobling' concluded a sequence of poems and prose passages in *Nonplus*,[50] introduced by the quatrain poem, 'Freedom'. In 'Freedom' the poet wished to station himself on an Olympian pedestal:

> Take me to the top of the high hill
> Mount Olympus laughter-roaring unsolemn
> Where no one is angry and satirical
> About a mortal creature on a tall column.

Stilts provide a more mobile and momentary public platform, altogether better adapted to his new comic muse. Another poem in the *Nonplus* sequence, 'Love in a Meadow', suggests that the future poet was from birth an Olympian or Parnassian, aloof, 'born on high ground':

> O the river flowed round and round
> The low meadows filled with buttercups
> In a place called Toprass.
> I was born on high ground.

Kavanagh customarily represented his relationship with his home country in sexual or filial terms. Here the river's encircling embrace of the lush, low-lying land suggests rural voluptuousness, yet the natal reference also invests the scene with maternal connotations. The local place-name, Toprass, has been chosen because it reinforces the image of eminence.

Reading 'Come Dance with Kitty Stobling' in the *Nonplus* sequence[51] adds a dimension of meta-commentary to the clause, 'as I moved/Through the colourful country', since the sequence included three sonnets, numbered 1, 2 and 3, instead of being titled, and referred to, as 'three coloured sonnets'. They were published as 'Yellow Vestment', 'Miss Universe' and 'The One' in both *Recent Poems* (1958) and *Come Dance with Kitty Stobling* (1960). Colour is obtrusive in the first and third of these sonnets; 'Miss Universe' is a colour piece only in a journalistic sense.

Like 'Come Dance with Kitty Stobling', 'Yellow Vestment' draws on journey imagery and on fantastic invention. What is invented here is a 'Superintendent', a combination of tour guide and overseer, who takes charge of the poet's creative itinerary. The effectiveness of such control is suspect. 'Yellow Vestment' marks a return to the defensiveness of Kavanagh's early fifties' verse. Its poet-priest persona hovers uneasily between pastoralism and sacerdotal arrogance, widening 'the field of the faithful's activity' with folk song and roundelay, or making pronouncements from the pulpit. As in so many of his hortatory poems his addressee appears to be the self, here struggling to suppress hate, resentment and susceptibility to public-house criticism. The sonnet reads like a morale-boosting auto-exhortation. Apart from the pun on 'grace' in the concluding line:

> And wear with grace the power-invoking habit

it lacks linguistic liveliness. While the text of 'Yellow Vestment' insists on poetic autonomy, the subtext exposes a remarkable dependence on popular esteem scarcely concealed beneath all the vestment trailing. Not merely 'happiness', but 'existence' itself, appears to derive from public opinion, as if the sonneteer, like his Superintendent, were himself a fiction. The other two 'coloured sonnets' jettison the Superintendent and proclaim the discovery of a nature-loving God. Both are country-based poems, set out of doors and out of earshot of the poet's detractors.

'Miss Universe' focuses on the belatedness of the poet's discovery of a caring God. God is represented as earth's lover, continually at her side, fondling her. He is patient and

presevering in his affection, never recriminatory. This is a
God who enables the poet to overlook past mistakes and
surrender himself to a present joy. The elation of such a
discovery is conveyed through triple repetition, a technique
to which Kavanagh often has recourse in these sonnets:

> I learned, I learned—when one might be inclined
> To think, too late, you cannot recover your
>   losses—
> I learned something of the nature of God's mind,
> Not the abstract Creator but He who caresses
> The daily and nightly earth; He who refuses
> To take failure for an answer till again and again is
>   worn.
> Love is waiting for you, waiting for the violence
>   that she chooses
> From the tepidity of the common round beyond
>   exhaustion or scorn.
> What was once is still and there is no need for
>   remorse;
> There are no recriminations in Heaven.

While God's love is portrayed as a gentle sustaining
relationship; the poet's attraction to earth is described, con-
trariwise, as a sudden onset of violent lust. Newly reinvigor-
ated after the 'scorn' of his satiric phase and the 'exhaustion'
of his recent illness, the sonneteer thrusts his sexuality into
the middle of a line, pushing 'Heaven' to one side and
interrupting pious reassurances. This is no 'abstract creator',
but a lecherous artist roused by the physical proximity and
aesthetic unattainability of country beauty. The sudden lunge
into eroticism dramatises love's 'violence':

> O the sensual throb
> Of the explosive body, the tumultuous thighs!
> Adown a summer lane comes Miss Universe
> She whom no lecher's art can rob
> Though she is not the virgin who was wise.

The personification of a country lane as a sex symbol works well and the present tense communicates the thrill of her presence, though the last line with its biblical knowingness is post-climactic. Kavanagh had often projected his relationship with the country in sexual terms, but the image of the Beauty Queen here gives an up-to-dateness and an ironic edge to his nature poetry.

The third coloured sonnet, 'The One', starts flamboyantly with four daubs of primary colour and three musical stresses, and the remainder of the quatrain maintains the momentum:

> Green, blue, yellow and red—
> God is down in the swamps and marshes
> Sensational as April and almost incred-
> ible the flowering of our catharsis.

The abrupt introduction of God at the beginning of the second line is a deliberate shock-tactic and the newsworthiness of the occasion is seized upon in the journalese, 'sensational'. 'Incred/ible', straddling two lines for the sake of rhyme, is one of Kavanagh's new outrageous effects, a cheeky gesture to sonnet convention. His God is once again brought 'down' to earth, situated on a wasteland, a disused bog. He is 'the gay, imaginative God who made the grass and the trees and the flowers'. ('A Goat Tethered Outside the Bailey', (1953)) The psychic 'flowering' experienced by the sonneteer is an aesthetic response to divine creativity. It is a burgeoning that follows on tragic purgation, tragedy developing into comic joy. That the euphoria described in this sonnet follows on a troubled period in the poet's personal life is hinted at, not spelt out as in 'Miss Universe'. Neither is the connection between privation and psycho-religious florescence explored as in the double sonnet, 'Advent'. Instead, pain is transposed to the dramatic plane of 'catharsis'.

Juxtaposition of the divine and the ordinary is perhaps over-laboured in the second quatrain:

> A humble scene in a backward place
> Where no one important ever looked

The raving flowers looked up in the face
Of the One and the Endless, the Mind that has
   baulked
The profoundest of mortals.

Subversion of customary notions of importance is such a recurring preoccupation that the sonnet momentarily lapses
into a preachy insistence. Naming restores its *élan*:

A primrose, a violet,
A violent wild iris—but mostly anonymous
   performers
Yet an important occasion as the Muse at her toilet
Prepared to inform the local farmers
That beautiful, beautiful, beautiful God
Was breathing His love by a cut-away bog.

'Violet' is a pivotal word, recalling the prismatic colours of the
opening line and preparing for the shift of emotional register
towards sensations of danger and craziness in 'violent'. The
wildness of the 'wild iris' and of wild flowers in general is
given zany, delirious connotations in this poem where bog
flowers are described as 'raving'. Naming is abandoned and
the dramatic metaphor resumed in 'anonymous performers'.
As in the first quatrain the dramatic spectacle provokes a
creative response. The divine breath that vitalises and sustains the world also inspires the poet. That Kavanagh should
have considered 'what happens in his own fields' to be 'stuff
for the Muses' is not new. What is novel is that he should be
prepared to bear witness to common-sense 'local farmers' of
the miracle in their midst. 'Beauty, who has described
beauty?', the poet questions in 'Come Dance with Kitty
Stobling'. Here, the beauty of God is manifest in his creation
of a beautiful world; the triple repetition of 'beautiful' is
emphatically exultant. God and 'cut-away bog' are permanently related in the rhyme of the concluding couplet. The
'One' is the exemplary casual God of Kavanagh's late poetics,
a divine poet, lavishing his love on the insignificant and the
commonplace.

§

Pride of place in *Come Dance with Kitty Stobling* is given to Kavanagh's two Canal sonnets, which are brought together on the opening page. 'Canal Bank Walk',[52] despite its urban setting, abounds in rural images: trees and grass, breeze and bird. The hyphenated opening phrase, 'Leafy-with-love', establishes the mood of the poem, passionate, profuse, generous. God's will is not that the poet repent his misspent years, but that he 'wallow', luxuriate, in the beauty of the world. So he gratefully abandons himself to present-tense delights and future hopes. Instead of looking back with nostalgia to his lost youth, he relives it in the here and now:

> Leafy-with-love banks and the green waters of the
> canal
> Pouring redemption for me, that I do
> The will of God, wallow in the habitual, the banal,
> Grow with nature again as before I grew.
> The bright stick trapped, the breeze adding a third
> Party to the couple kissing on an old seat,
> And a bird gathering materials for the nest for the
> Word
> Eloquently new and abandoned to its delirious beat.

Once again, as in 'Advent', 'life pours ordinary plenty'. The baptismal water of spiritual redemption is now as unstinted and accessible as canal water. To 'grow . . . again' is as easy and effortless as nature's seasonal renewal. His surroundings furnish the poet with images of his own condition: a twig, immobilised and helpless, but radiant; a couple, also stationary, but demonstrating love, accompanied by a comically intrusive, yet Romantic, breeze; a religio-Romantic bird, picking up the 'bits and pieces of Everyday' which will house a new *Logos*. Romantic expressive images gradually become more overt until the point where the bird becomes an objective correlative for the divinely inspired poet. This image suddenly takes off into the realms of poetic creativity, into language and rhythm. The line

> Eloquently new and abandoned to its delirious
> beat . . .

conjures up a poetry as fluent as canal water, as new as the spring season, as passive as the wallowing poet, as rhythmically rhapsodic as is demanded by the wonder of being alive and in love with a wonderful world.

The sestet is a hymn, not to the Christian God, but to his world:

> O unworn world enrapture me, encapture me in a web
> Of fabulous grass and eternal voices by a beech,
> Feed the gaping need of my senses, give me ad lib
> To pray unselfconsciously with overflowing speech
> For this soul needs to be honoured with a new dress
> woven
> From green and blue things and arguments that cannot
> be proven.

This sonnet is never orthodoxly Christian. It finds its religion out of doors, not in church or bible or creed. It divinises or sacramentalises the natural, turning the earth into an Eden where eternal voices are heard among the trees. It is a 'coloured sonnet', in which the poet wants to forego logic and rationality, not to achieve spiritual union with God, but to weave a worldly garment for the soul out of things sensual and natural, the greenness of beech leaves, grass and canal waters, the blue of the sky.

The sestet is an impassioned prayer for poetic inspiration. Emotional pressure is accelerated by the series of imperatives, and by the urgency of the internal rhymes, 'enrapture me, encapture me', 'feed the ... need'. 'Enrapture me' expressing a longing for ecstasy, is followed immediately by and associated with a desire to be encaptured, caught fast in a 'web', unable to escape, 'trapped' like the bright stick. There is a terrible self-distrust here, a fear of backsliding, of loss. For all its emotional urgency this sestet is a confession of personal inadequacy and deprivation, a prolonged, importunate cry for help. The word 'need' is repeated and this need is described as 'gaping', and further stressed by the rhyme with feed. It is as if the born-again poet seeks to be nurtured like a baby. Ultimately what he desires is to abandon himself to another will, an external power, to become a medium through which words flow freely, liberally, spontaneously, without strain or exertion or contrivance on his part. 'Not caring' here seems to lead not only to an abrogation of responsibility but to a complete surrender of self for the sake of poetry, a baptism by total immersion.

'Canal Bank Walk', though conversational, is carried forward by a powerful lyrical impulse. Its lines are lengthy, running to fourteen and fifteen syllables, very luxuriant for English poetry. The sense of fluidity and unstinted plenty, conjured up in words like 'pouring' and 'overflowing', is reproduced by the continuous flow of enjambment, lyrical statement spilling over from one line into the next, unchecked by the rhyme. Assonance also submerges the boundaries of line and rhyme, maintaining a spate of similar sound effects throughout the poem.

Its companion piece offers a complete contrast in pace and mood to 'Canal Bank Walk'. 'Lines Written On a Seat On the Grand Canal, Dublin'[53] is poised, assured, serene, as befits its monumental status. Where the first Canal sonnet pulsates with reburgeoning life, the second is an 'In Memoriam'. Consciousness of impending death lends a poignancy to Kavanagh's celebration of the living scene. The title is itself a memorial inscription, 'Lines Written On'. Moreover, it includes the tomb-like legend inscribed on the particular seat which inspired the poem, '"*Erected to the Memory of Mrs. Dermot O'Brien*".' The reiterated phrase, 'O commemorate me', frames the sonnet like a black mourning border and the image of the tomb is given a dominant position at the beginning of the concluding line.

Though 'full of repose' this sonnet is rich with life, 'stilly' and 'greeny' simultaneously. At the heart of the busy city the poet has discovered a quiet oasis on the banks of the Grand Canal. Here, where Dublin is at its most rural, the latter-day Romantic has islanded himself, discovered a bower as sensuous as any of Keats's, and withdrawn into contemplation:

> O commemorate me where there is water,
> Canal water preferably, so stilly
> Greeny at the heart of summer. Brother
> Commemorate me thus beautifully.
> Where by a lock niagarously roars
> The falls for those who sit in the tremendous silence
> Of mid-July. No one will speak in prose
> Who finds his way to these Parnassian islands.

Parnassus is now located in Dublin; urban canal water is 'preferred' to the rural 'river or the stream' for the muse's fount. An effect of intense localisation is created by the same comic parochial distortions of perspective as in 'Shancoduff' and 'Art McCooey'. So the canal waterfall 'niagarously roars' and Athy in the neighbouring county appears a 'far-flung' town:

> A swan goes by head low with many apologies,
> Fantastic light looks through the eyes of bridges—
> And look! a barge comes bringing from Athy
> And other far-flung towns mythologies.

Kavanagh has recovered, too, the 'spirit-shocking wonder' and transfiguring vision of his early forties' verse. Once again the ordinary is illuminated by 'fantastic light'. Canal bridges are anthropomorphised and a prosaic bargeload is transformed into a cargo of mythologies. Perhaps a playful allusion to Yeats may be detected in the collocation of humdrum mythologies and apologetic swan.

This poem's rite of self-immortalisation is curiously self-effacing. The introverted poet of the early 1950s is now determinedly extroverted, focusing on the external setting, not on his inner creative processes. For once the scene is more important than the figure in the scene and the 'I' is subsumed in the eye. Repetition of the verb 'look' which at first seems a blemish is really due to an anxiety of emphasis on the visual. Where the satiric and self-righteous Kavanagh was much given to constructing 'hero-courageous' monuments of his own magnificence, pedestalling himself or locating himself on Olympian heights, here he chooses an unegotistical tomb, a monument to his poetics rather than to his person:

> O commemorate me with no hero-courageous
> Tomb—just a canal-bank seat for the passer-by.

Future visitors are asked to sit with their backs turned to the memorial inscription, reading instead the scene before them. So the humble seat becomes an embodiment of a poetics which advocates 'watching', repose and contemplation. While the sonnet takes the form of an address, audience-consciousness does not, on this occasion, tempt the poet into didacticism and his doctrine remains implicit in his choice of tomb.

The Canal seat is also a monument to Kavanagh's posthumous influence on Irish poets:

> . . . No one will speak in prose
> Who finds his way to these Parnassian islands.

What Kavanagh bequeaths to Irish poets is an enabling legacy. His memorial sonnet offers a striking thematic contrast with Yeats's epitaph and magisterial advice to future Irish poets in 'Under Ben Bulben'. Where Yeats counsels the traveller to 'Cast a cold eye' and to 'pass by', Kavanagh, in the traditional manner of the memorial poet, endeavours to halt the passer-by and persuade him to contemplate the scene. Whereas Yeats proposes an Irish poetry that is craft-conscious and peopled with the dramatis personae from Irish history, Kavanagh typically eschews craftsmanship and history alike. His Canal school of poetry will focus on the fantastic beauty of an ordinary, unpopulated and unglamorous urban scene.

This sonnet is one of the poet's most controlled performances, and he has chosen to punctuate it musically, with pauses marking the rhythmic units of the quatrains and concluding couplet, even in defiance of the rules of syntax. He presents himself as one attuned to the harmonies of sound and silence, activity and contemplation. Those 'y' endings which proliferate at the beginning bring a swish of movement to a static waterscape. Commemoration dominates the poem through repetition of the verb and of words assonating with it: 'where there', 'preferably', 'where', 'niagarously', 'tremendous'. Assonance and internal rhyme recur throughout, unifying the poem musically. Kavanagh himself drew attention to his rhyming of 'bridges' with 'courageous' as indicative of his new nonchalant kind of poem. He might also have instanced the comic rhyming of 'roars' with 'prose'. Though he was greatly enamoured of obtrusive doggerel rhymes from the late 1950s, here his rhymes tend to be unobtrusive and he favours half-rhymes to avoid a full chime in 'water'/'brother', 'stilly'/'beautifully', as well as in 'bridges'/'courageous'.

Like the Canal sonnets, 'October'[54] has a *rus-in-urbe* setting, an 'arboreal street on the edge of a town'. Where the Canal sonnets sing of spring and summer, 'October' presents an autumnal epiphany. 'Leafy yellowness', which suggests the 'sere and yellow leaf' of life, offers instead an insight into eternity, the 'immortality' in things mortal. 'October' is a hymn of gratitude to a world where epiphany is still possible. Its middle-aged urban poet relives an experience from his country youth, his nineteen-year-old self's heartbreak at transitoriness and his proleptic sensation of the burden of old age:

> O leafy yellowness you create for me
> A world that was and now is poised above time,
> I do not need to puzzle out Eternity
> As I walk this arboreal street on the edge of a
>   town.
> The breeze, too, even the temperature
> And pattern of movement is precisely the same

As broke my heart for youth passing. Now I am
  sure
Of something. Something will be mine wherever I
  am.
I want to throw myself on the public street with-
  out caring
For anything but the prayering that the earth
  offers.
It is October over all my life and the light is
  staring
As it caught me once in a plantation by the fox
  coverts.
A man is ploughing ground for winter wheat
And my nineteen years weigh heavily on my feet.

This sonnet's focus is narrow and intense. The uncanny resemblance of arboreal street and country plantation becomes a visual and sensual correlative of the conflation of present and past. Such similarity of atmosphere, rhythm and scenic properties, lends psychological credibility to the epiphany of recurrence: 'It is October over all my life . . .'. Here the poet comes upon the atemporal poise he had been searching for since 'Auditors In' in a public street, a heaven that is under all our noses. The octet concludes on a note of joyful affirmation; the reiteration of 'something' increases the air of confidence.

This poem is completely devoid of audience-consciousness. The sonneteer who wants to prostrate himself on the street is not a histrionic exhibitionist, but one who acts spontaneously and instinctively, who utterly disregards public opinion. The relationship between 'without caring' and 'prayering' establishes the poet's affiliation with the worshipful earth and the lilt of the feminine rhyme conveys a mood of elation. Again Kavanagh discovers the religious through the natural, or finds corroboration of orthodox Christian teaching in his relationship with the world. Lighting plays a significant part in this poem as in the second Canal sonnet. Spiritual illumination is conferred by natural lighting; the staring light catches the poet in its radiance; he is 'caught', as he had prayed to be in 'Canal Bank Walk'. In the concluding couplet the present dissolves into the past; streetscape is metamorphosed into landscape. However, a reversal of the expected moods associated with youth and age counterpoints epiphany with gentle irony, giving an unobtrusive comic robustness to lyric grace.

In 'October' Kavanagh is utterly absorbed in the articulation of a private revelation to the exclusion of didacticism, dogmatism and rabble-baiting. 'Not caring' is here neither a defensive nor a defiant stance, but an expression of release from temporalities into a metaphysical dimension. Through time, time is conquered. The street is now consecrated ground like the earth of pre-*Great Hunger* poetry. That retrieval of youthful innocence in old age, a theme song in Kavanagh's post-operative poetics, is here played out without fuss or bravado. Though the image of 'winter wheat' suggests a belated crop of poetry, such poetic reflexiveness operates unobtrusively, almost subterraneanly, and the mood of rapture derives from an assurance of self-renewal and personal continuity in face of the implicit threat of death. 'Something will be mine wherever I am' indicates a larger frame of reference than Dublin and Inniskeen. Present-tense narration gives an appropriate air of spontaneity to the poet's rapture and it is peculiarly fitting in this sonnet, which, while it ranges over past, present and future, focuses on an experience of simultaneity. In 'October' Kavanagh succeeds in snatching out of time the passionate transitory.

'Question to Life'[55] is the least colourful and exuberant of Kavanagh's late fifties' sonnets. It is a peculiarly honest poem, the most disabusedly human of these lyrics. Rapture is deferred until the concluding couplet and, in the meantime, the sonneteer reflects with good-humoured sobriety on his less than idyllic life. His attitude to nature is cooler here. It is merely a backdrop to the human drama; left to itself, it only emphasises the human heroine's absence:

> Surely you would not ask me to have known
> Only the passion of primrose banks in May
> Which are merely a point of departure for the play
> And yearning poignancy when on their own.

Like so many of Kavanagh's apostrophes, the address to 'Life', though it begins with a conversational rebuttal, develops into a dialogue of self with self. Where other contemporary lyrics are rhapsodic, the mood here is self-consolatory, cheerfully determined to make the most of the second best that is all 'Life' has offered:

> Yet when all is said and done a considerable
> Portion of living is found in inanimate
> Nature, and a man need not feel miserable
> If fate should have decided on this plan of it.
> Then there is always the passing gift of affection
> Tossed from the windows of high charity
> In the office girl and civil servant section
> And these are no despisable commodity.

In this wry appraisal of emotional limitations, the sonneteer substitutes 'passing affection' for grand passion. Unlike his courtly love predecessors he does not serenade his high-placed lady. His status is rather that of a humble beggar who must make do with whatever casual scraps of kindness his women acquaintances can spare. The 'cloak of gold', the 'yellow vestment', the stilts, all the masks of bravado, are laid aside in this refreshingly frank poem. Its final joyful affirmation arises out of a calm, mature acceptance, instead of a questioning of life:

> So be reposed and praise, praise praise
> The way it happened and the way it is.

Contentment with an imperfect world transforms it into the 'positive world' in which celebratory poetry flourishes.

Despite his vehement denunciation of Dublin's artistic pretensions and his championship of London as a literary capital, Kavanagh's new poetry since *A Soul for Sale* (1947), with the notable exception of 'The Paddiad', had appeared in Irish periodicals and newspapers. He had no reputation outside Ireland and was more feared than honoured in his own country. In November 1955 he sent a third collection of his poems to Macmillan but they decided not to publish them,[56] thus finally severing all connection with the poet they had so often supported or subsidised for the previous twenty years.

Just when Kavanagh's literary fortunes seemed at their lowest ebb the tide began to turn in his favour. Not only did he succeed in having a selection of his poems accepted by the English literary quarterly, *Nimbus*, in March 1956, but the editor, David Wright pronounced himself 'incoherent with enthusiasm' about this verse.[57] Such praise from the co-editor of the Faber *Book of Twentieth Century Verse*, especially following so soon after Macmillan's rejection, was particularly gratifying. Wright brought out what effectively amounted to a mini-collection of Kavanagh's poems in the winter 1956 number of *Nimbus*. The nineteen poems he published included most of the best of his previously uncollected work: 'Intimate Parnassus', 'Auditors In', 'Prelude', 'On Looking into E. V. Rieu's Homer', 'Kerr's Ass', 'Shancoduff', 'Epic', 'I had a Future', 'God in Woman', 'In Memory of My Mother', 'Ante-Natal Dream'. *Nimbus* also collected some of the better and shorter satires, such as 'Who Killed James Joyce?' and 'Irish Stew', but excluded 'The Paddiad'. The concluding poem in the *Nimbus* collection was, significantly, 'The Hospital', the sonnet which ushered in the last great creative phase of Kavanagh's career and revealed that this renaissance had originated in illness and the euphoria of convalescence.

The short spate of poems which followed on his return to health and creativity were warmly welcomed by English journals. *Time and Tide* took the sonnets, 'Leaves of Grass' and 'Question to Life'. *The Times Literary Supplement* was 'delighted to print' 'Song at Fifty';[58] Stephen Spender at *Encounter* was particularly enthusiastic[59] and published 'October', 'Canal Bank Walk', 'Is', 'To Hell with Common-sense' and 'High Journey' ('Come Dance with Kitty Stobling'). Yet Kavanagh's new creed of 'not caring' seems to have extended to not bothering about placing his 'noo pomes' in prestigious journals. Two of the finest sonnets of the later 1950s, 'Miss Universe' and 'The One' together with 'Yellow Vestment', 'Winter', 'Love in a Meadow' and 'Freedom', appeared in the new Irish journal, *Nonplus*, edited by a friend, Patricia Murphy. His second Canal sonnet was dropped casually into an essay in the Irish Jesuit monthly, *Studies*, which also published 'Birth' and 'Requiem for a Mill'. Having just turned down the opportunity for a de luxe edition of his poems in England in 1958,[60] Kavanagh gave his blessing to the printing of a limited edition of twenty of his best uncollected poems on his brother Peter's newly acquired hand press. It was almost as if he were emulating Cézanne whom he had praised for tossing paintings into the bushes once he had finished with them.[61]

Peter Kavanagh's edition, entitled *Recent Poems*, was limited to fifty copies, twenty-five under the Peter Kavanagh hand press imprint.[62] His brother was a novice printer, but the fact that his handsetting led to mistakes, at first pleased Kavanagh rather than the reverse. 'Indeed the more mistakes —or nearly—the better', he wrote; such an impression of carelessness suited poems 'written in the spirit of "it doesn't matter"'.[63] Later, when he saw how printing errors could alter his meaning ('arising' substituted for 'arsing'); miss the contemporaneity of his language ('pre-cooken' for 'pre-cooked'); or spoil the spatial design of a sonnet, by printing one line as two in 'October'; he became agitated, and an errata slip had to be included in the volume to placate him.[64]

In England both Faber and Andre Deutsch proved uninterested in publishing Kavanagh's verse and, in Ireland, the recently founded Dolmen Press passed up the opportunity. By 1959, however, he was negotiating a commercial edition of his uncollected poems with Longmans, Green and Co. Ltd of London. There were to be thirty-five poems in all, including the twenty which had just appeared in *Recent Poems*, in fact all his new published poems with the exception of 'Birth' and 'Leaves of Grass'. Three satires, 'The Hero', 'House Party' and 'The Paddiad', were also collected and three early poems, unaccountably omitted from *A Soul for Sale*, 'To the Man after the Harrow', 'Peace' and 'Shancoduff'. This time Kavanagh's preoccupation with conveying an air of casualness was confined to the title. He actively involved himself in the selection process and was anxious that the three early poems should be dated, to distance them from more recent pieces. The publishers would like to have named the book after Shancoduff, but in spite of his promotion of this early poem, Kavanagh thought it unrepresentative of his recent work and vetoed it as a title. Instead he pressed for something inconsequential and more in keeping with his new poetics, such as *Dear Folks, Just a few lines*, or the title finally agreed, *Come Dance with Kitty Stobling*.[65]

Come Dance with Kitty Stobling was greeted with critical acclaim when it appeared in May 1960. It was the summer choice of the Poetry Book Society and was widely and enthusiastically reviewed in the major English as well as Irish journals. Alvarez's notice in *The Observer* would have been particularly heartening to Kavanagh on two counts. Firstly, because Alvarez compared his work advantageously with Auden's:

> *Come Dance with Kitty Stobling* has what Auden's latest so sadly lacks: that concentration which transforms outer and inner worlds into a single, compelling and fresh poetic whole.

Secondly, because although he found the quality of his longer poetry uneven, Alvarez considered that in his sonnets, Kavanagh was 'the most controlled, original and least pretentious Irish poet since Yeats'.[66] Auden had been Kavanagh's supreme exemplar and Yeats his reluctantly admired antagonist since 1942. Both were poets with whom he would have been honoured to sup at journey's end.

11

Thus a Poet Dies

> Though it is mid-summer I've
> No wish to rhapsodise,
> Thus a poet dies.[1]

THE publication of *Come Dance with Kitty Stobling* in 1960 signalled the end of Kavanagh's post-Canal creative phase. The impetus to celebrate a brave new poetic world had proved transitory. In a 1964 interview he confessed that he had begun 'to disbelieve' in his Canal myth[2] and in 'Living in the Country: 11' (1963) he made light of this loss of vision:

> We have no game no more
> Some one stole our game
> And left us high and dry
> On a beliefless shore . . .

Kavanagh's sixties' poetry is neither epiphanic nor edifying. It is altogether less rhapsodic, less optimistic and less consolatory than his late fifties' verse. His poetic enterprise has altered; what he is writing now is a poetry of predicament. The 'I' who speaks in these late poems is a man with whom the gods have ceased to commingle. He is an anti-hero, a poet in the grip of the demon drink, whose literary powers are failing. The technique of casualness which Kavanagh had been cultivating since the late 1950s is peculiarly appropriate to these confessional verses, bringing a tone of comic ruefulness to their sorry tale of alcoholic indignity and poetic disability. The poetics of 'not caring', which enabled him to write about the ugly, the indecorous and the trivial, had not been fully exploited in *Come Dance with Kitty Stobling*, where he still tended to aestheticise and eulogise such unconventional poetic subjects as a hospital ward, a 'cutaway bog' and a canal bank. In his sixties' poetry the sordid, repulsive aspects of human experience are rarely transformed by love. 'The way it happened and the way it is' are not glamourised. These late poems are the least transcendental, the most secular, of all Kavanagh's verses. Their mode is comic realism; their scale is human.

The speaker in these sixties' poems is primarily a poet: Kavanagh is acting out the final chapter in his poetic autobiography, dramatising his own decline. A sense of aftermath clings about these verses. Their authority derives from past accomplishment. They address a loyal readership, who have known their poet in happier times and are willing to hear him out to the end, to indulge his foibles and failings for *auld lang syne*. The poet, for his part, endeavours to be an entertaining companion to the last, and to talk cheerfully about his problems and his pain. The gap between the prophet and transcendentalist he once was and the ailing, fallible figure he has now become is life's final joke, and he is determined to enjoy it. Like Beckett in *Waiting for Godot*, he puts 'despair and futility' on the page 'for us to laugh at'.[3] The ageing poet, who humorously compared himself to the anti-hero of *Krapp's Last Tape*,[4] relished the terminal ironies of *Endgame*:

> Beckett's garbage-can
> Contains all our man
> Who without fright on his face
> Dominates the place
> And makes all feel
> That all is well.
>> ('Mermaid Tavern')

Gaiety transfigures all the dread in Kavanagh's late poems.

'News Item',[5] an oblique love poem to his future wife, Katherine Barry Maloney, in the guise of a poem of place, is the most ecstatic of Kavanagh's sixties' verses:

> I have taken roots of love
> And will find it pain to move.
> Betjeman, you've missed much of
>
> The secrets of London while
> Old churches you beguile
> I'll show you a holier aisle—
>
> The length of Gibson Square
> Caught in November's stare,
> That would set you to prayer . . .

Gibson Square, where Katherine lived,[6] joins those other places made holy by the heart's affections: Shancoduff, Raglan Road, the fields of 'Threshing Morning', the Grand Canal. The poem is less emotionally charged than 'October' (I want to throw myself on the public street without caring/For anything but the prayering that the earth offers.'); its private rapture is mediated through conversational polemic. Rhyming triplets neutralise the sense of emotional engagement, as if the poet was partly in earnest, and partly parodying an earlier mode.

Most of Kavanagh's sixties' poems are set in London or Inniskeen and the Inniskeen poems are sometimes written with a wry consciousness of the poet's previous rural verse. His romanticisation of his native village in a series of poems, from 'Christmas Eve Remembered' to 'Innocence', is mocked by the adoption of a common-sense attitude and a flat, prosaic utterance:

> I have to live here in the country till I get a
>   flat . . .
> Living in the country is a hard old station . . .
>   (Living in the Country: 11')

'Literary Adventures' begins with the knowingly anti-Romantic line:

> I am here in a garage in Monaghan . . .

However, its reportage of ordinary country happenings as if these were journalistic scoops ('exclusive/News stories that cannot be ignored') comes close to Kavanagh's customary play with techniques of inflation/deflation when dealing with 'the common and banal'. 'That Garage'[7] returns to the site of this poem and pronounces the writer's earlier delight in the countryside too 'facilely romantic', too 'Georgian'. He now plans 'More difficult dominion'. Perhaps this 'difficult dominion' includes the Inniskeen revisited in the 'Living in the Country' sequence, a poetry that does not spare self, milieu or reader.

'Living in the Country: 1'[8] is a poem enmeshed in local ironies and self-ironies, the central irony being that the elderly poet has been granted the privilege he had so often craved in his Dublin poems, a return to Inniskeen. The poem opens with a stanza on Inniskeen in Kavanagh's early 1940s' lyrical vein; its gracelessly titled 'Main Body' offers a jaundiced, contemporary commentary on the trials of 'living' there as a sophisticated adult. For his idyllic evocation the poet regresses to the childhood perspective adopted in 'A Christmas Childhood' and 'The Long Garden':

> It was the Warm Summer, that landmark
> In a child's mind, an infinite day
> Sunlight and burnt grass
> Green grasshoppers on the railway slopes
> The humming of wild bees
> The whole summer during the school holidays
> Till the blackberries appeared.
> Yes, a tremendous time that summer stands
> Beyond the grey finities of normal weather.

Here Kavanagh shows that he can still depict the country with all his old sensuousness, still prolong a happy time to infinity. Not only in the 1940s, but throughout his career, even in his Canal sonnets, he had privileged this innocent, unsophisticated bucolicism, had believed that poetry involved an escape from suffering and complexity into some childhood Eden or adult heaven of continuous love and nurture. When he confessed to his pain and frustration in poems like 'Auditors In' and 'Prelude', his narratives conducted towards a happy ending, the troubled poet rescued and residing in a 'placeless heaven', or blissfully counting his earthly blessings. Only rarely, in such sonnets as 'An Insult',[9] did he accept that suffering is an inevitable part of living:

> ... there is no golden rule
> For keeping out of suffering—if one lives.

The late poems endeavour to admit the whole adult man into verse, not to compartmentalise the satirist and the celebrant, or seek to purify the grouchy, quirky, opportunistic facets of the self. So in 'Living in the Country: 1' the depiction of Inniskeen as a pastoral childhood paradise is rudely interrupted:

> It's not nearly as bad as you'd imagine
> Living among small farmers in the north of Ireland
> They are for the most part the ordinary frightened
> Blind brightened, referred to sometimes socially
> As the underprivileged.
> They cannot perceive Irony or even Satire
> They start up with insane faces if
> You break the newspaper moral code.
> 'Language' they screech 'you effing so and so'
> And you withdraw into a precarious silence
> Organising in your mind quickly, for the situation
>   is tense,
> The theological tenets of the press.

The tense has now shifted from the past of 'Opening' to the present; lyricism has yielded to matter-of-fact conversational tones, and the scene has moved indoors from an unpeopled landscape to a country public house. The speaker is the experienced, social self, the 'living' man adroitly adjusting to his uncomfortable situation, not the ecstatic, pre-pubertal Romantic figure in the scene. The 'underprivileged', whose cause Kavanagh had championed so eloquently in *The Great Hunger*, are now presented in a comic light, dishonouring the prophet who has returned to his own country. The country, which had served as a symbol of vitality and incorruptibility, in such urban satires as 'Adventures in the Bohemian Jungle', now subscribes to the 'theological tenets of the press', and, deaf to its own obscenities, denies the poet freedom of speech. His stint among Dublin's offensive artisans has proved a useful preparatory training for 'living in the country'.

The social comedy in this poem depends largely on the reader's recognition of the stature of the poet who is being baited, and also gains added resonance from a knowledge of the public house episode in *The Great Hunger*. Similarly, the concluding stanza of 'Living in the Country: 1' presupposes an acquaintance with Kavanagh's previous verse:

> In many ways it is a good thing to be cast into exile
> Among strangers
> Who have no inkling
> Of The Other Man concealed
> Monstrously musing in a field.
> For me they say a Rosary
> With many a glossary.

Much of the irony of this portrayal of the poet amid the alien corn of Inniskeen would be lost on a reader unaware of the fact that exile from his native place was a dominant theme in Kavanagh's verse throughout the 1940s and early 1950s. Nevertheless, even a reader unfamiliar with Kavanagh's previous poetry will notice the very different roles played by the 'early blackberries' in the 'Opening' and penultimate stanza of this poem. In the 'Opening' they form a pastoral border; in the penultimate stanza they are chosen as the setting for a seduction. The passage from innocence to experience which would have been foregrounded and lamented in earlier poetry is now merely alluded to with a knowing wink.

'Living in the Country: 11',[10] originally published as 'The Poet's Ready Reckoner', is a belated, more cussed and careless, rewriting of 'Auditors In'. It is self-absorbed, a mood piece that catches the writer's volatility, his tetchiness, his bouts of gloom, self-pity and self-induced cheerfulness, his attempts to rally his failing powers:

> I know what I must write if I can
> This is the beginning of my Five Year Plan
> Concerned am I with the activities of my own man.
>
> And a week ago I idled,
> That is to say I roared and cursed over the position
> Broke, I had a good excuse for not caring
> Arts Council croppers harvesting and sharing
> And my deserted village all ill-faring
> Activity on every front
> And nought for the poor bastard who bore the brunt
> Of the day's battle—blood and sweat and grunt . . .

Here 'private problem[s]' have become 'subject matter/For ironic analysis':[11] vernacular directness, rural metaphor, literary allusion, comic rhyming, ensure that personal 'disturbances' are represented with an air of amused detachment, a self-knowingness that is also self-mocking.

In 'Living in the Country: 1' the poet had reverted to another earlier preoccupation, the renunciation of satire in favour of 'humaneness'. In the second part of the poem, this theme is broached in an incomplete line, as if there is no need to reiterate his views, since readers are already familiar with his association of satire with sterility:

> Satire a desert that yields no—

What such ellipsis may indicate is the writer's impatience with his own repetitiveness:

Plainly the only thing it not to be a bore
To ourselves . . .

In 'Living in the Country: 11' Kavanagh suddenly veers
from a passage of condescending benevolence towards his
readers to savage disdain:

Come London-Irish to me your voided souls
Shall not be left unfilled . . .
                              Into me never entered
Care for you. I am self-centred
But bunch of bums
I throw you these bewitching crumbs . . .

These last lines which portray the poet at his most obnoxious,
are immediately succeeded by a mood-swing to lyrical beatitude:

In the disused railway siding
(O railway that came up from Enniskillen)
A new living is spreading
Dandelions that grow from wagon-grease
I stand on the platform
And peace, perfect peace
Descends on me.

In earlier poems, even in *Come Dance with Kitty Stobling*, such
lyrical rhapsodies occurred in isolation, were contained in
sonnets or short poems. Kavanagh had previously tended to
separate his rapturous, celebratory moods from the less
edifying aspects of his personality, his rages, his grudges, his
doubts and yearnings; or to enact a lyrical triumph over less
worthy emotions. The project now is to represent the whole
man, a problematic and often dislikable personality, cro-
chety, complex, self-ironic and self-contradictory, torn by
conflicting impulses. The unevenness, the randomness, the
apparent lack of organisation, the *longueurs* of the 'Living in
the Country' sequence are deliberate. The poet is no longer
concerned to appear a consistently exemplary, admirable or

sympathetic figure. In 'Living in the Country: 11', especially, the poetics of 'not caring' dispenses with such literary constructs as the well-made poem and the well-meaning poet. However, this verse, though self-tolerant, is not reader-friendly, and places an impossible strain on the goodwill of all but the writer's most ardent disciples.

In the poems that treat of his alcoholism, the Kavanagh persona is less rebarbative. Most of his sixties' lyrics contain some allusion to pubs or drink. Ensconced in his Monaghan garage he thinks of 'Authority' whispering 'like Tyranny at the end of a bar'. His 'Gambler' is a pathetic alter-ego:

> While he plays his high jinks
> It's much later than he thinks
> He'll be alone with his drinks
> ('The Gambler: A Ballet')

When he ponders on other writers, Yeats, Hemingway, Beckett, he entitles the poem 'Mermaid Tavern', summoning up a longstanding connection between drink culture and literary culture. The technique of casualness was particularly suited to the portrayal of his own drink problem, enabling him to turn sickness and degradation into a comedy of indignity, while not blinking the uglier facets of drunkenness and hangover:

> On Christmas Day stretched out, how awful
> Not heeding the Church's orders lawful
> While everyone else is having a crawful.

> It is black all round as terror stricken
> I climb stone steps, trying not to weaken,
> My legs are taking a terrible licking.

> To the King Edward, empty of pudds
> Two friends and I in crumpled duds
> Go to talk with John Heath-Stubbs.

> O Charles Dickens with your Scrooge

I would gladly have taken refuge,
I was as sick as the devil's puke . . .
                    ('A Summer Morning Walk')

Kavanagh often resorts to couplets and tercets in his sixties' verse, and such playful foregrounding of rhyme prevents solemnity and self-pity, insists that alcoholic addiction, however reprehensible to the reader or uncomfortable for the writer, is a folly or a frolic. In the sonnet, 'The Same Again', whose title calls for another round, alcoholism is invoked to provide deflationary contrasts: 'bard' is humorously rhymed with 'hitting the bottle hard', and 'star', an image associated with poetic aspiration in the 1930s, is mismatched with 'the corner of a smoky bar'. When Kavanagh deplores the fact that alcoholism is handicapping him in the British poetry stakes and fantasises about the shock effects of his recovery of rude good health, rhyming couplets, even quadruplets, are drawn on to turn an egregiously arrogant and offensive poem into a piece of playful doggerel:

> But Kavanagh, the dog
> Took to the grog
> Leaving Larkin and Logue
> Manufacturing fog,
> And even MacNeice
> Making ground in the race . . .
>   ('Sensational Disclosures!')

'And even MacNeice' — he is displaying his customary ingratitude here. MacNeice is publicly demeaned, though he had generously introduced Kavanagh to a new audience, being responsible for his broadcast of *The Great Hunger* on the BBC's Third Programme in May 1960.

Kavanagh wanted a poetry that was 'at the same time light and adult', treating of his problems in 'an airy manner', a 'style whose meaning does not need a spanner', such as Auden had affected in the 1930s.[12] 'Let words laugh', he wrote in 'Mermaid Tavern'. In a 1964 interview he said that he enjoyed 'the fun and games of a lot of contemporary verse, even people like Ginsberg', because it released poetry from 'ponderosity'.[13] Consciously or unconsciously, his attraction to Beat verse, with its irreverent frankness about addiction to drugs or drink, may have influenced Kavanagh to write lighthearted rhymes about his own alcoholism. However, his doggerel/groggerel, an attempt to exude gay youthfulness through inconsequential rhyming, quickly palls. The verbal jokes are usually not quite funny enough and the continual sprightliness is so wearing that a wallow in self-pity would seem preferable.

Kavanagh was much enamoured of feminine rhymes in the 1960s, citing with approval his chiming of 'clichés', 'species', 'Nietzsche's'.[14] He enjoyed playing verbal games, getting into apparently inextricable difficulties with rhyme, to display his linguistic ingenuity:

> I sat on a deck-chair and started to work
>
> On a morning's walk not quite effectual,
> A little too unselectual
> But what does it count in the great perpetual?

Here the poem, 'A Summer Morning Walk', turns reflexive. Rhyme is exploited to draw attention to the process of composition[15] in

> The theme here invented . . .
>
> Is about a poor hero
> Who gambled on Zero
> There's no rhyme but Nero.
>
> ('The Gambler: A Ballet')

In 'Living in the Country: 11' the word 'marking' is left to dangle unrhymed and, ostentatiously, picked up five lines later:

> Must catch that rhyme that up there I left parking

Kavanagh maintained that 'the essence of any living art form is that it is amateur'[16] and his foregrounding of rhyme does

sometimes point up the improvisatory quality of his versifying. Unfortunately, and all too frequently, its function is
to provide him with a verbal framework when he has little to
say. His rhymed couplets and tercets, in particular, often
appear mechanical, a manufactured 'word-machine-to-live-
in-structure'.[17] He is merely performing certain rhythmic
routines, going through the motions like the dancer in 'The
Gambler: A Ballet with Words':

> Who demands of you no emotional moiety
> Or your attention as he capes his caper.

Another game with which Kavanagh sometimes amused
himself was a play with literary allusion and pastiche. The
conclusion of 'Living in the Country: 11', for instance,
displays a flippant familiarity with the work of certain
predecessors and contemporaries:

> My love lies at the gates of foam
> The last dear wreck of day
> And William H. Burroughs collages the poem
> As the curfew tolls the knell of Gray.

Here the allusion to Lord de Tabley's 'Churchyard on the
Sands'[18] is far fetched; the gaiety is forced; the pastiche is
tacked on to the conclusion of the poem as a comic cop-out.
Kavanagh sometimes seems to be joking for the sake of
saying something, writing to keep his spirits up. Poetry is
autotherapeutic, an antidote to alcoholism and depression:

> I just want to assure all
> That a poem made is a cure-all
> Of any soul-sickness. Toolooral!
>   ('A Summer Morning Walk')

He writes to assuage his guilt at not writing, to placate a
nagging poetic conscience:

> Now surely
>
> I can lie on the grass, feel no remorse

> For idling, I have worked at verse
> And exorcised a winter's curse.
>   ('A Summer Morning Walk')

There may be some truth in his facetious claim that he traded on his literary reputation to ensure the maintenance of a cash flow:

> I never suffer now from malnu–
> Trition. Or need for grog.
> I make a product I can easily flog.
> I am a small country exporting
> The pill of meaning to those
> Whom the condition is hurting ...
>   ('Living in the Country: 11')

'The Gambler: a Ballet with Words' and 'The Gambler: A Ballet', which are among the worst of his late offerings, were both commissioned.[19] The elderly poet was also over-indulged by eager young editors of new Irish journals. John Jordan at *Poetry Ireland* and James Liddy at *Arena* were grateful for the opportunity to publish anything by the old master.[20] Most of the late poems need revision and/or pruning; the poetics of 'not caring' encouraged sloppiness.

Much of Kavanagh's sixties' poetry is coterie verse, aimed at an audience of 'affectionados':[21]

> I have my friends, my public and they are waiting
> For me to come again as their one and only bard
> With a new statement that will repay all the waitment
> While I was hitting the bottle hard ...
>   ('The Same Again')

The poems contain in-allusions to such friends as John Betjeman, John Heath-Stubbs, Paul Potts or John Jordan. When he writes from Inniskeen in 'Living in the Country' he does so with the quizzical air of an exile in a primitive place addressing a circle of friends who will appreciate the ironies of his situation. His literary fun and games presuppose an endeared and protective readership, prepared to smile affectionately at his antics.

Since he was a poet who made no secret of his need for support and encouragement, the lionising Kavanagh enjoyed in his later years should have resulted in a fresh spate of creative vigour. But it was too late: booze and failing health had taken their toll. He had never been a prolific poet, and, as the 1960s progressed, his output flagged and finally petered out. By 1963, creative impotence had become a theme:

> I am here all morning with the familiar
> Blank page in front of me, I have perused
> An American anthology for stimulation
> But the result is not encouraging as it used
> To be when Walter Lowenfel's falling down words
> Like ladders excited me to chance my arm
> With nouns and verbs.
> But the wren, the wren got caught in the furze
> And the eagle turned turkey on my farm . . .
>
> ('In Blinking Blankness: Three Efforts')

The return to Inniskeen here serves to emphasise the gap between the eager country neophyte, spurred into verse by reading Walter Lowenfel's experimental stanzas in *The Irish Statesman*, and the jaded senior poet, incapable of being inspired. Inniskeen now provides metaphors of deterioration and decline. At the outset of his literary career, in 'Inniskeen Road: July Evening', Kavanagh had wryly compared himself to Cowper's solitary monarch. Now he is 'the king of all birds' who comes to an undignified end in the wren-boys' St Stephen's Day chant;[22] an eagle tamed into a farmyard turkey, ready for the slaughter. Country and Canal alike have failed him as poetic inspiration or poetic subject:

> Nature is not enough, I've used up lanes
> Waters that run in rivers or are stagnant . . .

'In Blinking Blankness' was among the first five pieces Kavanagh published in the new Irish journal, *Arena*, in spring

1963. 'Personal Problem', his contribution to the final number in spring 1965, and one of his last published poems returned, more sombrely, to the same theme:

> To take something as a subject, indifferent
> To personal affection, I have been considering
> Some old saga as an instrument
> To play upon without the person suffering
> From the tiring years. But I can only
> Tell of my problem without solving
> Anything. If I could rewrite a famous tale
> Or perhaps return to a midnight calving,
> This cow sacred on a Hindu scale—
> So there it is my friends. What am I to do
> With the void growing more awful every hour?
> I lacked a classical discipline. I grew
> Uncultivated and now the soil turns sour,
> Needs to be revived by a power not my own,
> Heroes enormous who do astounding deeds—
> Out of this world. Only thus can I attune
> To despair an illness like winter alone in Leeds.

The creative impasse, which Kavanagh analyses with such clear-sighted honesty here, is the dilemma of the Romantic extremist who privileges personal inspiration and devalues literary genres and traditions. 'To take something as a subject' was contrary to his poetics, in which the poet does not choose, but is chosen, in which naming is 'a love-act'. It was impossible for him to have recourse to a mode favoured by many of his Irish poetic predecessors and contemporaries, rewriting a prior text, adapting some 'old saga' or 'famous tale'. The implicit comparison in 'Personal Problem' is with Yeats who found poetic myths and metaphors in Gaelic and Indian literature, whereas Kavanagh's humble Monaghan heifer refused to be metamorphosed into a sacred cow, or to associate with the *Táin Bó Cuailne*. 'System' and 'Plan' are abjured as a 'Yeatsian invention' in 'Mermaid Tavern'. Throughout his career Kavanagh had shown no interest in constructing grand philosophical or rhetorical structures. He had put his faith in the passing lyrical impulse, had aimed at immediacy, sudden surprise, a fugitive intensity, a 'sniff' of personality. His mature poetics de-emphasised subject matter, sought to represent states of spiritual intoxication, to defy common sense and the laws of gravity, to become 'airborne', spurning the 'thought out' in favour of 'flight in the light'. As an unlearned poet, unconscious of his own Romantic ancestry, Kavanagh had groped his way by chance illuminations. He had lived precariously on the literary as well as the everyday plane, always subject to the hazards of chance and instinct; volatile, easily destabilised by financial insecurity or lack of esteem. It was a risky, hand-to-mouth existence, trusting to the pull of his affections to lure him into verse. In earlier years when his poetic crop failed, he blamed it on the 'sour soil' of his own psyche. He had erred through being motivated by disaffection, 'barren anger' and 'self-pitying melodrama'; he had neglected love's 'pure positive'. A change of heart, he believed, could set his poetic lands in order. The writer of 'Auditors In' had not foretold that the heart grows old.

When 'Personal Problem' appeared in spring 1964, Kavanagh was only fifty-nine, but he had lost a lung and the debilitating effects of alcoholic abuse had aged him. 'To write lively verse or prose, to be involved with Comedy, requires enormous physical and mental power,' he claimed, and in 'Personal Problem' he complains of 'suffering/From the tiring years'. Though Kavanagh is not confessing that a defective poetics has brought his career to a premature close, there is a wistful admission of inadequacy in the phrase, 'I lacked a classical discipline', a sad acknowledgment that if he were a neo-classical poet, he would still be writing. The 'un-cultivated' mode was, paradoxically, more difficult to sustain. 'To know that growth has stopped' signalled the death of the poet in 'To be Dead'. This nadir is reached in 'Personal Problem'. The last line of the poem is probably Kavanagh's bleakest, bringing together 'despair', 'illness', 'winter', isolation. The 'void' gapes and no rocky voice summons the poet to rejoice.

Though Kavanagh's sixties' poetry chronicles his losing battle with alcoholism, illness and failing inspiration, his final years brought the external success and recognition he had so long coveted. After the débâcle of *Kavanagh's Weekly*, he had been unable to obtain regular journalistic work throughout most of the 1950s. His cultural criticism was so extreme and so strident that newspaper and magazine editors considered him 'unsafe'. By 1955 his 'economic position' had 'reached the impossible'.[23] In February 1956, through the good offices of the Taoiseach, John A. Costello,[24] Kavanagh embarked on a series of extra-mural lectures on poetry at University College, Dublin, which was so successful that it became an annual event until 1959. He was delighted with this university platform, both with the academic establishment's acknowledgment of his poetic 'authority' and the fresh opportunity to preach his message. In 'Thank You, Thank You', an 'Epilogue to a series of lectures given at University College, Dublin', he wrote:

> I thank you and I say how proud
> That I have been by fate allowed
> To stand here having the joyful chance
> To claim my inheritance
> For most have died the day before
> The opening of that holy door.

Lecturing is here elevated into the performance of a sacred ministry; the podium is transformed into a pulpit. Kavanagh's magnification of his role reveals that he still entertained messianic pretensions in the late 1950s, but it also shows how starved he was for 'a holy hearing audience' at this time.

His instatement as a university lecturer may have lent Kavanagh respectability and allayed editorial doubts about his unsuitability as a columnist. He was asked to contribute a series of articles to the monthly fashion journal, *Creation*, from June to December 1957, and the editors of a new Irish monthly, the *National Observer*, engaged his services from July 1959 to January 1960. The clearest signal of Kavanagh's return to journalistic favour was the invitation to write a weekly column for *The Irish Farmers Journal* from June 1958. It was also a sign that he was regarded as an old dog who could be trusted to bark and not to bite, or, as he would have preferred to express it, a 'gentle tiger'. The readers of *The Irish Farmers Journal* were, by and large, conservative Catholic country people who expected their writers to observe 'the theological tenets of the press'. Kavanagh was content to oblige such readers by rehearsing benign memories of his life as a farmer in Inniskeen, in a reassuring 'I mind the time . . .' vein. By 1962 he was bored with this regressive weekly assignment and appears to have regarded it as an intrusion on his drinking time. His copy, which had become increasingly irregular, was sometimes so sloppy as to be unprintable,[25] and his employment was terminated by mutual consent in March 1963. Kavanagh was now such a national literary institution that he had no difficulty in finding a more congenial journalistic slot. The Irish radio and television journal, the *RTV Guide*, which addressed a more diverse readership than *The Irish Farmers Journal*, was delighted to have him contribute a weekly column. This ran from January 1964 until October 1966, approximately a year before his death. Writing for the *RTV Guide* went some way towards fulfilling Kavanagh's dream of being a media celebrity. He basked in the approbation of his new audience, endearing himself to his readers by treating them as close friends, chatting unpatronisingly about his own news and views.

In the prose of his last years, as in his poetry, Kavanagh was obsessed with himself as literary subject. He signed a contract to write his autobiography for Hutchinson in 1960, though he no longer had the stamina for such a sustained project and seems not to have embarked on it.[26] A half-hour script for an Irish television self-portrait series was a more manageable venture and allowed him to star in his own show on 30 October 1962.[27] His weekly columns in the *Irish Farmers Journal* and, later, in the *RTV Guide* were full of autobiographical reminiscences. From 1964 he was desultorily engaged in revising a rediscovered autobiographical novel from the early 1950s, a Dublin-based sequel to *Tarry Flynn*, to be published by MacGibbon and Kee. A draft of this unfinished novel was edited and published by Peter Kavanagh as *By Night Unstarred* in 1974.[28]

The most important literary event in the last years of Kavanagh's life was the publication of *Collected Poems* by MacGibbon and Kee in summer 1964. This collection, compiled by Martin Green and John Montague, was the first, albeit incomplete, attempt to establish the canon of Kavanagh's verse.[29] The poet was not asked to collaborate on the project, possibly because he was known to dislike so much of his own earlier verse that he would have insisted on a *Selected Poems*. *Collected Poems* included all the poems from the two collections, *Ploughman and Other Poems* (1936) and *A Soul for Sale* (1947), which had long been out of print, as well as from the recently published *Come Dance with Kitty Stobling* (1960). In addition, it assembled a large body of verse, both early and late, which had been published in journals, but never collected. Since Kavanagh printed very little verse after summer 1964, most of his *oeuvre* was available to the editors of *Collected Poems*, and they missed out on very few memorable poems. However, *Collected Poems* is an idiosyncratically organised compilation. It suffers from a lack of information as to the chronology of Kavanagh's work, and the ordering of the poems after the *Ploughman and Other Poems* section becomes increasingly confused. (Though chronology is eschewed in a prefatory bibliographical note, many of the problems with the book's arrangement, in fact, appear to derive from chronological misinformation.) Since the collection was made in the days before it was possible to photocopy from books or journals, numerous errors, in addition to obvious misprints, also entered the text. Kavanagh was given an opportunity to read the galley proofs, but he performed this task so perfunctorily that he even missed out on such misprints as the substitution of 'arising' for 'arsing', which he had fulminated about in the proofs of *Recent Poems*. In an 'Author's Note' to the volume he claimed that he 'was too indifferent, too lazy to eliminate, change or collect'. On the credit side, the editors and publishers of *Collected Poems* introduced Kavanagh's *oeuvre* to new generations of readers. Most of his thirties' and forties' poems, including *The Great Hunger*, were out of print until 1964. *Collected Poems* was, presumably, never intended to serve as the standard text which, *faute de mieux*, it became.[30]

In 1967 MacGibbon and Kee published a companion volume of Kavanagh's prose, edited by Niall Sheridan, and jokingly entitled by the author *Collected Pruse*.[31] This was altogether less scholarly and less complete than *Collected Poems*. It brought together excerpts from *The Green Fool* and *Tarry Flynn*, and a selection of journalism from the 1940s to the 1960s, including passages from *Kavanagh's Weekly*. More unexpectedly, in view of its title, it reprinted some of the *Irish Times* reportage of Kavanagh's libel action of 1954. *Collected Pruse* was a popular edition, which altered Kavanagh's essays without acknowledging the fact. Though it claimed to have indicated the original source of each item, it failed to do so for almost a third of them. The sources it did provide are, occasionally, incorrect. 'Three Glimpses of Life', published in *The Bell* in July 1944, for instance, is attributed to *Envoy*. So the reader is misled into thinking that this sequence of short fictions, instead of preceding *Tarry Flynn*, actually succeeded it. Some material from *Kavanagh's Weekly* is described as such, some is not. The most dubious piece of editing in the book is the last essay, entitled 'The Parish and the Universe', which weaves together materials from four different essays, three dating from 1952 and one from 1956.[32] *Collected Pruse* performed a useful service in collecting some of the best of Kavanagh's scattered journalism under a single cover and making it accessible to interested readers. Again, like *Collected Poems*, it was, presumably, not intended to have the status of a definitive text.

Had the salvaging of his life's work been left to Kavanagh, very little would have been preserved. He was always highly selective in his attitude to his own writings, prejudiced against or in favour of different pieces at different times, refusing anthologists permission to reprint poems he had come to dislike. What he saw fit to transmit to posterity in October 1963 was collected on a record entitled, *Almost Everything,*[33] on which he recited or read from his poems and prose, and sang 'If Ever You Go To Dublin Town'. On this occasion he took considerable liberties with the application of the word, 'almost', in the title of his record. In poetry, for instance, he chose to be remembered by only twenty pieces, which, unexpectedly, included excerpts from *The Great Hunger* and excluded the Canal sonnets. Predictably, since he always tended to value recent work, he began with 'The Same Again' and also read 'Living in the Country: 1'.

Kavanagh, who had always craved public esteem and financial reward, lived to reap at least some of the fruits of literary success. He experienced the pleasures and the profits of having much of his work republished in his lifetime: his novel, *Tarry Flynn*, his *Collected Poems* and his *Collected Pruse*. In his last years he was the much indulged old man of Irish letters, surrounded by disciples, honoured by younger Irish writers, hailed by critics as the finest Irish poet since Yeats. On 19 April 1967 he married Katherine Barry Maloney, a woman with whom he had enjoyed a long friendship. He even lived to accomplish that most difficult of human feats, being accepted as a prophet by his own people. His last public appearance, before his death on 30 November 1967, was at a staging of the dramatised version of *Tarry Flynn* in Dundalk on 23 November. He became ill during the performance and went from the Kavanagh homestead to a Dublin nursing home the following day. It was to be his last journey from Inniskeen to Dublin, retracing the route that he had first taken almost thirty-six years before when, as a just-published young poet, he had walked so hopefully towards his troubled destiny.

Conclusion

IN 'A Wreath for Tom Moore's Statue', Kavanagh protests against posterity's urge to categorise the dead writer, to petrify him in one attitude, appropriate him for one cause, memorialise him in one image. 'Peasant poet', 'People's poet', Love-poet; 'Post-colonial writer', 'Parochial writer', 'Comic writer', 'Mystic': such are the labels on the assorted wreaths that have been hung on Kavanagh by his 'affectionados' and/or critics. All of these labels offer a partial truth; none is adequate as a total description. And what has become of the angry, satiric, embattled writer? In Ireland, moreover, Kavanagh's notoriety as a picturesque 'character' almost exceeds his fame as an author. As he predicted in 'If Ever You Go To Dublin Town', Dubliners still love to swap anecdotes about his colourful doings and sayings.

Kavanagh himself is responsible for many of the simplifications surrounding his reputation, since he not only cultivated an idiosyncratic public persona, but also exerted a considerable influence on his readers' perception of his life and work. He had the publicist's talent for marketing his views in reiterated catch-phrases: 'parochialism' versus 'provincialism', 'comedy' versus 'tragedy'; 'simplicity', 'humourosity', 'not caring', 'kink'. He also provided a series of signposts to guide or misguide his readers, attaching particular viewpoints to the names of particular poems or places: 'simplicity' to 'Shancoduff', 'tragedy' to *The Great Hunger*, 'poetic birth' to the Grand Canal. In his latter years he published a number of official, edited accounts of his literary career, which have since been more often quoted than challenged. The 'Author's Note' to *Collected Poems*, and *Self-Portrait* as reprinted in *Collected Pruse*, have been especially influential in controlling and shaping his readers' responses, since they are, respectively, the opening essays in the two collections of his work which were most widely accessible throughout the 1960s, 1970s and 1980s. Both essays are entertaining propaganda exercises, designed to privilege his recent post-Canal verse, offering an endearing blend of confessional half-truths, falsifications and deliberate omissions.

'Author's Note' begins with a sentence which time has verified but which, at the date of utterance, was a blatant untruth: 'I have never been much considered by the English critics.' This was written just four years after *Come Dance with Kitty Stobling* had received rave reviews in the English press and had been the summer choice of the Poetry Book Society. It is succeeded almost immediately by another whopper: 'I am always shy of calling myself a poet . . .'. There follows the dubious anecdote about the often 'literally starved' writer. In 'Author's Note' Kavanagh is casting himself in the role of modest martyr, dangerous mystic and belated convert to comic insouciance. Everything he wrote between 1942 and 1955 (the only two dates in the note) vanishes into interlinear space, as he moves in a single short sentence from repudiating the 'tragic' *Great Hunger* towards a total surrender to his Canal poetics.

In *Self-Portrait*, where he promotes the cult of casual comedy and 'not caring', Kavanagh portrays his literary career as a journey from 'the simplicity of going away' to 'the simplicity of return', though, in fact, he was no more successful than Paddy Maguire in curving his life's circle 'to his own will'. Here the poetry that intervened between 'Shancoduff' and his post-Canal verses is summarily dismissed as complex, concerned or unloving. That the theme of departure and return had obsessed him since *The Green Fool* (1938) is ignored, as is his recurrent championship of humour, detachment, love, innocence, the wondrous beauty of 'ordinary things'.

Today Patrick Kavanagh occupies an anomalous critical position in that he is virtually unknown outside Ireland, while within Ireland, where his poetry is widely cherished, his achievement is at least partially obscured by a covering of embroideries from his own and others' mythologies. My aim in this book has been to introduce Kavanagh's *oeuvre* to a wider overseas readership, but also, since I am an Irish critic, to propose a demythologising, revisionist analysis. I read or rewrite Kavanagh as a Romantic *après la lettre*. I regard him as the unconscious and, therefore, innovative rather than derivative, heir of this nineteenth-century literary tradition, reincarnating the egocentricity, the subjective vision, the radical energies, the creative problematics of Romanticism in an Irish twentieth-century context. The conflictual relationships between innocence and experience, memory and imagination, realism and transcendentalism, subjectivity and didacticism, vernacular speech and abstract philosophical discourse, linguistic materialism and visionary communication: all these had been pondered before, but Kavanagh came to them afresh;[1] as he did to the importance of local affections and place-names, and the appropriation of a religious terminology to elevate the banal or to confer a visionary status on imaginative illuminations.

It would not have occurred to Kavanagh to situate himself among 'the last Romantics', since he spurned Yeats's ethnic and primitivist phantasmagoria. Literary romanticism in Ireland had become inextricably associated with the nationalist ideal of a separatist culture. Its project was to dialogue with the ancestral voices of a Gaelic-speaking past. Kavanagh refused to participate in this racial séance, preferring instead to praise or satirise his contemporary local world in a contemporary idiom and accent. The options between which the home-based, post-colonial Irish writer had to choose were to keep faith with an imagined past or to be true to the drab realities of the present. Both alternatives involved a conscious ethnicity, a subordination of individual identity to racial identity, a privileging of objectivity over subjectivity. Samuel Beckett pointed out in 1934 that, 'The device common to the poets of the Revival and after' was 'a flight from self-awareness' and that 'self-perception' was not for them 'an accredited theme'.[2] Though Kavanagh did not promulgate his creed of 'personality' until the early 1950s, the 'I' had played an obtrusive, if not always analytically self-aware, role in his work since *The Green Fool*. What vitiated Kavanagh's cultural criticism in *Lough Derg* and in the novel, *Stony Grey Soil*, and detracted from the dramatic autonomy of *The Great Hunger*, was this self-obtrusiveness. He was always either consciously or unconsciously his own hero.[3] In a post-colonial Irish society preoccupied with establishing or inventing an ethnic culture, such egocentricity was subversive and daringly *avant-garde*. The mature Kavanagh's insistence on subjective criteria of aesthetic importance, his fierce cherishing of his own cussed singularity, enabled him to refuse assimilation into any Irish poetic school or coterie, and to treat all literary allegiances, friendships or truces as temporary. He was 'a lone one', an impassioned believer in individualism, courageously championing personal values throughout a nationality-ridden era.

For me Patrick Kavanagh is a born-again Romantic; a literary category which seems sufficiently comprehensive to allow full and fair play to the complexities of this multi-faceted, self-contradictory, variable and volatile writer. However, just in case I have strait-jacketed him, I conclude by inviting 'the corpse' to 'put his elbows through' my 'jacket'. The last lines of this book are Kavanagh's own from 'A Wreath for Tom Moore's Statue', defending the poet's right to inconsistency against the categorising tendencies of hagiographer or critic:

> The poet would not stay poetical
> And his humility was far from being pliable,
> Voluptuary to-morrow, to-day ascetical,
> His morning gentleness was the evening's rage.

Notes

Chapter 1 (pp 1–51)

1. 'Diary', *Envoy*, July 1951.
2. 'Schoolbook Poetry', *Kavanagh's Weekly*, 10 May 1952.
3. Patrick Kavanagh, *The Complete Poems*, Peter Kavanagh ed, New York 1972, 339.
4. *Self-Portrait*, Dublin 1975, 9.
5. *Lapped Furrows*, Peter Kavanagh ed, New York 1969, 5.
6. 'Schoolbook Poetry'.
7. MS 3215, The National Library of Ireland.
8. *Self-Portrait*, 23.
9. 'Return in Harvest', *The Bell*, April 1954.
10. 'Schoolbook Poetry'.
11. *The Irish Times*, 11 April 1940.
12. *The Green Fool*, London 1971, 245.
13. *November Haggard*, Peter Kavanagh ed, New York 1971, 18; *The Green Fool*, chapter 24.
14. Kavanagh 'occasionally visited' the Carnegie Library in Dundalk, but his brother records that the 'pickings were very poor' and cannot recall that he ever 'borrowed anything worth reading'. See Peter Kavanagh, *Beyond Affection*, New York 1977, 22.
15. 'Schoolbook Poetry'.
16. Daniel Corkery, *Synge and Anglo–Irish Literature*, Cork 1966, 15.
17. 'A Poet's Country', *Ireland of the Welcomes*, March 1953.
18. *Poetry Book Society Bulletin*, June 1960.
19. This is the *Green Fool* version. A variant version is quoted in the *Poetry Book Society Bulletin*.
20. 'Return in Harvest'.
21. Kavanagh wrote jocular verses on local and family subjects in a family Commonplace Book between 1923 and 1927. These are collected in *Complete Poems*, 353ff.
22. 22 August 1925.
23. 24 October 1925 and 21 December 1929.
24. WR Rodgers, *Irish Literary Portraits*, BBC, London 1972, 200–201, ('country gobdough' in BBC-speak).

25. *Letters to W.B. Yeats*, vol 2, Richard J. Finneran, George Mills Harper, William M Murphy eds, London 1977, 533, 547–8.
26. James Matthews, *Voices, A Life of Frank O'Connor*, Dublin 1983, especially 165 and 184; Kavanagh stayed with Seán O'Faoláin and his wife in Wicklow in September 1933, *Lapped Furrows*, 27.
27. 'Ascetic', *John O'London's*, 2 May 1931; 'To a Blackbird' and 'Gold Watch', *The Spectator*, 9 May and 20 June 1931.
28. Realism was still associated with beauty in May 1934: 'Perhaps now that I have turned to objective reality I may be able to write something honest and beautiful, as chestnut trees or horses out on grass.' *Lapped Furrows*, 30.
29. 'Imagism', according to Kavanagh, 'paints pictures, telling us of the beauty perceived through the senses but does not comment on this beauty. It praises by showing.' *Lapped Furrows*, 111; 'Tinker's Wife' was published in *Ploughman and Other Poems*.
30. *Lapped Furrows*, 41.
31. Frank O'Connor, 'Awkward but Alive', *The Spectator*, 31 July 1964. What AE read was an ur-collection, c. 1933.
32. MS 9579, The National Library of Ireland. These poems have been collected in *Complete Poems*, but there are several variants from the MS version.
33. *Self-Portrait*, 26.
34. An early instance of the 'kink' that Kavanagh sees as characteristic of poets.
35. 'Fool', *The Irish Times*, 14 February 1938.
36. 'Poets on Poetry', X, March 1960.
37. *November Haggard*, 65.
38. 'Irish Poetry since the War', *The London Mercury*, April 1935.
39. See CK Stead, *The New Poetic*, Penguin, London 1967, 99.
40. The most extreme instance of this tendency is 'Remembered Country', *Complete Poems*, 49–50.
41. 'A Strange Irish Poet', *The Irish Times*, 30 and 31 March 1945.
42. MS 9579 notes that *The Seed and the Soil* was 'submitted to John Gawsworth when staying with him at 33 Great James Street and writing *The Green Fool* in 1937'. Gawsworth is saluted as his 'only literary mate' in 1938 in 'On the Centenary of the Birth of M.P. Shiel', *Complete Poems*, 348. John Gawsworth was the pen-name of Terence Ian Fytton Armstrong.
43. Cf compiler's note in *The Best Poems of 1930*, selected by Thomas Moult, London 1930.
44. *Fifty Years of Modern Verse, An Anthology*, chosen by John

Gawsworth, London 1938, includes Kavanagh's 'Plough-Horses', 'Old Soldier' and 'Ethical'. *Poems of Twenty Years, An Anthology, 1918–1938*, includes 'Morning' and 'Old Soldier'.

45. *The Spectator*, 16 September 1938.
46. 'Diary', *Envoy*, September 1950.
47. MS 9579.
48. The first three stanzas were published as 'A Reverie of Poor Piers' in 'City Commentary', *The Irish Press*, 27 September 1943.
49. Kavanagh, apparently, never spoke to Yeats. See Peter Kavanagh, *Sacred Keeper*, Ireland 1979, 48.
50. 'Irish Poetry since the War'.
51. See Donagh MacDonagh's review in *Ireland Today*, November 1936.
52. *Self-Portrait*, 20.
53. 'Yeats', *The Holy Door*, spring 1966.
54. *Ireland Today*, November 1936.
55. Variant version entitled 'Shanco Dubh' in *Dublin Magazine*, July–September 1937 and MS 9579. Revised version, entitled 'Shanco-duff', in *Nimbus*, winter 1956, *Come Dance with Kitty Stobling*, 1960 and *Collected Poems*, London 1964. In the latter two collections it is dated 1934, but I have found no MS evidence to support this early date.
56. 'Epic', *The Bell*, November 1951.
57. 'The Hospital,' *Nimbus*, winter 1956.
58. *Self-Portrait*, 26.

Chapter 2 (pp 52–86)
1. MS 9579, The National Library of Ireland.
2. My discussion of *The Green Fool* as autobiography is greatly indebted to Brian Finney, *The Inner I*, London 1985. Finney designates as 'allobiographical' those memoirs which focus on others as much as on the self.
3. *The Irish Farmers Journal*, 10 September 1960.
4. 'The Green Fool Notebook', Kav/A/8, The Kavanagh Archive, University College, Dublin.
5. See Peter Kavanagh, *Sacred Keeper*, Ireland 1979, 14.
6. A neighbour's death and funeral, rather than his own father's, is the subject of chapter 21, 'Death and Burial', probably in the interests of family privacy, but also to preserve comic distancing.
7. MS 3213–14, The National Library of Ireland. See also *Lapped Furrows*, Peter Kavanagh ed, New York 1969, 33.

8. 750 copies from which the libellous page 300 had been removed were issued in 1939 by Harper and Brothers, New York. See Peter Kavanagh, *Garden of the Golden Apples*, New York 1972, 8.
9. Peter Kavanagh attributes the absence of writs to the book's withdrawal from local libraries (*Lapped Furrows*, 42–3), but the serialised newspaper version was read in Inniskeen.
10. 'Feasts and Feasts', (excerpt from *The Green Fool*), *The Standard*, 4 April 1947.
11. *RTV Guide*, 7 August 1964.
12. *Sacred Keeper*, 19.
13. John Wilson Foster, *Fictions of the Revival*, Dublin 1987, 323.
14. 'The Green Fool Notebook'.
15. See *Self-Portrait*, Dublin 1975, 24.
16. James Olney suggests that autobiographies present a better picture of an author at the time of writing than at the times written about. See his *Metaphors of the Self*, Princeton 1972, 44.
17. *November Haggard*, Peter Kavanagh ed, New York 1971, 88.
18. 'From Monaghan to the Grand Canal', *Studies*, spring 1959.
19. *November Haggard*, 70.
20. Preface to *The Autobiography of William Carleton*, London 1968.
21. 'A Poet's Country', *Ireland of the Welcomes*, March 1953.
22. 'From Monaghan to the Grand Canal'.
23. 'Diary', *Envoy*, July 1951.
24. MS 3213–14.
25. According to Peter Kavanagh, he considered naming the book, *The Iron Fool*. 'Iron fool' was a local expression for someone who was pretending to be a fool for self-protection. See *Sacred Keeper*, 58.
26. See Enid Welsford, *The Fool: His Social and Literary History*, London 1935.
27. Notebook of Patrick Kavanagh's Jottings, c. 1927–1930, MS 3218, The National Library of Ireland.
28. *The Inner I*, 24.
29. Kavanagh never 'went out for hire', *Sacred Keeper*, 60 and see also 42.
30. Kavanagh's athletic exploits are not mentioned, for instance. See *Sacred Keeper*, 43. Such material was put to comic use in 'Diary', *Envoy*, August 1950.
31. His sister, Celia, considered that the 'year of forced inactivity', following on Patrick's hospitalisation for typhoid fever in 1923, 'really stimulated his mental growth'. See *Lapped Furrows*, 14.

32. MS 3213–14.
33. *Sacred Keeper*, 59.
34. ibid 58. *The Green Fool* MS is untitled.
35. MS 3213–14.
36. ibid.
37. James Matthews, *Voices, A Life of Frank O'Connor*, Dublin 1983, 165.
38. 'Irish Poetry since the War', *The London Mercury*, April 1935.
39. The book was warmly reviewed not only in Irish journals such as *The Dublin Magazine* and *The Irish Press*, but in *The Daily Telegraph and Morning Post*, *The Observer* and *The New York Times* among others. *The Spectator* reviewer was particularly euphoric: '*The Green Fool* is a book of so many qualities that it is difficult to speak of it with restraint. It is, of its kind, almost perfect; and the kind is worthy.'

Chapter 3 (pp 87–122)
1. *Self-Portrait*, Dublin 1975, 11.
2. 'City Commentary', *The Irish Press*, 25, 26, 28 December 1942.
3. *The Dublin Magazine*, October–December 1939.
4. 'From Monaghan to the Grand Canal', *Studies*, spring 1959.
5. *The Bell*, October 1940.
6. *Lough Derg*.
7. *The Irish Independent*, 23 December 1939.
8. The first part was published in *The Irish Press*, 24 December 1943; the second in *The Bell*, December 1940.
9. *The Listener*, 11 December 1941.
10. See chapter 5 for a discussion of 'Why Sorrow?'.
11. 'Spraying the Potatoes', *The Irish Times*, 27 July 1940; 'Art McCooey', *The Bell*, April 1941.
12. 'The Hospital'.
13. 'A Poet's Country', *Ireland of the Welcomes*, March 1953.
14. This count is based on the Cuala Press edition, 1942. 24 lines were bowdlerised and other changes introduced in the *A Soul for Sale* version. Further changes were introduced in *Collected Poems*, London 1964 and *Complete Poems*, New York 1972.
15. Review of *The Great Hunger* in *The Bell*, September 1942.
16. I did consider that the reference might be to masturbation, but this does not fit the context.
17. Kav/A/2 in the Kavanagh Archive, University College, Dublin.
18. Based on Joseph Lee and Gearóid Ó Tuathaigh, *The Age of de*

Valera, Dublin 1982 and FSL Lyons, *Ireland since the Famine*, Fontana, London 1973.

19. Frank O'Connor, *The Backward Look*, London 1967, 224–5.
20. Seán O'Faoláin, *Vive Moi!*, London 1967, 245.
21. Based on Terence Brown's reading in *Ireland, A Social and Cultural History, 1922–1985*, Fontana, London 1986, 156–7.
22. 'Silent Ireland', *The Bell*, August 1943.
23. *Horizon*, vol v, no 25, January 1942.
24. *The Backward Look*, 224.
25. *The Bell*, December 1940; April 1941; July 1944; June 1945; January 1952.
26. *The Irish Times*, 27 July 1940; 14 October 1944.
27. *An Irish Journey*, London 1940, 288. O'Faoláin notes that the builders of the 'Anti-Christ Hall' appealed the case and were granted their licence.
28. Peter Kavanagh, *Sacred Keeper*, Ireland 1979, 66.
29. Kav/B/14, 15, 16, Kavanagh Archive.
30. 'The Future of Irish Literature', *Horizon*, January 1942.
31. *The Backward Look*, 229.
32. This account of Peadar O'Donnell draws on Grattan Freyer, *Peadar O'Donnell*, USA, 1973. Freyer's short study does not treat of O'Donnell's connections with Kavanagh. Their friendship probably pre-dated the founding of *The Bell*, and may account for the leftward bent in Kavanagh's poetry from 'The Hired Boy', 1936. Kavanagh often contributed to *The Bell* under O'Donnell's editorship. O'Donnell is described in 'Diary', *Envoy*, December 1949, as one who has 'the giving quality'. This is not altogether complimentary, since the implication is that he is not an artist in his own right.
33. *The Backward Look*, 224.
34. *Horizon*, January 1942.
35. According to his brother, he wrote it in little more than ten days, *Sacred Keeper*, 103, or 'slightly less than three weeks', *Complete Poems*, 393.
36. 'The Irish Year', *The New Statesman*, 9 December 1933.
37. 'Ireland after Yeats', *The Bell*, summer 1953.
38. A note in *Horizon*, January 1942, states that 'The Old Peasant', as *The Great Hunger* was then entitled, 'is a long poem of 30 pages of which only the beginning is here given'. Parts I, II, III and 26 lines from Part IV were printed. There are several variants between this version and the Cuala Press version and Part IV is substantially different.

39. James Matthews, *Voices, A Life of Frank O'Connor*, Dublin 1983, 184–6.
40. 'The Future of Irish Literature'.
41. John Montague, *The Irish Times*, 2 December 1967.

Chapter 4 (pp 123–158)
  1. Canon Bernard Maguire, ('Salamanca Barney'), Rector of the Irish College, Salamanca, 1898–1907; Parish Priest of Inniskeen, 1915–48.
  2. Kavanagh's cinematic technique was first noticed by James Plunkett in a pioneering article on *The Great Hunger*, 'The Pulled Weeds on the Ridge', *The Bell*, March 1952. Kavanagh became film critic for *The Standard* in 1946.
  3. This image, which appears in the Cuala Press edition only, explains the part played by the personified Hope in later versions of the poem.
  4. 'A Strange Irish Poet', *The Irish Times*, 30 and 31 March 1945.
  5. Kavanagh was visited by two Gardaí Siochana in connection with the January 1942 number of *Horizon*, though the interview appears to have been conducted in a friendly manner. Some copies of this number of the journal were seized but, while there appears to be no consensus as to why the Irish authorities took exception to it, it is generally agreed that 'The Old Peasant', as the excerpt from *The Great Hunger* was entitled, was not the reason.
  6. See Terence Brown, *Ireland, A Social and Cultural History, 1922–1985*, Fontana, London 1986, 21.
  7. 'From Monaghan to the Grand Canal', *Studies*, spring 1959.
  8. 'Liberators', *The Irish Times*, 15 August 1942.
  9. Kavanagh later quoted these lines from Auden's 1935 poem, 'To a Writer on his Birthday' in 'Auden and the Creative Mind', *Envoy*, June 1951.
  10. 'Apronful' in the Cuala Press and *A Soul for Sale* versions. 'Armful', introduced in *Collected Poems* and *Complete Poems*, does not make sense and would seem to be a misprint.
  11. *The Irish Press*, 18 March 1943.
  12. Brown, op cit, 187.
  13. 'Author's Note', *Collected Poems*.
  14. ibid.
  15. *November Haggard*, Peter Kavanagh ed, New York 1977, 59.

Chapter 5 (pp 159–194)
  1. See chapter 1 of *Synge and Anglo–Irish Literature*, London 1931.
  2. This will be discussed in chapter 6, 204–6 and in chapter 7, 268–9.

3. 'William Carleton', *The Irish Times*, 13 January 1945.
4. *The Listener*, 11 December 1941.
5. The dedication is in Gaelic (Peadar O Comhraidhe), an uncharacteristic touch. Kavanagh quarrelled with Curry in summer 1949, and lost his job with *The Standard*. 'Petty Curry's ego is small', he wrote to his brother. See Peter Kavanagh, *Sacred Keeper*, Ireland 1979, 132–5, 189.
6. 'The Anglo–Irish Mind', 28 May 1943.
7. *The Standard*, 12 March 1943.
8. 'Sean O'Casey Grows Up', *The Irish Times*, 14 March 1942.
9. *The Bell*, February 1951.
10. 'Diary', *Envoy*, July 1951.
11. ibid, March 1951.
12. 'Paris in Aran', *Kavanagh's Weekly*, 7 June 1952.
13. 'The Gallivanting Poet', *Irish Writing*, December 1947.
14. 'Diary', *Envoy*, September 1950.
15. ibid, March 1951.
16. 'William Butler Yeats', *The Kilkenny Magazine*, spring 1962.
17. 'Nationalism and Literature', *Nonplus*, October 1959.
18. See *Sacred Keeper*, 191 and *Lapped Furrows*, Peter Kavanagh ed, New York 1969, 57.
19. *RTV Guide*, 7 August 1964.
20. 'Croagh Patrick', *The Irish Independent*, 29 July 1940.
21. 'Pilgrim without Petrol', *The Standard*, 8 May 1942.
22. 'Pageantry with a Meaning', *The Standard*, 24 August 1945.
23. *Sacred Keeper*, 191–6.
24. The *Lough Derg* typescript, Kav/B/2, Kavanagh Archive, University College, Dublin, differs in several respects from both published versions of the poem. I follow the Kav/B/2 version.
25. *Sacred Keeper*, 86.
26. *The Standard*, 30 August 1946.
27. *Sacred Keeper*, 86–7.
28. *The Standard*, 12 June 1942.
29. He read the written petitions placed by pilgrims on the altar, in order to discover their private wishes. See *Lapped Furrows*, 57.
30. 'Lough Derg' was included by Peter Kavanagh in *November Haggard* in 1971. However, it was its simultaneous publication as a single volume by Martin Brian and O'Keeffe, London, and by The Goldsmith Press, Ireland, in 1978, that brought it to the attention of many reviewers and readers.
31. *Kavanagh's Weekly*, 24 May 1952.
32. I detect O'Donnell's influence here.

33. I follow Kav/B/2 here.

34. Kavanagh showed Kav/B/2, the *Lough Derg* typescript, to Frank O'Connor, who made a number of markings on it. Sometimes he suggests cutting, otherwise it is difficult to interpret his markings. Peter Kavanagh states that O'Connor suggested expanding the poem in several places. See *Complete Poems*, Peter Kavanagh ed, Ireland 1984, 394.

35. In *The Irish Times*.

Chapter 6 (pp 195–253)

 1. *Kavanagh's Weekly*, 24 May 1952.
 2. *The Standard*.
 3. 'No Social Conscience' in *Collected Poems*, London 1964, and thereafter.
 4. *Kavanagh's Weekly*, 24 May 1952.
 5. *November Haggard*, Peter Kavanagh ed, New York 1971, 69.
 6. 'From Monaghan to the Grand Canal', *Studies*, spring 1959.
 7. *Kavanagh's Weekly*, 24 May 1952.
 8. 'William Carleton', *The Irish Times*, 13 January 1945.
 9. *November Haggard*, 69.
10. ibid.
11. 'Nationalism and Literature', *Nonplus*, October 1959.
12. *November Haggard*, 69–70.
13. ibid, 33–4.
14. 'From Monaghan to the Grand Canal'.
15. 'William Carleton'.
16. 'Diary', *Envoy*, April 1950.
17. *Kavanagh's Weekly*, 24 May 1952.
18. 'William Carleton'.
19. *Kavanagh's Weekly*, 24 May 1952.
20. 'Diary', *Envoy*, April 1950.
21. 'From Monaghan to the Grand Canal', 'Nationalism in Literature', *Self-Portrait*, 11.
22. 'Diary', *Envoy*, February 1950.
23. 'Paris in Aran', *Kavanagh's Weekly*, 7 June 1952.
24. WB Yeats and Thomas Kinsella, *Davis, Mangan, Ferguson?*, *Tradition and the Irish Writer*, Dolmen Press, Ireland 1970, 57–66.
25. *The Bell*, January 1948.
26. *Kavanagh's Weekly*, 12 April 1952.
27. *Kavanagh's Weekly*, 14 June 1952.

28. Kavanagh's animosity towards Clarke and Farren is dealt with in the next chapter.
29. 'From Monaghan to the Grand Canal'.
30. Letter from Frank O'Connor to Jean Hendrick, 1941, *The Journal of Irish Literature*, vol iv, no 1, January 1975, 52.
31. 'From Monaghan to the Grand Canal'.
32. 'Living under Ben Bulben', *The Kilkenny Magazine*, 1966.
33. See 'Unhappy and at Home', Interview with Seamus Heaney by Seamus Deane, *The Crane Bag Book of Irish Studies, 1977–1981*, Dublin 1982, 71.
34. Kav/B/10, Kavanagh Archive, University College, Dublin.
35. Peter Kavanagh, *Sacred Keeper*, Ireland 1979, 88.
36. *The Standard*, 5 October 1945.
37. *Irish Writing*, no 1, October 1946.
38. *Self-Portrait*, 8.
39. *Sacred Keeper*, 176.
40. Kav/B/14, 15, 16.
41. *Sacred Keeper*, 174.
42. 'Spraying the Potatoes' in Kav/B/14, 'Art McCooey' in Kav/B/15.
43. Kav/B/16.
44. *The Irish Press*, 15 June 1946.
45. *Lapped Furrows*, Peter Kavanagh ed, New York 1969, 119.
46. *November Haggard*, 91.
47. *Lapped Furrows*, 119.
48. Chapter 1, May 1947; chapter 3, June 1947; part of chapter 4, July 1947; chapter 8, September 1947.
49. *Sacred Keeper*, 178 and *Lapped Furrows*, 134.
50. Robert Farren seems to have been largely responsible for the unbanning of *Tarry Flynn* (see *Lapped Furrows*, 176), a magnanimous gesture, since Kavanagh repeatedly attacked him in print. See next chapter.
51. 'From Monaghan to the Grand Canal'.
52. 'Diary', *Envoy*, September 1950.
53. *November Haggard*, 17.
54. *Self-Portrait*, 9.
55. 'William Carleton'.
56. The phrase is used by Seán O'Faoláin of the Inniskeen parish priest's sermon in *An Irish Journey*, London 1940, 288.
57. 'William Carleton'.
58. Kav/B/80.
59. Kavanagh printed the report of a court case from *The Dundalk Democrat*, under the title, 'Tarry Flynn's Neighbours', in

Kavanagh's Weekly, 19 April 1952, which helps to demonstrate the novel's authenticity.

60. 'A Voice of Gaelic Ireland', *Hibernia*, July 1962.
61. 'Anna Quinn', *Dublin Magazine*, October–December 1939; 'My Room', *Dublin Magazine*, April–June 1933.
62. See chapter 1 for a discussion of the concluding poem. This is the first time the entire poem was published.
63. *Self-Portrait*, 10.
64. The first three sonnets were published in *The Irish Times* on 1 September 1945; the final two on 29 June 1946.
65. Kav/B/80.
66. Patrick Kavanagh in *Poetry Book Society Bulletin*, June 1960.
67. Kav/B/88.
68. The 1972 edition of *Tarry Flynn*, published by Martin Brian and O'Keeffe, was republished by Penguin in 1978. It was reprinted in 1980, 1984, 1987, 1988 and 1989.
69. Hugh Kenner, *A Colder Eye*, London 1983, 235.
70. A phrase used by Kavanagh in 'Diary', *Envoy*, September 1950.
71. Peter Kavanagh attributes Patrick's loss of his job as film critic for *The Standard* to the banning of *Tarry Flynn*. It may have been a contributory factor, but he did not lose this job until July 1949, and it would appear that it came about because he insulted the editor. See *Sacred Keeper*, 178 and 179.
72. The text of PJ O'Connor's dramatisation of *Tarry Flynn* was published in *The Journal of Irish Literature*, vol vi, no 1, January 1977, 83–155.

Chapter 7 (pp 254–307)

1. *Self-Portrait*, Dublin 1975, 11.
2. 'Diary', *Envoy*, December 1949.
3. The 1939 prize was presented in January 1940. Kavanagh was 35 in October 1939.
4. *The Irish Press*, 14 September 1942 to 8 February 1944.
5. The poems 'A Knight at the Tournament', *Irish Press*, 21 December 1942 and 'Candida', *Irish Press*, 23 September 1943 both result from this friendship which is also referred to in 'I had a Future', *Kavanagh's Weekly*, 12 April 1952.
6. *Self-Portrait*, 9.
7. 'Diary', *Envoy*, March 1950.
8. *Self-Portrait*, 11.
9. Seán O'Faoláin, *An Irish Journey*, Dublin 1940, 298.
10. Letter from Frank O'Connor to Sean Hendrick, 1941, published

in *The Journal of Irish Literature*, vol iv, no 1, January 1975.

11. This comment is maliciously attributed to AE by George Moore in *Hail and Farewell*.

12. *An Irish Journey*, 299.

13. 'Comment', *Horizon*, January 1942.

14. 'The Paddiad'.

15. See Peter Kavanagh, *Sacred Keeper*, Ireland 1979, 92–5.

16. Cf 'A Letter and an Environment from Dublin', *Nimbus*, autumn 1956.

17. 'City Commentary', *The Irish Press*, 14 September 1942.

18. ibid, 22 January 1943.

19. 'Beyond the Headlines', 'City Commentary', 29 March 1943.

20. ibid, 31 December 1942.

21. ibid, 1 October 1943; 12 July 1943.

22. ibid, 5 October 1942.

23. ibid, 1 October 1943.

24. ibid, 22 January 1944.

25. 'Diary', *Envoy*, April 1951.

26. 'City Commentary', 8 March 1943.

27. 'Auditors In'.

28. 'Fifty Years' Achievement', *The Standard*, 7 September 1945.

29. 'Diary', *Envoy*, March 1950.

30. 'The Gallivanting Poet', *Irish Writing*, November 1947.

31. *Poems from Ireland*, edited with an introduction by Donagh MacDonagh, *The Irish Times*, 1944. This included 'Spraying the Potatoes', 'Renewal' ('Advent'), 'Statue, Symbol and Poet' ('A Wreath for Tom Moore's Statue'), 'A Glut on the Market' ('Pegasus'), 'Memory of Brother Michael'.

32. Robert Greacen and Valentin Iremonger, *Contemporary Irish Poetry*, Dublin 1949.

33. 'Diary', *Envoy*, December 1949.

34. ibid, September 1950.

35. *Lapped Furrows*, Peter Kavanagh ed, New York 1969, 105.

36. Kavanagh attacked Austin Clarke's weekly poetry programme on Radio Éireann in *Envoy*, July 1951 and in *Kavanagh's Weekly*, 5 July 1952.

37. Based on Patrick Kavanagh's letter in *The New Statesman and Nation*, 5 February 1949.

38. Kavanagh maintained his friendship with the Archbishop of Dublin, John Charles McQuaid.

39. Hubert Butler, 'Envoy and Mr Kavanagh', *The Bell*, September 1951.

40. 'Diary', *Envoy*, April 1951.
41. 'Poetry in Ireland Today', *The Bell*, April 1948.
42. ibid.
43. 'Expressive' is the term used by MH Abrams to describe the aesthetic theory 'in which the artist himself becomes the major element, generating both the artistic product and the criticism by which it is to be judged', *The Mirror and the Lamp*, Oxford 1977, 21–2.
44. 'Poetry in Ireland Today'.
45. 'The Gallivanting Poet'.
46. Peter Kavanagh, *Beyond Affection*, New York 1977, 131–8 and *Kavanagh's Weekly*, 5 July 1952.
47. *Kavanagh's Weekly*, 3 May 1952.
48. ibid, 5 July 1952.
49. ibid, 17 and 31 May, 28 June 1952.
50. ibid, 10 May 1952.
51. ibid, 24 May 1952.
52. ibid, 7 June 1952.
53. ibid, 12 April 1952.
54. ibid, 17 May 1952.
55. ibid, 10 May 1952.
56. ibid, 28 June 1952.
57. Introduction to *Poisoned Lands*, Dublin 1977, 9.
58. *Beyond Affection*, 131–8.
59. The Victor Waddington Gallery, and Drogheda Grammar School. The headmaster of the latter complained about the high cost of the advertisement.
60. *Kavanagh's Weekly*, 26 April 1952.
61. ibid, 10 May 1952.
62. 'Diary', *Envoy*, January 1950.
63. 'Auditors In'. He married Katherine Barry Maloney on 19 April 1967.
64. 'Baudelaire and Kavanagh', *Envoy*, November 1950.
65. *November Haggard*, 90 and 94.
66. 'Dear Folks' and cf *Envoy*, July 1951.
67. *Kavanagh's Weekly*, 14 June 1952.
68. ibid, 5 July 1952.
69. 1944. Published in *The Irish Times*, 14 October 1944.
70. 'From Monaghan to the Grand Canal', *Studies*, spring 1959.
71. Originally 'Statue, Symbol and Poet', *The Irish Times*, 4 March 1944. Moore's statue was an object of ridicule since it was first erected. See Terence de Vere White, *Tom Moore*, London 1977, xii. White himself refers to the statue as a 'libel in metal'.

72. *The Irish Times*, 1 July 1944.
73. 'A Wreath for Tom Moore's Statue'.
74. *Kavanagh's Weekly*, 19 April 1952.
75. *The Irish Times*, 25 September 1948.
76. 'Diary', *Envoy*, January 1950 and March 1951.
77. 'Bardic Dust', *The Irish Times*, 9 December 1944. A review of Austin Clarke's *The Viscount of Blarney and Other Plays*.
78. *Nimbus*, winter 1954.
79. 'Tale of Two Cities', untitled in *Envoy*, October 1950. Titled in *Collected Poems*, London 1964, 115; 'A Sonnet Sequence for the Defeated' in *Envoy*, February 1951, 'The Defeated' in *Collected Poems*, 97–9.
80. 'Farren, Clarke, MJ McManus are the chief characters in it', *Lapped Furrows*, 140; in Kav/B/80, Kavanagh Archive, University College, Dublin, Kavanagh identifies the Paddies as follows: Paddy of the Celtic Mist—Austin Clarke and other personalities; Paddy Connemara West—just a personification of provincialism; Chestertonian Paddy Frog—Robert Farren; in their middle sits a fellow—Maurice Walsh and other personalities; Paddy Conscience—the author among others.
81. The twelfth stanza probably alludes, not only to Kavanagh's own views, but to Joyce's self-dissociation from the Literary Revival in 'The Holy Office':
    But I must not accounted be
    One of that mumming company . . .
82. July 1954.
83. Attributed to Eusebius Cassidy in *The Bell*, July 1947, probably by way of acknowledgment that it is not much better than the rural ballads of Kavanagh's youth.
84. A collection of nineteen poems. Cronin's essay is entitled 'Innocence and Experience: The Poetry of Patrick Kavanagh'.
85. The full title is 'House Party to Celebrate the Destruction of the Roman Catholic Church in Ireland'. It was first published in *Nimbus*, winter 1956. Cf 'Pages from a Literary Novel', *The Bell*, February 1954.
86. *Kavanagh's Weekly*, 3 May 1952, under the pen-name, Laurence Pepper.
87. 'Diary', *Envoy*, May 1950.

Chapter 8 (pp 308–339)
1. *Collected Poems*, London 1964, 114.
2. 'Tale of Two Cities'.

3. Cf especially *Envoy*, July 1950, where he writes about the 'Diary' as a mode of self-revelation and experiments with writing a 'true diary' for a day in June 1950.

4. *Kavanagh's Weekly*, 31 May and 19 April 1952.

5. ibid, 12 April 1952.

6. ibid, 26 April 1952.

7. ibid, 28 June 1952.

8. ibid, 21 June 1952.

9. ibid, 24 May 1952.

10. ibid, 7 June 1952.

11. ibid.

12. 'Diary', *Envoy*, September 1950.

13. *Kavanagh's Weekly*, 7 June 1952.

14. Samuel Beckett, 'Recent Irish Poetry', *The Bookman*, August 1934, under the pseudonym, Andrew Belis.

15. 'Diary', *Envoy*, July 1950.

16. In a biographical note on Kavanagh in *Poems from Ireland*, Dublin 1944, Donagh MacDonagh writes, 'A Monaghan man, he speaks with the ruggedness of the country and the strength of one who can afford to break the rules.'

17. 'Meet Mr. Patrick Kavanagh', *The Bell*, April 1948.

18. 'A Goat Tethered outside the Bailey', *The Bell*, September 1953.

19. *The Irish Press*, 10 January 1946.

20. *By Night Unstarred* was an unfinished and unrevised novel, Peter Kavanagh ed, and published in Ireland in 1977.

21. *Dublin Magazine*, July–September 1936.

22. 'Dark Haired Miriam Ran Away', the original title of 'On Raglan Road', *The Irish Press*, 3 October 1946.

23. *The Bell*, March 1954.

24. 'God in Woman'.

25. Cf *Self-Portrait*, Dublin 1975, 15.

26. *The Irish Press*, 3 October 1946; *The Bell*, January 1954.

27. The omitted lines are added at the back of *Complete Poems*, Ireland 1984, but the final 8-line stanza is divided into two quatrains.

28. *Kavanagh's Weekly*, 21 June 1952.

29. 'A Ballad', initialled K.H. in *Kavanagh's Weekly*, 14 June 1952. Both *Collected Poems* and *Complete Poems* print 'remedies' instead of the original vernacular word, 'readies'.

30. *The Bell*, June 1945.

31. *The Bell*, March 1954.

32. 'Diary', *Envoy*, February 1950.

33. 'After Forty Years of Age'.
34. 'No Social Conscience' was entitled 'The Hero' in *The Irish Times*, 15 July 1949; 'Dublin', *The Bell*, March 1954, was entitled 'The Hero' in *Nimbus*, winter 1956 and in *Collected Poems*.
35. *Envoy*, March and September 1950.
36. ibid, September 1950.
37. ibid.
38. *The Irish Times*, 21 March 1953.
39. *Collected Pruse*, London 1967, includes a condensed version of *The Irish Times*'s extensive reportage of Kavanagh's libel action. Kavanagh was referred to as a novelist rather than a poet in the paper's headlines.
40. Kavanagh appealed from the high court to the supreme court and his appeal was allowed on 4 March 1955. A retrial was ordered, but the court was informed on 23 May 1955, the date for which it was listed as a jury action, that the case had been settled. The terms of the settlement were not disclosed.

Chapter 9 (pp 340–375)
1. 'Auditors In'.
2. 'Having Confessed' in *Collected Poems*, London 1964, 149.
3. *The Bell*, October 1951.
4. See chapter 1, 6.
5. *The Standard*, 7 December 1945.
6. *Kavanagh's Weekly*, 28 June 1952.
7. *Envoy*, July 1950.
8. 'Innocence', *The Bell*, October 1951; 'Epic', *The Bell*, November 1951.
9. ibid, November 1951.
10. ibid, March 1954.
11. 'Diary', *Envoy*, October 1950.
12. 'From a Prelude', *The Irish Times*, 12 February 1955.
13. See *Lapped Furrows*, 185, where John A Costello on his Christmas card compliments Kavanagh on 'the grace and substance of "From a Prelude"'.

Chapter 10 (pp 376–433)
1. 'On a Liberal Education', *X*, August 1961.
2. *Self-Portrait*, Dublin 1975, 26.
3. 'From Monaghan to the Grand Canal', *Studies*, spring 1959.
4. Published by The Dolmen Press, Dublin.

5. Published by MacGibbon and Kee, London.
6. 'A Letter and an Environment from Dublin', *Nimbus*, summer 1956.
7. 'Birth' was published in *Studies*, spring 1958.
8. *Self-Portrait*, 24.
9. 'From Monaghan to the Grand Canal'.
10. *Self-Portrait*, 16.
11. ibid, 24–5.
12. ibid, 11.
13. 'From Monaghan to the Grand Canal'.
14. ibid.
15. *Self-Portrait*, 8.
16. 'Some Reflections on *Waiting for Godot*', *The Irish Times*, 28 January 1956.
17. 'William Butler Yeats', *The Kilkenny Magazine*, spring 1962.
18. ibid.
19. *November Haggard*, Peter Kavanagh ed, New York 1971, 62.
20. 'From Monaghan to the Grand Canal'.
21. ibid.
22. ibid.
23. *Self-Portrait*, 19.
24. *November Haggard*, 15.
25. 'From Monaghan to the Grand Canal'.
26. 'Lines Written on a Seat on the Grand Canal, Dublin'.
27. 'From Monaghan to the Grand Canal'.
28. *November Haggard*, 73.
29. 'Diary', *Envoy*, June 1951.
30. *Time and Tide*, 1 December 1956.
31. 'From Monaghan to the Grand Canal'.
32. *Self-Portrait*, 19.
33. 'From Monaghan to the Grand Canal'.
34. Published by Longmans, Green and Co.
35. *Lapped Furrows*, Peter Kavanagh ed, New York 1969, 206.
36. ibid, 202.
37. ibid, 203.
38. ibid, 206.
39. 'The Self-slaved', *Recent Poems*, 1958.
40. 'Lecture Hall', *X*, November 1969.
41. Title of a Kavanagh poem attributed to Ann McKenna in *Kavanagh's Weekly*, 24 May 1952.
42. In *Nimbus*.
43. Cf *Self-Portrait*, 26.

44. ibid, 23.
45. *Lapped Furrows*, 203.
46. First published in *Recent Poems*, 1958.
47. *The Irish Times*, 12 July 1958 and *Recent Poems*.
48. *Recent Poems* and *The Times Literary Supplement*, 19 December 1958.
49. Published as 'High Journey' in *Encounter*, May 1958 and in *Recent Poems* 1958.
50. Untitled in *Nonplus*, October 1959.
51. 'The One', 'Yellow Vestment', 'Love in a Meadow', 'High Journey'/'Come Dance with Kitty Stobling' and 'Miss Universe' were informally grouped in both *Recent Poems* and in *Come Dance with Kitty Stobling*, as well as in *Nonplus*.
52. First published in *Encounter*, May 1958.
53. First published in *Recent Poems*; later in *Studies*, spring 1959.
54. First published in *Encounter*, January 1958.
55. First published in *Time and Tide*, 12 April 1958.
56. *Lapped Furrows*, 192.
57. ibid, 196.
58. Letter from the editor, 28 October 1958, Kav/B/84, Kavanagh Archive.
59. *Lapped Furrows*, 203–4. Spender found the poems 'very beautiful', not 'violently beautiful', as Kavanagh quotes him. 'Violent' was one of Kavanagh's favourite terms of praise at this time.
60. 'I've had offer of de luxe publication of poems by David Archer' (The Parton Press, London), *Lapped Furrows*, 206.
61. 'From Monaghan to the Grand Canal'.
62. Peter Kavanagh, *Garden of the Golden Apples*, 8.
63. *Lapped Furrows*, 212.
64. ibid, 215.
65. Kav/B/85, Kavanagh Archive.
66. *The Observer*, 10 July 1960.

Chapter 11 (pp 434–455)
1. The title of and a refrain in an unpublished late poem collected in Patrick Kavanagh, *The Complete Poems*, Peter Kavanagh ed, New York 1972, 335–6.
2. 'Poetry is not really an Art', Patrick Kavanagh talks to Máirín O'Farrell, *Hibernia*, vol 28, no 5, May 1964.
3. 'Some Reflections on *Waiting for Godot*', *The Irish Times*, 28 January 1956.

4. 'Kavanagh's First Tape', *November Haggard*, Peter Kavanagh ed, New York 1971, 48–52.

5. First published in *The Observer*, 20 November 1960.

6. Katherine Barry Maloney had an apartment at 47 Gibson Square in 1960. Kavanagh was a frequent visitor to London in the 1960s.

7. 'Literary Adventures' was first published in *Poetry Ireland*, autumn 1962; 'That Garage' in *Arena*, spring 1963.

8. First published in *X*, November 1959.

9. First published in *The New Statesman*, 21 February 1964, but included in a bound collection of poems, which Kavanagh sent to Macmillan in November 1955. See Kav/B/47, Kavanagh Archive, and *Lapped Furrows*, 191.

10. *Arena*, autumn 1963.

11. 'Intimate Parnassus'.

12. WH Auden, Preface to *The Oxford Book of Light Verse*, Oxford 1938; the rhymed lines are from 'Letter to Lord Byron'.

13. *Hibernia*, May 1964. 'I like Corso, Ferlinghetti, and Allen Ginsberg very much', *Tri-quarterly*, no 4, 1965.

14. 'I have learned the magical, imagination-stimulating quality of outrageous rhyming: clichés, species, Nietzsche's', he wrote in a note to introduce 'Important Statement' ('News Item') in an American anthology, *Poet's Choice*, Paul Engle and Joseph Langland eds, New York 1966, 66.

15. Auden may still have been an influence. Cf, for instance,
    Though it's in keeping with the best traditions
    For Travel Books to wander from the point
    (There is no other rhyme except anoint) . . .
    ('Letter to Lord Byron')

16. *RTV Guide*, 12 September 1963.

17. 'In Blinking Blankness: Three Efforts'.

18. *The Collected Poems* of Lord de Tabley, London 1903, 303–6. The parodied lines are the first lines of 'The Churchyard in the Sands':
    My love lies in the gates of foam
    The last dear wreck of shore . . .

19. 'The Gambler: a Ballet with Words' was commissioned by Guinness who asked for a poem of between 50 and 200 lines on a subject of the poet's choice, for first publication during the Festival of Poetry that the Poetry Book Society was organising at the Mermaid Theatre, London, from 16–23 July 1961. The poem was first printed in the festival programme. 'The Gambler: A Ballet' was commissioned for Patricia Ryan's Ballet Company. It was spoken by a narrator in the wings during the ballet and had

its première at the Olympia Theatre, Dublin, on 31 May 1961. See Kav/B/88.

20. John Jordan, for instance, would have liked Kavanagh to submit 'one or more or a hundred poems for consideration', Kav/B/87. Most of Kavanagh's late poems were published in *Arena*.

21. 'Affectionados' is a term Kavanagh uses in the *Hibernia* interview, May 1964.

22. It was a St Stephen's Day custom in parts of rural Ireland for groups of youths, known as 'wren-boys', to call at neighbours' houses, collecting money. Originally, they would have carried a dead wren. The verse or verses they recited varied from place to place; the Inniskeen version was as follows:

    The wren, the wren, the king of all birds
    On St Stephen's Day he was caught in the furze,
    Although he was little, his fame it was great
    So get up Mrs ——, and give us a treat.

    The 'wren' and 'the eagle turned turkey' ('turned turtle') both allude to the killing of a regal bird in the country at Christmastime, but the context is comic and festive.

23. Letter of 16 February 1955 from Patrick Kavanagh to the Taoiseach (Prime Minister), John A Costello, who as defence barrister had cross-examined him in his libel action.

24. Costello replied the next day to say that he was in touch with the president of University College, Dublin, to arrange a lecturing post. Kavanagh became seriously ill in March 1955, so he did not begin lecturing until the following spring. *Lapped Furrows*, 186. Extracts from ten of these lectures were published in *November Haggard*, 55–76.

25. Letter dated 8 January 1960, from the Farm Home editor of the *Irish Farmers Journal*. Kav/B/87, Kavanagh Archive.

26. Hutchinson wrote on 15 August 1960, welcoming Kavanagh's suggestion that he write his autobiography. They paid him an advance of £300, but despite numerous reminders, received no part of the MS. See Kav/B/88–90, Kavanagh Archive.

27. The 'Self-Portrait' was one of a series on Irish television, a talk to camera by the subject about himself and his own life, lasting about 27 minutes. Kavanagh agreed to contribute only if there were absolutely no censorship of his script. He was displeased with the Dolmen Press publication of this script, both with its pretentious appearance and the photographs used, which he found 'vulgar, ostentatious and grossly stage-Irish'. Kav/B/89–90, Kavanagh Archive.

28. This MS was mislaid in 1951, and recovered in November 1961. MacGibbon and Kee had it typed up for revision by Kavanagh in 1964. *Lapped Furrows*, 233, 241, 246. Peter Kavanagh's edition was published by Goldsmith Press, Ireland, 1977.

29. For two divergent accounts of the making of this collection, see John Montague, 'Collecting Kavanagh', *The Irish Times*, 5 February 1980 and Martin Green, 'Kavanagh plain', *Books Ireland*, September 1987. A revised version of Montague's essay, 'Patrick Kavanagh: A Speech from the Dock', is included in *The Figure in the Cave, Selected Prose of John Montague*, Antoinette Quinn ed, Lilliput Press, Ireland 1989.

30. No other edition of Kavanagh's poetry was published in the British Isles until *Complete Poems* was reprinted by Goldsmith Press in 1984.

31. 'Pruse' was intended as a mimicry of genteel Irish speech.

32. Excerpts from *Kavanagh's Weekly* of 17, 24 May and 28 June and 'A Letter and an Environment from Dublin', *Nimbus*, autumn 1956.

33. *Almost Everything: Written and Spoken by Patrick Kavanagh*, 16 October 1963, published by Claddagh Records, Dublin 1965.

Conclusion (pp 456–459)

1. Kavanagh comments succinctly on the 'originality' of his own Romanticism: 'Originality is the old truths re-experienced immersed in a new personality', *November Haggard*, Peter Kavanagh ed, New York 1971, 58. Originality is, of course, a Romantic aesthetic criterion.

2. Samuel Beckett, 'Recent Irish Poetry', *The Bookman*, August 1934, under the pseudonym, Andrew Belis.

3. Even nature is personalised, cf 'Prelude': 'the weeds that grew/ Somewhere specially for you'.

Select Bibliography

Primary Sources

Books
Ploughman and Other Poems, Macmillan, London 1936.
The Green Fool, Michael Joseph, London 1938.
The Great Hunger, Cuala Press, Dublin 1942.
A Soul for Sale, Macmillan, London 1947.
Tarry Flynn, Pilot Press, London 1948.
Recent Poems, Peter Kavanagh Hand Press, New York 1958.
Come Dance with Kitty Stobling and Other Poems, Longmans, Green and Co, London 1960.
Self-Portrait, Dolmen Press, Dublin 1964.
Lapped Furrows, Correspondence 1933–1967 between Patrick and Peter Kavanagh with Other Documents, edited by Peter Kavanagh, Peter Kavanagh Hand Press, New York, 1969.
November Haggard, Uncollected Prose and Verse of Patrick Kavanagh, selected, arranged and edited by Peter Kavanagh, Peter Kavanagh Hand Press, New York 1971.
Patrick Kavanagh, The Complete Poems, collected, arranged and edited by Peter Kavanagh, Peter Kavanagh Hand Press, New York 1972.
By Night Unstarred, An Autobiographical Novel, edited by Peter Kavanagh, Goldsmith Press, The Curragh, Ireland 1977.

Serial Publications
The Green Fool, *The Irish Weekly and Ulster Examiner*, 3 December 1938 to 13 May 1939.
'Literary Scene', *The Standard*, a weekly column from 26 February 1943 to 11 June 1943.
'City Commentary', a twice weekly column under the name, Piers Plowman, *The Irish Press*, 14 September 1942 to 8 February 1944.
'Round the Cinemas', a weekly column, *The Standard*, 22 February 1946 to 8 July 1949.
'Diary', *Envoy*, a monthly column, December 1949 to July 1951.
Kavanagh's Weekly, 12 April 1952 to 5 July 1952.
Creation, a monthly column, June 1957 to December 1957.

The Irish Farmers Journal, a weekly column, 14 June 1958 to 9 March 1963.

'A Column', *National Observer,* a monthly column, July 1959 to January 1960.

RTV Guide, a weekly column, 17 January 1964 to 7 October 1966.

Record

Almost Everything, Written and Spoken by Patrick Kavanagh, Ceirnini Cladaigh, Dublin 1965.

Note: Information about the first publication of the individual poems and prose items I discuss is provided in the text or Notes.

Manuscripts

The Kavanagh Archive is in the library of University College, Dublin. The following MSS are in The National Library of Ireland:

Cobbler's Account Book of James Kavanagh, 1911–29 (Patrick's father), MS 3220

Cobbler's Account Book of Patrick Kavanagh, 1929–39, MS 3217

Notebook, miscellaneous jottings by Patrick Kavanagh, c. 1927–30, MS 3218

The Green Fool, untitled holograph draft, MS 3213–14.

Untitled holograph collection of poems (1929–40), MS 3215.

The Seed and the Soil, 1937 and *To Anna Quinn,* 1938, two unpublished collections of poems, MS 9579.

The Great Hunger (holograph fair copy), MS 3216.

Secondary Sources

M.H. Abrams, *The Mirror and the Lamp,* Oxford University Press 1977.

W.H. Auden, *Collected Poems,* Faber and Faber, London 1976.

W.H. Auden, *The Oxford Book of Light Verse, Chosen by W.H. Auden,* Oxford University Press 1938.

Terence Brown, *Ireland, A Social and Cultural History, 1922–85,* Fontana, London 1985.

Terence Brown and Nicholas Grene (eds), *Tradition and Influence in Anglo–Irish Poetry,* Macmillan, London 1989.

Hubert Butler, *Escape from the Anthill,* Lilliput Press, Ireland 1985.

Joseph Campbell, *The Poems of Joseph Campbell,* Austin Clarke ed, Allen Figgis, Dublin 1963.

William Carleton, *Traits and Stories of the Irish Peasantry,* in 2 volumes, Garland Publishing, New York and London 1979.

William Carleton, *Autobiography*, with a preface by Patrick Kavanagh, MacGibbon and Kee, London 1968.

Austin Clarke, *Collected Poems*, Dolmen Press, Dublin 1974.

Padraic Colum, *The Collected Poems*, Macmillan, London 1932.

Daniel Corkery, *Synge and Anglo–Irish Literature*, The Mercier Press, Cork 1966.

D. Felicitas Corrigan, *Helen Waddell, a Biography*, London 1986.

Anthony Cronin, *Dead as Doornails*, Dolmen Press, Dublin 1976.

Lord de Tabley, *The Collected Poems*, Chapman and Hall, London 1903.

Terence de Vere White, *Tom Moore, The Irish Poet*, Hamish Hamilton, London 1977.

T.S. Eliot, *Collected Poems*, Faber and Faber, London 1963.

Robert Farren, *The Course of Irish Verse in English*, Macmillan, London 1948.

R.J. Finneran, George Mills Harper, William M. Murphy, eds, *Letters to W.B. Yeats*, vol 2, London 1977.

Brian Finney, *The Inner I*, Faber and Faber, London 1985.

John Wilson Foster, *Fictions of the Irish Literary Revival*, Gill and Macmillan, Dublin 1987.

R.F. Foster, *Modern Ireland, 1600–1972*, Allen Lane, England 1988.

Grattan Freyer, *Peadar O'Donnell*, Bucknell University Press, Lewisburg 1973.

F.R. Higgins, *The Dark Breed*, Macmillan, London 1927, *The Gap of Brightness*, Macmillan, London 1940.

Patrick Kavanagh, *Collected Poems*, MacGibbon and Kee, London 1964.

Patrick Kavanagh, *Collected Pruse*, MacGibbon and Kee, London 1967.

Patrick Kavanagh, *Lough Derg*, Martin Brian and O'Keeffe, London 1978 and Goldsmith Press, The Curragh, Ireland 1978.

Peter Kavanagh, *Garden of the Golden Apples, A Bibliography of Patrick Kavanagh*, compiled and researched by Peter Kavanagh, Peter Kavanagh Hand Press, New York 1972.

Peter Kavanagh, *Beyond Affection, An Autobiography*, Peter Kavanagh Hand Press, New York 1977.

Peter Kavanagh, *Sacred Keeper, a biography of Patrick Kavanagh*, Goldsmith Press, The Curragh, Ireland 1979.

Peter Kavanagh ed, *Patrick Kavanagh: Man and Poet*, Goldsmith Press, Newbridge, Ireland 1987.

Hugh Kenner, *A Colder Eye*, Allen Lane, London 1983.

J.J. Lee ed, *Ireland, 1945–70*, Gill and Macmillan, Dublin 1979.

Joseph Lee and Gearóid Ó Tuathaigh, *The Age of de Valera*, Ward River Press, Dublin 1982.

F.S.L. Lyons, *Ireland since the Famine*, Fontana, London 1973.

James Matthews, *Voices, A Life of Frank O'Connor*, Gill and Macmillan, Dublin 1983.

Larry Meegan, *The Inniskeen Story, A History 1888–1988*, published by Inniskeen Grattans GFC, Ireland 1988.

John Montague, *Poisoned Lands*, Dolmen Press, Dublin 1977.

John Nemo, 'A Bibliography of Materials by and about Patrick Kavanagh', *Irish University Review*, spring 1973.

John Nemo ed, *The Journal of Irish Literature*, A Patrick Kavanagh Number, January 1977.

John Nemo, *Patrick Kavanagh*, Twayne, Boston, Mass 1979.

Darcy O'Brien, *Patrick Kavanagh*, Bucknell University Press, Lewisburg 1975.

Frank O'Connor, *The Backward Look*, London 1967.

Seán O'Faoláin, *An Irish Journey*, Longmans, Green and Co, London 1940.

Seán O'Faoláin, *Vive Moi!*, Rupert Hart-Davis Ltd, London 1965.

Michael O'Loughlin, *After Kavanagh*, Raven Arts Press, Dublin 1985.

James Olney, *Metaphors of the Self*, Princeton 1972.

W.R. Rodgers, *Irish Literary Portraits*, BBC, London 1972.

John Ryan, *Remembering How We Stood*, Gill and Macmillan, Dublin 1975.

C.K. Stead, *The New Poetic*, Penguin Books 1967.

Alan Warner, *Clay is the Word*, Dolmen Press, Dublin 1973.

Enid Welsford, *The Fool: His Social and Literary History*, London 1935.

W.B. Yeats and Thomas Kinsella, *Davis, Mangan, Ferguson?, Tradition and the Irish Writer*, Dolmen Press, Dublin 1970.

W.B. Yeats, *Collected Poems*, Macmillan, London 1967.

General Index

Index of Kavanagh's Work